YOU AND SCIENCE FICTION

YOU AND SCIENCE FICTION

Bernard Hollister

National Textbook Company
a division of *NTC Publishing Group* • Lincolnwood, Illinois USA

Acknowledgments

The author wishes to acknowledge Bobbi Anderson, Tom Clareson, and Leonard Fiddle for their valuable help.

"Who Am I This Time?" excerpted from *Welcome to the Monkey House* by Kurt Vonnegut, Jr. Copyright © 1961 by Kurt Vonnegut, Jr. Originally appeared in *The Saturday Evening Post* as "My Name Is Everyone." Reprinted by permission of Delacorte Press/ Seymour Lawrence.

"Profession" (edited version) by Isaac Asimov. Copyright © 1957 by Street & Smith Publications, Inc. Reprinted by permission of the author.

"Rat Race" by Raymond E. Jones. Copyright © 1965 by Condé Nast Publications, Inc. First published in *Analog Science Fact and Fiction,* April 1966. Reprinted by permission of the author and the author's agents, Scott Meredith Literary Agency, Inc., 845 Third Avenue, New York, New York 10022.

"Survival Ship" by Judith Merril . Copyright © 1950, 1976 by Judith Merril. Reprinted by permission of the author and the author's agent, Virginia Kidd.

"The Smile" by Ray Bradbury. Copyright 1952 by Ray Bradbury. Reprinted by permission of The Harold Matson Company, Inc.

"Gilead" by Zenna Henderson from *Pilgrimage: A Book of the People* by Zenna Henderson. Copyright © 1961 by Zenna Henderson. Copyright 1952 by Mercury Press, Inc.

"All Summer in a Day" by Ray Bradbury. Copyright 1958 by Ray Bradbury. Reprinted by permission of The Harold Matson Company, Inc.

"Day of Truce" by Clifford D. Simak. Copyright © 1962 by Galaxy Publishing Corp. Reprinted by permission of the author's agents, Robert P. Mills, Ltd.

"The Subliminal Man" by J. G. Ballard. Copyright © 1961 by J. G. Ballard. Reprinted by permission of the author and the author's agents, Scott Meredith Literary Agency, Inc., 845 Third Avenue, New York, New York 10022.

"It's Such a Beautiful Day" by Isaac Asimov. Copyright 1954 by Ballantine Books, Inc. Reprinted by permission of the author.

"Now Let Us Sleep" by Avram Davidson. Copyright © 1957 by Mercury Press, Inc. Reprinted by permission of Kirby McCauley, Literary Agent.

"What To Do Till the Analyst Comes" from *Alternating Currents* by Frederik Pohl. Copyright © 1956 by Frederik Pohl. Reprinted by permission of the author.

"Consumers' Report" by Theodore R. Cogswell, from *SF: Authors' Choice,* edited by Harry Harrison, published by Berkley Publishing Corp. 1968. Copyright © 1955 by Imagination. Reprinted by permission of the author.

1995 Printing

INTRODUCTION

Ask a half dozen science fiction fans to define science fiction, and you'll probably get a half dozen different definitions. One fan might enjoy what is called space opera SF: space ships pursue one another far into unknown galaxies. Space operas are based on the old Western theme of the hero pursuing the bad guy; the space ship just replaces the horse. *Flash Gordon, Buck Rogers,* and the old television show *Captain Video* are examples of space operas. Another SF buff might like science fiction fantasy such as the *Lord of the Rings* books, which are populated by hobbits and other mythical creatures. Still a third person could be interested in what is called sword and sorcery SF, a literary experience with fabled kingdoms inhabited by witches and the like. Social commentary SF is a fourth example. Here the author uses fiction to make a social comment on the present and the future. For example, population explosions, the computer, or the growth of all-powerful governments are just a few of the themes that science fiction writers have made statements about.

So asking SF readers to define what they understand science ficiton to be is like asking the six blind men in the famous fable to feel a different part of an elephant in order to describe the whole elephant. Remember, one man grabbed the elephant's trunk, the second a leg, the third the tail. Of course each experienced the elephant very differently, and when asked, "What is an elephant?", each gave a different answer. So it is with science fiction. Science fiction is a rich and varied type of literature, depending upon which part of the elephant you enjoy. Therefore, no single definition of SF will be attempted here.

This is a book *about* science fiction that uses SF stories to view the human condition by raising four very important questions: Who am I? How do I relate to others? What kind of society do I want to live in? What kind of world do I seek? These four questions have been asked and pondered ever since humans first began to think and to discuss ideas among themselves.

You, too, are being asked in this book to think about these questions, and in a very personal way. After reading the following stories and doing the activities, it is hoped that you will better understand yourself, the people with whom you associate, and the society and the world in which you will live tomorrow. Remember, you will be living far longer in the future than you have lived in the past. Yet most of the courses that you've taken in school have been past-oriented—history, literature written by authors long dead.

For each of the stories in this book there are provided numerous opportunities for you to use science fiction to view the future. Before and after each story are exercises and activities that will help you to consider what some of the consequences of the story might be. In this way, you are being encouraged to think in new ways about yourself, your relations with others, and your relations with your society and your world.

This book is different because it is oriented to the future—your future, that is. However, the good science fiction writer not only projects us into the future, whatever it might hold, but also forces us to look at ourselves today and to examine our present values. Even if some of the SF stories never "come true," at least we have been given a creative glimpse of what might be. In this way, we are better able to make choices in a world of maybes.

SECTION 1
WHO AM I?

SECTION 2
HOW DO I RELATE TO OTHERS?

SECTION 3
WHAT KIND OF SOCIETY DO I WANT?

SECTION 4
WHAT KIND OF WORLD DO I SEEK?

SECTION 1
WHO AM I?

WHO AM I?

At one time, people, young and old alike, never raised the question: Who am I? There was no such thing as an identity crisis. It was naturally assumed that the young would follow in the footsteps of their parents, just as those parents had followed in the paths of their elders. There was no need to disturb this pattern. To be better than one's parents was unheard of among most families. What need was there to be different from one's father or mother?

In the past, most people were tied, in one way or another, to the land. With the coming of industrialization, however, massive numbers of people were uprooted and sought their destinies in the cities' factories. This led to the birth of new lifestyles, as people pursued hundreds and even thousands of different careers.

How easy it seems now to have simply followed the well-worn path of generations of relatives. How difficult it has become for a young person to choose an occupation from among the many available. Often we hear high school and college students saying, "I really don't know what I want to be."

Certainly, occupational roles play a most important part in shaping futures. Many people, in fact, structure their entire identities from their jobs. This identification can be positive or negative; for example, we frequently hear comments like, "I'm only a housewife." In recent years, however, the work week has been getting shorter, and as people have worked less, they have sought other means of fulfilling themselves. From camping and raising plants to skiing and hang-gliding, people are discovering that there is more to life than a 9 to 5 job. We have, in fact, had a leisure revolution in this country.

But we have had an even more dramatic revolution as blacks, women, and other groups have demonstrated and persuasively argued that they too must have the promised opportunity to find themselves. They have asked the question, "Who am I?", and have also made a statement, "I am somebody." Thus another revolution is taking place today, as one group after another seeks to define itself, its values, and its new roles.

In this first section of the book, you'll be reading stories and doing activities that will bring you into this revolutionary world of today and tomorrow. In this section, the most important questions are—Who am I? How do I define myself? Where am I going?

YOU AND THE FUTURE: YOUR FUTURE AUTOBIOGRAPHY

We are all to some degree interested in the future. When we glance at a horoscope, scan the stockmarket report in the daily newspaper, or listen to the local weather report, we are involving ourselves in the short range future. Most of us, however, don't think too carefully about the long range future ten or twenty years in the distance.

Ideally, how do you want to be living in the future? What lifestyle and interests would you like to have? Where would you like to live? These are very personal questions that can be answered only by you, and the answers can shape the next five and ten years of your life. Possibly these answers could affect the rest of your life. Nobody can predict with absolute accuracy that your "ideal" future will come true, but you are being asked to consider your tomorrows in the "future autobiography" that follows.

Five Years from Now
1. Where would you like to be living? (Which state or country?) Describe what the area looks like. Why do you want to live here?

2. Specifically, would you like to live in a house, an apartment, a mobile home, or other?
3. What kind of lifestyle would you like to have? Do you picture yourself as single? Married? How about a family?
4. What kind of a job would you like to have? Specifically, what do you picture yourself doing for a living? Do you think that you would enjoy this job?
5. What will your hobbies and interests be? (Pets, plants, cars, crafts, etc.)

Ten Years from Now
Answer the same questions

Twenty-Five Years from Now
Answer the same questions

Fifty Years from Now
Answer the same questions

Of course, in the last two categories it will be harder to project yourself into the future. However, see if any pattern emerges in the five and ten year categories, and this should make it easier to fill in the twenty-five year and fifty year categories.

FINDING AN IDENTITY

1

Erik Erikson, a famous psychiatrist, has spent his adult life exploring how we humans develop a sense of identity. Unfortunately, as Erikson notes, many people, young and old alike, never do "find themselves" and consequently they suffer what he calls an identity crisis. They are never too sure of who they are or what their values are or what they want in life. In this first section, you are going to look at the identities of some fictional characters. At the same time, however, you are asked to think about how you would respond to the questions: Who am I? What kind of person do I want to be?

We all play roles—son or daughter, brother or sister, friend, boyfriend or girl friend, employee, or student. In fact, each of us plays literally dozens of different roles. For each of these roles one wears different clothes, uses a different vocabulary, and also behaves differently. Being a boyfriend or girl friend leads us to act in a manner unlike that of a son or daughter.

In this first story, Kurt Vonnegut's "Who Am I This Time?," we are being asked to put ourselves in the place of a couple who have no real identity until they take up the roles created in the make-believe world of drama. Or is it such a make-believe world . . .?

1. Which cartoon of the future best represents your own view?
2. Draw your own cartoon about the future. What images did you use? Is your cartoon pessimistic or positive? Why?

PROJECTIONS

"We've called you here today to announce that, according to our computer, by the year 2000 everything is going to be peachy."

WHO AM I THIS TIME?

—Kurt Vonnegut

The North Crawford Mask and Wig Club, an amateur theatrical society I belong to, voted to do Tennessee Williams's *A Streetcar Named Desire* for the spring play. Doris Sawyer, who always directs, said she couldn't direct this time because her mother was so sick. And she said the club ought to develop some other directors anyway, because she couldn't live forever, even though she'd made it safely to seventy-four.

So I got stuck with the directing job, even though the only thing I'd ever directed before was the installation of combination aluminum storm windows and screens I'd sold. That's what I am, a salesman of storm windows and doors, and here and there a bathtub enclosure. As far as acting goes, the highest rank I ever held on stage was either butler or policeman, whichever's higher.

I made a lot of conditions before I took the directing job, and the biggest one was that Harry Nash, the only real actor the club has, had to take the Marlon Brando part in the play. To give you an idea of how versatile Harry is, inside of one year he was Captain Queeg in *The Caine Mutiny Court Martial,* then Abe Lincoln in *Abe Lincoln in Illinois* and then the young architect in *The Moon is Blue.* The year after that, Harry Nash was Henry the Eighth in *Anne of the Thousand Days* and Doc in *Come Back Little Sheba,* and I was after him for Marlon Brando in *A Streetcar Named Desire.* Harry wasn't at the meeting to say whether he'd take the part or not. He never came to meetings. He was too shy. He didn't stay away from meetings because he had something else to do. He wasn't married, didn't go out with women—didn't have any close men friends either. He stayed away from all kinds of gatherings because he never could think of anything to say or do without a script.

So I had to go down to Miller's Hardware Store, where Harry was a clerk, the next day and ask him if he'd take the part. I stopped off at the telephone company to complain about a bill I'd gotten for a call to Honolulu, I'd never called Honolulu in my life.

And there was this beautiful girl I'd never seen before behind the counter at the phone company, and she explained that the company had put in an automatic billing machine and that the machine didn't have all the bugs out of it yet. It made mistakes. "Not only did I not call Honolulu," I told her, "I don't think anybody in North Crawford ever has or will."

So she took the charge off the bill, and I asked her if she was from around North Crawford. She said no. She said she just came with the new billing machine to teach local girls how to take care of it. After that, she said, she would go with some other machine to someplace else. "Well," I said, "as long as people have to come along with the machines, I guess we're all right."

"What?" she said.

"When machines start delivering themselves," I said, "I guess that's when the people better start really worrying."

"Oh," she said. She didn't seem very interested in that subject, and I wondered if she was interested in anything. She seemed kind of numb, almost a machine herself, an automatic phone-company politeness machine.

"How long will you be in town here?" I asked her.

"I stay in each town eight weeks, sir," she said. She had pretty blue eyes, but there sure wasn't much hope or curiosity in them. She told me she had been going from town to town like that for two years, always a stranger.

And I got it in my head that she might make a good Stella for the play. Stella was the wife of the Marlon Brando character, the wife of the character I wanted Harry Nash to play. So I told her where and when we were going to hold tryouts, and said the club would be very happy if she'd come.

She looked surprised, and she warmed up a little. "You know," she said, "that's the first time anybody ever asked me to participate in any community thing."

"Well," I said, "there isn't any other way to get to know a lot of nice people faster than to be in a play with 'em."

She said her name was Helene Shaw. She said she might just surprise me—and herself. She said she just might come.

You would think that North Crawford would be fed up with Harry Nash in plays after all the plays he'd been in. But the fact was that North Crawford probably could have gone on enjoying Harry forever, because he was never Harry on stage. When the maroon curtain went up on the stage in the gymnasium of the Consolidated Junior-Senior High School, Harry, body and soul, was exactly what the script and the director told him to be.

Somebody said one time that Harry ought to go to a psychiatrist so he could be something important and colorful in real life, too—so he could get married anyway, and maybe get a better job than just clerking in Miller's Hardware Store for fifty dollars a week. But I don't know what a psychiatrist could have turned up about him that the town didn't already know. The trouble with Harry was he'd been left on the doorstep of the Unitarian Church when he was a baby, and he never did find out who his parents were.

When I told him there in Miller's that I'd been appointed director, that I wanted him in my play, he said what he always said to anybody who asked him to be in a play—and it was kind of sad, if you think about it.

"Who am I this time?" he said.

So I held the tryouts where they're always held—in the meeting room on the second floor of the North Crawford Public Library. Doris Sawyer, the woman who usually directs, came to give me the benefit of all her experience. The two of us sat in state upstairs, while the people who wanted parts waited below. We called them upstairs one by one.

Harry Nash came to the tryouts, even though it was a waste of time. I guess he wanted to get that little bit more acting in.

For Harry's pleasure, and our pleasure, too, we had him read from the scene where he beats up his wife. It was a play in itself, the way Harry did it, and Tennessee Williams hadn't written it all either. Tennessee Williams didn't write the part, for instance, where Harry, who weighs about one hundred forty-five, who's about five feet eight inches tall, added fifty pounds to his weight and four inches to his height by just picking up a playbook. He had a short little double-breasted bellows-back grade-school graduation suit coat on and a dinky little red tie with a horsehead on it. He took off the coat and tie, opened his collar, then turned his back to Doris and me, getting up steam for the part. There was a great big rip in the back of his shirt, and it looked like a fairly new shirt too. He'd ripped it on purpose, so he could be that much more like Marlon Brando, right from the first.

When he faced us again, he was huge and handsome and conceited and cruel. Doris read the part of Stella, the wife, and Harry bullied that old, old lady into believing that she was a sweet, pregnant girl married to a sexy gorilla who was going to beat her brains out. She had me believing it too. And I read the lines of Blanche, her sister in the play, and darned if Harry didn't scare me into feeling like a drunk and faded Southern belle.

And then, while Doris and I were getting over our emotional experiences, like people coming out from under ether, Harry put down the playbook, put on his coat and tie, and turned into the pale hardware-store clerk again.

"Was—was that all right?" he said, and he seemed pretty sure he wouldn't get the part.

"Well," I said, "for a first reading, that wasn't too bad."

"Is there a chance I'll get the part?" he said. I don't know why he always had to pretend there was some doubt about his getting a part, but he did.

"I think we can safely say we're leaning powerfully in your direction," I told him.

He was very pleased. "Thanks! Thanks a lot!" he said, and he shook my hand.

"Is there a pretty new girl downstairs?" I said, meaning Helene Shaw.

"I didn't notice," said Harry.

It turned out that Helene Shaw *had* come for the tryouts, and Doris and I had our hearts broken. We thought the North Crawford Mask and Wig Club was finally going to put a really good-looking, really young girl

9

on stage, instead of one of the beat-up forty-year-old women we generally have to palm off as girls.

But Helene Shaw couldn't act for sour apples. No matter what we gave
her to read, she was the same girl with the same smile for anybody who
had a complaint about his phone bill.

Doris tried to coach her some, to make her understand that Stella in
the play was a very passionate girl who loved a gorilla because she
needed a gorilla. But Helene just read the lines the same way again. I
don't think a volcano could have stirred her up enough to say, "Oo."

"Dear," said Doris, "I'm going to ask you a personal question."

"All right," said Helene.

"Have you ever been in love?" said Doris. "The reason I ask," she said,
"remembering some old love might help you put more warmth in your
acting."

Helene frowned and thought hard. "Well," she said, "I travel a lot, you
know. And practically all the men in the different companies I visit are
married and I never stay anyplace long enough to know many people
who aren't."

"What about school?" said Doris. "What about puppy love and all the
other kinds of love in school?"

So Helene thought hard about that, and then she said, "Even in school
I was always moving around a lot. My father was a construction worker,
following jobs around, so I was always saying hello or good-by to someplace, without anything in between."

"Um," said Doris.

"Would movie stars count?" said Helene. "I don't mean in real life. I
never knew any. I just mean up on the screen."

Doris looked at me and rolled her eyes. "I guess that's love of a kind,"
she said.

And then Helene got a little enthusiastic. "I used to sit through movies
over and over again," she said, "and pretend I was married to whoever
the man movie star was. They were the only people who came with us.
No matter where we moved, movie stars were there."

"Uh huh," said Doris.

'Well, thank you, Miss Shaw," I said. "You go downstairs and wait with
the rest. We'll let you know."

So we tried to find another Stella. And there just wasn't one, not one
woman in the club with the dew still on her. "All we've got are
Blanches," I said, meaning all we had were faded women who could play
the part of Blanche, Stella's faded sister. "That's life, I guess—twenty
Blanches to one Stella."

"And when you find a Stella," said Doris, "it turns out she doesn't
know what love is."

Doris and I decided there was one last thing we could try. We could
get Harry Nash to play a scene along with Helene. "He just might make
her bubble the least little bit," I said.

"That girl hasn't got a bubble in her," said Doris.

So we called down the stairs for Helene to come back on up, and we told somebody to go find Harry. Harry never sat with the rest of the people at tryouts—or at rehearsals either. The minute he didn't have a part to play, he'd disappear into some hiding place where he could hear people call him, but where he couldn't be seen. At tryouts in the library he generally hid in the reference room, passing the time looking at flags of different countries in the front of the dictionary.

Helene came back upstairs, and we were very sorry and surprised to see that she'd been crying.

"Oh, dear," said Doris. "Oh, my—now what on earth's the trouble, dear?"

"I was terrible, wasn't I?" said Helene, hanging her head.

Doris said the only thing anybody can say in an amateur theatrical society when somebody cries. She said, "Why, no dear—you were marvelous."

"No, I wasn't," said Helene. "I'm a walking icebox, and I know it."

"Nobody could look at you and say that," said Doris.

"When they get to know me, they can say it," said Helene. "When people get to know me, that's what they *do* say." Her tears got worse. "I don't want to be the way I am," she said. "I just can't help it, living the way I've lived all my life. The only experiences I've had have been in crazy dreams of movie stars. When I meet somebody nice in real life, I feel as though I were in some kind of big bottle, as though I couldn't touch that person, no matter how hard I tried." And Helene pushed on air as though it were a big bottle all around her.

"You ask me if I've ever been in love," she said to Doris. "No—but I want to be. I know what this play's about. I know what Stella's supposed to feel and why she feels it. I—I—I—" she said, and her tears wouldn't let her go on.

"You what, dear?" said Doris gently.

"I—" said Helene, and she pushed on the imaginary bottle again. "I just don't know how to begin," she said.

There was heavy clumping on the library stairs. It sounded like a deep-sea diver coming upstairs in his lead shoes. It was Harry Nash, turning himself into Marlon Brando. In he came, practically dragging his knuckles on the floor. And he was so much in character that the sight of a weeping woman made him sneer.

"Harry," I said, "I'd like you to meet Helene Shaw. Helene—this is Harry Nash. If you get the part of Stella, he'll be your husband in the play." Harry didn't offer to shake hands. He put his hands in his pockets, and he hunched over, and he looked her up and down, gave her looks that left her naked. Her tears stopped right then and there.

"I wonder if you two would play the fight scene," I said, "and then the reunion scene right after it."

"Sure," said Harry, his eyes still on her. Those eyes burned up clothes faster than she could put them on. "Sure," he said, "if Stell's game."

"What?" said Helene. She'd turned the color of cranberry juice.

"Stell—Stella," said Harry. "That's you. Stell's my wife."

I handed the two of them playbooks. Harry snatched his from me without a word of thanks. Helene's hands weren't working very well, and I had to kind of mold them around the book.

"I'll want something I can throw," said Harry.

"What?" I said.

"There's one place where I throw a radio out a window," said Harry. "What can I throw?"

So I said an iron paperweight was the radio, and I opened the window wide. Helene Shaw looked scared to death.

"Where you want us to start?" said Harry, and he rolled his shoulders like a prizefighter warming up.

"Start a few lines back from where you throw the radio out the window," I said.

"O.K., O.K.," said Harry, warming up, warming up. He scanned the stage directions. "Let's see," he said, "after I throw the radio, she runs off stage, and I chase her, and I sock her one."

"Right," I said.

"O.K., baby," Harry said to Helene, his eyelids drooping. What was about to happen was wilder than the chariot race in *Ben Hur.* "On your mark," said Harry. "Get ready, baby. Go!"

When the scene was over, Helene Shaw was as hot as a hod carrier, as limp as an eel. She sat down with her mouth open and her head hanging to one side. She wasn't in any bottle any more. There wasn't any bottle to hold her up and keep her safe and clean. The bottle was gone.

"Do I get the part or don't I?" Harry snarled at me.

"You'll do," I said.

"You said a mouthful!" he said. "I'll be going now. . . . See you around, Stella," he said to Helene, and he left. He slammed the door behind him.

"Helene?" I said. "Miss Shaw?"

"Mf?" she said.

"The part of Stella is yours," I said. "You were great!"

"I was?" she said.

"I had no idea you had that much fire in you, dear," Doris said to her.

"Fire?" said Helene. She didn't know if she was afoot or on horseback.

"Skyrockets! Pinwheels! Roman candles!" said Doris.

"Mf," said Helene. And that was all she said. She looked as though she were going to sit in the chair with her mouth open forever.

"Stella," I said.

"Huh?" she said.

"You have my permission to go."

So we started having rehearsals four nights a week on the stage of the Consolidated School. And Harry and Helene set such a pace that everybody in the production was half crazy with excitement and exhaustion before we'd rehearsed four times. Usually a director has to beg people to learn their lines, but I had no such trouble. Harry and Helene were working so well together that everybody else in the cast regarded it as a duty and an honor and a pleasure to support them.

I was certainly lucky—or thought I was. Things were going so well, so hot and heavy, so early in the game that I had to say to Harry and Helene after one love scene, "Hold a little something back for the actual performance, would you please? You'll burn yourselves out."

I said that at the fourth or fifth rehearsal, and Lydia Miller, who was playing Blanche, the faded sister, was sitting next to me in the audience. In real life, she's the wife of Verne Miller. Verne owns Miller's Hardware Store. Verne was Harry's boss.

"Lydia," I said to her, "have we got a play or have we got a play?"

"Yes," she said, "you've got a play, all right." She made it sound as though I'd committed some kind of crime, done something just terrible. "You should be very proud of yourself."

"What do you mean by that?" I said.

Before Lydia could answer, Harry yelled at me from the stage, asked if I was through with him, asked if he could go home. I told him he could and, still Marlon Brando, he left, kicking furniture out of his way and slamming doors. Helene was left all alone on the stage, sitting on a couch with the same gaga look she'd had after the tryouts. That girl was drained.

I turned to Lydia again and I said, "Well—until now, I thought I had every reason to be happy and proud. Is there something going on I don't know about?"

"Do you know that girl's in love with Harry?" said Lydia.

"In the play?" I said.

"What play?" said Lydia. "There isn't any play going on now, and look at her up there." She gave a sad cackle. "You aren't directing this play."

"Who is?" I said.

"Mother Nature at her worst," said Lydia. "And think what it's going to do to that girl when she discovers what Harry really is." She corrected herself. "What Harry really isn't," she said.

I didn't do anything about it, because I didn't figure it was any of my business. I heard Lydia try to do something about it, but she didn't get very far.

"You know," Lydia said to Helene one night, "I once played Ann Rutledge, and Harry was Abraham Lincoln."

Helene clapped her hands. "That must have been heaven!" she said.

"It was, in a way," said Lydia. "Sometimes I'd get so worked up, I'd love Harry the way I'd love Abraham Lincoln. I'd have to come back to earth and remind myself that he wasn't ever going to free the slaves, that he was just a clerk in my husband's hardware store."

"He's the most marvelous man I ever met," said Helene.

"Of course, one thing you have to get set for, when you're in a play with Harry," said Lydia, "is what happens after the last performance."

"What are you talking about?" said Helene.

"Once the show's over," said Lydia, "whatever you thought Harry was just evaporates into thin air."

"I don't believe it," said Helene.

"I admit it's hard to believe," said Lydia.

Then Helene got a little sore. "Anyway, why tell me about it?" she said. "Even if it is true, what do I care?"

"I—I don't know," said Lydia, backing away. "I—I just thought you might find it interesting."

"Well, I don't," said Helene.

And Lydia slunk away, feeling about as frowzy and unloved as she was supposed to feel in the play. After that nobody said anything more to Helene to warn her about Harry, not even when word got around that she'd told the telephone company that she didn't want to be moved around anymore, that she wanted to stay in North Crawford.

So the time finally came to put on the play. We ran it for three nights—Thursday, Friday, and Saturday—and we murdered those audiences. They believed every word that was said on stage, and when the maroon curtain came down they were ready to go to the nut house along with Blanche, the faded sister.

On Thursday night the other girls at the telephone company sent Helene a dozen red roses. When Helene and Harry were taking a curtain call together, I passed the roses over the footlights to her. She came forward for them, took one rose from the bouquet to give to Harry. But when she turned to give Harry the rose in front of everybody, Harry was gone. The curtain came down on that extra little scene—that girl offering a rose to nothing and nobody.

I went backstage, and I found her still holding that one rose. She'd put the rest of the bouquet aside. There were tears in her eyes. "What did I do wrong?" she said to me. "Did I insult him some way?"

"No," I said. "He always does that after a performance. The minute it's over, he clears out as fast as he can."

"And tomorrow he'll disappear again?"

"Without even taking off his makeup."

"And Saturday?" she said. "He'll stay for the cast party on Saturday, won't he?"

"Harry never goes to parties," I said. "When the curtain comes down on Saturday, that's the last anybody will see of him till he goes to work on Monday."

"How sad," she said.

Helene's performance on Friday night wasn't nearly so good as Thursday's. She seemed to be thinking about other things. She watched Harry take off after curtain call. She didn't say a word.

On Saturday she put on the best performance yet. Ordinarily it was Harry who set the pace. But on Saturday Harry had to work to keep up with Helene.

When the curtain came down on the final curtain call, Harry wanted to get away, but he couldn't. Helene wouldn't let go his hand. The rest of the cast and the stage crew and a lot of well-wishers from the audience were all standing around Harry and Helene, and Harry was trying to get his hand back.

"Well," he said, "I've got to go."

"Where?" she said.

"Oh," he said, "home."

"Won't you please take me to the cast party?" she said.

He got very red. "I'm afraid I'm not much on parties," he said. All the Marlon Brando in him was gone. He was tongue-tied, he was scared, he was shy—he was everything Harry was famous for being between plays.

"All right," she said. "I'll let you go—if you promise me one thing."

"What's that?" he said, and I thought he would jump out a window if she let go of him then.

"I want you to promise to stay here until I get you your present," she said.

"Present?" he said, getting even more panicky.

"Promise?" she said.

He promised. It was the only way he could get his hand back. And he stood there miserably while Helene went down to the ladies' dressing room for the present. While he waited, a lot of people congratulated him on being such a fine actor. But congratulations never made him happy. He just wanted to get away.

Helene came back with the present. It turned out to be a little blue book with a big red ribbon for a place marker. It was a copy of *Romeo and Juliet.* Harry was very embarrassed. It was all he could do to say "Thank you."

"The marker marks my favorite scene," said Helene.

"Um," said Harry.

"Don't you want to see what my favorite scene is?" she said.

So Harry had to open the book to the red ribbon.

Helene got close to him, and read a line of Juliet's. " 'How cam'st thou hither, tell me, and wherefore?' " she read. " 'The orchard walls are high and hard to climb, and the place death, considering who thou art, if any of my kinsmen find thee here.' " She pointed to the next line. "Now, look what Romeo says," she said.

"Um," said Harry.

"Read what Romeo says," said Helene.

Harry cleared his throat. He didn't want to read the line, but he had to. " 'With love's light wings did I o'erperch these walls,' " he read out loud in his everyday voice. But then a change came over him. " 'For stony limits cannot hold love out,' " he read, and he straightened up, and eight years dropped away from him, and he was brave and gay. " 'And what love can do, that dares love attempt,' " he read, " 'therefore thy kinsmen are no let to me.' "

" 'If they do see thee they will murther thee,' " said Helene, and she started him walking toward the wings.

" 'Alack!' " said Harry, " 'there lies more peril in thine eye than twenty of their swords.' " Helene led him toward the backstage exit. " 'Look thou but sweet,' " said Harry, " 'and I am proof against their enmity.' "

" 'I would not for the world they saw thee here,' " said Helene, and that was the last we heard. The two of them were out the door and gone.

They never did show up at the cast party. One week later they were married.

They seem very happy, although they're kind of strange from time to time, depending on which play they're reading to each other at the time.

I dropped into the phone company office the other day, on account of the billing machine was making dumb mistakes again. I asked her what plays she and Harry'd been reading lately.

"In the past week," she said, "I've been married to Othello, been loved by Faust and kidnaped by Paris. Wouldn't you say I was the luckiest girl in town?"

I said I thought so, and I told her most of the women in town thought so too.

"They had their chance," she said.

"Most of 'em couldn't stand the excitement," I said. And I told her I'd been asked to direct another play. I asked if she and Harry would be available for the cast. She gave me a big smile and said, "Who are we this time?"

PROBINGS

1. List all the different roles that you play in life and keep a role diary for two weeks. Include in this diary all the different clothes, props (such as cigarettes and jewelry), behavior that you use to play the role. For example, what special clothes do you wear as an employee? As a girl friend or boyfriend? Are there certain clothes that your parents don't like you to wear? Why?

2. Analyze your diary. Which of the roles are most important to you? Least important? Why? One way of analzing our roles is by constucting a role graph. Try to figure out how much time you spend on an average day playing various roles, then figure out an *approximate* percentage of your total time spent on the role. For example, if you work six hours out of twenty-four, then the percentage of your day spent as an employee is 25%.

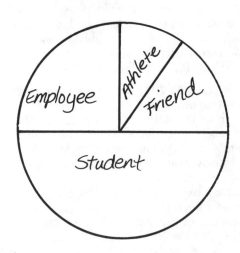

3. Watch at least two TV shows or films and construct a role diary for the following characters. What clothes or costumes do they wear? What props do they use?

   Cowboy
   Teacher
   Detective
   Doctor
   Lawyer
   Homemaker

4. By using a tape recorder or keeping a written journal, record an interview with someone at least sixty-five years old. Attempt to find out what the person feels about his or her life. What gave your inerviewee the greatest satisfaction in life? What made him or her the happiest? Saddest? If the interviewee could change his or her life in any way, what would he or she have done differently? Why?

    Caution: You are to be more of a listener than a talker. The mark of a good interviewer is an ability to draw out the interviewee and to encourage him or her to talk. Therefore, try not to make judgments about the person, even if you don't find his or her life particularly appealing. Your job is to find out what roles were most important to the person you are interviewing, and how they contributed to this person's identity.

5. If you could place five personal things in a time capsule or an "identity" capsule, things that would tell people about the you of today, which items would you choose? (This capsule would be opened in the year 3000). Why did you select these items? Do you think that these items will still represent you ten years from now? Twenty years from now? Fifty years? Why or Why not?

6. Assuming that you are very, very old, write a will. What things, ideas, advice, and qualities would you leave and to whom? Why? If you had to write a will today, what things, ideas, advice, or qualities would you leave and to whom? Why?

7. Fill out the following "Note From the Future."

    The year is between 2021 and 2025. I am a (occupation) _____ living in the state or country of _____. I am living there because I enjoy what about the state or country _____. The type of dwelling that I live in is best described as a (house, apartment, condominium, cabin, other) _____. As I am getting older, I find more time to do things that I always wanted to do. Some of these things are _____, _____, and _____.

    As I look back over my life, I feel that my three greatest accomplishments have been (1) _____, (2) _____, and, (3) _____. The greatest source(s) of joy and comfort for me is (are) _____.

    I fully expect to live to be (what age) _____. I consider _____ as the best years of my life because _____. When I die, I hope that I'll be best remembered for _____.

8. How would your life be changed—
    a. If most embryos were developed in artificial wombs?
    b. If people mostly worked at home via TV and computers?

OCCUPATIONAL ROLES

2

In some cultures when one meets a stranger the question raised is: "Who is your family?" or "What is your village?" In this way, a person is immediately identified by his or her association with a particular family or village. Consequently, the person gains a specific identity.

In our culture, we ask the stranger: "What do you do?" Of course, we are asking about the individual's job. Once we have the answer to that question, we can usually tell a great deal about the person, for example, his or her interests, lifestyle, and income. In effect, we create little biographies for people once we know their occupation. Sometimes our biographies are wrong, but often they are right. Teachers are supposed to have certain interests; doctors, different ones; laborers, still other ones. In our society, we spend many years going to school in order to "be something" or be "somebody" eventually. We are urged by teachers and parents alike to find an occupation with which we can be happy.

But what if there came a time when you would never have to go to school? Rather, on a magical day, at age eighteen, you would be programmed for your life's work. This is the world that Isaac Asimov describes in his story "Profession."

1. Headlines from Tomorrow:

**BOY REBELS AGAINST
JOB PROGRAMMING**

**JOB QUOTAS NOT
MET—MORE BABIES
NEEDED**

PROJECTIONS

2. A scientist in Maryland has perfected a machine, he claims, that measures the thinking efficiency of the human brain. He proposes to test children at age five or six to determine which children should pursue specific occupations. Children who score high on the tests would be allowed to become lawyers, doctors, and engineers; those who score lower would have to pursue less "desirable" occupations. Would you be in favor of testing children at this age? Why or why not? Discuss the moral, ethical, and political consequences of such a system.

"PROFESSION"

—Isaac Asimov

There was a time, four or five thousand years ago when mankind was confined to the surface of Earth. Even then, his culture had grown quite technological and his numbers had increased to the point where any failure in technology would have meant mass starvation and disease. To maintain the technological level and advance it in the face of an increasing population, more and more technicians and scientists had to be trained, and yet, as science advanced, it took longer and longer to train them.

As first interplanetary and then interstellar travel was developed, the problem grew more acute. In fact, actual colonization of extra-Solar planets was impossible for about fifteen hundred years because of a lack of properly trained men.

The turning point came when the mechanics of the storage of knowledge within the brain was worked out. Once that had been done, it became possible to devise Educational tapes that would modify the mechanics in such a way as to place within the mind a body of knowledge ready-made, so to speak. . . .

Once that was done, trained men could be turned out by the thousands and millions, and we could begin what someone has since called the "Filling of the Universe." There are now fifteen hundred inhabited planets in the Galaxy and there is no end in sight.

Do you see all that is involved? Earth exports Education tapes for low-specialized professions and that keeps the Galactic culture unified. For instance, the Reading tapes insure a single language for all of us. . . .

Earth also exports highly specialized professionals and keeps its own population at an endurable level. Since they are shipped out in a balanced sex ratio, they act as self-reproductive units and help increase the populations on the Outworlds where an increase is needed. Furthermore, tapes and men are paid for in material which we much need and on which our economy depends.

For most of the first eighteen years of his life, George Platen had headed firmly in one direction, that of Registered Computer Programmer. There were those in his crowd who spoke wisely of Spationautics, Refrigeration Technology, Transportation Control, and even Administration. But George held firm.

He argued relative merits as vigorously as any of them, and why not? Education Day loomed ahead of them and was the great fact of their existence. It approached steadily, as fixed and certain as the calendar—the first day of November of the year following one's eighteenth birthday.

After that day, there were other topics of conversation. One could discuss with others some detail of the profession, or the virtues of one's wife and children. . . .

Before Education Day, however, there was only one topic that unfailingly and unwearyingly held everyone's interest, and that was Education Day.

"What are you going for? Think you'll make it? That's no good. Look at the records; quota's been cut. Logistics now—"

Or Hypermechanics now— Or Communications now— Or Gravitics now—

Especially Gravitics at the moment. Everyone had been talking about Gravitics in the few years just before George's Education Day because of the development of the Gravitic power engine.

Any world within ten light-years of a dwarf star, everyone said, would give its eyeteeth for any kind of Registered Gravitics Engineer.

The thought of that never bothered George. Sure it would; all the eyeteeth it could scare up. But George had also heard what had happened before in a newly developed technique. Rationalization and simplification followed in a flood. New models each year; new types of gravitic engines; new principles. Then all those eyeteeth gentlemen would find themselves out of date and superseded by later models with later educations. The first group would then have to settle down to unskilled labour or ship out to some backwoods world that wasn't quite caught up yet.

Now Computer Programmers were in steady demand year after year, century after century. The demand never reached wild peaks; there was never a howling bull market for Programmers; but the demand climbed steadily as new worlds opened up and as older worlds grew more complex.

He had argued with Trevelyan about that constantly. As best friends, their arguments had to be constant and vitriolic and, of course, neither ever persuaded or was persuaded.

But then Trevelyan had had a father who was a Registered Metallurgist and had actually served on one of the Outworlds, and a grandfather who had also been a Registered Metallurgist. He himself was intent on becoming a Registered Metallurgist almost as a matter of family right and was firmly convinced that any other profession was a shade less than respectable.

"There'll always be metal," he said, "and there's an accomplishment in moulding alloys to specification and watching structures grow. Now what's a Programmer going to be doing. Sitting at a coder all day long, feeding some fool machine."

Even at sixteen, George had learned to be practical. He said simply, "There'll be a million Metallurgists put out along with you."

"Because it's good. A good profession. The best."

"But you get crowded out, Stubby. You can be way back in line. Any world can tape out its own Metallurgists, and the market for advanced

Earth models isn't so big. And it's mostly the small worlds that want them. You know what percent of the turnout of Registered Metallurgists get tabbed for worlds with a Grade A rating. I looked it up. It's just 13.3 percent. That means you'll have seven chances in eight of being stuck in some world that just about has running water. You may even be stuck on Earth; 2.3 percent are."

Trevelyan said belligerently, "There's no disgrace in staying on Earth. Earth needs technicians, too. Good ones." His grandfather had been an Earthbound Metallurgist, and Trevelyan lifted his finger to his upper lip and dabbed at an as yet non-existent moustache.

George knew about Trevelyan's grandfather and, considering the Earthbound position of his own ancestry, was in no mood to sneer. He said diplomatically, "No intellectual disgrace. Of course not. But it's nice to get into a Grade A world, isn't it?

"Now you take Programmers. Only the Grade A worlds have the kind of computers that really need first-class Programmers so they're the only ones in the market. And Programmer tapes are complicated and hardly any one fits. They need more Programmers than their own population can supply. It's just a matter of statistics. There's one first-class Programmer per million, say. A world needs twenty and has a population of ten million, they have to come to Earth for five to fifteen Programmers. Right?

"And you know how many Registered Computer Programmers went to Grade A planets last year? I'll tell you. Every last one. If you're a Programmer, you're a picked man. Yes, sir."·

Trevelyan frowned. "If only one in a million makes it, what makes you think *you*'ll make it?"

George said guardedly, "I'll make it."

He never dared tell anyone; not Trevelyan; not his parents; of exactly what he was doing that made him so confident. But he wasn't worried. He was simply confident. . . .

He was as blandly confident as the average eight-year-old kid approaching Reading Day—that childhood preview of Education Day.

Of course, Reading Day had been different. Partly, there was the simple fact of childhood. A boy of eight takes many extraordinary things in his stride. One day you can't read and the next day you can. That's just the way things are. Like the sun shining.

And then not so much depended upon it. There were no recruiters just ahead, waiting and jostling for the lists and scores. . . . A boy or girl who goes through the Reading Day is just someone who has ten more years of undifferentiated living upon Earth's crawling surface; just someone who returns to his family with one new ability.

By the time Education Day came, ten years later, George wasn't even sure of most of the details of his own Reading Day.

Most clearly of all, he remembered it to be a dismal September day with a mild rain falling. . . . George had dressed by the wall lights, with his parents far more excited than he himself was. His father was a Registered Pipe Fitter and had found his occupation on earth. This fact had always been a humiliation to him, although, of course, as anyone could see plainly, most of each generation must stay on Earth in the nature of things.

There had to be farmers and miners and even technicians on Earth. It was only the late-model, high-specialty professions that were in demand on the Outworlds, and only a few millions a year out of Earth's eight billion population could be exported. Every man and woman on Earth couldn't be among that group.

But every man and woman could hope that at least one of his children could be one, and Platen, Senior, was certainly no exception. It was obvious to him (and, to be sure, to others as well) that George was notably intelligent and quick-minded. He would be bound to do well and he would have to, as he was an only child. If George didn't end on an Outworld, they would have to wait for grandchildren before a next chance would come along, and that was too far in the future to be much consolation.

Reading Day would not prove much, of course, but it would be the only indication they would have before the big day itself. Every parent on Earth would be listening to the quality of reading when his child came home with it; listening for any particularly easy flow of words and building that into certain omens of the future. There were few families that didn't have at least one hopeful who, from Reading Day on, was the great hope because of the way he handled his trisyllabics.

Dimly, George was aware of the cause of his parents' tension, and if there was any anxiety in his young heart that drizzly morning, it was only the fear that his father's hopeful expression might fade out when he returned home with his reading.

The children met in the large assembly room of the town's Education hall. All over Earth, in millions of local halls, throughout that month, similar groups of children would be meeting. George felt depressed by the greyness of the room and by the other children, strained and stiff in unaccustomed finery.

Automatically, George did as all the rest of the children did. He found the small clique that represented the children on his floor of the apartment house and joined them. . . .

A woman's voice sounded loudly over the public address system. There was instant silence everywhere. . . .

"Children," said the voice, "we are going to call out your names. As each child is called, he or she is to go to one of the men waiting along the side walls. Do you see them? They are wearing red uniforms so they will be easy to find. The girls will go to the right. The boys will go to the left. Now look about and see which man in red is nearest to you—"

George found his man at a glance and waited for his name to be called off. He had not been introduced before this to the sophistications of the alphabet, and the length of time it took to reach his own name grew disturbing.

The crowd of children thinned; little rivulets made their way to each of the red-clad guides.

When the name "George Platen" was finally called, his sense of relief was exceeded only by the feeling of pure gladness at the fact that Trevelyan still stood in his place, uncalled. . . .

He was herded into a line and directed down corridors in the company of strange children. They all looked at one another, large-eyed and concerned, but beyond a snuffling, "Quitcher pushing" and "'Hey, watch out" there was no conversation.

They were handed little slips of paper which they were told must remain with them. George stared at his curiously. Little black marks of different shapes. He knew it to be printing but how could anyone make words out of it? He couldn't imagine.

He was told to strip; he and four other boys who were all that now remained together. All the new clothes came shucking off and four eight-year-olds stood naked and small, shivering more out of embarrassment than cold. Medical technicians came past, probing them, testing them with odd instruments, pricking them for blood. Each took the little cards and made additional marks on them with black rods that produced the marks, all neatly lined up, with great speed. George stared at the new marks, but they were no more comprehensible than the old. The children were ordered back into their clothes.

They sat on separate little chairs then and waited again. Names were called again and "George Platen" came third.

He moved into a large room, filled with frightening instruments with knobs and glassy panels in front. There was a desk in the very centre, and behind it a man sat, his eyes on the papers piled before him.

He said, "George Platen?"

"Yes, sir" said George, in a shaky whisper. All this waiting and all this going here and there was making him nervous. He wished it were over.

The man behind the desk said, "I am Dr. Lloyd, George. How are you?"

The doctor didn't look up as he spoke. It was as though he had said those words over and over again and didn't have to look up any more.

"I'm all right."

"Are you afraid, George?"

"N-no sir," said George, sounding afraid even in his own ears.

"That's good," said the doctor, "because there's nothing to be afraid of, you know. Let's see, George. It says here on your card that your father is named Peter and that he's a Registered Pipe Fitter and your mother is named Amy and is a Registered Home Technician. Is that right?"

"Y-yes, sir."

"And your birthday is February 13, and you had an ear infection about a year ago. Right?"

"Yes, sir."

"Do you know how I know all these things?"

"It's on the card, I think, sir."

"That's right." The doctor looked up at George for the first time and smiled. He showed even teeth and looked much younger than George's father. Some of George's nervousness vanished.

The doctor passed the card to George. "Do you know what all those things there mean, George?"

Although George knew he did not he was startled by the sudden request into looking at the card as though he might understand now through some sudden stroke of fate. But they were just marks as before and he passed the card back. "No, sir."

"Why not?"

George felt a sudden pang of suspicion concerning the sanity of this doctor. Didn't he know why not?

George said, "I can't read, sir."

"Would you like to read?"

"Yes, sir."

"Why, George?"

George stared, appalled. No one had ever asked him that. He had no answer. He said falteringly, "I don't know, sir."

"Printed information will direct you all through your life. There is so much you'll have to know even after Education Day. Cards like this one will tell you. Books will tell you. Television screens will tell you. Printing will tell you such useful things and such interesting things that not being able to read would be as bad as not being able to see. Do you understand?"

"Yes, sir."

"Are you afraid, George?"

"No, sir."

"Good. Now I'll tell you exactly what we'll do first. I'm going to put these wires on your forehead just over the corners of your eyes. They'll stick there but they won't hurt at all. Then, I'll turn on something that will make a buzz. It will sound funny and it may tickle you, but it won't hurt. Now if it does hurt, you tell me, and I'll turn it off right away, but it won't hurt. All right?"

George nodded and swallowed.

"Are you ready?"

George nodded. He closed his eyes while the doctor busied himself. His parents had explained this to him. They, too, had said it wouldn't hurt, but then there were always the older children. There were the ten- and twelve-year-olds who howled after the eight-year-olds waiting for Reading Day, "Watch out for the needle." There were the others who took you off in confidence and said, "They got to cut your head open. They use a sharp knife that big with a hook on it," and so on into horrifying details.

George had never believed them but he had had nightmares, and now he closed his eyes and felt pure terror.

He didn't feel the wires at his temple. The buzz was a distant thing, and there was the sound of his own blood in his ears, ringing hollowly as though it and he were in a large cave. Slowly he chanced opening his eyes.

The doctor had his back to him. From one of the instruments a strip of paper unwound and was covered with a thin, wavy purple line. The doctor tore off pieces and put them into a slot in another machine. He did it over and over again. Each time a little piece of film came out, which the doctor looked at. Finally, he turned toward George with a queer frown between his eyes.

The buzzing stopped.

George said breathlessly, "Is it over?"

The doctor said, "Yes," but he was still frowning.

"Can I read now?" asked George. He felt no different.

The doctor said, "What?" then smiled very suddenly and briefly. He said, "It works fine, George. You'll be reading in fifteen minutes. Now we're going to use another machine this time and it will take longer. I'm going to cover your whole head, and when I turn it on you won't be able to see or hear anything for a while, but it won't hurt. Just to make sure I'm going to give you a little switch to hold in your hand. If anything hurts, you press the little button and everything shuts off. All right?"

In later years, George was told that the little switch was strictly a dummy; that it was introduced solely for confidence. He never did know for sure, however, since he never pushed the button.

A large smoothly curved helmet with a rubbery inner lining was placed over his head and left there. Three or four little knobs seemed to grab at him and bite into his skull, but there was only a little pressure that faded. No pain.

The doctor's voice sounded dimly. "Everything all right, George?"

And then, with no real warning, a layer of thick felt closed down all about him. He was disembodied, there was no sensation, no universe, only himself and a distant murmur at the very ends of nothingness telling him something—telling him—telling him—

He strained to hear and understand but there was all that thick felt between.

Then the helmet was taken off his head, and the light was so bright that it hurt his eyes while the doctor's voice drummed at his ears.

The doctor said, "Here's your card, George. What does it say?"

George looked at his card again and gave out a strangled shout. The marks weren't just marks at all. They made up words. They were words just as clearly as though something were whispering them in his ears. He could *hear* them being whispered as he looked at them.

"What does it say, George?"

"It says—it says—'Platen, George. Born 13 February 6492 of Peter and Amy Platen in . . .'" He broke off.

"You can read, George," said the doctor. "It's all over."

"For good? I won't forget how?"

"Of course not." The doctor leaned over to shake hands gravely. "You will be taken home now."

It was days before George got over this new and great talent of his. He read for his father with such facility that Platen, Senior, wept and called relatives to tell the good news.

George walked about town, reading every scrap of printing he could find and wondering how it was that none of it had ever made sense to him before.

He tried to remember how it was not to be able to read and he couldn't. As far as his feeling about it was concerned, he had always been able to read. Always.

At eighteen, George was rather dark, of medium height, but thin enough to look taller. Trevelyan, who was scarcely an inch shorter, had a stockiness of build that made "Stubby" more than ever appropriate, but in his last year he had grown self-conscious. The nickname could no longer be used without reprisal. And since Trevelyan disapproved of his proper first name even more strongly, he was called Trevelyan or any decent variant of that. As though to prove his manhood further, he had most persistently grown a pair of sideburns and a bristly moustache. . . .

They were in the same large hall they had been in ten years before (and not since). It was as if a vague dream of the past had come to sudden reality. In the first few minutes George had been distinctly surprised at finding everything seem smaller and more cramped than his memory told him; then he made allowance for his own growth.

The crowd was smaller than it had been in childhood. It was exclusively male this time. The girls had another day assigned them.

Trevelyan leaned over to say, "Beats me the way they make you wait."

"Red tape," said George. "You can't avoid it."

Trevelyan said, "What makes *you* so damned tolerant about it?"

"I've got nothing to worry about."

"Oh, brother, you make me sick. I hope you end up Registered Manure Spreader just so I can see your face when you do." His sombre eyes swept the crowd anxiously.

George looked about, too. It wasn't quite the system they used on the children. Matters went slower, and instructions had been given out at the start in print (an advantage over the pre-Readers). The names Platen and Trevelyan were well down the alphabet still, but this time the two knew it.

Young men came out of the education rooms, frowning and uncomfortable, picked up their clothes and belongings, then went off to analysis to learn the results.

Each, as he came out, would be surrounded by a clot of the thinning crowd. "How was it?" "How'd it feel?" "Whacha think ya made?" "Ya feel any different?"

Answers were vague and noncommittal.

George forced himself to remain out of those clots. You only raised your own blood pressure. Everyone said you stood the best chance if you remained calm. Even so, you could feel the palms of your hands grow cold. Funny that new tensions came with the years.

For instance, high-specialty professionals heading out for an Outworld were accompanied by a wife (or husband). It was important to keep the sex ratio in good balance on all worlds. And if you were going out to a Grade A world, what girl would refuse you? George had no specific girl in mind yet; he wanted none. Not now! Once he made Programmer; once he could add to his name, Registered Computer Programmer, he could take his pick, like a sultan in a harem. The thought excited him and he tried to put it away. Must stay calm.

Trevelyan muttered, "What's it all about anyway? First they say it works best if you're relaxed and at ease. Then they put you through this and make it impossible for you to be relaxed and at ease."

"Maybe that's the idea. They're separating the boys from the men to begin with. Take it easy, Trev."

"Shut up."

George's turn came. His name was not called. It appeared in glowing letters on the notice-board.

He waved at Trevelyan. "Take it easy. Don't let it get you."

He was happy as he entered the testing chamber. Actually happy.

The man behind the desk said, "George Platen?"

For a fleeting instant there was a razor-sharp picture in George's mind of another man, ten years earlier, who had asked the same question, and it was almost as though this were the same man and he, George, had turned eight again as he had stepped across the threshold.

But the man looked up and, of course, the face matched that of the sudden memory not at all. The nose was bulbous, the hair thin and stringy, and the chin wattled as though its owner had once been grossly overweight and had reduced.

The man behind the desk looked annoyed. "Well?"

George came to Earth. "I'm George Platen, sir."

"Say so, then. I'm Dr. Zachary Antonelli, and we're going to be intimately acquainted in a moment."

He stared at small strips of film, holding them up to the light owlishly.

George winced inwardly. Very hazily, he remembered that other doctor (he had forgotten the name) staring at such film. Could these be the same? The other doctor had frowned and this one was looking at him now as though he were angry.

His happiness was already just about gone.

Dr. Antonelli spread the pages of a thickish file out before him now and put the films carefully to one side. "It says here you want to be a Computer Programmer."

"Yes, doctor."

"Still do?"

"Yes, sir."

"It's a responsible and exacting position. Do you feel up to it?"

"Yes, sir."

"Most pre-Educates don't put down any specific profession. I believe they are afraid of queering it."

"I think that's right, sir."

"Aren't you afraid of that?"

"I might as well be honest, sir."

Dr. Antonelli nodded, but without any noticeable lightening of his expression. "Why do you want to be a Programmer?"

"It's a responsible and exacting position as you said, sir. It's an important job and an exciting one. I like it and I think I can do it."

Dr. Antonelli put the papers away, and looked at George sourly. He said, "How do you know you like it? Because you think you'll be snapped up by some Grade A planet?"

George thought uneasily: He's trying to rattle you. Stay calm and stay frank.

He said, "I think a Programmer has a good chance, sir, but even if I were left on Earth, I know I'd like it." (That was true enough. I'm not lying, thought George.)

"All right, how do you know?"

He asked it as though he knew there was no decent answer and George almost smiled. He had one.

He said, "I've been reading about Programming, sir."

"You've been *what?*" Now the doctor looked genuinely astonished and George took pleasure in that.

"Reading about it, sir. I bought a book on the subject and I've been studying it."

"A book for Registered Programmers?"

"Yes, sir."

"But you couldn't understand it."

"Not at first. I got other books on mathematics and electronics. I made out all I could. I still don't know much, but I know enough to know I like it and to know I can make it." (Even his parents never found that secret cache of books or knew why he spent so much time in his own room or exactly what happened to the sleep he missed.)

The doctor pulled at the loose skin under his chin. "What was your idea in doing that, son?"

"I wanted to make sure I would be interested, sir."

"Surely you know that being interested means nothing. You could be devoured by a subject and if the physical make-up of your brain makes it more efficient for you to be something else, something else you will be. You know that, don't you?"

"I've been told that," said George cautiously.

"Well, believe it. It's true."

George said nothing.

Dr. Antonelli said, "Or do you believe that studying some subject will bend the brain cells in that direction, like that other theory that a pregnant woman need only listen to great music persistently to make a composer of her child. Do you believe that?"

George flushed. That had certainly been in his mind. By forcing his intellect constantly in the desired direction, he had felt sure that he would be getting a head start. Most of his confidence had rested on exactly that point.

"I never—" he began, and found no way of finishing.

"Well, it isn't true. Good Lord, youngster, your brain pattern is fixed at birth. It can be altered by a blow hard enough to damage the cells or by a burst blood vessel or by a tumour or by a major infection—each time, of course, for the worse. But it certainly can't be affected by your thinking special thoughts." He stared at George thoughtfully, then said, "Who told you to do this?"

George, now thoroughly disturbed, swallowed and said, "No one, doctor. My own idea."

"Who knew you were doing it after you started?"

"No one. Doctor, I meant to do no wrong."

"Who said anything about wrong? Useless is what I would say. Why did you keep it to yourself?"

"I-I thought they'd laugh at me." (He thought abruptly of a recent exchange with Trevelyan. George had very cautiously broached the thought as of something merely circulating distantly in the very outermost reaches of his mind, concerning the possibility of learning something by ladling it into the mind by hand, so to speak, in bits and pieces. Trevelyan had hooted, "George, you'll be tanning your own shoes next and weaving your own shirts." He had been thankful then for his policy of secrecy.)

Dr. Antonelli shoved the bits of film he had first looked at from position to position in morose thought. Then he said, "Let's get you analysed. This is getting me nowhere."

The wires went to George's temples. There was the buzzing. Again there came a sharp memory of ten years ago.

George's hands were clammy; his heart pounded. He should never have told the doctor about his secret reading.

It was his damned vanity, he told himself. He had wanted to show how enterprising he was, how full of initiative. Instead, he had showed himself superstitious and ignorant and aroused the hostility of the doctor. (He could tell the doctor hated him for a wise guy on the make.)

And now he had brought himself to such a state of nervousness, he was sure the analyser would show nothing that made sense.

He wasn't aware of the moment when the wires were removed from his temples. The sight of the doctor, staring at him thoughtfully, blinked into his consciousness and that was that; the wires were gone. George dragged himself together with a tearing effort. He had quite given up his ambition to be a Programmer. In the space of ten minutes, it had all gone.

He said dismally, "I suppose no?"

"No what?"

"No Programmer?"

The doctor rubbed his nose and said, "You get your clothes and whatever belongs to you and go to room 15-C. Your files will be waiting for you there. So will my report."

George said in complete surprise. "Have I been Educated already? I thought this was just to—"

Dr. Antonelli stared down at his desk. "It will all be explained to you. You do as I say."

George felt something like panic. What was it they couldn't tell him? He wasn't fit for anything but Registered Labourer. They were going to prepare him for that; adjust him to it.

He was suddenly certain of it and he had to keep from screaming by main force.

He stumbled back to his place of waiting. Trevelyan was not there, a fact for which he would have been thankful if he had had enough self-possession to be meaningfully aware of his surroundings. Hardly anyone was left, in fact, and the few who were looked as though they might ask him questions were it not that they were too worn out by their tail-of-the-alphabet waiting to buck the fierce, hot look of anger and hate he cast at them.

What right had *they* to be technicians and he, himself, a Labourer? Labourer! He was *certain*!

He was led by a red-uniformed guide along the busy corridors lined with separate rooms each containing its groups, here two, there five: the Motor Mechanics, the Construction Engineers, the Agronomists—there were hundreds of specialized Professions and most of them would be represented in this small town by one or two anyway.

He hated them all just then: the Statisticians, the Accountants, the lesser breeds and the higher. He hated them because they owned their smug knowledge now, knew their fate, while he himself, empty still, had to face some kind of further red tape.

He reached 15-C, was ushered in and left in an empty room. For one moment, his spirits bounded. Surely, if this were the Labour classification room, there would be dozens of youngsters present.

A door sucked into its recess on the other side of a waist-high partition and an elderly, white-haired man stepped out. He smiled and showed even teeth that were obviously false, but his face was still ruddy and his voice had vigour.

He said, "Good evening, George. Our own sector has only one of you this time, I see."

"Only one?" said George blankly.

"Thousands over the Earth, of course. Thousands. You're not alone."

George felt exasperated. He said, "I don't understand, sir. What's my classification? What's happening?"

"Easy, son. You're all right. It could happen to anyone." He held out his hand and George took it mechanically. It was warm and it pressed George's hand firmly. "Sit down, son. I'm Sam Ellenford."

George nodded impatiently. "I want to know what's going on, sir."

"Of course. To begin with, you can't be a Computer Programmer, George. You've guessed that, I think."

"Yes, I have," said George bitterly. 'What will I be, then?"

"That's the hard part to explain, George." He paused, then said with careful distinctness, "Nothing."

"What!"

"Nothing!"

"But what does that mean? Why can't you assign me a profession?"

"We have no choice in the matter, George. It's the structure of your mind that decides that."

George went a sallow yellow. His eyes bulged. "There's something wrong with my mind?"

"There's *something* about it. As far as professional classification is concerned. I suppose you can call it wrong."

"But why?"

Ellenford shrugged. "I'm sure you know how Earth runs its Educational programme, George. Practically any human being can absorb practically any body of knowledge, but each individual brain pattern is better suited to receiving some types of knowledge than others. We try to match mind to knowledge as well as we can within the limits of the quota requirements for each profession."

George nodded. "Yes, I know."

"Every once in a while, George, we come up against a young man whose mind is not suited to receiving a superimposed knowledge of any sort."

"You mean I can't be Educated?"

"That is what I mean."

"But that's crazy. I'm intelligent. I can understand—" He looked helplessly about as though trying to find some way of proving that he had a functioning brain.

"Don't misunderstand me, please," said Ellenford gravely. "You're intelligent. There's no question about that. You're even above average in intelligence. Unfortunately that has nothing to do with whether the mind ought to be allowed to accept superimposed knowledge or not. In fact, it is almost always the intelligent person who comes here."

"You mean I can't even be a Registered Labourer?" babbled George. Suddenly even that was better than the blank that faced him. "What's there to know to be a Labourer?"

"Don't underestimate the Labourer, young man. There are dozens of subclassifications and each variety has its own corpus of fairly detailed knowledge. Do you think there's no skill in knowing the proper manner of lifting a weight? Besides, for the Labourer, we must select not only minds suited to it, but bodies as well. You're not the type, George, to last long as a Labourer."

George was conscious of his slight build. He said, "But I've never heard of anyone without a profession."

"There aren't many," conceded Ellenford. "And we protect them."

"Protect them?" George felt confusion and fright grow higher inside him.

"You're a ward of the planet, George. From the time you walked through that door, we've been in charge of you." And he smiled.

It was a fond smile. To George it seemed the smile of ownership; the smile of a grown man for a helpless child.

He said. "You mean, I'm going to be in prison?"

"Of course not. You will simply be with others of your kind."

Your kind. The words made a kind of thunder in George's ear.

Ellenford said, "You need special treatment. We'll take care of you."

To George's own horror, he burst into tears. Ellenford walked to the other end of the room and faced away as though in thought.

George fought to reduce the agonized weeping to sobs and then to strangle those. He thought of his father and mother, of his friends, of Trevelyan, of his own shame—

He said rebelliously, "I learned to read."

"Everyone with a whole mind can do that. We've never found exceptions. It is at this stage that we discover—exceptions. And when you learned to read, George, we were concerned about your mind pattern. Certain peculiarities were reported even then by the doctor in charge."

"Can't you try Educating me? You haven't even tried. I'm willing to take the risk."

"The law forbids us to do that, George. But look, it will not be bad. We will explain matters to your family so they will not be hurt. At the place to which you'll be taken, you'll be allowed privileges. We'll get you books and you can learn what you will."

"Dab knowledge in by hand," said George bitterly. "Shred by shred. Then, when I die I'll know enough to be a Registered Junior Office Boy, Paper-Clip Division."

"Yet I understand you've already been studying books."

George froze. He was struck devastatingly by sudden understanding. "That's it . . ."

"What is?"

"That fellow Antonelli. He's knifing me."

"No, George. You're quite wrong."

"Don't tell me that." George was in an ecstasy of fury. "That lousy bastard is selling me out because he thought I was a little too wise for him. I read books and tried to get a head start toward programming. Well, what do you want to square things? Money? You won't get it. I'm getting out of here and when I finish broadcasting this—"

He was screaming.

Ellenford shook his head and touched a contact.

Two men entered on catfeet and got on either side of George. They pinned his arms to his sides. One of them used an air-spray hypodermic in the hollow of his right elbow and the hypnotic entered his vein and had an almost immediate effect.

His screams cut off and his head fell forward. His knees buckled and only the men on either side kept him erect as he slept . . .

PROBINGS

1. If you could learn anything from education tapes like those mentioned in the story, what would it be and why?
2. If you lived in the society that Asimov portrays, what would you find most appealing about it? Least appealing? Why?
3. If you had been the young person in "Profession," how would you have felt when you were told that you could have no profession? What specifically would you have done? Write a short story, keep a journal, or write a letter to a favorite friend describing your feelings.
4. Rank twenty occupations according to your personal preference. Number one would be the occupation that you see as being most desirable; number twenty would be the occupation that you would see as being least desirable. Number ten would be the median, the one that you don't feel strongly about one way or the other. Give reasons for each of your rankings.
5. Interview at least two older people about their jobs. What do they find most rewarding about their job? Least rewarding? Why? Why did they select the job they did? If they could have any job they wanted, what would it be? Why?
6. If you could select the ideal occupation for you that would make you happy for the rest of your life, what would it be? Why? What specifically would you expect from your job? Money? Power? Status? Romance? Other?
7. What interests, hobbies, or training do you already have that might prepare you for your "ideal" occupation?
8. Roosevelt (Rosey) Grier does needlepoint, a hobby that does not fit the role he is supposed to play as a former professional football player. Can you think of other people who do not completely fit the "proper" occupational mold in terms of their lifestyle, interests, or

hobbies? Do you know anyone personally who doesn't follow his or her "proper" occupational role?

9. What if everybody could be programmed for their life's work? One technique used by futurists to study the world of tomorrow is called a future wheel. This can be used to study some of the hidden consequences of an invention or a trend. Through future wheels, we can see how our society might move from the reality of today to an almost science fiction tomorrow.

The following future wheel, done by one of my classes, shows what might happen if gasoline prices climbed to $2.00 per gallon. As you can see from the wheel, gasoline prices could have a dynamic effect on many different areas of society: the family, recreation patterns, the economy, and so on.

Construct a future wheel based on the idea that *nobody* has to work in the future. For each future wheel that you make, place a + after all those consequences you feel would be positive; place a − after all these consequences you feel would be negative; place a ? after all those you feel unsure of. In this way, comparisons can be made with other people in your class.

LEISURE ROLES

3

Futurists, or people who seriously study the future, are in agreement that we Americans are going to be working fewer years in the future. In some professions and trades, people are already being encouraged to retire at ages fifty and fifty-five to make room for younger workers. Earlier in our history, it was not at all unusual for men, women, and even children to work twelve hours per day, six or seven days per week. In fact, not too many years ago the fortyh-hour work week was considered to be a wild dream. Today some unions are actively advocating a thirty-hour work week. How many hours you'll work in the future is open to speculation, but most futurists feel that it will be less than thirty hours per week. As a result, we do know that Americans are going to have an enormous amount of leisure time, and what we will do with that time has become somewhat of a problem already.

The average American watches approximately 1200 hours of television per year, but reads only five hours per year. Jerzy Kosinski, a writer, has called us a nation of "vididiots" because of our attachment to "the tube." The Japanese have already perfected two new types of television that could revolutionize our viewing habits still further. On the one hand, the Japanese are now marketing a television screen the size of the average wall of a room. On the other hand, they are also experimenting with 3-dimensional television. Maybe our world of the future will be populated with giant-sized actors, football players, and "Big Birds" right in our homes. Further, if we can't go to the Rockies or the beach, why not bring the mountains or the seashore in living 3-D color to our homes? Just turn on your set, dial any part of the world, sit back and enjoy.

What if there were an even more "far out" world—a world where nobody had to work at all? This is exactly what happens in Raymond Jones' short story "Rat Race." There is no need to work because all of the society's needs are supplied by the Computer, at least until one man makes a most interesting discovery. What would you do with yourself if you never had to work? How would you occupy your time to keep from becoming bored—and perhaps even going mad?

1. Headlines from Tomorrow:

LEISURE RIOTS BREAK OUT IN OMAHA

PEOPLE REBEL AGAINST LEISURE—DEMAND WORK

Construct a future wheel for the above headlines.

PROJECTIONS

2. Look at the "B.C." cartoon below.
   a. What point is the cartoonist trying to make?
   b. What has already occurred in our society that would have inspired this cartoon?

RAT RACE

—Raymond E. Jones

The big run of HO model railroad activity began that summer, and George Sims-Howton was responsible for it. He had a penchant for old things like that and came across a description of HO model trains one day while browsing in the public archives. It was characteristic of George that he would go down there and finger the old volumes rather than make a computer search for subject matter in a fraction of the time.

"If I just want to find out what's there, how can I ask for it by subject?" he'd argue.

He brushed off the answer that he could use random search on the library computer. He said he liked to feel the old things with his hands.

There was no objection to it. Nobody else had asked for access to the original archives these past ten years. Actually, most of the stuff had been long since destroyed, because it was preserved on tape or film. Why it hadn't all gone that way worried no one.

Anyway, it was there, and it gave George a lot of pleasure to wade through the stuff, and that's how he came up with this model railroad thing. It seems there used to be whole magazines and books devoted to the subject about 150 years ago, but it's almost certain that no one living had ever seen a model train until George came up with it.

Right away, George wanted an HO railroad, and the idea intrigued some of the other fellows who lived in the same condomin. They all belonged to the same *bali-putsch* team and had beat every other outfit in their league and in several leagues around. They were ripe for some new excitement when George made his discovery.

They debated about where to get the train. Sam Bowlerman was sure the proper place would be a sporting goods store. Dave Estes said an appliance store. But George was convinced that a hardware store would be the place, and since the idea was his, that was where they went.

There was a shopping center just across the mall from their condomin. George had obtained veri-copies of some plans in an old model-railroading magazine in the archives and brought them along. He sat in the small booth and fed the veri-copies of the model train plans to the scanner, while Sam and Dave stuck their heads in the door. George had the feeling the scanner gulped as it absorbed the strange image on the paper. But the order was not rejected, and presently, the light went out, the plans were returned, and a slip of printout paper reported: Manufacture— Oklahoma City. Delivery—two days.

Sam growled in disgust. "Why do you think they schedule a little order like that two-thirds of the way across the country? It could have been made in Buffalo and we could have had it this afternoon."

"Question not the wisdom of the computer," said Dave. "It provideth all. But that kills it for the rest of the day." He glanced at his watch. "Only eleven o'clock. How about a game after lunch?"

Sam shook his head. "You're getting stale from too much playing. Ellie wants to go for a ride. I'm going to take her to Rio this afternoon. We'll get back in time to see what the train looks like."

"I'm going back to the library," said George.

"Call us when it comes in," said Dave.

George wandered back to the library, but he didn't go in. He drove past the utility complex of nuclear-powered machinery that kept the community going. He remembered that once, about five years ago, he had actually seen a Workman performing some manual repairs on the power station. He could still recall the deep envy he had felt for the man's privileged position. There had been a time when he thought he might even have a chance in the annual quota of Workmen chosen from among the Citizens. But his community had been bypassed entirely in the last two quotas, and George no longer had any illusions about himself. He lacked the qualifications in the first place, and he was too old now—at 27—in the second place.

He'd spend the rest of his life playing *bali-putsch,* wandering from one continent to another in aimless visiting with others like himself, occasionally doing something vigorous—like a six-month sprint in the Antarctic. That would be it.

The trouble was, the others—most of them—weren't like him. They seemed to be thoroughly enjoying this Age of Abundance, which had reached its full-blown state about three-quarters of a century ago. But George felt himself steadily eaten by a sick discontent and dissatisfaction.

He wasn't even sure what he was discontented about, but the history and the artifacts of a century or two ago gave him the feeling that he belonged in some such age as that. Not in an age of assured luxury that demanded absolutely nothing of a man. George sometimes had the vague, anachronistic sense that he ought to be contributing. But he had no idea what he would contribute, nor to whom.

Thinking again of the little model trains, he felt an utterly irrational pleasure. He had read of the long-vanished rail carriers, both Diesel and steam, but he had never heard until now of the model trains, which men used to play with. He had the feeling that he had rediscovered some long hidden pleasure that men had not known for generations.

It made no sense at all.

The train—engine, to be exact—arrived on schedule. Paula was there when it arrived and couldn't believe her eyes. It was a child's wheeled toy. George's tender caress of it frightened her.

"What in the world are you going to do with that thing?" she cried.

"Run it," he said, "when we get some track." He realized for the first time that they had forgotten to order track to go with it. "And some cars.

I'm going to get some bright yellow and red reefers, some cattle cars, and some tankers."

He guessed they had been so excited about the whole thing that they'd forgotten all about cars. It really had been hard to believe they'd actually get the engine.

He held it now up to the light, letting his fingers touch the tiny, realistic rivets on the dull black body of the boiler. He gently turned the drivers and delighted in the motion of the rods and valve mechanism.

"I'm going over to show it to Sam and Dave," he said. "They'll love it."

"Then they must be as crazy as you are!" shouted Paula as he went out.

She didn't really mean it. She was just frightened. George was always doing such incredibly odd things. Why couldn't he just be satisfied with *bali-putsch* and long talks on philosophy in the condomin mall like the other men?

Sam and Dave thought it was great.

"How do we make it go?" asked Sam.

George was baffled. He remembered reading about motors and electric power packs. But he hadn't thought any more about them than he had about tracks or cars.

Dave had been poking around the insides of the engine. Finally he looked up with exasperation. "This isn't ever going to go. The idiot computer just didn't put a motor in it!"

In dismay, and without looking at the engine, George knew Dave was right. They had submitted plans showing the external structure of the engine, but there were no details of the motor. If the plans had even stated that one was required, the computer probably would have whomped up something to make it go. As it was, they had an empty shell.

But that could be remedied. "We can get a motor at the same time we order track and cars. There are lots of other things you can get, too—realistic landscapes, ancient towns. This is going to be more fun than *bali-putsch* ever was." He held the little engine up again. "Did you ever see anything as beautiful as that!"

George hunted for two days in the archives, trying to find plans for a motor, but these simply didn't appear. It finally dawned on him that the plans he did find were for making by hand the parts of the models that it was practical to make in that way. Other items were factory built. This astonished him more than anything else he had discovered up to now. That such things could be handmade by the model engineers themselves—

They got a motor simply by telling the computer they needed one and referring to the previously submitted plans. The order was sent to Manchester, England, and brought back a realistic steam engine powered by a miniature nuclear-isotope core. A complete radio control was furnished.

George recognized that this was considerable of an anachronism, but it gave a more realistic performance than any of the electric motors he saw referred to. He let it go.

They ordered track by the quarter-mile. George installed it in the all-purpose room of his condomin over the protests of Paula. By the time it was up the group had grown to 15 HO enthusiasts, and track layouts were being planned by at least four other members of the group. There was more excitement than the condomin had seen since it was built.

It was the men, of course. The women stood around on the fringes looking bewildered, wondering if their men had gone utterly insane. George, at his operating cab, wore coveralls, an engineer's long-billed cap, and a blue kerchief around his neck. With intoxicated enthusiasm he jerked the cord above his head and sent a wild, shrill whistle through the room. His 2-8-8-2 Mallet chuffed into motion with a long string of brilliant reefers, cattle cars, tankers, and a couple of Pullmans for good measure. He was vaguely aware that the passenger cars didn't belong with the others. But he'd work out the details later. For now, he had something going, the like of which the world had not seen for a century and a half.

In the freight yards, Sam was busy making up a freight that was due out in two hours, and Dave was putting together a passenger express near the station.

Assorted other members of the group were making up train orders, checking the accuracy of the present team of engineers, or waiting impatiently their turn at the controls.

The wives were near hysteria.

They met three times a week, at least. In between, there was incessant tinkering with the layout and the rolling stock. The local hardware store did a land office business in HO. Within a month it was agreed they simply had to have better facilities. A new wing was ordered for the recreation center at the south end of the mall. It was approved by the computer without a murmur. The parts were fabricated, and a couple of days later a Workman was sent out to erect the wing.

Normally, Citizens watched the erection of a building both with envy of the Workman and ghoulish anticipation. For occasionally—not often but occasionally—the computer controlling the job went awry with hilarious consequences in the form of an unholy mess. It had happened once in the condomin when a small eight-story medical building was going up. With six floors completed the thing simply shivered and fell apart. Two other Workmen had to come out to help program new tapes to get the site cleaned up.

But the model railroaders didn't want that to happen to their structure. They watched anxiously and gave the Workman all their silent good wishes for speedy success. He had it, and the huge room was ready for occupancy three days later.

They wanted to elect George president of the group, but he side-stepped that one and got Sam elected to the position. Sam was an organizer, captain of the *bali-putsch* team, and the most logical one for the position.

George wanted to do some thinking.

It would be more fun if they could do their own building of equipment. According to the old journals in the archives, that's the way the most advanced old-time modelers used to do it, and George could see why. What greater pleasure could there be than to take raw metal and shape one of these delicate engines out of it? It was a pleasure that no man in the Abundant Society could know—unless he was a Workman or an Artist. And George and his friends were neither.

The question of metal stock was something of a problem. He supposed the hardware store would be the right source and tried it. He ordered some sheet brass and copper and pot metal alloy.

His order was totally rejected.

He realized long after that this should have been a warning. But at the time he was too hell-bent to pay attention to storm signals. After an evening of intense concentration on the problem he came up with the solution of ordering various artifacts that had large quantities of the material he needed and cutting them up.

It worked. He got some large boilers of copper and brass, and some pots and ladles of the alloy.

But there was the matter of tools. George dug up all the descriptions he could find of cutters, drills, files, screwdrivers, and soldering tools. He had never seen any of these. Nobody in the condomin had. Probably they were used by Workmen, but he didn't know.

He wondered if he would be rejected on those.

He tried an order for tinsnips, showing the computer reader a picture from an ancient catalog. The snips came through.

He tried a screwdriver and got it.

One by one he ordered the hand tools the journals indicated he'd need and he practiced shaping the stock he cut out of the tubs and boilers. It began to go quite easy, and he was drunk with the ecstasy of it.

There was one other thing it looked as if he'd need in the near future—a lathe. A 3-inch swing and a 16-inch bed would be plenty big enough. But he couldn't find any complete plans, and it was too complex to derive from a picture alone. He began drawing his own plans. They were rough, but the computer could work it out from the specs he wrote alongside his drawings.

When he'd completed a sketch of the lathe bed he ordered it as a trial. It came back in a couple of days and was perfect. He followed with the other parts, the head, chuck, screw, tailstock. He let the computer supply its own specification for a nuclear-isotope motor. When the whole thing was finally assembled, George put a piece of ⅜-inch rod into the chuck and touched it with the tool. A thin spiral of steel curled up in bright beauty.

George's hands began to shake so he couldn't hold the tool any longer. He shut the motor off and sat down. The steel spiral lay on the bench now. He regarded it with wonder, and then looked down at his own hands.

The visitors came early the next morning. There were two of them. They greeted him pleasantly and asked to come in.

He knew everyone in the local condomin. He wondered who these strangers were. Then he glimpsed the small blue symbol on the breasts of their coats, and his knees began to tremble.

"Please sit down," he said. "Refreshments?"

"No," said the taller one. "It's early. You're George Sims-Howton, I believe?" He had a miniature writer on his knee and was punching buttons as he talked.

George licked his dry lips. He was glad Paula was out. "Yes, I'm on the championship *bali-putsch* team for this district," he added, irrelevantly.

His visitors were bright-looking young men. They weren't any older than he was, George thought. One was tall and one was short. Except for that, you could hardly tell them apart. The expressions on their faces were the same: Friendly, courteous, smiling—implacable.

"You have been ordering some unusual devices recently," the tall one said. "Some tools."

"Oh, yes!" said George warmly. "Would you like to see them . . . see what we're doing with them?"

Both visitors shook their heads.

"It was quite ingenious of you to order them one by one," said the tall one. "And the lathe—piece by piece. Very ingenious."

"I don't know what you're talking about."

"You certainly knew that if you had ordered all the hand tools at once, or the complete lathe, the order would have been rejected."

"No . . . I didn't know that. And I don't understand what this is all about. Will you please tell me?"

"I don't believe that you don't know. But for the sake of the record we'll go over it. Production. The accumulation of hand tools which you now have is a production facility. The lathe is a production tool."

"I suppose it is," said George. "I got them to build some model railroads. If you'd only let me show you—"

"What kind of production is unimportant. *All* private production is prohibited. You know that."

"Yes, of course I know that. But this is not *production*—it's just making some little trains. I—"

"The only reason our society exists today is that production is properly controlled. Since the beginning of man's history the world has been more than capable of providing all that men could consume. The only trouble mankind ever had was with systems of distribution and conflicting philosophies of creation and accumulation.

"It was all so very easy once we took man out of the picture and made of the problem only a matter of logics and control. So very easy—you want a toy train and the computer determines that it will fit into the overall matrix of construction and distribution and orders one built for you. The factory builds it. You receive. You give nothing in return, neither service nor what was once called money.

"The population next year will be 3.8 million greater than this year. The computer has already determined this, and the food for those extra bodies is in production. They will never starve. They will never want for any device or product they can conceive. The earth can provide for ten times the bodies it now supports. Would you upset that provision for abundance?"

"No . . . no, of course not! I still don't know what you are talking about. I just wanted to make a little train—"

"The computer will determine if the trains should be made, and it will direct the factories to make them. It will supply you with the wildest contraptions you can dream of. But *it* controls the production. Do you understand that?"

The other one spoke up now. "A little train here. In another condomin, a piece of fabric and simple clothes. Somewhere else a strange food or a new device. All over the world—and people begin to trade these things and value them because they are different. And control is lost. The computer does not know what products, what food, what clothes are needed tomorrow and next year. The Abundant Society breaks down."

The tall one nodded. "It is for this reason that production tools and equipment are prohibited. They are not needed; ask for anything your heart desires, and the Abundant Society will give it to you—free. But, more important, the Abundant Society exists in the face of human-controlled production."

George was aware that his breath had been stifled. He had known none of this; he had never cared to know it. These were things that were discussed by the would-be philosophers who sat in the sun in the mall and refused to join in the *bali-putsch* games.

But what was the penalty?

"You will return these tools through the distribution channels by which they came. Your condomin will be marked with a warning which must remain for the next 60 days. That is all. You must watch yourself carefully. Order that which you please. If it is approved, it will be received. But keep out of anything resembling production.

"We stop smiling on the second offense. There is no appeal. For a second offense the penalty is reduction to subsistence status for the rest of your life and removal to the subsistence reservation. Do you have any questions?"

George shook his head numbly and felt that he was still shaking it as he stood by the window, watching them go as their little car took off and flew high over the mall.

He went outside then and looked at the wall by the door. They had pasted a blue banner there that announced to the world and all his friends that George Sims-Howton had been given a subsistence-reservation warning.

He wondered what would happen to the model railroad group. He wondered if Paula would divorce him. He put on a light coat and left the condomin, walking through the mall, where he waved to the philosophers in the sun and answered a call from players on the *bali-putsch* court. He continued on through the parklike fields and woods beyond the community.

On the top of a small hill he stopped and looked back. A paradise, and he was a snake in it, he thought; somewhere he'd heard of an allusion to something like that. But what kind of a paradise was it that could be threatened by a model train?

He sat down and began to think about that. Somewhere here was a problem, but he couldn't define it; he could only feel it. He had felt it all his life, he thought. That vague discontent that had always plagued him. He remembered how it had vanished when he watched the bright shining spirals curl up from the stock in his lathe.

It must be as simple as that, he thought after a while. That was the missing element of the Abundant Society. And if that were so, what a mockery the name was. It was not abundant; it was the most impoverished of all imaginable societies. A man's supreme joy was the joy of building, molding, changing, assembling—creating—with his own two hands and his mind. And this was the single thing the Abundant Society could not tolerate for fear of coming apart at the seams. Only a narrow elite, isolated from all other citizens, could be permitted the luxury of creation—of work.

He'd have to do something about that, George Sims-Howton thought again after a long while. He had an idea that maybe there was something he could do about it. Maybe the notion that he should be contributing, which had plagued him ever since he became an adult, was not so crazy, after all.

When he got near home he saw that small groups of his neighbors were still standing around his doorway, looking at the blue banner. Nothing like it had ever happened in the condomin before. He didn't know how they would react. He didn't know how he should act, himself.

As it turned out, things were better than he expected. He explained the situation about 50 different times before the day was out, and everyone was sympathetic and understanding. He wasn't marked as a Jonah, to be run out of the condomin by ostracizing.

There was only Paula. She didn't understand. She was frightened. There was nothing he could say to explain away her fears. And then he remembered that she had seen in her childhood someone who had been sent away to the subsistence reservation for some crime. The talk of the adults at that time had burned itself into her mind: ". . . No shelter except what they build themselves; only half enough food to keep alive; heat from open fires; no protection in the summer. . . ."

"You'll give up all this crazy toy railroad business, now, won't you?" Paula begged.

"They didn't ask me to do that," George said. "It was the tools, and I'm going to take them back. I made a mistake, and I won't make it again, because they told me where I was wrong."

Paula didn't understand. She couldn't separate it from the trains.

George remained awake most of the night. He had no reason to doubt that the terrors of the subsistence reservation as remembered by Paula from conversations overheard in childhood were less than real. He had heard some of them himself. But he had never seen anyone who knew firsthand. No one ever returned.

He would be risking it, he knew, if he tempted the powers of the Abundant Society any further. He did not know the details of the law. Citizens were not taught those things. Somewhere in the upper echelons of the Workers who governed by, for, and with the mammoth, world-wide computer system there were those who knew the law and passed it down to bright young men like those who had visited him today. He wondered how it was that so many of them escaped entanglement with the law when they knew so little about it.

But that was not the problem. Should he go on or not? Was there anything worth while that one man, by himself, could accomplish? The system had existed for a century and a half. It would go on for centuries more. Who was he to challenge it?

And risk a life sentence to subsistence reservation?

He went to the railroad room of the recreation center the next morning. He was the only one there. That night was the regular meeting. Only about half the usual number came around. George put on his coveralls and his kerchief and his long-billed cap, and he jerked the whistle cord with abandon. But it was no good. It was like a pall of dread had settled over the whole operation. They listened to George's explanations all over again, but they were afraid. *Bali-putsch* was safe. The HO trains seemed like a fearful unknown, now.

He made his decision after the meeting. If he failed to go ahead now, the whole project would die.

He went to the hardware store the next morning with a complex order. It took him half the day to feed it in. And then he went out and sat in the sun.

Two days later a sizable shipment came in. He took it to the empty railroad room and spread it out. Thousands of parts, precisely labeled and packaged, just as he had ordered. That gave him some small comfort. If the order were illegal, the computer surely would not have approved and delivered it.

He began gathering the parts and repackaging them. He had even ordered brightly colored boxes to put them in, just like the ones he had seen in the old journals. Kits, they called them there. You could get all the parts and just put them together yourself—with the help of one small screwdriver. George had ordered the screwdrivers and put one in each kit.

Was it production?

He'd soon find out.

He presented the first one to Sam. Sam saw the box cover and shook his head. "I think I'm going to give it up, George," he said. "My game's been lousy since I started fooling with the trains, and I've got to get it back. I really think you ought to do the same. We're never going to have a chance against Monmouth unless we get back in shape."

"Open it up," said George.

Sam hesitated, then removed the cover. "What the devil?"

"A kit," said George. "You have all the fun of putting it together yourself—and you get around the anti-production law at the same time."

Sam looked up cautiously. "You're sure this is all right?"

"Absolutely clean. The computer put the order through without a murmur. If it hadn't been right it would have been bounced, wouldn't it?

"I don't know. You almost got clobbered for the tools, and the computer sent them through all right—and then tattled."

"It's safe," George repeated.

Sam couldn't help lifting out the delicate parts and touching them. His eyes were bright as he speculated on how they fit together. He tried the cab against the boiler casting.

"Here's the instruction sheet," said George. "I had it printed up to go along with the kits."

It was nearly midnight when he finally got the engine assembled, a beautiful little 2-8-2 Mikado. Sam's eyes were bleary with the unaccustomed close work. But there was serenity and joy in his face. "Boy, isn't she a beauty!" he exclaimed. "But say, I ought to give you something for this; you can't just give them away."

"Why not? They were given to me."

"You went to all the trouble of ordering them. And you packed the parts into kits."

"O.K. You pay me two blue chips. That'll square us."

Sam nodded and handed over a couple of the worthless chips that were used to bet on the *bali-putsch* games. "It's a deal," he said.

They were at the railroad room almost by sunrise to break in the new Mikado and check it out. By mid-morning George had disposed of 15 more of the kits. Nobody moved from the room. If they couldn't find table space, they sat down on the floor and began assembling them. Most wanted engines of their own, to start with. But some began work on bright reefers or complex specialty cars, such as wreckers or hoppers.

At noon George leaned back and began to breathe easy. He had it going again. Most of the old group was there, and a couple of new fellows had dropped by to see what was going on and had got hooked by the fascination of assembling the kits.

George wondered, with a sigh of anxiety, how much time he had. Certainly the report of his order had gone through to a desk at some upper echelon. They had their eye on him. Or perhaps the computer had already ticked him off as a two-time loser.

It was five days before they showed up again. The same two. The tall one and the short one, with the same implacable faces.

George took them to the recreation center, into the new model railroad wing. A half dozen engineer's cabs were occupied on the huge layout. Eight or ten men were at worktables, assembling new models. They all stopped their work and blanched at the sight of the two men with George Sims-Howton. George had tricked them. Now they were all in for it!

George sensed their reaction. "Just a check," he said as calmly as he could. "On me—not you."

The two investigators conferred together with some uncertainty, "You put together the parts ordered from the hardware computer," said the tall one to George. "You put them together with a screwdriver into their finished form."

"That is right," said George.

"Why?"

"We like to. It's fun. Why do we play *bali-putsch?* It gives us pleasure. So does assembling the kits."

"The object is to run them around the track, is it not? Then why is it not more efficient and more pleasurable to order them in completed form? You could run them that much sooner."

George felt his hand beginning to go sweaty. "Both forms of activity give us pleasure. Who is to say it makes sense? *Bali-putsch* doesn't make sense when you try to rationalize it."

"But you are assuming for yourselves a part of the production process, which would normally be completed at the factory."

"No, no—" said George. "Production is the creation of something that has not existed before. These parts—they are already in existence. Their purpose is to form an engine or a car. We only carry out that purpose. Forgive me if I argue the point, for I realize that if I have made a mistake again it is a fatal mistake for me. But I do not think I have made a mistake. I have very carefully observed the law."

"It is our opinion," said the tall one coldly, "that you are very carefully trying to break the law. But we fail to understand why or how. I think the computer will be able to clarify these matters. We will return as soon as we have its analysis and its decision."

George wandered out into the sunshine of the mall after they were gone. The model railroaders were uneasy. Some of them had slipped out as quietly as possible while the investigators were in the recreation hall. Maybe even if the decision were favorable too much damage would have been done. No one had ever seen investigators around the condomin before. The most casual visit was terifying.

And a third one was coming this afternoon.

He sat down at a distance from the groups of arguing philosophers lounging in the sun. He looked about the peaceful landscape, the aesthetically satisfying structures. Total lack of want, he thought, except for the one thing—the delight of individual creation. Without that, every-thing else was an empty shell. He had felt it all his life. The driving discontent. The vague compulsion to take things in his own hands, to feel and shape them.

Maybe it was stronger in him than in the others. But they felt it, too. Their pleasure in the little trains was proof of that. And that pleasure would stir and ferment if only it could be nurtured with a little care.

He had risked all he had here, against the unknown terrors of subsis-tence reservation, to provide that care. It was all he could do. It was what he had to do.

The sun was low and shadows were lengthening when they returned. They were walking slowly as they approached, and their faces were more puzzled than ever.

"The computer cleared you," the tall one said. "It pronounced your activities nonproductive and legal."

"Thanks," said George.

"Don't thank us. We merely carry the message. You are going to be watched. Everything you do will be evaluated by the computer for con-formance to the inte t of the law. An automatic alarm will indicate when you slip. We're with you night and day, George Sims-Howton."

He was all alone in the mall when he finally got up to go. It was dark except for the moonlight and the glow from the buildings. He could see lights in the railroad room. Some of them—it looked like quite a number —were gathering for the evening run.

Hundreds would learn what it meant to put something together with their own hands. They would learn the pleasure of touching materials that were fine and delicate and smooth and well-formed—the pleasure of forming and shaping and putting together.

A few hundred, maybe. It wasn't much, but it would spread. And then someone would take the supreme risk of going out in a forlorn country-side and picking up rocks and putting together a house. And struggling for his own food right from the ground itself—for the mere pleasure of it.

Would he have to convince Paula it was not insane?

He thought of the computer. The idiot computer. It gave out only what was put in—plus an illusion of great omniscience. It could not distinguish between mechanical production and creative pleasure because those who had built it understood no such distinction. He was safe until greater men touched the computer.

But for now there were many things to do. More trains to put in kits. And he'd just learned about model airplanes, and animals and people, too. The field seemed endless.

It was just a question of how far he could go with it.

He had a feeling he was going a long way.

PROBINGS

1. Why is George a danger to his society?
2. Why do you think the author selected the title "Rat Race" for his story? Just what is a rat race?
3. Why does George admire the Workman who repaired the power station? Have you ever felt a similar kind of admiration for someone who has built something or fixed something? What? Why? Have you ever had a sense of fulfillment at creating something? What is the most creative thing you have ever done?
4. If you lived in the society described in "Rat Race," how would you fit in—or would you? Would you enjoy living in a society where you would never have to work? What would *you* do in this society?
5. If you could ask the "Rat Race's" computer for any five things, in order of preference, what would they be? Why would you want these things? After each item indicate whether you want this thing for money, status, creativity, self-fulfillment, sex symbol, other.
6. What things can you now do that give you a sense of accomplishment comparable to George's? Knitting, hobbies, working on cars, athletics, plants, cooking, etc. Rank twenty things that you really like doing. At the top of the list would be those things you enjoy most; at the bottom of the list would be those things that you enjoy but that are not priority items. Put a plus after all of the things that you think you would still enjoy doing next year. Place a 5 after those things you think you'll still enjoy in five years; a 10 after those things you'll still enjoy in ten years; a 20 for twenty years; a 50 for fifty years.

7. Project yourself fifty years into the future and do one of the following: write a radio play and tape it, write a short story, or draw a cartoon about what people will do with their leisure time. Will there be more spectator sports? 3-D television is just around the corner—how will this change our use of leisure?
8. Develop a futuristic advertisement advertising 3-D television. Develop an advertisement for a Westworld-type of amusement park. Perhaps each park could have a theme: the Civil War; the Depression; World War II, etc.

SEXUAL ROLES

4

From birth we have been raised to be good little girls and boys; we have been brought up to be either feminine or masculine. Traditionally, little boys have been encouraged to play with guns, trucks and cars; little girls have been encouraged to play with nurse's kits, dolls, and play dishes. Sexual roles are changing, however, and there is much controversy over the changes. In the words of the popular song: "The times, they are a changin'." Women are beginning to find themselves and to gain recognition in jobs that were closed to them only five years ago.

As women have asserted their new identities in recent years, we have seen some very dramatic, and some very subtle, changes occurring. With the increase in availability of various birth control methods, millions of women are able to decide whether they want children. In many occupations, the discrimination against women has been lessened. But men have also been changed by the sexual revolution; the so-called unisex mode of dress is just one consequence. Men are talking about how they feel about themselves, their careers, and how they relate to others.

What of the future? What if our sexual roles disappear completely? Would an important part of our identity be replaced as we assumed newer roles? One consequence might be new names for people. Consider that women have traditionally been taught to give up a very personal part of their identities when they marry—their last names. Today some couples are combining both their names for a new name; for example, Valerie Smith and Bob Jones marry and each takes the last name Smith-Jones. Perhaps in the future a couple could merge parts of each of their last names and create a new shared name to symbolize the new relationship.

Certainly, like our jobs, sexual roles have been an important source of our identities. In "Survival Ship" we are being asked to question just what our sexual roles are. What does it mean to be feminine? What does it mean to be masculine? How do the sexes view one another? How do you feel about your own sexual identity?

1. Headlines from Tomorrow:

HOUSEHUSBANDS PICKET CONGRESS FOR EQUAL RIGHTS

Washington, January 3, 2009. In reaction to the demands of thousands of irate househusbands, Congress has established a special subcommittee to investigate charges of sexual discrimination. . . .

2. Assume that you are about to be married. Develop a new name that reflects your new relationship. For example, your name might be Smith and your partner's might be Jones, therefore, your new name could be Smones.

PROJECTIONS

3. Examine the cartoon below, which deals with sexual roles.

Is this cartoon funny? Why or why not? Would you react in the same way as the men in the cartoon?

If the cartoonist had included women as passengers, how might he have drawn their reaction to the announcement?

"Welcome aboard. This is your captain, Margaret Williamson, speaking."

SURVIVAL SHIP

—Judith Merril

Half a million people actually made the round trip to Space Station One that day to watch the take-off in person. And back on Earth a hundred million video screens flashed the picture of Captain Melnick's gloved hand waving a dramatic farewell at the port, while the other hand slowly pressed down the lever that would fire the ship out beyond the orbit of the artifical satellite, past the Moon and the planets, into unknown space.

From Station One, Earth, and Moon, a hundred million winged wishes added their power to the surge of the jets, as a rising spiral of fire inside the greatest rocket tower ever built marked the departure of the thrice-blessed ship, *Survival*. In the great churches, from pole to pole, services were held all day, speeding the giant vessel on its way, calling on the aid of the Lord for the Twenty and Four who manned the ship.

At mountain-top telescopes a dozen cameras faithfully transmitted the messages of great unblinking glass eyes. Small home sets and massive pulpit screens alike looked to the sky to follow the flare dimming in the distance, to watch the man-made star falling away.

Inside the great ship Melnick's hand left the firing lever, then began adjusting the chin rest and the earphones of the acceleration couch. The indicator dashboard, designed for prone eye level, leaped into focus. Securing the couch straps with the swift competence of habit, the captain intently watched the sweep of the big second hand around the take-off timer, aware at the same time that green lights were beginning to glow at the other end of the board. The indicator reached the first red mark.

"The show's over, everybody. We're in business!" The mike built into the chin rest carried the captain's taut voice all over the ship. "Report, all stations!"

"Number one, all secure!" Melnick mentally ticked off the first green light, glowing to prove the astrogator's couch was in use.

"Number two, all secure!"

"Number three ..." "Four ..." "Five." The rhythmic sing-song of pinpoint timing in take-off was second nature by now to the whole crew. One after another, the green lights glowed for safety, punctuating the litany, and the gong from the timer put a period neatly in place after the final "All secure!"

"Eight seconds to black out," the captain's voice warned. "Seven ... six ... stand by." The first wave of acceleration shock reeled into twenty-four helmet-sheathed heads on twenty-four individually designed head rests. "Five——" *It's got to work*, Melnick was thinking, fighting off unconsciousness with fierce intensity. "Four——" *It's got to ... got to ... "Three——" got to ... got to ... "Two——" got to ...*

At the space station, a half-million watchers were slowly cleared from

57

the giant take-off platform. They filed in long orderly lines down the ramps to the interior, and waited there for the smaller Earth rockets that would take them home. Waiting, they were at once elated and disappointed. They had seen no more than could be seen at the same place on any other day. The entire rocket area had been fenced off, with a double cordon of guards to make sure that too-curious visitors stayed out of range. Official explanations mentioned the new engine, the new fuel, the danger of escaping gases—but nobody believed it. Every one of the half-million visitors knew what the mystery was: the crew, and nothing else. Giant video screens all over the platform gave the crowd details and closeups, the same they would have seen had they stayed comfortably at home. They saw the captain's gloved hand, at the last, but not the captain's face.

There was muttering and complaining, but there was something else too. Each man, woman, and child who went to the station that day would be able to say, years later, "I was there when the *Survival* took off. You never saw anything so big in your life."

Because it wasn't just another planet hop. It wasn't just like the hundreds of other take-offs. It was the *Survival,* the greatest spaceship ever engineered. People didn't think of the *Survival* in terms of miles-per-second; they said, "Sirius in fifteen years!"

From Sunday supplements to dignified periodicals, nearly every medium of communication on Earth had carried the story. Brightly colored graphs made visibly simple the natural balance of life forces in which plants and animals could maintain a permanently fresh atmosphere as well as a self-perpetuating food supply. Lecture demonstrations and videocasts showed how centrifugal force would replace gravity.

For months before take-off, the press and video followed the preparations with daily intimate accounts. The world over, people knew the nicknames of pigs, calves, chickens, and crew members—and even the proper botanical name of the latest minor masterpiece of the biochemists, a hybrid plant whose root, stems, leaves, buds, blossoms, and fruit were all edible, nourishing, and delicious, and which had the added advantage of being the thirstiest CO_2 drinker ever found.

The public knew the nicknames of the crew, and the proper name of the plant. But they never found out, not even the half million who went to the field to see for themselves, the real identity of the Twenty and Four who comprised the crew. They knew that thousands had applied; that it was necessary to be single, under twenty-five, and a graduate engineer in order to get as far as the physical exam; that the crew was mixed in sex, with the object of filling the specially equipped nursery and raising a second generation for the return trip, if, as was hoped, a lengthy stay on Sirius's planet proved possible. They knew, for that matter, all the small characteristics and personal idiosyncrasies of the crew members— what they ate, how they dressed, their favorite games, theaters, music, books, cigarettes, preachers, and political parties. There were only two things the public didn't know, and couldn't find out: the real names of

58

the mysterious Twenty and Four, and the reason why those names were kept secret.

There were as many rumors as there were newsmen or radio reporters, of course. Hundreds of explanations were offered at one time or another. But still nobody knew—nobody except the half hundred Very Important Persons who had planned the project, and the Twenty and Four themselves.

And now, as the pinpoint of light faded out of the screens of televisors all over Earth, the linear and rotary acceleration of the great ship began to adjust to the needs of the human body. "Gravity" in the living quarters gradually approached Earth-normal. Tortured bodies relaxed in the acceleration couches, where the straps had held them securely positioned through the initial stage, so as to keep the blood and guts where they belonged, and to prevent the stomach from following its natural tendency to emerge through the backbone. Finally, stunned brain cells awoke to the recognition that danger signals were no longer coming through from shocked, excited tissues.

Captain Melnick was the first to awake. The row of lights on the board still glowed green. Fumbling a little with the straps, Melnick watched tensely to see if the indicator lights were functioning properly, sighing with relief as the one at the head of the board went dead, operated automatically by the removal of body weight from the couch.

It was right—it was essential—for the captain to wake up first. If any of the men had showed superior recuperative powers, it could be bad. Melnick thought wearily of the years and years ahead during which this artificial dominance had to be maintained in defiance of all Earth conditioning. But of course it would not be that bad, really. The crew had been picked for ability to conform to the unusual circumstances; they were all without strong family ties or prejudices. Habit would establish the new castes soon enough, but the beginning was crucial. Survival was more than a matter of plant-animal balance and automatic gravity.

While the captain watched, another light went out, and then another. Officers, both of them. Good. Three more lights died out together. Then men were beginning to awaken, and it was reassuring to know that their own couch panels would show them that the officers had revived first. In any case, there was no more time for worrying. There were things to be done.

A detail was sent off immediately to attend to the animals, release them from the confinement of the specially prepared acceleration pens, and check them for any possible damage incurred in spite of precautions. The proportions of human, animal, and plant life had been worked out carefully beforehand for maximum efficienty and for comfort. Now that the trip had started, the miniature world had to maintain its status quo or perish.

As soon as enough of the crew were awake, Lieutenant Johnson, the third officer, took a group of eight out to make an inspection of the hydroponic tanks that lined the hull. Nobody expected much trouble here. Being at the outermost part of the ship, the plants were exposed to high "gravity." The outward pull exerted on them by rotation should have held their roots in place, even through the tearing backward thrust of the acceleration. But there was certain to be a large amount of minor damage, to stems and leaves and buds, and whatever there was would need immediate repair. In the ship's economy the plants had the most vital function of all—absorbing carbon dioxide from dead air already used by humans and animals, and deriving from it the nourishment that enabled their chlorophyll systems to release fresh oxygen for re-use in breathing.

There was a vast area to inspect. Row upon row of tanks marched solidly from stem to stern of the giant ship, all around the inner circumference of the hull. Johnson split the group of eight into four teams, each with a biochemist in charge to locate and make notes of the extent of the damage, and an unclassified man as helper, to do the actual dirty work, crawling out along the catwalks to mend each broken stalk.

Other squads were assigned to check the engines and control mechanisms, and the last two women to awake got stuck with the booby prize—first shift in the galley. Melnick squashed their immediate protests with a stern reminder that they had hardly earned the right to complain; but privately the captain was pleased at the way it had worked out. This first meal on board was going to have to be something of an occasion. A bit of ceremony always helped; and above all, social procedures would have to be established immediately. A speech was indicated—a speech Melnick did not want to have to make in the presence of all twenty-four crew members. As it worked out, the Four would almost certainly be kept busy longer than the others. If these women had not happened to wake up last . . .

The buzzing of the intercom broke into the captain's speculations. "Lieutenant Johnson reporting, sir." Behind the proper, crisp manner, the young lieutenant's voice was frightened. Johnson was third in command, supervising the inspection of the tanks.

"Having trouble down there?" Melnick was deliberately informal, knowing the men could hear over the intercom, and anxious to set up an immediate feeling of unity among the officers.

"One of the men complaining, sir." The young lieutenant sounded more confident already. "There seems to be some objection to the division of work."

Melnick thought it over quickly and decided against any more public discussion on the intercom. "Stand by. I'll be right down."

All over the ship airducts and companionways led from the inner-level living quarters "down" to the outer level of tanks; Melnick took the steps three at a time and reached the trouble zone within seconds after the conversation ended.

"Who's the troublemaker here?"

"Kennedy—on assignment with Petty Officer Giorgio for plant maintenance."

"You have a complaint?" Melnick asked the swarthy, dungareed man whose face bore a look of sullen dissatisfaction.

"Yeah." The man's voice was deliberately insolent. The others had never heard him speak that way before, and he seemed to gain confidence from the shocked surprise they displayed. "I thought I was supposed to be a pampered darling this trip. How come I do all the dirty work here, and Georgie gets to keep so clean?"

His humor was too heavy to be effective. "Captain's orders, that's why," Melnick snapped. "Everybody has to work double time till things are squared away. If you don't like the job here, I can fix you up fine in the brig. Don't worry about your soft quarters. You'll get 'em later and plenty of 'em. It's going to be a long trip, and don't forget it." The captain pointed significantly to the chronometer built into the overhead. "But it's not much longer to dinner. You'd better get back to work if you want to hit the chow while it's hot. Mess call in thirty minutes."

Melnick took a chance and turned abruptly away, terminating the interview. It worked. Sullen but defeated, Kennedy hoisted himself back up on the catwalk, and then began crawling out to the spot Giorgio pointed out. Not daring to express their relief, lieutenant and captain exchanged one swift look of triumph before Melnick walked wordlessly off.

In the big control room that would be mess hall, social hall, and general meeting place for all of them for fifteen years to come—or twice that time if Sirius's planet turned out to be uninhabitable—the captain waited for the crew members to finish their checkup assignments. Slowly they gathered in the lounge, ignoring the upholstered benches around the sides and the waiting table in the center, standing instead in small awkward groups. An undercurrent of excitement ran through them all, evoking deadly silences and erupting in bursts of too-noisy conversation, destroying the joint attempt at an illusion of nonchalance. They all knew —or hoped they knew—what the subject of the captain's first speech would be, and behind the facade of bronzed faces and trimly muscled bodies they were all curious, even a little afraid.

Finally there were twenty of them in the room, and the captain rose and rapped for order.

"I suppose," Melnick began, "you will all want to know our present position and the results of the checkup." Nineteen heads turned as one, startled and disappointed at the opening. "However," the captain continued, smiling at the change of expressions the single word brought, "I imagine you're all as hungry and—er—impatient as I am, so I shall put off the more routine portions of my report until our other comrades have joined us. There is only one matter which should properly be discussed immediately."

Everyone in the room was acutely conscious of the Four. They had all known, of course, how it would be. But on Earth there had always been other, ordinary men around to make them less aware of it. Now the general effort to maintain an air of artificial ease and disinterest was entirely abandoned as the captain plunged into the subject most on everyone's mind.

"Our ship is called the *Survival*. You all know why. Back on Earth, people think they know why too; they think it's because of our planets and artificial gravity, and the hundreds of other engineering miracles that keep us going. Of course, they also know that our crew is mixed, and that our population is therefore"—the captain paused, letting an anticipatory titter circle the room—"is therefore by no means fixed. What they don't know, naturally, is the division of sexes in the crew.

"You're all aware of the reason for the secrecy. You know that our organization is in direct opposition to the ethical principles on which the peace was established after World War IV. And you know how the planners of this trip had to struggle with the authorities to get this project approved. When consent was granted, finally, it was only because the highest prelates clearly understood that the conditions of our small universe were in every way different from those on Earth—and that the division proposed was *necessary for survival.*"

The captain paused, waiting for the last words to sink in, and studying the attitudes of the group. Even now, after a year's conditioning to counteract earthly mores, there were some present who listened to this public discussion of dangerous and intimate matters with flushed faces and embarrassed smiles.

"You all realize, of course, that this consent was based, finally, on the basic principle itself." Automatically, out of long habit unbroken by that year's intensive training, the captain made the sign of the olive branch. *"Survival of the race is the first duty of every ethical man and woman."* The command was intoned meaningfully, almost pontifically, and brought its reward as confusion cleared from some of the flushed faces. "What we are doing, our way of life now, has the full approval of the authorities. We must never forget that.

"On Earth, survival of the race is best served by the increasing strength of family ties. It was not thought wise to endanger those ties by letting the general public become aware of our—unorthodox—system here on board. A general understanding, on Earth, of the true meaning of the phrase, 'the Twenty and the Four,' could only have aroused a furor of discussion and argument that would, in the end, have impeded survival both there and here.

"The knowledge that there are twenty of one sex on board, and only four of the other—that children will be born outside of normal family groups, and raised jointly—I need not tell you how disastrous that would have been." Melnick paused, raising a hand to dispel the muttering in the room.

"I wanted to let you know, before the Four arrive, that I have made some plans which I hope will carry us through the initial period in which difficulties might well arise. Later, when the groups of six—five of us, and one of them in each—have been assigned their permanent quarters, I think it will be possible, in fact necessary, to allow a greater amount of autonomy within those groups. But for the time being, I have arranged a—shall we call it a dating schedule?" Again the captain paused, waiting for tension to relieve itself in laughter. "I have arranged dates for all of you with each of them during convenient free periods over the next month. Perhaps at the end of that time we will be able to choose groups; perhaps it will take longer. Maternity schedules, of course, will not be started until I am certain that the grouping is satisfactory to all. For the time being, remember this:

"We are not only more numerous than they, but we are stronger and, in our social placement here, more fortunate. We must become accustomed to the fact that they are our responsibility. It is because we are hardier, longer-lived, less susceptible to pain and illness, better able to withstand, mentally, the difficulties of a life of monotony, that we are placed as we are—and not alone because we are the bearers of children."

Over the sober silence of the crew, the captain's voice rang out. "Lieutenant Johnson," Melnick called to the golden-haired, sun-tanned woman near the door, "will you call the men in from the tank rooms now? They can finish their work after dinner."

PROBINGS

1. What clues are you given within the story that tell you what the sex of the main characters is? Why does Kennedy expect to be a "pampered darling"? Were you aware as you read the story that the characters are referred to only by name and rank, never by the pronouns "he" or "she"?
2. Read and evaluate at least three children's books. How are little girls and boys portrayed? What kinds of activities do girls engage in? Boys? What do the mothers and fathers do in the stories?
3. Analyze three comic strips in your local newspaper. How are men treated? Women? What kinds of jobs do they hold?
4. View at least three TV soap operas. What kinds of occupations do women pursue? Men? What kind of images are presented for females and males to follow? Is the man strong and decisive? The woman weak and clinging? Are you personally able to identify with any of the problems explored in the soapers? Which?
5. Write an SF story in which there is *total* sexual equality. What might be some of the consequences? Would you enjoy living in such a society?
6. How would our future sexual roles be changed—
    a. if embryos were grown in artificial wombs?
    b. if men and women adopted exactly the same hair and clothing styles?
    c. if there was no such thing as marriage?

VALUES

5

What we most value is what our identities are really all about. What is valuable to me might not be valuable to you. To some, religion offers a great deal of comfort and joy; others receive satisfaction from sports, music, art, or woodworking. One person needs a lot of money for fulfillment; another person might only need the sun, wind, and some wild flowers.

Many arguments and disagreements develop, of course, because we do have different lifestyles and values. To some young people, the so-called older generation is living all wrong. On the other hand, many older people can't comprehend why younger people think the things they do. Pick up any newspaper and these value conflicts become all too obvious. "Don't use pot or other drugs," many people admonish their children—who stare in wonderment at their elders' martinis. Recently in an advice-to-the-lovelorn column, a grandmother wrote in pleading for some insight into the changing lifestyles of the young. It seems she had just attended her granddaughter's wedding on the top of a sand dune; the bride wore a long plain dress and had wild flowers woven into her hair. To the grandmother, it seemed almost as if she were attending the wedding of a Martian. What we had here was, of course, a conflict over values—and a subsequent failure to communicate. To the older woman, weddings always involved solemn organ music, stately churches, and white wedding gowns.

Alvin Toffler coined the term "future shock" to express the effects of the large number of rapid changes that our society is undergoing. For example, it took more than forty years before a majority of Americans owned a car; it took less than a decade before TV ownership became widespread. Future shocks often force us to change our values very quickly. What might be valuable today might be equally valueless tomorrow. For a few years, for example, almost every American child wanted a hula-hoop, but then, suddenly, nobody wanted them.

How would you like to live in a society where values changed from week to week or even day to day? Or is this too impossible to contemplate, even in the future?

In Ray Bradbury's "The Smile," one small piece of the painting "The Mona Lisa" becomes the most treasured item for one little boy. As you read "The Smile," think about just what you treasure most—exactly what is most valuable to you?

1. Headlines from Tomorrow:

TEACHERS STRIKE FOR LESS PAY, MORE WORKING HOURS

2. Construct your own future wheel, projecting your values 20 years into the future.
3. Assume that you are going on a space voyage to another planet; you will be away for at least forty years. What five personal things, things that mean a lot to you, would you take with you? What practical things, such as contact

PROJECTIONS

lenses, would you take? Why? If you could take with you any five people whom you wished, who would they be? Why? Being away for so long, you might want to preserve something from Earth that would remind you of home. What sights, sounds, and odors would you like to take along? Why? Assuming that children would be born on the flight or while you are on distant planets, what kinds of things would you want them to know about Earth? Or would you prefer that they suffer from cultural amnesia and forget about Earth?

THE SMILE

—Ray Bradbury

In the town square the queue had formed at five in the morning while cocks were crowing far out in the rimed country and there were no fires. All about, among the ruined buildings, bits of mist had clung at first, but now with the new light of seven o'clock it was beginning to disperse. Down the road, in twos and threes, more people were gathering in for the day of marketing, the day of festival.

The small boy stood immediately behind two men who had been talking loudly in the clear air, and all of the sounds they made seemed twice as loud because of the cold. The small boy stomped his feet and blew on his red, chapped hands, and looked up at the soiled gunnysack clothing of the men and down the long line of men and women ahead.

"Here boy, what're you doing out so early?" said the man behind him.

"Got my place in line, I have," said the boy.

"Whyn't you run off, give your place to someone who appreciates?"

"Leave the boy alone," said the man ahead, suddenly turning.

"I was joking." The man behind put his hand on the boy's head. The boy shook it away coldly. "I just thought it strange, a boy out of bed so early."

"This boy's an appreciator of arts, I'll have you know," said the boy's defender, a man named Grigsby. "What's you name, lad?"

"Tom."

"Tom here is going to spit clean and true, right, Tom?"

"I sure am!"

Laughter passed down the line.

A man was selling cracked cups of hot coffee up ahead. Tom looked and saw the little hot fire and the brew bubbling in a rusty pan. It wasn't really coffee. It was made from some berry that grew on the meadowlands beyond town, and it sold a penny a cup to warm their stomachs; but not many were buying, not many had the wealth.

Tom stared ahead to the place where the line ended, beyond a bombed-out stone wall.

"They say she *smiles,*" said the boy.

"Aye, she does," said Grigsby.

"They say she's made of oil and canvas."

"True. And that's what makes me think she's not the original one. The original, now, I've heard, was painted on wood a long time ago."

"They says she's four centuries old."

"Maybe more. No one knows what year this is, to be sure."

"It's 2061!"

"That's what they say, boy, yes. Liars. Could be 3000 or 5000, for all we know. Things were in a fearful mess there for a while. All we got now is bits and pieces."

They shuffled along the cold stones of the street.

"How much longer before we see her?" asked Tom uneasily.

"Just a few more minutes. They got her set up with four brass poles and velvet rope, all fancy, to keep folks back. Now mind, no rocks, Tom; they don't allow rocks thrown at her."

"Yes, sir."

The sun rose higher in the heavens, bringing heat which made the men shed their grimy coats and greasy hats.

"Why're we all here in line?" asked Tom at last. "Why're we all here to spit?"

Grigsby did not glance down at him, but judged the sun. "Well, Tom, there's lots of reasons." He reached absently for a pocket that was long gone, for a cigarette that wasn't there. Tom had seen the gesture a million times. "Tom, it has to do with hate. Hate for everything in the Past. I ask you, Tom, how did we get in such a state, cities all junk, roads like jigsaws from bombs, and half the cornfields glowing with radioactivity at night? Ain't that a lousy stew, I ask you?"

"Yes, sir, I guess so."

"It's this way, Tom. You hate whatever it was that got you all knocked down and ruined. That's human nature. Unthinking, maybe, but human nature anyway."

"There's hardly nobody or nothing we don't hate," said Tom.

"Right! The whole blooming kaboodle of them people in the Past who run the world. So here we are on a Thursday morning with our guts plastered to our spines, cold, live in caves and such, don't smoke, don't drink, don't nothing except have our festivals, Tom, our festivals."

And Tom thought of the festivals in the past few years. The year they tore up all the books in the square and burned them and everyone was drunk and laughing. And the festival of science a month ago when they dragged in the last motorcar and picked lots and each lucky man who won was allowed one smash of a sledge hammer at the car.

"Do I remember *that,* Tom? Do I *remember?* Why, I got to smash the front window, the window, you hear? My God, it made a lovely sound! *Crash!*"

Tom could hear the glass fall in glittering heaps.

"And Bill Henderson, he got to bash the engine. Oh, he did a smart job of it, with great efficiency. Wham!"

"But best of all," recalled Grigsby, "there was the time they smashed a factory that was still trying to turn out airplanes."

"Lord, did we feel good blowing it up!" said Grigsby. "And then we found that newspaper plant and the munitions depot and exploded them together. Do you understand, Tom?"

Tom puzzled over it. "I guess."

It was high noon. Now the odors of the ruined city stank on the hot air and things crawled among the tumbled buildings.

"Won't it ever come back, mister?"

"What, civilization? Nobody wants it. Not me!"

"I could stand a bit of it," said the man behind another man. "There were a few spots of beauty in it."

"Don't worry your heads," shouted Grigsby. "There's no room for that, either."

"Ah," said the man behind the man. "Someone'll come along someday with imagination and patch it up. Mark my words. Someone with a heart."

"No," said Grigsby.

"I say yes. Someone with a soul for pretty things. Might give us back a kind of *limited* sort of civilization, the kind we could live in in peace."

"First thing you know there's war!"

"But maybe next time it'd be different."

At last they stood in the main square. A man on horseback was riding from the distance into the town. He had a piece of paper in his hand. In the center of the square was the roped-off area. Tom, Grigsby, and the others were collecting their spittle and moving forward—moving forward prepared and ready, eyes wide. Tom felt his heart beating very strongly and excitedly, and the earth was hot under his bare feet.

"Here we go, Tom, let fly!"

Four policemen stood at the corners of the roped area, four men with bits of yellow twine on their wrists to show their authority over other men. They were there to prevent rocks being hurled.

"This way," said Grigsby at the last moment, "everyone feels he's had his chance at her, you see, Tom? Go on, now!"

Tom stood before the painting and looked at it for a long time.

"Tom, spit!"

His mouth was dry.

"Get on, Tom! Move!"

"But," said Tom, slowly, "she's *beautiful!*"

"Here, I'll spit for you!" Grigsby spat and the missile flew in the sunlight. The woman in the portrait smiled serenely, secretly, at Tom, and he looked back at her, his heart beating, a kind of music in his ears.

"She's beautiful," he said.

"Now get on, before the police——"

"Attention!"

The line fell silent. One moment they were berating Tom for not moving forward, now they were turning to the man on horseback.

"What do they call it, sir?" asked Tom, quietly.

"The picture? *Mona Lisa,* Tom, I think. Yes, the *Mona Lisa.*"

"I have an announcement," said the man on horseback. "The authorities have decreed that as of high noon today the portrait in the square is to be given over into the hands of the populace there, so they may participate in the destruction of——"

Tom hadn't even time to scream before the crowd bore him, shouting and pummeling about, stampeding toward the portrait. There was a sharp ripping sound. The police ran to escape. The crowd was in full cry, their hands like so many hungry birds pecking away at the portrait. Tom felt himself thrust almost through the broken thing. Reaching out in blind imitation of the others, he snatched a scrap of oily canvas, yanked, felt the canvas give, then fell, was kicked, sent rolling to the outer rim of the mob. Bloody, his clothing torn, he watched old women chew pieces of canvas, men break the frame, kick the ragged cloth, and rip it into confetti.

Only Tom stood apart, silent in the moving square. He look down at his hand. It clutched the piece of canvas close to his chest, hidden.

"Hey there, Tom!" cried Grigsby.

Without a word, sobbing, Tom ran. He ran out and down the bomb-pitted road, into a field, across a shallow stream, not looking back, his hand clenched tightly, tucked under his coat.

At sunset he reached the small village and passed on through. By nine o'clock he came to the ruined farm dwelling. Around back, in the half silo, in the part that still remained upright, tented over, he heard the sounds of sleeping, the family—his mother, father, and brother. He slipped quickly, silently, through the small door and lay down, panting.

"Tom?" called his mother in the dark.

"Yes."

"Where've you been?" snapped his father. "I'll beat you in the morning."

Someone kicked him. His brother, who had been left behind to work their little patch of ground.

"Go to sleep," cried his mother, faintly.

Another kick.

Tom lay getting his breath. All was quiet. His hand was pushed to his chest, tight, tight. He lay for half an hour this way, eyes closed.

Then he felt something, and it was a cold white light. The moon rose very high and the little square of light moved in the silo and crept slowly over Tom's body. Then, and only then, did his hand relax. Slowly, carefully, listening to those who slept about him, Tom drew his hand forth. He hesitated, sucked in his breath, and then, waiting, opened his hand and uncrumpled the tiny fragment of painted canvas.

All the world was asleep in the moonlight.

And there on his hand was the Smile.

He looked at it in the white illumination from the midnight sky. And he thought, over and over to himself, quietly, *the Smile, the lovely Smile.*

An hour later he could still see it, even after he had folded it carefully and hidden it. He shut his eyes and the Smile was there in the darkness. And it was still there, warm and gentle, when he went to sleep and the world was silent and the moon sailed up and then down the cold sky toward morning.

PROBINGS

1. What is the most beautiful thing that you have ever seen, heard, or experienced in your life?
2. In the film *Soylent Green,* people are allowed to go to suicide parlors in order to end their lives if they wish. However, they are allowed to recall via film the beautiful experiences that they have had in the past. If you could recapture the ten most beautiful experiences in your life, what would they be?
3. In the future, which of the following would be the most meaningful to you? Rank them in order.
    a. a fulfilling religious life?
    b. having a lot of power over other people?
    c. owning the biggest and most beautiful house in the neighborhood?
    d. having a one-of-a-kind sports car or designer dress?
    e. having a satisfying relationship with someone of the opposite sex?

f.   having friends that really care for you, and you for them?

g.   having a lot of children?

h.   being able to create something that no one else has created? (what would it be?)

i.   having a lot of money?

j.   having a stimulating career?

k.   finding a cure for a disease?

l.   becoming a well-known sports star?

m. simply being like most other people?

n.   working with your hands?

o.   having a white-collar job?

p.   living in the mountains away from most people?

q.   other?

Why did you rank the items the way you did?

4.   Write a story about a future world in which there are really no group values or each individual has his own values. Could such a society function?

SECTION 2
HOW DO I
RELATE
TO OTHERS?

HOW DO I RELATE TO OTHERS?

Homo sapiens—humans—obviously live in groups, but so do other species. What makes human groups unique is that we don't associate with one another simply to procure food, to keep warm, or to obtain protection. Humans also congregate for a variety of social, political, and religious reasons.

From infancy we are taught how to fit in with our family, friends, and neighbors. What is "proper" behavior for a child is quickly learned by the infant, or else the child suffers the consequences. We punish children when they are bad; we reward them when they are good. Of course, what is considered "bad" in one culture may be "good" in another.

By our third and fourth years, we enter the politics of the neighborhood and nursery schools, and our social horizons expand. We come in contact with a variety of other children, some very much like us, others very different. Again, though, we are rewarded for proper behavior.

By age five, we take another giant social step—off to kindergarten, where we begin school, which will dominate our lives for at least twelve more years. New friends are gained and often these become life-long ones. In school, too, we learn how to "get along with others" or become a member of the group that gets check marks on our report card after the comment: "Doesn't play well with others."

From school age throughout the rest of our lives, those whom psychologists term "significant others"—relatives, friends, neighbors, playmates, and our peers—contribute to forming and pressuring us into a social being. From our teen-age years in particular, our peers, or our equals, play an increasingly important role in helping us shape an identity for ourselves.

In this section of the book, you'll be asked to look at the "significant others" in your own life. You'll also be asked to evaluate how they relate to you—and you to them.

Also in this section, you'll meet some unusual persons who just can't seem to conform and follow the leader. These are the rebels, the mavericks, the "strange" ones who can't seem to do what the silent majority wants to do. Two writers called us a "nation of sheep" because Americans don't like to rock the boat or appear too different. Another writer coined the term the "gray flannel man" to describe the corporate employee who looked, acted, and thought like his fellows. The people in this section are far from being sheep, and they most definitely would not fit easily, if at all, into the corporate structure.

FAMILY

6

Without doubt the family is the most important single group in our earliest years. In movies, television programs, books, and even comic strips we are constantly being offered models of the "ideal" American family, such as *The Brady Bunch* or *The Partridge Family.* Until fairly recently, however, most of these families consisted of a father, a mother, and one or more children. Now we are offered examples of widows, divorced parents, and even single parents. Numerous models are also presented in family-type TV shows and commercials of the "ideal" husband and father, wife and mother, and children. But what is an *ideal* family? How does a good mother or father behave? How does a proper child behave?

Certain families are termed "close"; these are families that seem to share many common experiences. Often these families are what we call extended families; aunts, uncles, cousins, and grandparents participate in family activities together. Other families, however, are close-knit but consist only of the parents and the children; these families are called nuclear families.

The nuclear family has been sharply criticized recently. Indeed, some people are raising the question: Is the family still necessary? Once children reach their teens it seems to

be the rare family that still does things together—or for that matter even eats a meal
together. Almost everyone over the age of
sixteen can drive a car, and this has given the
family unprecedented mobility. Within
minutes, family members can scatter themselves over the landscape as each member
pursues his or her own "thing."

At one time, families were forced to enter-
tain themselves, but now the magic tube
(television) has taken over that function. Still
other tremors have rocked the traditional
family. For example, some people are merg-
ing their families into one large communal
family; single parents are adopting children;
and many young and old people are even
rejecting the idea of marriage in favor of "living together."

What the future might bring for the family
is hard to project, but interesting to consider.
Or is there any future for the family? Might
children belong to everybody?

In the following story by Zenna Henderson, we share the experiences of a strange
family, whose members have some very
special gifts that make them rather different
—uniquely different, to say the least. While
reading this story, consider what your own
family is really like, and also consider just
what is a "perfect" family; what is an "ideal"
husband and father, or wife and mother;
what is an "ideal" child?

1. Headlines from Tomorrow:

Couple Married in West Virginia—First Wedding in State in 10 Years

The wedding on November 26, 2550, makes West Virginia the nation's leader in traditional marriages. The second in rank, Oregon, averages one wedding in every 10.75 years.

PROJECTIONS

2. How might the family of the future be changed—
   a. if most people worked at home using TV and computers?
   b. if education were conducted primarily by TV and computer?
   c. if most leisure were also provided by TV?

   Would these changes bring the family closer together or not?

GILEAD

—Zenna Henderson

I don't know when it was that I found out that our family was different from other families. There was nothing to point it out. We lived in a house very like the other houses in Socorro. Our pasture lot sloped down just like the rest through arrowweed and mesquite trees to the sometime Rio Gordo that looped around town. And on occasion our cow bawled just as loudly across the river at the Jacobses' bull as all the other cows in all the other pasture lots. And I spent as many lazy days as any other boy in Socorro lying on my back in the thin shade of the mesquites, chewing on the beans when work was waiting somewhere. It never occurred to me to wonder if we were different.

I suppose my first realization came soon after I started to school and fell in love—with the girl with the longest pigtails and the widest gap in her front teeth of all the girls in my room. I think she was seven to my six.

My girl and I had wandered down behind the school woodshed, under the cottonwoods, to eat our lunch together, ignoring the chanted "Peter's got a gir-ul! Peter's got a gir-ul!" and the whittling fingers that shamed me for showing my love. We ate our sandwiches and pickles and then lay back, arms doubled under our heads, and blinked at the bright sky while we tried to keep the crumbs from our cupcakes from falling into our ears. I was so full of lunch, contentment and love that I suddenly felt I just had to do something spectacular for my ladylove. I sat up, electrified by a great idea and by the knowledge that I could carry it out.

"Hey! Did you know that I can fly?" I scrambled to my feet, leaving my love sitting gape-mouthed in the grass.

"You can't neither fly! Don't be crazy!"

"I can too fly!"

"You can not neither!"

"I can so! You just watch!" And lifting my arms I swooped up to the roof of the shed. I leaned over the edge and said, "See there? I can, too!"

"I'll tell teacher on you!" she gasped, wide-eyed, staring up at me. "You ain't supposed to climb up on the shed."

"Oh, poof," I said, "I didn't climb. Come on, you fly up too. Here, I'll help you."

And I slid down the air to the ground. I put my arms around my love and lifted. She screamed and wrenched away from me and fled shrieking back to the schoolhouse. Somewhat taken aback by her desertion, I gathered up the remains of my cake and hers and was perched comfortably on the ridgepole of the shed, enjoying the last crumbs, when teacher arrived with half the school trailing behind her.

"Peter Merrill! How many times have you been told not to climb things at school?"

I peered down at her, noting with interest that the spit curls on her cheeks had been jarred loose by her hurry and agitation and one of them was straightening out, contrasting oddly with the rest of her shingled bob.

"Hang on tight until Stanley gets the ladder!"

"I can get down," I said, scrambling off the ridgepole. "It's easy."

"Peter!" teacher shrieked. "Stay where you are!"

So I did, wondering at all the fuss.

By the time they got me down and teacher yanked me by one arm back up to the schoolhouse I was bawling at the top of my voice, outraged and indignant because no one would believe me, even my girl denying obstinately the evidence of her own eyes. Teacher, annoyed at my persistence, said over and over, "Don't be silly, Peter. You can't fly. Nobody can fly. Where are your wings?"

"I don't need wings," I bellowed. "People don't need wings. I ain't a bird!"

"Then you can't fly. Only things with wings can fly."

So I alternately cried and kicked the schoolhouse steps for the rest of the noon hour, and then I began to worry for fear teacher would tattle to Dad. After all I had been on forbidden territory, no matter how I got there.

As it turned out she didn't tell Dad, but that night after I was put to bed I suddenly felt an all-gone feeling inside me. Maybe I *couldn't* fly. Maybe teacher was right. I sneaked out of bed and cautiously flew up to the top of the dresser and back. Then I pulled the covers up tight under my chin and whispered to myself, "I can so fly," and sighed heavily. Just another fun stuff that grownups didn't allow, like having cake for breakfast or driving the tractor or borrowing the cow for an Indian-pony-on-a-warpath.

And that was all of that incident except that when teacher met Mother and me at the store that Saturday she ruffled my hair and said, "How's my little bird?" Then she laughed and said to Mother, "He thinks he can fly!"

I saw Mother's fingers tighten whitely on her purse, and she looked down at me with all the laughter gone from her eyes. I was overflooded with incredulous surprise mixed with fear and dread that made me want to cry, even though I knew it was Mother's emotions and not my own that I was feeling.

Mostly Mother had laughing eyes. She was the laughingest mother in Socorro. She carried happiness inside her as if it were a bouquet of flowers and she gave part of it to everyone she met. Most of the other mothers seemed to have hardly enough to go around to their own families. And yet there were other times, like at the store, when laughter fled and fear showed through—and an odd wariness. Other times she made me think of a caged bird, pressing against the bars. Like one night I remember vividly.

Mother stood at the window in her ankle-length flannel nightgown, her long dark hair lifting softly in the draft from the rattling window frames. A high wind was blowing in from a spectacular thunderstorm in the Huachucas. I had been awakened by the rising crescendo and was huddled on the sofa wondering if I was scared or excited as the house shook with the constant thunder. Dad was sitting with the newspaper in his lap.

Mother spoke softly, but her voice came clearly through the tumult.

"Have you ever wondered what it would be like to be up there in the middle of the storm with clouds under your feet and over your head and lightning lacing around you like hot golden rivers?"

Dad rattled his paper. "Sounds uncomfortable," he said.

But I sat there and hugged the words to me in wonder. I knew! *I remembered!* " 'And the rain like icy silver hair lashing across your lifted face,' " I recited as though it were a loved lesson.

Mother whirled from the window and stared at me. Dad's eyes were on me, dark and troubled.

"How do you know?" he asked.

I ducked my head in confusion. "I don't know," I muttered.

Mother pressed her hands together, hard, her bowed head swinging the curtains of her hair forward over her shadowy face. "He knows because I know. I know because my mother knew. She knew because our People used to—" Her voice broke. "Those were her words—"

She stopped and turned back to the window, leaning her arm against the frame, her face pressed to it, like a child in tears.

"Oh, Bruce, I'm sorry!"

I stared, round-eyed in amazement, trying to keep tears from coming to my eyes as I fought against Mother's desolation and sorrow.

Dad went to Mother and turned her gently into his arms. He looked over her head at me. "Better run on back to bed, Peter. The worst is over."

I trailed off reluctantly, my mind filled with wonder. Just before I shut my door I stopped and listened.

"I've never said a word to him, honest." Mother's voice quivered. "Oh, Bruce, I try so hard, but sometimes—oh sometimes!"

"I know, Eve. And you've done a wonderful job of it. I know it's hard on you, but we've talked it out so many times. It's the only way, honey."

"Yes," Mother said. "It's the only way, but—oh, be my strength, Bruce! Bless the Power for giving me you!"

I shut my door softly and huddled in the dark in the middle of my bed until I felt Mother's anguish smooth out to loving warmness again. Then for no good reason I flew solemnly to the top of the dresser and back, crawled into bed and relaxed. And remembered. Remembered the hot golden rivers, the clouds over and under and the wild winds that buffeted like foam-frosted waves. But with all the sweet remembering was the reminder, *You can't because you're only eight. You're only eight. You'll have to wait.*

And then Bethie was born, almost in time for my ninth birthday. I remember peeking over the edge of the bassinet at the miracle of tiny fingers and spun-sugar hair. Bethie, my little sister. Bethie, who was whispered about and stared at when Mother let her go to school, though mostly she kept her home even after she was old enough. Because Bethie was different—too.

When Bethie was a month old I smashed my finger in the bedroom door. I cried for a quarter of an hour, but Bethie sobbed on and on until the last pain left my finger.

When Bethie was six months old our little terrier, Glib, got caught in a gopher trap. Bethie screamed until Glib fell asleep over his bandaged paw.

Dad had acute appendicitis when Bethie was two, but it was Bethie who had to be given a sedative until we could get Dad to the hospital.

One night Dad and Mother stood over Bethie as she slept restlessly under sedatives. Mr. Tyree-next-door had been cutting wood and his axe slipped. He lost a big toe and a pint or so of blood, but as Doctor Dueff skidded to a stop on our street it was into our house that he rushed first and then to Mr. Tyree-next-door who lay with his foot swathed and propped up on a chair, his hands pressed to his ears to shut out Bethie's screams.

"What can we do, Eve?" Dad asked. "What does the doctor say?"

"Nothing. They can do nothing for her. He hopes she will outgrow it. He doesn't understand it. He doesn't know that she—"

"What's the matter? What makes her like this?" Dad asked despairingly.

Mother winced. "She's a Sensitive. Among my People there were such—but not so young. Their perception made it possible for them to help sufferers. Bethie has only half the Gift. She has no control."

"Because of me?" Dad's voice was ragged.

Mother looked at him with steady loving eyes. "Because of us, Bruce. It was the chance we took. We pushed our luck after Peter."

So there we were, the two of us—different—but different in our differences. For me it was mostly fun, but not for Bethie.

We had to be careful for Bethie. She tried school at first, but skinned knees and rough rassling and aching teeth and bumped heads and the janitor's Monday hangover sent her home exhausted and shaking the first day, with hysteria hanging on the flick of an eyelash. So Bethie read for Mother and learned her numbers and leaned wistfully over the gate as the other children went by.

It wasn't long after Bethie's first day in school that I found a practical use for my difference. Dad sent me out to the woodshed to stack a cord of mesquite that Delfino dumped into our back yard from his old wood wagon. I had a date to explore an old fluorspar mine with some other guys and bitterly resented being sidetracked. I slouched out to the woodpile and stood, hands in pockets, kicking the heavy rough stove lengths. Finally I carried in one armload, grunting under the weight, and afterward sucking the round of my thumb where the sliding wood had peeled me. I hunkered down on my heels and stared as I sucked. Suddenly something prickled inside my brain. If I could fly why couldn't I make the wood fly? *And I knew I could!* I leaned forward and flipped a finger under half a dozen sticks, concentrating as I did so. They lifted into the air and hovered. I pushed them into the shed, guided them to where I wanted them and distributed them like dealing a pack of cards. It didn't take me long to figure out the maximum load, and I had all the wood stacked in a wonderfully short time.

I whistled into the house for my flashlight. The mine was spooky and dark, and I was the only one of the gang with a flashlight.

"I told you to stack the wood." Dad looked up from his milk records.

"I did," I said, grinning.

"Cut the kidding," Dad grunted. "You couldn't be done already."

"I am, though," I said triumphantly. "I found a new way to do it. You see—" I stopped, frozen by Dad's look.

"We don't need any new ways around here," he said evenly. "Go back out there until you've had time to stack the wood right!"

"It *is* stacked," I protested. "And the kids are waiting for me!"

"I'm not arguing, son," said Dad, white-faced. "Go back out to the shed."

I went back out to the shed—past Mother, who had come in from the kitchen and whose hand half went out to me. I sat in the shed fuming for a long time, stubbornly set that I wouldn't leave till Dad told me to.

Then I got to thinking. Dad wasn't usually unreasonable like this. Maybe I'd done something wrong. Maybe it was bad to stack wood like that. Maybe—my thoughts wavered as I remembered whispers I'd overheard about Bethie. Maybe it—it was a crazy thing to do—an insane thing.

I huddled close upon myself as I considered it. Crazy means not doing like other people. Crazy means doing things ordinary people don't do. Maybe that's why Dad made such a fuss. Maybe I'd done an insane thing! I stared at the ground, lost in bewilderment. What *was* different about our family? And for the first time I was able to isolate and recognize the feeling I must have had for a long time—the feeling of being on the outside looking in—the feeling of apartness. With this recognition came a wariness, a need for concealment. If something was wrong no one else must know—I must not betray . . .

Then Mother was standing beside me. "Dad says you may go now," she said, sitting down on my log.

"Peter—" She looked at me unhappily. "Dad's doing what is best. All I can say is: remember that whatever you do, wherever you live, different is dead. You have to conform or—or die. But Peter, don't be ashamed. Don't ever be ashamed!" Then swiftly her hands were on my shoulders and her lips brushed my ear. "Be different!" she whispered. "Be as different as you can. But don't let anyone see—don't let anyone know!" And she was gone up the back steps, into the kitchen.

As I grew further into adolescence I seemed to grow further and further away from kids my age. I couldn't seem to get much of a kick out of what they considered fun. So it was that with increasing frequency in the years that followed I took Mother's whispered advice, never asking for explanations I knew she wouldn't give. The wood incident had opened up a whole vista of possibilities—no telling what I might be able to do—so I got in the habit of going down to the foot of our pasture lot. There, screened by the brush and greasewood, I tried all sorts of experiments, never knowing whether they would work or not. I sweated plenty over some that didn't work—and some that did.

I found that I could snap my fingers and bring things to me, or send them short distances from me without bothering to touch them as I had the wood. I roosted regularly in the tops of the tall cottonwoods, swandiving ecstatically down to the ground, warily, after I got too ecstatic once and crashlanded on my nose and chin. By headaching concentration that left me dizzy, I even set a small campfire ablaze. Then blistered and charred both hands unmercifully by confidently scooping up the crackling fire.

Then I guess I got careless about checking for onlookers because some nasty talk got started. Bub Jacobs whispered around that I was "doing things" all alone down in the brush. His sly grimace as he whispered made the "doing things" any nasty perversion the listeners' imaginations could conjure up, and the "alone" damned me on the spot. I learned bitterly then what Mother had told me. Different is dead—and one death is never enough. You die and die and die.

Then one day I caught Bub cutting across the foot of our wood lot. He saw me coming and hit for tall timber, already smarting under what he knew he'd get if I caught him. I started full speed after him, then plowed to a stop. Why waste effort? If I could do it to the wood I could do it to a blockhead like Bub.

He let out a scream of pure terror as the ground dropped out from under him. His scream flatted and strangled into silence as he struggled in mid-air, convulsed with fear of falling and the terrible thing that was happening to him. And I stood and laughed at him, feeling myself a giant towering above stupid dopes like Bub.

Sharply, before he passed out, I felt his terror, and an echo of his scream rose in my throat. I slumped down in the dirt, sick with sudden realization, knowing with a knowledge that went beyond ordinary experience that I had done something terribly wrong, that I had prostituted whatever powers I possessed by using them to terrorize unjustly.

I knelt and looked up at Bub, crumpled in the air, higher than my head, higher than my reach, and swallowed painfully as I realized that I had no idea how to get him down. He wasn't a stick of wood to be snapped to the ground. He wasn't me, to dive down through the air. I hadn't the remotest idea how to get a human down.

Half dazed, I crawled over to a shaft of sunlight that slit the cottonwood branches overhead and felt it rush through my fingers like some- thing to be lifted—and twisted—and fashioned and *used! Used on Bub!* But how? *How?* I clenched my fist in the flood of light, my mind beating against another door that needed only a word or look or gesture to open, but I couldn't say it, or look it, or make it.

I stood up and took a deep breath. I jumped, batting at Bub's heels that dangled a little lower than the rest of him. I missed. Again I jumped and the tip of one finger flicked his heel and he moved sluggishly in the air. Then I swiped the back of my hand across my sweaty forehead and laughed—laughed at my stupid self.

Cautiously, because I hadn't done much hovering, mostly just up and down, I lifted myself up level with Bub. I put my hands on him and pushed down hard. He didn't move.

I tugged him up and he rose with me. I drifted slowly and deliberately away from him and pondered. Then I got on the other side of him and pushed him toward the branches of the cottonwood. His head was beginning to toss and his lips moved with returning consciousness. He drifted through the air like a waterlogged stump, but he moved and I draped him carefully over a big limb near the top of the tree, anchoring his arms and legs as securely as I could. By the time his eyes opened and he clutched frenziedly for support I was standing down at the foot of the tree, yelling up at him.

"Hang on, Bub! I'll go get someone to help you down!"

So for the next week or so people forgot me, and Bub squirmed under "Who treed you, feller?" and "How's the weather up there?" and "Get a ladder, Bub, get a ladder!"

Even with worries like that it was mostly fun for me. Why couldn't it be like that for Bethie? Why couldn't I give her part of my fun and take part of her pain?

Then Dad died, swept out of life by our Rio Gordo as he tried to rescue a fool Easterner who had camped on the bone-dry white sands of the river bottom in cloudburst weather. Somehow it seemed impossible to think of Mother by herself. It had always been Mother and Dad. Not just two parents but Mother-and-Dad, a single entity. And now our thoughts must limp to Mother-and, Mother-and. And Mother—well, half of her was gone.

After the funeral Mother and Bethie and I sat in our front room, looking at the floor. Bethie was clenching her teeth against the stabbing pain of Mother's fingernails gouging Mother's palms.

I unfolded the clenched hands gently and Bethie relaxed.

"Mother," I said softly, "I can take care of us. I have my part-time job at the plant. Don't worry. I'll take care of us."

I knew what a trivial thing I was offering to her anguish, but I had to do something to break through to her.

"Thank you, Peter," Mother said, rousing a little. "I know you will—" She bowed her head and pressed both hands to her dry eyes with restrained desperation. "Oh, Peter, Peter! I'm enough of this world now to find death a despair and desolation instead of the solemnly sweet calling it is. Help me, help me!" Her breath labored in her throat and she groped blindly for my hand.

"If I can, Mother," I said, taking one hand as Bethie took the other.

"Then help me remember. Remember with me."

And behind my closed eyes I remembered. Unhampered flight through a starry night, a flight of a thousand happy people like birds in the sky, rushing to meet the dawn—the dawn of the Festival. I could smell the flowers that garlanded the women and feel the quiet exultation that went with the Festival dawn. Then the leader sounded the magnificent opening notes of the Festival song as he caught the first glimpse of the rising sun over the heavily wooded hills. A thousand voices took up the song. A thousand hands lifted in the Sign . . .

I opened my eyes to find my own fingers lifted to trace a sign I did not know. My own throat throbbed to a note I had never sung. I took a deep breath and glanced over at Bethie. She met my eyes and shook her head sadly. She hadn't seen. Mother sat quietly, eyes closed, her face cleared and calmed.

"What was it, Mother?" I whispered.

"The Festival," she said softly. "For all those who had been called during the year. For your father, Peter and Bethie. We remembered it for your father."

"Where was it?" I asked. "Where in the world—?"

"Not in this—" Mother's eyes flicked open. "It doesn't matter, Peter. You are of this world. There is no other for you."

"Mother," Bethie's voice was a hesitant murmur, "what do you mean, 'remember'?"

Mother looked at her and tears welled into her dry burned-out eyes.

"Oh, Bethie, Bethie, all the burdens and none of the blessings! I'm sorry, Bethie, I'm sorry." And she fled down the hall to her room.

Bethie stood close against my side as we looked after Mother.

"Peter," she murmured, "what did Mother mean, 'none of the blessings'?"

"I don't know," I said.

"I'll bet it's because I can't fly like you."

"Fly!" My startled eyes went to hers. "How do you know?"

"I know lots of things," she whispered. "But mostly I know we're different. Other people aren't like us. Peter, what made us different?"

"Mother?" I whispered. "Mother?"

"I guess so," Bethie murmured. "But how come?"

We fell silent and then Bethie went to the window where the late sun haloed her silver blond hair in fire.

"I can do things too," she whispered. "Look."

She reached out and took a handful of sun, the same sort of golden sun-slant that had flowed so heavily through my fingers under the cotton-woods while Bub dangled above me. With flashing fingers she fashioned the sun into an intricate glowing pattern. "But what's it for," she murmured, "except for pretty?"

"I know," I said, looking at my answer for lowering Bub. "I know, Bethie." And I took the pattern from her. It strained between my fingers and flowed into darkness.

The years that followed were casual uneventful years. I finished high school, but college was out of the question. I went to work in the plant that provided work for most of the employables in Socorro.

Mother built up quite a reputation as a midwife—a very necessary calling in a community which took literally the injunction to multiply and replenish the earth and which lay exactly seventy-five miles from a hospital, no matter which way you turned when you got to the highway.

Bethie was in her teens and with Mother's help was learning to control her visible reactions to the pain of others, but I knew she still suffered as much as, if not more than, she had when she was smaller. But she was able to go to school most of the time now and was becoming fairly popular in spite of her quietness.

So all in all we were getting along quite comfortably and quite ordinarily except—well, I always felt as though I were waiting for something to happen or for someone to come. And Bethie must have, too, because she actually watched and listened—especially after a particularly bad spell. And even Mother. Sometimes as we sat on the porch in the long evenings she would cock her head and listen intently, her rocking chair still. But when we asked what she heard she'd sigh and say, "Nothing. Just the night." And her chair would rock again.

Of course I still indulged my differences. Not with the white fire of possible discovery that they had kindled when I first began, but more like the feeding of a small flame just "for pretty." I went farther afield now for my "holidays," but Bethie went with me. She got a big kick out of our excursions, especially after I found that I could carry her when I flew, and most especially after we found, by means of a heart-stopping accident, that though she couldn't go up she could control her going down. After that it was her pleasure to have me carry her up as far as I could and she would come down, sometimes taking an hour to make the descent, often weaving about her the intricate splendor of her sunshine patterns.

It was a rustling russet day in October when our world ended—again. We talked and laughed over the breakfast table, teasing Bethie about her date the night before. Color was high in her usually pale cheeks, and, with all the laughter and brightness the tingle of fall, everything just felt good.

But between one joke and another the laughter drained out of Bethie's face and the pinched set look came to her lips.

"Mother!" she whispered, and then she relaxed.

"Already?" asked Mother, rising and finishing her coffee as I went to get her coat. "I had a hunch today would be the day. Reena would ride that jeep up Peppersauce Canyon this close to her time."

I helped her on with her coat and hugged her tight.

"Bless-a-mama," I said, "when are you going to retire and let someone else snatch the fall and spring crops of kids?"

"When I snatch a grandchild or so for myself," she said, joking, but I felt her sadness. "Besides she's going to name this one Peter—or Bethie, as the case may be." She reached for her little black bag and looked at Bethie. "No more yet?"

Bethie smiled. "No," she murmured.

"Then I've got plenty of time. Peter, you'd better take Bethie for a holiday. Reena takes her own sweet time and being just across the road makes it bad on Bethie."

"Okay, Mother," I said. "We planned one anyway, but we hoped this time you'd go with us."

Mother looked at me, hesitated and turned aside. "I—I might sometime."

"Mother! Really?" This was the first hesitation from Mother in all the times we'd asked her.

"Well, you've asked me so many times and I've been wondering. Wondering if it's fair to deny our birthright. After all there's nothing wrong in being of the People."

"What people, Mother?" I pressed . "*Where* are you from? Why can—?"

"Some other time, son," Mother said. "Maybe soon. These last few months I've begun to sense—yes, it wouldn't hurt you to know even if nothing could ever come of it; and perhaps soon something *can* come, and you will have to know. But no," she chided as we clung to her. "There's no time now. Reena might fool us after all and produce before I get there. You kids scoot, now!"

We looked back as the pickup roared across the highway and headed for Mendigo's Peak. Mother answered our wave and went in the gate of Reena's yard, where Dalt, in spite of this being their sixth, was running like an anxious puppy dog from Mother to the porch and back again.

It was a day of perfection for us. The relaxation of flight for me, the delight of hovering for Bethie, the frosted glory of the burning-blue sky, the russet and gold of grasslands stretching for endless miles down from the snow-flecked blue and gold Mendigo.

At lunchtime we lolled in the pleasant warmth of our favorite baby box canyon that held the sun and shut out the wind. After we ate we played our favorite game, Remembering. It began with my clearing my mind so that it lay as quiet as a hidden pool of water, as receptive as the pool to every pattern the slightest breeze might start quivering across its surface.

Then the memories would come—strange un-Earthlike memories that were like those Mother and I had had when Dad died. Bethie could not remember with me, but she seemed to catch the memories from me almost before the words could form in my mouth.

So this last lovely "holiday" we remembered again our favorite. We walked the darkly gleaming waters of a mountain lake, curling our toes in the liquid coolness, loving the tilt and sway of the waves beneath our feet, feeling around us from shore and sky a dear familiarity that was stronger than any Earth ties we had yet formed.

Before we knew it the long lazy afternoon had fled and we shivered in the sudden chill as the sun dropped westward, nearing the peaks of the Huachucas. We packed the remains of our picnic in the basket, and I turned to Bethie, to lift her and carry her back to the pickup.

She was smiling her soft little secret smile.

"Look, Peter," she murmured. And flicking her fingers over her head she shook out a cloud of snowflakes, gigantic whirling tumbling snow-flakes that clung feather-soft to her pale hair and melted, glistening, across her warm cheeks and mischievous smile.

"Early winter, Peter!" she said.

"Early winter, punkin!" I cried and snatching her up, boosted her out of the little canyon and jumped over her, clearing the boulders she had to scramble over. "For that you walk, young lady!"

But she almost beat me to the car anyway. For one who couldn't fly she was learning to run awfully light.

Twilight had fallen before we got back to the highway. We could see the headlights of the scurrying cars that seldom even slowed down for Socorro. "So this is Socorro, wasn't it?" was the way most traffic went through.

We had topped the last rise before the highway when Bethie screamed. I almost lost control of the car on the rutty road. She screamed again, a wild tortured cry as she folded in on herself.

"Bethie!" I called, trying to get through to her. "What is it? Where is it? Where can I take you?"

But her third scream broke off short and she slid limply to the floor. I was terrified. She hadn't reacted like this in years. She had never fainted like this before. Could it be that Reena hadn't had her child yet? That she was in such agony—but even when Mrs. Allbeg had died in childbirth Bethie hadn't—I lifted Bethie to the seat and drove wildly homeward, praying that Mother would be—

And then I saw it. In front of our house. The big car skewed across the road. The kneeling cluster of people on the pavement.

The next thing I knew I was kneeling too, beside Dr. Dueff, clutching the edge of the blanket that mercifully covered Mother from chin to toes. I lifted a trembling hand to the dark trickle of blood that threaded crookedly down from her forehead.

"Mother," I whispered. "Mother!"

Her eyelids fluttered and she looked up blindly. "Peter." I could hardly hear her. "Peter, where's Bethie?"

"She's fainted. She's in the car—" I faltered. "Oh, Mother!"

"Tell the doctor to go to Bethie."

"But, Mother!" I cried. "You—"

"I am not called yet. Go to Bethie."

We knelt by her bedside, Bethie and I. The doctor was gone. There was no use trying to get Mother to a hospital. Just moving her indoors had started a dark oozing from the corner of her mouth. The neighbors were all gone except Gramma Reuther who always came to troubled homes and had folded the hands of the dead in Socorro from the founding of the town. She sat now in the front room holding her worn Bible in quiet hands, after all these years no longer needing to look up the passages of comfort and assurance.

The doctor had quieted the pain for Mother and had urged sleep upon Bethie, not knowing how long the easing would last, but Bethie wouldn't take it.

Suddenly Mother's eyes were open.

"I married your father," she said clearly, as though continuing a conversation. "We loved each other so, and they were all dead—all my People. Of course I told him first, and oh, Peter! He believed me! After all that time of having to guard every word and every move I had someone to talk to—someone to believe me. I told him all about the People and lifted myself and then I lifted the car and turned it in mid-air above the highway—just for fun. It pleased him a lot but it made him thoughtful and later he said, 'You know, honey, your world and ours took different turns way back there. We turned to gadgets. You turned to the Power.'"

Her eyes smiled. "He got so he knew when I was lonesome for the Home. Once he said, 'Homesick, honey? So am I. For what this world could have been. Or maybe—God willing—what it may become.'

"Your father was the other half of me." Her eyes closed, and in the silence her breath became audible, a harsh straining sound. Bethie crouched with both hands pressed to her chest, her face dead white in the shadows.

"We discussed it and discussed it," Mother cried. "But we had to decide as we did. We thought I was that last of the People. I had to forget the Home and be of Earth. You children had to be of Earth, too, even if—That's why he was so stern with you, Peter. Why he didn't want you to—experiment. He was afraid you'd do too much around other people if you found out—" She stopped and lay panting. "Different is dead," she whispered, and lay scarcely breathing for a moment.

"I knew the Home." Her voice was heavy with sorrow. "I remember the Home. Not just because my People remembered it but because I saw it. I was born there. It's gone now. Gone forever. There is no Home. Only a band of dust between the stars!" Her face twisted with grief and Bethie echoed her cry of pain.

Then Mother's face cleared and her eyes opened. She half propped herself up in her bed.

"You have the Home, too. You and Bethie. You will have it always. And your children after you. Remember, Peter? Remember?"

Then her head tilted attentively and she gave a laughing sob. "Oh, Peter! Oh, Bethie! Did you hear it? I've been called! I've been called!" Her hand lifted in the Sign and her lips moved tenderly.

"Mother!" I cried fearfully. "What do you mean? Lie down. Please lie down!" I pressed her back against the pillows.

"I've been called back to the Presence. My years are finished. My days are totaled."

"But Mother," I blubbered like a child, "what will we do without you?"

"Listen!" Mother whispered rapidly, one hand pressed to my hair. "You must find the rest. You must go right away. They can help Bethie. They can help you, Peter. As long as you are separated from them you are not complete. I have felt them calling the last year or so, and now that I am on the way to the Presence I can hear them clearer, and clearer." She paused and held her breath. "There is a canyon—north. The ship crashed there, after our life slips—here, Peter, give me your hand." She reached urgently toward me and I cradled her hand in mine.

And I saw half the state spread out below me like a giant map. I saw the wrinkled folds of the mountains, the deceptively smooth roll of the desert up to the jagged slopes. I saw the blur of timber blunting the hills and I saw the angular writhing of the narrow road through the passes. Then I felt a sharp pleasurable twinge, like the one you feel when seeing home after being away a long time.

"There!" Mother whispered as the panorama faded. "I wish I could have known before. It's been lonely—

"But you, Peter," she said strongly. "You and Bethie must go to them."

"Why should we, Mother?" I cried in desperation. "What are they to us or we to them that we should leave Socorro and go among strangers?"

Mother pulled herself up in bed, her eyes intent on my face. She wavered a moment and then Bethie was crouched behind her, steadying her back.

"They are not strangers," she said clearly and slowly. "They are the People. We shared the ship with them during the Crossing. They were with us when we were out in the middle of emptiness with only the fading of stars behind and the brightening before to tell us we were moving. They, with us, looked at all the bright frosting of stars across the blackness, wondering if on one of them we would find a welcome.

"You are woven of their fabric. Even though your father was not of the People—"

Her voice died, her face changed. Bethie moved from in back of her and lowered her gently. Mother clasped her hands and sighed.

"It's a lonely business," she whispered. "No one can go with you. Even with them waiting it's lonely."

In the silence that followed we heard Gramma Reuther rocking quietly in the front room. Bethie sat on the floor beside me, her cheeks flushed, her eyes wide with a strange dark awe.

"Peter, it didn't hurt. It didn't hurt at all. It—healed!"

But we didn't go. How could we leave my job and our home and go off to—where? Looking for—whom? Because—why? It was mostly me, I guess, but I couldn't quite believe what Mother had told us. After all she hadn't said anything definite. We were probably reading meaning where it didn't exist. Bethie returned again and again to the puzzle of Mother and what she had meant, but we didn't go.

And Bethie got paler and thinner, and it was nearly a year later that I came home to find her curled into an impossible tight ball on her bed, her eyes tight shut, snatching at breath that came out again in sharp moans.

I nearly went crazy before I at last got through to her and uncurled her enough to get hold of one of her hands. Finally, though, she opened dull dazed eyes and looked past me.

"Like a dam, Peter," she gasped. "It all comes in. It should—it should! I was born to—" I wiped the cold sweat from her forehead. "But it just piles up and piles up. It's supposed to go somewhere. I'm supposed to do something! Peter, Peter, Peter!" She twisted on the bed, her distorted face pushing into the pillow.

"What does, Bethie?" I asked, turning her face to mine. "What does?"

"Glib's foot and Dad's side and Mr. Tyree-next-door's toe—" and her voice faded down through the litany of years of agony.

"I'll go get Dr. Dueff," I said hopelessly.

"No." She turned her face away. "Why build the dam higher? Let it break. Oh, soon, soon!"

"Bethie, don't talk like that," I said, feeling inside me my terrible aloneness that only Bethie could fend off now that Mother was gone. "We'll find something—some way—"

"Mother could help," she gasped. "A little. But she's gone. And now I'm picking up mental pain too! Reena's afraid she's got cancer. Oh, Peter, Peter!" Her voice strained to a whisper. "Let me die! Help me die!"

Both of us were shocked to silence by her words. Help her die? I leaned against her hand. Go back into the Presence with the weight of unfinished years dragging at our feet? For if she went I went too.

Then my eyes flew open and I stared at Bethie's hand. What Presence? Whose ethics and mores were talking in my mind?

And so I had to decide. I talked Bethie into a sleeping pill and sat by her even after she was asleep. And as I sat there all the past years wound through my head. The way it must have been for Bethie all this time and I hadn't let myself know.

Just before dawn I woke Bethie. We packed and went. I left a note on the kitchen table for Dr. Dueff saying only that we were going to look for help for Bethie and would he ask Reena to see to the house. And thanks.

I slowed the pickup over to the side of the junction and slammed the brakes on.

"Okay," I said hopelessly. "You choose which way this time. Or shall we toss for it? Heads straight up, tails straight down! I can't tell where to go, Bethie. I had only that one little glimpse that Mother gave me of this country. There's a million canyons and a million side roads. We were fools to leave Socorro. After all we have nothing to go on but what Mother said. It might have been delirium."

"No," Bethie murmured. "It can't be. It's got to be real."

"But, Bethie," I said, leaning my weary head on the steering wheel, "you know how much I want it to be true, not only for you but for myself too. But look. What do we have to assume if Mother was right? First, that space travel is possible—was possible nearly fifty years ago. Second, that Mother and her People came here from another planet. Third, that we are, bluntly speaking, half-breeds, a cross between Earth and heaven knows what world. Fourth, that there's a chance—in ten million—of our finding the other People who came at the same time Mother did, presupposing that any of them survived the Crossing.

"Why, any one of these premises would brand us as crazy crackpots to any normal person. No, we're building too much on a dream and a hope. Let's go back, Bethie. We've got just enough gas money along to make it. Let's give it up."

"And go back to what?" Bethie asked, her face pinched. "No, Peter. Here."

I looked up as she handed me one of her sunlight patterns, a handful of brilliance that twisted briefly in my fingers before it flickered out.

"Is that Earth?" she asked quietly. "How many of our friends can fly? How many—" she hesitated, "how many can Remember?"

"Remember!" I said slowly, and then I whacked the steering wheel with my fist. "Oh, Bethie, of all the stupid—! Why, it's Bub all over again!"

I kicked the pickup into life and turned on the first faint desert trail beyond the junction. I pulled off even that suggestion of a trail and headed across the nearly naked desert toward a clump of ironwood, mesquite, and catclaw that marked a sand wash against the foothills. With the westering sun making shadow lace through the thin foliage we made camp.

I lay on my back in the wash and looked deep into the arch of the desert sky. The trees made a typical desert pattern of warmth and coolness on me, warm in the sun, cool in the shadow, as I let my mind clear smoother, smoother, until the soft intake of Bethie's breath as she sat beside me sent a bright ripple across it.

And I remembered. But only Mother-and-Dad and the little campfire I had gathered up, and Glib with the trap on his foot and Bethie curled, face to knees on the bed, and the thin crying sound of her labored breath.

I blinked at the sky. I *had* to Remember. I just had to. I shut my eyes and concentrated and concentrated, until I was exhausted. Nothing came now, not even a hint of memory. In despair I relaxed, limp against the chilling sand. And all at once unaccustomed gears shifted and slipped into place in my mind and there I was, just as I had been, hovering over the life-sized map.

Slowly and painfully I located Socorro and the thin thread that marked the Rio Gordo. I followed it and lost it and followed it again, the finger of my attention pressing close. Then I located Vulcan Springs Valley and traced its broad rolling to the upsweep of the desert, to the Sierra Cobreña Mountains. It was an eerie sensation to look down on the infinitesimal groove that must be where I was lying now. Then I handspanned my thinking around our camp spot. Nothing. I probed farther north, and east, and north again. I drew a deep breath and exhaled it shakily. There it was. The Home twinge. The call of familiarity.

I read it off to Bethie. The high thrust of a mountain that pushed up baldly past its timber, the huge tailings dump across the range from the mountain. The casual wreathing of smoke from what must be a logging town, all forming sides of a slender triangle. Somewhere in this area was the place.

I opened my eyes to find Bethie in tears.

"Why, Bethie!" I said. "What's wrong? Aren't you glad—?"

Bethie tried to smile but her lips quivered. She hid her face in the crook of her elbow and whispered. "I saw, too! Oh, Peter, this time I saw, too!"

We got out the road map and by the fading afternoon light we tried to translate our rememberings. As nearly as we could figure out we should head for a place way off the highway called Kerry Canyon. It was apparently the only inhabited spot anywhere near the big bald mountain. I looked at the little black dot in the kink in the third-rate road and wondered if it would turn out to be a period to all our hopes or the point for the beginning of new lives for the two of us. Life and sanity for Bethie, and for me . . . In a sudden spasm of emotion I crumpled the map in my hand. I felt blindly that in all my life I had never known anyone but Mother and Dad and Bethie. That I was a ghost walking the world. If only I could see even one other person that felt like our kind! Just to know that Bethie and I weren't all alone with our unearthly heritage!

I smoothed out the map and folded it again. Night was on us and the wind was cold. We shivered as we scurried around looking for wood for our campfire.

Kerry Canyon was one business street, two service stations, two saloons, two stores, two churches, and a handful of houses flung at random over the hillsides that sloped down to an area that looked too small to accommodate the road. A creek which was now thinned to an intermittent trickle that loitered along, waited for the fall rains to begin. A sudden speckling across our windshield suggested it hadn't long to wait.

We rattled over the old bridge and half through the town. The road swung up sharply over a rusty single-line railroad and turned left, shying away from the bluff that was hollowed just enough to accommodate one of the service stations.

We pulled into the station. The uniformed attendant came alongside.

"We just want some information," I said, conscious of the thinness of my billfold. We had picked up our last tankful of gas before plunging into the maze of canyons between the main highway and here. Our stopping place would have to be soon whether we found the People or not.

"Sure! Sure! Glad to oblige." The attendant pushed his cap back from his forehead. "How can I help you?"

I hesitated, trying to gather my thoughts and words—and some of the hope that had jolted out of me since we had left the junction.

"We're trying to locate some—friends—of ours. We were told they lived out the other side of here, out by Baldy. Is there anyone—?"

"Friends of *them* people?" he asked in astonishment. "Well, say, now, that's interesting! You're the first I ever had come asking after them."

I felt Bethie's arm trembling against mine. Then there *was* something beyond Kerry Canyon!

"How come? What's wrong with them?"

"Why, nothing, Mac, nothing. Matter of fact they're dern nice people. Trade here a lot. Come in to church and the dances."

"Dances?" I glanced around the steep sloping hills.

"Sure. We ain't as dead as we look." The attendant grinned. "Come Saturday night we're quite a town. Lots of ranches around these hills. Course, not much out Cougar Canyon way. That's where your friends live, didn't you say?"

"Yeah. Out by Baldy."

"Well, nobody else lives out that way." He hesitated. "Hey, there's something I'd like to ask."

"Sure. Like what?"

"Well, them people pretty much keep themselves to themselves. I don't mean they're stuck-up or anything, but—well, I've always wondered. Where they from? One of them overrun countries in Europe? They're foreigners, ain't they? And seems like most of what Europe exports any more is DP's. Are them people some?"

"Well, yes, you might call them that. Why?"

"Well, they talk just as good as anybody and it must have been a war a long time ago because they've been around since my Dad's time, but they just—feel different." He caught his upper lip between his teeth reflectively. "Good different. Real nice different." He grinned again. "Wouldn't mind shining up to some of them gals myself. Don't get no encouragement, though.

"Anyway, keep on this road. It's easy. No other road going that way. Jackass Flat will beat the tar outa your tires, but you'll probably make it, less'n comes up a heavy rain. Then you'll skate over half the county and most likely end up in a ditch. Slickest mud in the world. Colder'n hell— beg pardon, lady—out there on the flat when the wind starts blowing. Better bundle up."

"Thanks, fella," I said. "Thanks a lot. Think we'll make it before dark?"

"Oh, sure. 'Tain't so awful far but the road's lousy. Oughta make it in two-three hours, less'n like I said, comes up a heavy rain."

We knew when we hit Jackass Flat. It was like dropping off the edge. If we had thought the road to Kerry Canyon was bad we revised our opinions, but fast. In the first place it was choose your own ruts. Then the tracks were deep sunk in heavy clay generously mixed with sharp splintery shale and rocks as big as your two fists that were like a gigantic gravel as far as we could see across the lifeless expanse of the flat.

But to make it worse, the ruts I chose kept ending abruptly as though the cars that had made them had either backed away from the job or jumped over! I drove, in and out of ruts, so wrapped up in surmises that I hardly noticed the rough going until a cry from Bethie aroused me.

"Stop the car!" she cried. "Oh, Peter! Stop the car!"

I braked so fast that the pickup swerved wildly, mounted the side of a rut, lurched and settled sickeningly down on the back tire which sighed itself flatly into the rising wind.

"What on earth!" I yelped, as near to being mad at Bethie as I'd ever been in my life. "What was that for?"

Bethie, white-faced, was emerging from the army blanket she had huddled in against the cold. "It just came to me. Peter, supposing they don't want us?"

"Don't want us? What do you mean?" I growled, wondering if that lace doily I called my spare tire would be worth the trouble of putting it on.

"We never thought. It didn't even occur to us. Peter, we—we don't belong. We won't be like them. We're partly of Earth—as much as we are of wherever else. Supposing they reject us? Supposing they think we're undesirable—?" Bethie turned her face away. "Maybe we don't belong anywhere, Peter, not anywhere at all."

I felt a chill sweep over me that was not of the weather. We had assumed so blithely that we would be welcome. But how did we know? Maybe they *wouldn't* want us. We weren't of the People. We weren't of Earth. Maybe we didn't belong—not anywhere.

"Sure they'll want us," I forced out heartily. Then my eyes wavered away from Bethie's and I said defensively, "Mother said they would help us. She said we were woven of the same fabric—"

"But maybe the warp will only accept genuine woof. Mother couldn't know. There weren't any—half-breeds—when she was separated from them. Maybe our Earth blood will mark us—"

"There's nothing wrong with Earth blood," I said defiantly. "Besides, like you said, what would there be for you if we went back?"

She pressed her clenched fists against her cheeks, her eyes wide and vacant. "Maybe," she muttered, "maybe if I'd just go on and go completely insane it wouldn't hurt so terribly much. It might even feel good."

"Bethie!" my voice jerked her physically. "Cut out that talk right now! We're going on. The only way we can judge the People is by Mother. She would never reject us or any others like us. And that fellow back there said they were good people."

I opened the door. "You better try to get some kinks out of your legs while I change the tire. By the looks of the sky we'll be doing some skating before we get to Cougar Canyon."

But for all my brave words it wasn't just for the tire that I knelt beside the car, and it wasn't only the sound of the lug wrench that the wind carried up into the darkening sky.

I squinted through the streaming windshield, trying to make out the road through the downpour that fought our windshield wiper to a standstill. What few glimpses I caught of the road showed a deceptively smooth-looking chocolate river, but we alternately shook like a giant maraca, pushed out sheets of water like a speedboat, or slithered aimlessly and terrifyingly across sudden mud flats that often left us yards off the road. Then we'd creep cautiously back until the soggy squelch of our tires told us we were in the flooded ruts again.

Then all at once it wasn't there. The road, I mean. It stretched a few yards ahead of us and then just flowed over the edge, into the rain, into nothingness.

"It couldn't go there," Bethie murmured incredulously. "It can't just drop off like that."

"Well, I'm certainly not dropping off with it, sight unseen," I said, huddling deeper into my army blanket. My jacket was packed in back and I hadn't bothered to dig it out. I hunched my shoulders to bring the blanket up over my head. "I'm going to take a look first."

I slid out into the solid wall of rain that hissed and splashed around me on the flooded flat. I was soaked to the knees and mudcoated to the shins before I slithered to the drop-off. The trail—call that a road?—tipped over the edge of the canyon and turned abruptly to the right, then lost itself along a shrub-grown ledge that sloped' downward even as it paralleled the rim of the canyon. If I could get the pickup over the rim and onto the trail it wouldn't be so bad. But—I peered over the drop-off at the turn. The bottom was lost in shadows and rain. I shuddered.

Then quickly, before I could lose my nerve, I squelched back to the car.

"Pray, Bethie. Here we go."

There was the suck and slosh of our turning tires, the awful moment when we hung on the brink. Then the turn. And there we were, poised over nothing, with our rear end slewing outward.

The sudden tongue-biting jolt as we finally landed, right side up, pointing the right way on the narrow trail, jarred the cold sweat on my face so it rolled down with the rain.

I pulled over at the first wide spot in the road and stopped the car. We sat in the silence, listening to the rain. I felt as though something infinitely precious were lying just before me. Bethie's hand crept into mine and I knew she was feeling it, too. But suddenly Bethie's hand was snatched from mine and she was pounding with both fists against my shoulder in most un-Bethie-like violence.

"I can't stand it, Peter!" she cried hoarsely, emotion choking her voice. "Let's go back before we find out any more. If they should send us away! Oh, Peter! Let's go before they find us! Then we'll still have our dream.

We can pretend that someday we'll come back. We can never dream again, never hope again!" She hid her face in her hands. "I'll manage somehow. I'd rather go away, hoping, than run the risk of being rejected by them."

"Not me," I said, starting the motor. "We have as much chance of a welcome as we do of being kicked out. And if they can help you—Say, what's the matter with you today? I'm supposed to be the doubting one, remember? You're the mustard seed of this outfit!" I grinned at her, but my heart sank at the drawn white misery of her face. She almost managed a smile.

The trail led steadily downward, lapping back on itself as it worked back and forth along the canyon wall, sometimes steep, sometimes almost level. The farther we went the more rested I felt, as though I were shutting doors behind or opening them before me.

Then came one of the casual miracles of mountain country. The clouds suddenly opened and the late sun broke through. There, almost frighteningly, a huge mountain pushed out of the featureless gray distance. In the flooding light the towering slopes seemed to move, stepping closer to us as we watched. The rain still fell, but now in glittering silver-beaded curtains; and one vivid end of a rainbow splashed color recklessly over trees and rocks and a corner of the sky.

I didn't watch the road. I watched the splendor and glory spread out around us. So when, at Bethie's scream, I snatched back to my driving all I took down into the roaring splintering darkness was the thought of Bethie and the sight of the other car, slanting down from the bobbing top branches of a tree, seconds before it plowed into us broadside, a yard above the road.

I thought I was dead. I was afraid to open my eyes because I could feel the rain making little puddles over my closed lids. And then I breathed. I was alive, all right. A knife jabbed itself up and down the left side of my chest and twisted itself viciously with each reluctant breath I drew.

Then I heard a voice.

"Thank the Power they aren't hurt too badly. But, oh, Valancy! What will Father say?" The voice was young and scared.

"You've known him longer than I have," another girl-voice answered. "You should have some idea."

"I never had a wreck before, not even when I was driving instead of lifting."

"I have a hunch that you'll be grounded for quite a spell," the second voice replied. "But that isn't what's worrying me, Karen. Why didn't we know they were coming? We always can sense Outsiders. We should have known—"

"Q. E. D. then," said the Karen-voice.

" 'Q. E. D.'?"

"Yes. If we didn't sense them, then they're not Outsiders—" There was the sound of a caught breath and then, "Oh, what I said, Valancy! You don't suppose!" I felt a movement close to me and heard the soft sound of breathing. "Can it really be two more of us? Oh, Valancy, they must be second generation—they're about our age. How did they find us? Which of our Lost Ones were their parents?"

Valancy sounded amused. "Those are questions they're certainly in no condition to answer right now, Karen. We'd better figure out what to do. Look, the girl is coming to."

I was snapped out of my detached eavesdropping by a moan beside me. I started to sit up. "Bethie—" I began, and all the knives twisted through my lungs. Bethie's scream followed my gasp.

My eyes were open now, but good, and my leg was an agonized burning ache down at the far end of my consciousness. I gritted my teeth but Bethie moaned again.

"Help her, help her!" I pleaded to the two fuzzy figures leaning over us as I tried to hold my breath to stop the jabbing.

"But she's hardly hurt," Karen cried. "A bump on her head. Some cuts."

With an effort I focused on a luminous clear face—Valancy's—whose deep eyes bent close above me. I licked the rain from my lips and blurted foolishly, "You're not even wet in all this rain!" A look of consternation swept over her face. There was a pause as she looked at me intently and then said, "Their shields aren't activated, Karen. We'd better extend ours."

"Okay, Valancy." And the annoying sibilant wetness of the rain stopped.

"How's the girl?"

"It must be shock or maybe internal—"

I started to turn to see, but Bethie's sobbing cry pushed me flat again.

"Help her," I gasped, grabbing wildly in my memory for Mother's words. "She's a—a Sensitive!"

"A Sensitive?" The two exchanged looks. "Then why doesn't she—?" Valancy started to say something, then turned swiftly. I crooked my arm over my eyes as I listened.

"Honey—Bethie—hear me!" The voice was warm but authoritative. "I'm going to help you. I'll show you how, Bethie."

There was a silence. A warm hand clasped mine and Karen squatted close beside me.

"She's sorting her," she whispered. "Going into her mind. To teach her control. It's so simple. How could it happen that she doesn't know?"

I heard a soft wondering "Oh!" from Bethie, followed by a breathless "Oh, thank you, Valancy, thank you!"

I heaved myself up onto my elbow, fire streaking me from head to foot, and peered over at Bethie. She was looking at me, and her quiet face was happier than smiles could ever make it. We stared for the space of two relieved tears, then she said softly, "Tell them now, Peter. We can't go any farther until you tell them."

I lay back again, blinking at the sky where the scattered raindrops were still falling, though none of them reached us. Karen's hand was warm on mine and I felt a shiver of reluctance. If they sent us away . . . ! But then they couldn't take back what they had given to Bethie, even if— I shut my eyes and blurted it out as bluntly as possible.

"We aren't of the People—not entirely. Father was not of the People. We're half-breeds."

There was a startled silence.

"You mean your mother married an Outsider?" Valancy's voice was filled with astonishment. "That you and Bethie are—?"

"Yes she did and yes we are!" I retorted. "And Dad was the best—" My belligerence ran thinly out across the sharp edge of my pain. "They're both dead now. Mother sent us to you."

"But Bethie is a Sensitive . . ." Valancy's voice was thoughtful.

"Yes, and I can fly and make things travel in the air and I've even made fire. But Dad—" I hid my face and let it twist with the increasing agony.

"Then we *can!*" I couldn't read the emotion in Valancy's voice. "Then the People and Outsiders— But it's unbelievable that you . . ." Her voice died.

In the silence that followed, Bethie's voice came fearful and tremulous, "Are you going to send us away?" My heart twisted to the ache in her voice.

"Send you away! Oh, my people, my people! Of course not! As if there were any question!" Valancy's arm went tightly around Bethie, and Karen's hand closed warmly on mine. The tension that had been a hard twisted knot inside me dissolved, and Bethie and I were home.

Then Valancy became very brisk.

"Bethie, what's wrong with Peter?"

Bethie was astonished. "How did you know his name?" Then she smiled. "Of course. When you were sorting me!" She touched me lightly along my sides, along my legs. "Four of his ribs are hurt. His left leg is broken. That's about all. Shall I control him?"

"Yes," Valancy said. "I'll help."

And the pain was gone, put to sleep under the persuasive warmth that came to me as Bethie and Valancy came softly into my mind.

"Good," Valancy said. "We're pleased to welcome a Sensitive. Karen and I know a little of their function because we are Sorters. But we have no full-fledged Sensitive in our Group now."

She turned to me. "You said you know the inanimate lift?"

"I don't know," I said. "I don't know the words for lots of things."

"You'll have to relax completely. We don't usually use it on people. But if you let go all over we can manage."

They wrapped me warmly in our blankets and lightly, a hand under my shoulders and under my heels, lifted me carrying-high and sped with me through the trees, Bethie trailing from Valancy's free hand.

Before we reached the yard the door flew open and warm yellow light spilled out into the dusk. The girls paused on the porch and shifted me to the waiting touch of two men. In the wordless pause before the babble of question and explanation I felt Bethie beside me draw a deep wondering breath and merge like a raindrop in a river into the People around us.

But even as the lights went out for me again, and I felt myself slide down into comfort and hunger-fed belongingness, somewhere deep inside of me was a core of something that couldn't quite—no, *wouldn't* quite dissolve—wouldn't yet yield itself completely to the People.

PROBINGS

1. Is your family a close one or not? What kinds of activities do you do together as a family?
2. Report on your family rituals or customs in an essay. What specific events, holidays, or celebrations do you observe? How do you celebrate them? Does your family cook special or ethnic foods on some occasions? Some families, for example, gather together for Christmas and have certain rituals they observe year in and year out.
3. Who is the most important member of your family? Why?
4. Who is the most important or famous person on your family tree? Why?
5. All members of the class should cooperate to make a large display of the ethnic backgrounds of your families. Place several large maps on a bulletin board, maps of the world, of Europe, of the United States, and of your community. For each racial or ethnic group select a different color pin to place on each of the maps. For example, you could use red pins for Italians. (These pins are available at dime stores and stationery stores.)

   Use one pin for each different household that's a part of your family. Include your grandparents, aunts, and uncles, even if they live in another town or city. After you have finished, you should see some patterns showing where various racial and ethnic groups settled in the United States and your community. If you live in a suburb, you might want to include a map of the city, also.

6. Write a scenario or a story about your family in the year 2025. How will you be living? Where? Refer back to the "Headlines from Tomorrow."
7. Collect at least five comic strips that deal with the American family. How is the family portrayed? The father? The mother? The children?
8. Observe at least two family-type TV shows. Do they accurately reflect family life as you know it? How? Which shows deal with themes such as divorce or single parents?
9. If you could have special gifts like the children in the story "Gilead," which gifts would you like to have? Why?
10. Write another story based on Hendersons. What else could have happened to the children after their mother died?

FRIENDS

7

There is a very old saying that my mother used to tell me that goes something like this: "Thank God we can choose our friends, because we can't choose our relatives." As we grow older, friends become a very important part of our lives; they influence our opinions and our very identities.

One sociologist has offered the suggestion that every human needs at least two or three intimate friends with whom he or she can share almost anything. It is a very sad person who has no friends. In fact, people without friends consider themselves lonely and are considered lonely by others—and usually pitied, too. Social scientists use the term "the lonely crowd," to describe the fact that people can be surrounded by others but still feel very lonely in today's world.

Of course, we all feel lonely at times, even though our culture has so many instruments to help us communicate, like TV, stereo, radio, and the telephone. However, for one reason or another, at the same time that we have perfected many technological inventions to help people communicate electronically, many of us have become even more fearful and lonely. How many times have you walked into an empty house or apartment and turned on the radio, TV, or stereo for company?

In Ray Bradbury's beautiful short story "All Summer in a Day," we meet one little girl who is friendless and lonely. A little girl who wants to trust—but who finds her needs rebuffed by her potential friends.

1. Headlines from Tomorrow:

CONGRESS ENACTS A LIMIT: ONLY ONE FRIEND PER PERSON

Howard Rapp, Leader of the Senate, announced today a new law that allows a person to have only one friend, to be seen a maximum of three times a year. For special circumstances, a person may file a "Request to Visit Form" with the Personal Relations Bureau.

PROJECTIONS

Reasons for the new law are:

How would you react to this new law?

2. A friend I would like to have twenty years from now is _____.
Why did you choose this person?

ALL SUMMER IN A DAY

—Ray Bradbury

"Ready?"

"Ready."

"Now?"

"Soon."

"Do the scientists really know? Will it happen today, will it?"

"Look, look; see for yourself!"

The children pressed to each other like so many roses, so many seeds, intermixed, peering out for a look at the hidden sun.

It rained.

It had been raining for seven years; thousands upon thousands of days compounded and filled from one end to the other with rain, with the drum and gush of water, with the sweet crystal fall of showers and the concussion of storms so heavy they were tidal waves come over the islands. A thousand forests had been crushed under the rain and grown up a thousand times to be crushed again. And this was the way life was forever on the planet Venus, and this was the schoolroom of the children of the rocket men and women who had come to a raining world to set up civilization and live out their lives.

"It's stopping, it's stopping!"

"Yes, yes!"

Margot stood apart from them, from these children who could never remember a time when there wasn't rain and rain and rain. They were all nine years old, and if there had been a day, seven years ago, when the sun came out for an hour and showed its face to the stunned world, they could not recall. Sometimes, at night, she heard them stir, in remembrance, and she knew they were dreaming and remembering gold or a yellow crayon or a coin large enough to buy the world with. She knew that they thought they remembered a warmness, like a blushing in the face, in the body, in the arms and legs and trembling hands. But then they always awoke to the tatting drum, the endless shaking down of clear bead necklaces upon the roof, the walk, the gardens, the forest, and their dreams were gone.

All day yesterday they had read in class, about the sun. About how like a lemon it was, and how hot. And they had written small stories or essays or poems about it:

> I think the sun is a flower,
> That blooms for just one hour.

That was Margot's poem, read in a quiet voice in the still classroom while the rain was falling outside.

"Aw, you didn't write that!" protested one of the boys.

"I did," said Margot. "I *did.*"

"William!" said the teacher.

But that was yesterday. Now, the rain was slackening, and the children were crushed to the great thick windows.

"Where's teacher?"

"She'll be back."

"She'd better hurry, we'll miss it!"

They turned on themselves, like a feverish wheel, all tumbling spokes.

Margot stood alone. She was a very frail girl who looked as if she had been lost in the rain for years and the rain had washed out the blue from her eyes and the red from her mouth and the yellow from her hair. She was an old photograph dusted from an album, whitened away, and if she spoke at all her voice would be a ghost. Now she stood, separate, staring at the rain and the loud wet world beyond the huge glass.

"What're *you* looking at?" said William.

Margot said nothing.

"Speak when you're spoken to." He gave her a shove. But she did not move; rather she let herself be moved only by him and nothing else.

They edged away from her, they would not look at her. She felt them go away. And this was because she would play no games with them in the echoing tunnels of the underground city. If they tagged her and ran, she stood blinking after them and did not follow. When the class sang songs about happiness and life and games, her lips barely moved. Only when they sang about the sun and the summer did her lips move, as she watched the drenched windows.

And then, of course, the biggest crime of all was that she had come here only five years ago from Earth, and she remembered the sun and the way the sun was and the sky was, when she was four, in Ohio. And they, they had been on Venus all their lives, and they had been only two years old when last the sun came out, and had long since forgotten the color and heat of it and the way that it really was. But Margot remembered.

"It's like a penny," she said, once, eyes closed.

"No, it's not!" the children cried.

"It's like a fire," she said, "in the stove."

"You're lying, you don't remember!" cried the children.

But she remembered and stood quietly apart from all of them, and watched the patterning windows. And once, a month ago, she had refused to shower in the school shower rooms, had clutched her hands to her ears and over her head, screaming the water mustn't touch her head. So after that, dimly, dimly, she sensed it, she was different and they knew her difference and kept away.

There was talk that her father and mother were taking her back to Earth next year; it seemed vital to her that they do so, though it would mean the loss of thousands of dollars to her family. And so the children hated her for all these reasons, of big and little consequence. They hated her pale snow face, her waiting silence, her thinness and her possible future.

"Get away!" The boy gave her another push. "What're you waiting for?"

Then, for the first time, she turned and looked at him. And what she was waiting for was in her eyes.

"Well, don't wait around here!" cried the boy, savagely. "You won't see nothing!"

Her lips moved.

"Nothing!" he cried. "It was all a joke, wasn't it?" He turned to the other children. "Nothing's happening today. *Is* it?"

They all blinked at him and then, understanding, laughed and shook their heads. "Nothing, nothing!"

"Oh, but," Margot whispered, her eyes helpless. "But, this is the day, the scientists predict, they say, they *know,* the sun . . ."

"All a joke!" said the boy, and seized her roughly. "Hey, everyone, let's put her in a closet before teacher comes!"

"No," said Margot, falling back.

They surged about her, caught her up and bore her, protesting, and then pleading, and then crying, back into a tunnel, a room, a closet, where they slammed and locked the door. They stood looking at the door and saw it tremble from her beating and throwing herself against it. They heard her muffled cries. Then, smiling, they turned and went out and back down the tunnel, just as the teacher arrived.

"Ready, children?" She glanced at her watch.

"Yes!" said everyone.

"Are we all here?"

"Yes!"

The rain slackened still more.

They crowded to the huge door.

The rain stopped.

It was as if, in the midst of a film concerning an avalanche, a tornado, a hurricane, a volcanic eruption, something had, first, gone wrong with the sound apparatus, thus muffling and finally cutting off all noise, all of the blasts and repercussions and thunders, and then secondly, ripped the film from the projector and inserted in its place a peaceful tropical slide which did not move or tremor. The world ground to a standstill. The silence was so immense and unbelievable that you felt that your ears had been stuffed or you had lost your hearing altogether. The children put their hands to their ears. They stood apart. The door slid back and the smell of the silent, waiting world came in to them.

The sun came out.

It was the color of flaming bronze and it was very large. And the sky around it was a blazing blue tile color. And the jungle burned with sunlight as the children, released from their spell, rushed out, yelling, into the summertime.

"Now, don't go too far," called the teacher after them. "You've only one hour, you know. You wouldn't want to get caught out!"

But they were running and turning their faces up to the sky and feeling the sun on their cheeks like a warm iron; they were taking off their jackets and letting the sun burn their arms.

"Oh, it's better than the sun lamps, isn't it?"

"Much, much better!"

They stopped running and stood in the great jungle that covered Venus, that grew and never stopped growing, tumultuously, even as you watched it. It was a nest of octopuses, clustering up great arms of fleshlike week, weavering, flowering in this brief spring. It was the color of rubber and ash, this jungle, from the many years without sun. It was the color of stones and white cheeses and ink.

The children lay out, laughing, on the jungle mattress, and heard it sigh and squeak under them, resilient and alive. They ran among the trees, they slipped and fell, they pushed each other, they played hide-and-seek and tag, but most of all they squinted at the sun until tears ran down their faces, they put their hands up at that yellowness and that amazing blueness and they breathed of the fresh fresh air and listened and listened to the silence which suspended them in a blessed sea of no sound and no motion. They looked at everything and savored everything. Then, wildly, like animals escaped from their caves, they ran and ran in shouting circles. They ran for an hour and did not stop running.

And then—

In the midst of their running, one of the girls wailed.

Everyone stopped.

The girl, standing in the open, held out her hand.

"Oh, look, look," she said, trembling.

They came slowly to look at her opening palm.

In the center of it, cupped and huge, was a single raindrop.

She began to cry, looking at it.

They glanced quickly at the sky.

"Oh. Oh."

A few cold drops fell on their noses and their cheeks and their mouths. The sun faded behind a stir of mist. A wind blew cool around them. They turned and started to walk back toward the underground house, their hands at their sides, their smiles vanishing away.

A boom of thunder startled them and like leaves before a new hurricane, they tumbled upon each other and ran. Lightning struck ten miles away, five miles away, a mile, a half mile. The sky darkened into midnight in a flash.

They stood in the doorway of the underground for a moment until it was raining hard. Then they closed the door and heard the gigantic sound of the rain falling in tons and avalanches everywhere and forever.

"Will it be seven more years?"

"Yes. Seven."

Then one of them gave a little cry.

"Margot!"

"What?"

"She's still in the closet where we locked her."

"Margot."

They stood as if someone had driven them, like so many stakes, into the floor. They looked at each other and then looked away. They glanced out at the world that was raining now and raining and raining steadily. They could not meet each other's glances. Their faces were solemn and pale. They looked at their hands and feet, their faces down.

"Margot."

One of the girls said, "Well . . . ?"

No one moved.

"Go on," whispered the girl.

They walked slowly down the hall in the sound of cold rain. They turned through the doorway to the room, in the sound of the storm and thunder, lightning on their faces, blue and terrible. They walked over to the closet door slowly and stood by it.

Behind the closet door was only silence.

They unlocked the door, even more slowly, and let Margot out.

PROBINGS

1. Why do the children in the story discriminate against the little girl? Can you think of incidents from your own childhood when you saw children discriminate against another child? What were they?
2. "All Summer in a Day" is a story about friendship, but it is also a story about ecology and about the possible problems of life on another planet. Write a short essay (a few paragraphs) on drastic changes in the ecology—and how these changes might affect your relations with other people.
3. Who is your best friend? Your next best friend? Why? What specific qualities do these friends have that you value?
4. The greatest thing that a friend could do for me is _____. The greatest thing I could do for my best friend is _____. Something that I could tell my best friend and nobody else is _____. The best experience I have ever had with my best friend is _____. Why was it the best _____? One thing I would never do, even if my best friend asked me to, is to _____. If I could give my best friend one thing that would make him or her happy, it would be _____.
5. List all of the things you enjoy doing with the following groups:

	BEST FRIEND(S)	FRIENDS	OTHERS (NOT NECESSARILY FRIENDS)
Hanging around			
Sports			
Driving around			
Hobbies			
Other			

6. Although surrounded by other humans, many of us feel alone. What would happen if everybody felt alone in a society where no one trusted anyone else?
7. Robert Silverberg wrote a story called "To See The Invisible Man." In his story a man is branded "invisible" for one year because he is emotionally cold. Everyone can see him, but because he is branded invisible, nobody may have any contact with him. Write a SF story on this idea.
8. *Headlines from Tomorrow:* "Man sentenced for Emotional Coldness." Develop at least another dozen headlines following the man's progress for one year.

GENERATIONS

8

Just a few years ago, there was much controversy about something called the generation gap. Somehow a chasm seemingly opened between the younger and older generations. At one time in our society, all the generations lived, worked, and played together and gave no thought to a "gap." However, things seem to have changed. For example, some bars are now designated for "singles" only; apartments are rented only to single people; whole suburbs are populated by young couples and their children, without an "old" person within miles.

What of the aged? We refer to them using euphemisms like "senior citizens" and "golden-agers." These names imply honor and respect. Yet the aged are frequently put away in special homes. One scholar has noted that when Americans don't want to think about people whose problems we find disagreeable, such as the aged or the mentally ill, we create special places to hide them away. He calls this the "toilet assumption"; it's just like flushing our waste away—out of sight, therefore, out of mind.

In the following story outright war breaks out between the generations. As you read the story, consider how well you relate to the older generations and the younger generation coming up behind you.

1. Headlines from Tomorrow:

WASHINGTON, 2001...GOVERNMENT ANNOUNCES ABOLITION OF OLD AGE

Write a two or three paragraph follow-up story.

PROJECTIONS

2. Draw a future wheel using the idea that the generations may disappear in the future. People might all look and dress "young." Would you like to live in this type of society?

DAY OF TRUCE
—Clifford D. Simak

The evening was quiet. There was no sign of the Punks. Silence lay heavily across the barren and eroded acres of the subdivision, and there was nothing moving—not even one of the roving and always troublesome dog packs.

It was too quiet, Max Hale decided.

There should have been some motion and some noise. It was as if everyone had taken cover against some known and coming violence—another raid perhaps. Although there was only one place against which a raid could possibly be aimed. Why should others care, Max wondered; why should they cower indoors, when they had long since surrendered?

Max stood upon the flat lookout-rooftop of the Crawford stronghold and watched the streets to north and west. It was by one of these that Mr. Crawford would be coming home. No one could guess which one, for he seldom used the same road. It was the only way one could cut down the likelihood of ambush or of barricade. Although ambush was less frequent now. There were fewer fences, fewer trees and shrubs; there was almost nothing behind which one could hide. In this barren area it called for real ingenuity to effect an ambuscade. But, Max reminded himself, no one had ever charged the Punks with lack of ingenuity.

Mr. Crawford had phoned that he would be late and Max was getting nervous. In another quarter hour, darkness would be closing in. It was bad business to be abroad in Oak Manor after dark had fallen. Or for that matter, in any of the subdivisions. For while Oak Manor might be a bit more vicious than some of the others of them, it still was typical.

He lifted his glasses again and swept the terrain slowly. There was no sign of patrols or hidden skulkers. There must be watchers somewhere, he knew. There were always watchers, alert to the slightest relaxation of the vigilance maintained at Crawford stronghold.

Street by street he studied the sorry houses, with their broken windowpanes and their peeling paint, still marked by the soap streaks and the gouges and the red-paint splashes inflicted years before. Here and there dead trees stood stark, denuded of their branches. Browned evergreens, long dead, stood rooted in the dusty yards—yards long since robbed of the grass that once had made them lawns.

And on the hilltop, up on Circle Drive, stood the ruins of Thompson stronghold, which had fallen almost five years before. There was no structure standing. It had been leveled stone by stone and board by board. Only the smashed and dying trees, only the twisted steel fence posts marked where it had been.

Now Crawford stronghold stood alone in Oak Manor. Max thought of it with a glow of pride and a surge of painful memory. It stood because of him, he thought, and he would keep it standing.

In this desert it was the last oasis, with its trees and grass, with its summerhouses and trellises, with the massive shrubbery and the wondrous sundial beside the patio, with its goldfish-and-lily pond and the splashing fountain.

"Max," said the walkie-talkie strapped across his chest.

"Yes, Mr. Crawford."

"Where are you located, Max?"

"Up on the lookout, sir."

"I'll come in on Seymour Drive," said Mr. Crawford's voice. "I'm about a mile beyond the hilltop. I'll be coming fast."

"The coast seems to be quite clear, sir."

"Good. But take no chances with the gates."

"I have the control box with me, sir. I can operate from here. I will keep a sharp lookout."

."Be seeing you," said Crawford.

Max picked up the remote-control box and waited for his returning master.

The car came over the hill and streaked down Seymour Drive, made its right-hand turn on Dawn, roared toward the gates.

When it was no more than a dozen feet away, Max pushed the button that unlocked the gates. The heavy bumper slammed into them and pushed them open. The buffers that ran along each side of the car held them aside as the machine rushed through. When the car had cleared them, heavy springs snapped them shut, and they were locked again.

Max slung the control-box strap over his shoulder and went along the rooftop catwalk to the ladder leading to the ground.

Mr. Crawford had put away the car and was closing the garage door as Max came around the corner of the house.

"It does seem quiet," said Mr. Crawford. "Much quieter, it would seem to me, than usual."

"I don't like it, sir. There is something brewing."

"Not very likely," said Mr. Crawford. "Not on the eve of Truce Day."

"I wouldn't put nothing past them dirty Punks," said Max.

"I quite agree," said Mr. Crawford, "but they'll be coming here tomorrow for their day of fun. We must treat them well for, after all, they're neighbors and it is a custom. I would hate to have you carried beyond the bounds of propriety by overzealousness."

"You know well and good," protested Max, "I would never do a thing. I am a fighter, sir, but I fight fair and honorable."

Mr. Crawford said, "I was thinking of the little gambit you had cooked up last year."

"It would not have hurt them, sir. Leastwise, not permanently. They might never have suspected. Just a drop or two of it in the fruit punch was all we would have needed. It wouldn't have taken effect until hours after they had left. Slow-acting stuff, it was."

"Even so," said Mr. Crawford sternly, "I am glad I found out in time.

And I don't want a repeat performance, possibly more subtle, to be tried this year. I hope you understand me."

"Oh, certainly, sir," said Max. "You can rely upon it, sir."

"Well, good night, then, I'll see you in the morning."

It was all damn foolishness, thought Max—this business of a Day of Truce. It was an old holdover from the early days when some do-gooder had figured maybe there would be some benefit if the stronghold people and the Punks could meet under happy circumstances and spend a holiday together.

It worked, of course, but only for the day. For twenty-four hours there were no raids, no flaming arrows, no bombs across the fence. But at one second after midnight the feud took up again, as bitter and relentless as it had ever been.

It had been going on for years. Max had no illusions about how it all would end. Some day Crawford stronghold would fall, as had all the others in Oak Manor. But until that day, he pledged himself to do everything he could. He would never lower his guard nor relax his vigilance. Up to the very end, he would make them smart for every move they made.

He watched as Mr. Crawford opened the front door and went across the splash of light that flowed out from the hall. Then the door shut, and the house stood there, big and bleak and black, without a sliver of light showing anywhere. No light ever showed from the Crawford house. Well before the fall of night he always threw the lever on the big control board to slam steel shutters closed against all the windows in the place. Lighted windows made too good a nighttime target.

Now the raids always came at night. There had been a time when some had been made in daylight, but that was too chancy now. Year by year, the defenses had been built up, to a point where an attack in daylight was plain foolhardiness.

Max turned and went down the driveway to the gates. He drew on rubber gloves and with a small flashlight examined the locking mechanism. It was locked. It had never failed, but there might come a time it would. He never failed to check it once the gates had closed.

He stood beside the gates and listened. Everything was quiet, although he imagined he could hear the faint singing of the electric current running through the fence. But that, he knew, was impossible, for the current was silent.

He reached out with a gloved hand and stroked the fence. Eight feet high, he told himself, with a foot of barbed wire along the top of it, and every inch of it alive with the surging current.

And inside of it, a standby, auxiliary fence into which current could be introduced if the forward fence should fail.

A clicking sound came padding down the driveway and Max turned from the gate.

"How you, boy," he said.

It was too dark for him to see the dog, but he could hear it snuffling and snorting with pleasure at his recognition.

It came bumbling out of the darkness and pushed against his legs. He squatted down and put his arms about it. It kissed him sloppily.

"Where are the others, boy?" he asked, and it wriggled in its pleasure.

Great dogs, he thought. They loved the people in the stronghold almost to adoration, but had an utter hatred for every other person. They had been trained to have.

The rest of the pack, he knew, was aprowl about the yard, alert to every sound, keyed to every presence. No one could approach the fence without their knowing it. Any stranger who got across the fence they would rip to bits.

He stripped off the rubber gloves and put them in his pocket.

"Come on, boy," he said.

He turned off the driveway and proceeded across the yard—cautiously, for it was uneven footing. There was no inch of it that lay upon the level. It was cleverly designed so that any thrown grenade or Molotov cocktail would roll into a deep and narrow bomb trap.

There had been a time, he recalled, when there had been a lot of these things coming over the fence. There were fewer now, for it was a waste of effort. There had been a time, as well, when there had been flaming arrows, but these had tapered off since the house had been fireproofed.

He reached the side yard and stopped for a moment, listening, with the dog standing quietly at his side. A slight wind had come up, and the trees were rustling. He lifted his head and stared at the delicate darkness of them, outlined against the lighter sky.

Beautiful things, he thought. It was a pity there were not more of them. Once this area had been named Oak Manor for the stately trees that grew here. There, just ahead of him, was the last of them—a rugged old patriarch with its massive crown blotting out the early stars.

He looked at it with awe and appreciation—and with apprehension too. It was a menace. It was old and brittle and it should be taken down, for it leaned toward the fence and someday a windstorm might topple it across the wire. He should have mentioned it long ago to Mr. Crawford, but he knew the owner held this tree in a sentimental regard that matched his own. Perhaps it could be made safe by guywires to hold it against the wind, or at least to turn its fall away from the fence should it be broken or uprooted. Although it seemed a sacrilege to anchor it with guywires, an insult to an ancient monarch.

He moved on slowly, threading through the bomb traps, with the dog close at his heels, until he reached the patio, and here he stopped beside the sundial. He ran his hand across its rough stone surface and wondered why Mr. Crawford should set such store by it. Perhaps because it was a link to the olden days before the Punks and raids. It was an old piece that had been brought from a monastery garden somewhere in France. That in itself, of course, would make it valuable. But perhaps Mr. Crawford

120

saw in it another value, far beyond the fact that it was hundreds of years old and had come across the water.

Perhaps it had grown to symbolize for him the day now past when any man might have a sundial in his garden, when he might have trees and grass without fighting for them, when he might take conscious pride in the unfenced and unmolested land that lay about his house.

Bit by bit, through the running years, those rights had been eroded.

II

First it had been the little things—the casual, thoughtless trampling of the shrubbery by the playing small fry, the killing of the evergreens by the rampaging packs of happy dogs that ran with the playing small fry. For each boy, the parents said, must have himself a dog.

The people in the first place had moved from the jam-packed cities to live in what they fondly called the country, so that they could keep a dog or two and where their children would have fresh air and sunlight and room in which to run.

But too often this country was, in reality, no more than another city, with its houses cheek by jowl—each set on acre or half-acre lots, but still existing cheek by jowl.

Of course, a place to run. The children had. But no more than a place to run. There was nothing more to do. Run was all they could do—up and down the streets, back and forth across the lawns, up and down the driveways, leaving havoc in their trail. And in time the toddlers grew up, and in their teen-age years they still could only run. There was no place for them to go, nothing they might do. Their mothers foregathered every morning at the coffee klatches and their fathers sat each evening in the backyards, drinking beer. The family car could not be used because gasoline cost money and the mortgages were heavy and the taxes terrible and the other costs were high.

So to find an outlet for their energies, to work off their unrealized resentments against having nothing they could do, these older fry started out, for pure excitement only, on adventures in vandalism. There was a cutting of the backyard clotheslines, a chopping into bits of watering hoses left out overnight, a breaking and ripping up of the patios, ringing of the doorbells, smashing of the windows, streaking of the siding with a cake of soap, splashing with red paint.

Resentments had been manufactured to justify this vandalism, and now the resentments were given food to grow upon. Irate owners erected fences to keep out the children and the dogs, and this at once became an insult and a challenge.

And that first simple fence, Max told himself, had been the forerunner of the eight-foot barrier of electricity which formed the first line of defense in the Crawford stronghold. Likewise, those small-time soap-cake vandals, shrieking their delight at messing up a neighbor's house, had been the ancestors of the Punks.

He left the patio and went down the stretch of backyard, past the goldfish-and-lily pond and the tinkling of the fountain, past the clump of weeping willows, and so out to the fence.

"Psst!" said a voice just across the fence.

"That you, Billy?"

"It's me," said Billy Warner.

"All right. Tell me what you have."

"Tomorrow is Truce Day and we'll be visiting—"

"I know all that," said Max.

"They're bringing in a time bomb."

"They can't do that," said Max, disgusted. "The cops will frisk them at the gates. They would spot it on them."

"It'll be all broken down. Each one will have a piece. Stony Stafford hands out the parts tonight. He has a crew that has been practicing for weeks to put a bomb together fast—even in the dark, if need be."

"Yeah," said Max, "I guess they could do it that way. And once they get it put together?"

"The sundial," Billy said. "Underneath the sundial."

"Well, thanks," said Max. "I am glad to know. It would break the boss' heart should something happen to the sundial."

"I figure," Billy said, "this might be worth a twenty."

"Yes," Max agreed. "Yes, I guess it would."

"If they ever knew I told, they'd take me out and kill me."

"They won't ever know," said Max. "I won't ever tell them."

He pulled his wallet from his pocket, turned on the flash, and found a pair of tens.

He folded the bills together, lengthwise, twice. Then he shoved them through an opening in the fence.

"Careful there," he cautioned. "Do not touch the wire."

Beyond the fence he could see the faint white outline of the other's face. And a moment later, the hand had reached out carefully and grabbed the corner of the folded bills.

Max did not let loose of the money immediately. They stood, each of them, with their grip upon the bills.

"Billy," said Max solemnly, "you would never kid me, would you? You would never sell me out. You would never feed me erroneous information."

'You know me, Max," said Billy. "I've played square with you. I'd never do a thing like that."

Max let go of the money and let the other have it.

"I am glad to hear you say that, Billy. Keep on playing square. For the day you don't, I'll come out of here and hunt you down and cut your throat myself."

But the informer did not answer. He was already moving off, out into the deeper darkness.

Max stood quietly, listening. The wind still blew in the leaves and the fountain kept on splashing, like gladsome silver bells.

"Hi, boy," Max said softly, but there was no snuffling answer. The dog had left him, was prowling with the others up and down the yard.

Max turned about and went up the yard toward the front again, completing his circuit of the house. As he rounded the corner of the garage, a police car was slowing to a halt before the gates.

He started down the drive, moving ponderously and deliberately.

"That you, Charley?" he called softly.

"Yes, Max," said Charley Pollard. "Is everything all right?"

"Right as rain," said Max.

He approached the gates and saw the bulky loom of the officer on the other side.

"Just dropping by," said Pollard. "The area is quiet tonight. We'll be coming by one of these days to inspect the place. It looks to me you're loaded."

"Not a thing illegal," Max declared. "All of it's defensive. That is still the rule."

"Yes, that is the rule," said Pollard, "but it seems to me that there are times you become a mite too enthusiastic. A full load in the fence, no doubt."

"Why, certainly," said Max. "Would you have it otherwise?"

"A kid grabs hold of it and he could be electrocuted, at full strength."

"Would you rather I had it set just to tickle them?"

"You're playing too rough, Max."

"I doubt it rather much," said Max. "I watched from here, five years ago, when they stormed Thompson stronghold. Did you happen to see that?"

"I wasn't here five years ago. My beat was Farview Acres."

"They took it apart," Max told him. "Stone by stone, brick by brick, timber by timber. They left nothing standing. They left nothing whole. They cut down all the trees and chopped them up. They uprooted all the shrubs. They hoed out all the flower beds. They made a desert out of it. They reduced it to their level. And I'm not about to let it happen here, not if I can help it. A man has got the right to grow a tree and a patch of grass. If he wants a flower bed, he has a right to have a flower bed. You may not think so, but he's even got the right to keep other people out."

"Yes," said the officer, "all you say is true. But these are kids you are dealing with. There must be allowances. And this is a neighborhood. You folks and the others like you wouldn't have this trouble if you only tried to be a little neighborly."

"We don't dare be neighborly," said Max. "Not in a place like this. In Oak Manor, and in all the other manors and all the other acres and the other whatever-you-may-call-thems, neighborliness means that you let people over-run you. Neighborliness means you give up your right to live your life the way you want to live it. This kind of neighborliness is rooted way back in those days when the kids made a path across your lawn as a shortcut to the school bus and you couldn't say a thing for fear that they would sass you back and so create a scene. It started when your neighbor borrowed your lawn mower and forgot to bring it back and when you went to get it you found that he had broken it. But he pretended that he hadn't and for the sake of neighborliness, you didn't have the guts to tell him that he had and to demand that he pay the bill for the repairing of it."

"Well, maybe so," said Pollard, "but it's gotten out of hand. It has been carried too far. You folks have got too high and mighty."

"There's a simple answer to everything," Max told him stoutly. "Get the Punks to lay off us and we'll take down the fence and all the other stuff."

Pollard shook his head. "It has gone too far," he said. "There's nothing anyone can do."

He started to go back to the car, then turned back.

"I forgot," he said. "Tomorrow is your Truce Day. Myself and a couple of the other men will be here early in the morning."

Max didn't answer. He stood in the driveway and watched the car pull off down the street. Then he went up the driveway and around the house to the back door.

Nora had a place laid at the table for him and he sat down heavily, glad to be off his feet. By this time of the evening he was always tired. Not as young, he thought, as he once had been.

"You're late tonight," said the cook, bringing him the food. "Is everything all right?"

"I guess so. Everything is quiet. But we may have trouble tomorrow. They're bringing in a bomb."

"A bomb!" cried Nora. "What will you do about it? Call in the police, perhaps."

Max shook his head. "No, I can't do that. The police aren't on our side. They'd take the attitude we'd egged on the Punks until they had no choice but to bring in the bomb. We are on our own. And, besides, I must protect the lad who told me. If I didn't the Punks would know and he'd be worthless to me then. He'd never get to know another thing. But knowing they are bringing something, I can watch for it."

He still felt uneasy about it all, he realized. Not about the bomb, itself, perhaps, but something else, something that was connected with it. He wondered why he had this feeling. Knowing about the bomb, he all but had it made. All he'd have to do would be to locate it and dig it out from beneath the sundial.

He would have the time to do it. The day-long celebration would end at six in the evening and the Punks could not set the bomb to explode earlier than midnight. Any blast before midnight would be a violation of the truce.

He scooped fried potatoes from the dish onto his plate and speared a piece of meat. Nora poured his coffee and pulling out a chair, sat down opposite him.

"You aren't eating?" he asked.

"I ate early, Max."

He ate hungrily and hurriedly, for there were still things to do. She sat and watched him eat. The clock on the kitchen wall ticked loudly in the silence.

Finally she said: "It is getting somewhat grim, Max."

He nodded, his mouth full of food and unable to speak.

"I don't see," said the cook. "why the Crawfords want to stay here. There can't be much pleasure in it for them. They could move into the city and it would be safer there. There are the juvenile gangs, of course, but they mostly fight among themselves. They don't make life unbearable for all the other people."

"It's pride," said Max. "They won't give up. They won't let Oak Manor beat them. Mr. and Mrs. Crawford are quality. They have some steel in them."

"They couldn't sell the place, of course," said Nora. "There would be no one to buy it. But they don't need the money. They could just walk away from it."

"You misjudge them, Nora. The Crawfords in all their lives have never walked away from anything. They went through a lot to live here. Sending Johnny off to boarding school when he was a lad, since it wouldn't have been safe for him to go to school with the Punks out there. I don't suppose they like it. I don't see how they could. But they won't be driven out. They realize someone must stand up to all that trash out there, or else there's no hope."

Nora sighed. "I suppose you're right. But it is a shame. They could live so safe and comfortable and normal if they just moved to the city."

He finished eating and got up.

"It was a good meal, Nora," he said. "But then you always fix good meals."

"Ah, go on with you," said Nora.

He went into the basement and sat down before the shortwave set. Systematically, he started putting in his calls to the other strongholds. Wilson stronghold, over in Fair Hills, had had a little trouble early in the evening—a few stink bombs heaved across the fence—but it had quieted down. Jackson stronghold did not answer. While he was trying to get through to Smith stronghold in Harmony Settlement, Curtis stronghold in Lakeside Heights began calling him. Everything was quiet, John Hennessey, the Curtis custodian told him. It had been quiet for several days.

He stayed at the radio for an hour and by that time had talked with all the nearby strongholds. There had been scattered trouble here and there, but nothing of any consequence. Generally it was peaceful.

He sat and thought about the time bomb and there was still that nagging worry. There was something wrong, he knew, but he could not put his finger on it.

Getting up, he prowled the cavernous basement, checking the defense material—extra sections of fencing, piles of posts, pointed stakes, rolls of barb wire, heavily flexible wire mesh and all the other items for which some day there might be a need. Tucked into one corner, hidden, he found the stacked carboys of acid he had secretly cached away. Mr. Crawford would not approve, he knew, but if the chips should ever be down, and there was need to use those carboys, he might be glad to have them.

He climbed the stairs and went outside to prowl restlessly about the yard, still upset by that nagging something about the bomb he could not yet pin down.

The moon had risen. The yard was a place of interlaced light and shadow, but beyond the fence the desert acres that held the other bombs lay flat and bare and plain, without a shadow on them except the shadows of the houses.

Two of the dogs came up and passed the time of night with him and then went off into the shrubbery.

He moved into the backyard and stood beside the sundial.

The wrongness still was there. Something about the sundial and the bomb—some piece of thinking that didn't quite run true.

He wondered how they knew that the destruction of the sundial would be a heavy blow to the owner of the stronghold. How could they possibly have known?

The answer seemed to be that they couldn't. They didn't. There was no way for them to know. And even if, in some manner, they had learned, a sundial most certainly would be a piddling thing to blow up when that single bomb could be used so much better somewhere else.

Stony Stafford, the leader of the Punks, was nobody's fool. He was a weasel—full of cunning, full of savvy. He'd not mess with any sundial when there was so much else that a bomb could do so much more effectively.

And as he stood there beside the sundial, Max knew where that bomb would go—knew where he would plant it were he in Stafford's place.

At the roots of that ancient oak which leaned toward the fence.

He stood and thought about it and knew that he was right. Billy Warner, he wondered. Had Billy double-crossed him?

Very possibly he hadn't. Perhaps Stony Stafford might have suspected long ago that his gang harbored an informer and for that reason, had given out the story of the sundial rather than the oak tree. And that, of course, only to a select inner circle which would be personally involved with the placing of the bomb.

In such a case, he thought, Billy Warner had not done too badly.

Max turned around and went back to the house, walking heavily. He climbed the stairs to his attic room and went to bed. It had been, he thought just before he went to sleep, a fairly decent day.

III

The police showed up at eight o'clock. The carpenters came and put up the dance platform. The musicians appeared and began their tuning up. The caterers arrived and set up the tables, loading them with food and two huge punch bowls, standing by to serve.

Shortly after nine o'clock the Punks and their girls began to straggle in. The police frisked them at the gates and found no blackjacks, no brass knuckles, no bicycle chains on any one of them.

The band struck up. The Punks and their girls began to dance. They strolled through the yard and admired the flowers, without picking any of them. They sat on the grass and talked and laughed among themselves. They gathered at the overflowing boards and ate. They laughed and whooped and frolicked and everything was fine.

"You see?" Pollard said to Max. "There ain't nothing wrong with them. Give them a decent break and they're just a bunch of ordinary kids. A little hell in them, of course, but nothing really bad. It's your flaunting of this place in their very faces that makes them the way they are."

"Yeah," said Max.

He left Pollard and drifted down the yard, keeping as inconspicuous as he could. He wanted to watch the oak, but he knew he didn't dare to. He knew he had to keep away from it, should not even glance toward it. If he should scare them off, then God only knew where they would plant the bomb. He thought of being forced to hunt wildly for it after they were gone and shuddered at the thought.

There was no one near the bench at the back of the yard, near the flowering almond tree, and he stretched out on it. It wasn't particularly comfortable, but the day was warm and the air was drowsy. He dropped off to sleep.

When he woke he saw that a man was standing on the gravel path just beyond the bench.

He blinked hard and rubbed his eyes.

"Hello, Max," said Stony Stafford.

"You should be up there dancing, Stony."

"I was waiting for you to wake up," said Stony. "You are a heavy sleeper. I could of broke your neck."

Max sat up. He rubbed a hand across his face.

"Not on Truce Day, Stony. We all are friends on Truce Day."

Stony spat upon the gravel path.

"Look," said Max, "why don't you just run off and forget about it? You'll break your back if you try to crack this place. Pick up your marbles, Stony, and go find someone else who's not so rough to play with."

"Someday we'll make it," Stony said. "This place can't stand forever."

"You haven't got a chance," said Max.

"Maybe so," said Stony. "But I think we will. And before we do, there is just one thing I want you to know. You think nothing will happen to you even if we do. You think that all we'll do is just rip up the place, not harming anyone. But you're wrong, Max. We'll do it the way it is supposed to be with the Crawfords and with Nora. We won't hurt them none. But we'll get you, Max. Just because we can't carry knives or guns doesn't mean there aren't other ways. There'll be a stone fall on you or a timber hit you. Or maybe you'll stumble and fall into the fire. There are a lot of ways to do it and we plan to get you plenty."

"So," said Max, "you hate me. It makes me feel real bad."

"Two of my boys are dead," said Stony. "There are others who are crippled pretty bad."

"There wouldn't nothing happen to them, Stony, if you didn't send them up against the fence."

He looked up and saw the hatred that lay in Stony Stafford's eyes, but washing across the hatred was a gleam of triumph.

"Goodbye, dead man," said Stony.

He turned and stalked away.

Max sat quietly on the bench, remembering that gleam of triumph in Stony Stafford's eyes. And that meant he had been right. Stony had something up his sleeve and it could be nothing else but the bomb beneath the oak.

The day wore on. In the afternoon, Max went up to the house and into the kitchen. Nora fixed him a sandwich, grumbling.

"Why don't you go out and eat off the tables?" she demanded. "There is plenty there."

"Just as soon keep out of their way," said Max. "I have to fight them all the rest of the year. I don't see why I should pal up with them today."

"What about the bomb?"

"Shhh," said Max. "I know where it is."

Nora stood looking out the window. "They don't look like bad kids," she said. "Why can't we make a peace of some sort with them?"

Max grunted. "It's gone too far," he said.

Pollard had been right, he thought. It was out of hand. Neither side could back down now.

The police could have put a stop to it to start with, many years ago, if they had cracked down on the vandals instead of adopting a kids-will-be-kids attitude and shrugging it all off as just an aggravated case of quarreling in the neighborhood. The parents could have stopped it by paying some attention to the kids, by giving them something that would have stopped their running wild. The community could have put a stop to it by providing some sort of recreational facilities.

But no one had put a stop to it. No one had even tried.

And now it had grown to be a way of life and it must be fought out to the bitter end.

Max had no illusions as to who would be the winner.

Six o'clock came and the Punks started drifting off. By six-thirty the last of them had gone. The musicians packed up their instruments and left. The caterers put away their dishes and scooped up the leftovers and the garbage and drove away. The carpenters came and got their lumber.

128

Max went down to the gates and checked to see that they were locked.

"Not a bad day," said Pollard, speaking through the gates to Max. "They really aren't bad kids, if you'd just get to know them."

"I know them plenty now," said Max.

He watched the police car drive off, them turned back up the driveway.

He'd have to wait for a while, he knew, until the dusk could grow a little deeper, before he started looking for the bomb. There would be watchers outside the fence. It would be just as well if they didn't know that he had found it. It might serve a better purpose if they could be left to wonder if it might have been a dud. For one thing, it would shake their confidence. For another, it would protect young Billy Warner. And while Max could feel no admiration for the kid, Billy had been useful in the past and still might be useful in the future.

He went down to the patio and crawled through the masking shrubbery until he was only a short distance from the oak.

He waited there, watching the area out beyond the fence. There was as yet no sign of life out there. But they would be out there watching. He was sure of that.

The dusk grew deeper and he knew he could wait no longer. Creeping cautiously, he made his way to the oak. Carefully, he brushed away the grass and leaves, face held close above the ground.

Halfway around the tree, he found it—the newly up-turned earth, covered by a sprinkling of grass and leaves, and positioned neatly between two heavy roots.

He thrust his hand against the coolness of the dirt and his fingers touched the metal. Feeling it, he froze, then very slowly, very gently, pulled his hand away.

He sat back on his heels and drew in a measured breath.

The bomb was there, all right, just as he had suspected. But set above it, protecting it, was a contact bomb. Try to get the time bomb out and the contact bomb would be triggered off.

He brushed his hands together, wiping off the dirt.

There was, he knew, no way to get out the bombs. He had to let them stay. There was nothing he could do about it.

No wonder Stony's eyes had shown a gleam of triumph. For there was more involved than just a simple time bomb. This was a foolproof setup. There was nothing that could be done about it. If it had not been for the roots, Max thought, he might have taken a chance on working from one side and digging it all out. But with the heavy roots protecting it, that was impossible.

Stony might have known that he knew about it and then had gone ahead, working out a bomb set that no one would dare to mess around with.

It was exactly the sort of thing that would be up Stony's alley. More than likely, he was setting out there now, chuckling to himself.

Max stayed squatted, thinking.

He could string a line of mesh a few feet inside the tree, curving out to meet the auxiliary fence on either side. Juice could be fed into it and it might serve as a secondary defense. But it was not good insurance. A determined rush would carry it, for at best it would be flimsy. He'd not be able to install it as he should, working in the dark.

Or he could rig the tree with guywires to hold it off the fence when it came crashing down. And that, he told himself, might be the thing to do.

He got up and went around the house, heading for the basement to look up some wire that might serve to hold the tree.

He remembered, as he walked past the short-wave set, that he should be signing in on the regular evening check among the nearby strong-holds. But it would have to wait tonight.

He walked on and then stopped suddenly as the thought came to him. He stood for a moment, undecided, then swung around and went back to the set.

He snapped on the power and turned it up.

He'd have to be careful what he said, he thought, for there was the chance the Punks might be monitoring the channels.

John Hennessey, custodian of the Curtis stronghold, came in a few seconds after Max had started calling.

"Something wrong, Max?"

"Nothing wrong, John. I was just wondering—do you remember tell-ing me about those toys that you have?"

"Toys?"

"Yeah. The rattles."

He could hear the sound of Hennessey sucking in his breath.

Finally he said: "Oh, those. Yes, I still have them."

"How many would you say?"

"A hundred, probably. Maybe more than that."

"Could I borrow them?"

"Sure," said Hennessey. "Would you want them right away?"

"If you could," said Max.

"Okay. You'll pick them up?"

"I'm a little busy."

"Watch for me," said Hennessey. "I'll box them up and be there in an hour."

"Thanks, John," said Max.

Was it wrong? he wondered. Was it too much of a chance?

Perhaps he didn't have the right to take any chance at all.

But you couldn't sit forever, simply fending off the Punks. For if that was all you did, they'd keep on coming back. But hit back hard at them and they might get a bellyfull. You might end it once for all. The trouble was, he thought, you could strike back so seldom. You could never act except defensively, for if you took any other kind of action, the police were down on you like a ton of bricks.

He licked his lips.

It was seldom one had a chance like this—a chance to strike back lustily and still be legally defensive.

IV

He got up quickly and walked to the rear of the basement, where he found the heavy flexible mesh. He carried out three rolls of it and a loop of heavy wire to hang it on. He'd have to use some trees to stretch out the wire. He really should use some padding to protect the trees against abrasion by the wire, but he didn't have the time.

Working swiftly, he strung the wire, hung the mesh upon it, pegged the bottom of the mesh tight against the ground, tied the ends of it in with auxiliary fence.

He was waiting at the gates when the truck pulled up. He used the control box to open the gates and the truck came through. Hennessey got out.

"Outside is swarming with Punks," he told Max. "What is going on?"

"I got troubles," said Max.

Hennessey went around to the back of the truck and lowered the tail gate. Three large boxes, with mesh insets, rested on the truck bed.

"They're in there?" asked Max.

Hennessey nodded. "I'll give you a hand with them."

Between them they lugged the boxes to the mesh curtain, rigged behind the oak.

"I left one place unpegged," said Max. "We can push the boxes under."

"I'll unlock the lids first," said Hennessey. "We can reach through with the pole and lift the lids if they are unlocked. Then use the pole again to tip the boxes over."

They slid the boxes underneath the curtain, one by one. Hennessey went back to the truck to get the pole. Max pegged down the gap.

"Can you give me a bit of light?" asked Hennessey. "I know the Punks are waiting out there. But probably they'd not notice just a squirt of it. They might think you were making just regular inspection of the grounds."

Max flashed the light and Hennessey, working with the pole thrust through the mesh, flipped back the lids. Carefully, he tipped the boxes over. A dry slithering and frantic threshing sounds came out of the dark.

"They'll be nasty customers," said Hennessey. "They'll be stirred up and angry. They'll do a lot of circulating, trying to get settled for the night and that way, they'll get spread out. Most of them are big ones. Not many of the small kinds."

He put the pole over his shoulder and the two walked back to the truck.

Max put out his hand and the two men shook.

"Thanks a lot, John."

"Glad to do it, Max. Common cause, you know. Wish I could stay around. . ."

"You have a place of your own to watch."

They shook hands once again and Hennessey climbed into the cab.

"You better make it fast the first mile or so," said Max. "Our Punks may be laying for you. They might have recognized you."

"With the bumpers and the power I have," said Hennessey, "I can get through anything."

"And watch out for the cops. They'd raise hell if they knew we're helping back and forth."

"I'll keep an eye for them."

Max opened the gates and the truck backed out, straightened in the road and swiftly shot ahead.

Max listened until it was out of hearing, then checked to see that the gates were locked.

Back in the basement, he threw the switch that fed the current into the auxiliary fence—and now into the mesh as well.

He sighed with some contentment and climbed the stairs out to the yard.

A sudden flash of light lit up the grounds. He spun swiftly around, then cursed softly at himself. It was only a bird hitting the fence in flight. It happened all the time. He was getting jittery, and there was no need of it. Everything was under control—reasonably so.

He climbed a piece of sloping ground and stood behind the oak. Staring into the darkness, it seemed to him that he could see shadowy forms out beyond the fence.

They were gathering out there and they would come swarming in as soon as the tree went down, smashing the fences. Undoubtedly they planned to use the tree as a bridge over the surging current that still would flow in the smashed-down fence.

Maybe it was taking too much of a chance, he thought. Maybe he should have used the guywires on the tree. That way there would have been no chance at all. But, likewise, there would have been no opportunity.

They might get through, he thought, but he'd almost bet against it.

He stood there, listening to the angry rustling of a hundred rattlesnakes, touchy and confused, in the area beyond the mesh.

The sound was a most satisfying thing.

He moved away, to be out of the line of blast when the bomb exploded, and waited for the Day of Truce to end. . . .

132

PROBINGS

1. How well do you get along with your parents? Grandparents? Other older people?
2. Refer back to what you said you value most in the first section of this book. In the following activity, you will compare your values with those of your parents and grandparents. You are being asked to set up a scale of values that you think your parents and grandparents hold.

	YOU	FATHER	MOTHER	GRANDPARENTS
Values Most				
1.				
2.				
3.				
4.				
5.				
6.				
7.				
8.				
9.				
10.				
Values Least				

   Compare the lists. Do you find any similarities? Differences? Why?
3. The most important contribution that my mother has given me is_____
   _____.
   The most important contribution that my father has given me is_____
   _____.
   The most important contribution that my grandparents have given me is_____.

4. Ray Bradbury wrote of a "living time machine" in his novel *Dandelion Wine*. This "living time machine" was simply a very old man with a remarkable memory of the past. Children were fascinated by his stories. Think of five questions you would like to ask a "living time machine" in your own neighborhood or community. Many old people love to be interviewed about their lives, and they are all around you. Some students I know have gone to nursing homes to interview older people.

Asking good questions is an art. Don't ask questions that lead the person to answer with a simple "yes" or "no." Ask open-ended questions that allow the person to open up. Let the person talk and don't make judgments. Either record the conversation on tape or take notes. Some topics you might consider:

Life during the Depression
Life during World War I or II on the Home Front
Coming to This Country (or City)
The Greatest Joy in My Life

5. Construct a list of terms that refer to different age groups. For example, department stores have sections for infants, toddlers, preschoolers, etc. What other age categories can you think of?

CONFORMITY

9

In the American media, two of the most popular heroes are the cowboy and the detective. Both of these types are usually strong-willed, tough, and independent. Like Marshal Kane in the film *High Noon* or Kojak in the TV series, our media heroes have their "heads right," as the popular saying goes— they know what course to follow. Social scientists call this type of person inner-directed; such people have their own personal code of values that they follow regardless of how others might feel about it. In the 19th century, American industrialists such as Andrew Carnegie and John D. Rockefeller were such inner-directed men, people who were out to make fortunes and couldn't be bothered by what others might think of them.

By the middle of this century, however, a new type of American had appeared—the other-directed person. These were people who were brought up to fit in, conform, be pleasant, and not make waves. Advertising, in particular, manipulates us by urging us to be well liked. Us the right underarm deodorant or cologne, and immediately people will like you, or so claim the ads. According to the ads, if you have bad breath, athlete's foot, dandruff, and jock itch, you will be the ultimate social outcast.

Further, children are encouraged to "play nice" with other children; adults pay the supreme compliment to one another by saying that he or she is "nice." But just what does it mean to be "nice"? In Arthur Miller's play *The Death of a Salesman,* Willy Loman constantly chides his sons to be "well-liked." To Willy, the most important thing in life was to put up a good front so that people would like him. American corporations urge their employees to be part of the "family" or to join "the team." Of course, this all goes to say that we have become a people out to please others.

In J. G. Ballard's story that follows, "The Subliminal Man," the pressure to conform is even more insidious because the government uses subliminal advertising to motivate citizens to consume more goods. Subliminal messages are those delivered on a preconscious or subconscious level; you are not aware that you are receiving the message. For example, a number of years ago experiments were conducted using subliminal messages to encourage movie audiences to buy more popcorn. A message was flashed on the screen so rapidly that the audience was not conscious of it—but the message was being registered on their brains. The result? Audiences bought more popcorn.

While reading "The Subliminal Man," let your mind play around with the consequences of subliminal advertising that can motivate us to fit in, conform, be nice, and be well-liked.

1. Headlines from Tomorrow:

WASHINGTON, MARCH 17, 2010. CONGRESS PASSES "TOTAL EQUALITY" BILL

Finish the story. Develop a scenario showing how our society got from today to this possible world of tomorrow.

"The World Council announced today that people in Region I,

PROJECTIONS

which in the 20th century was known as the Western Hemisphere, must wear black clothing; and people in Region II, formerly the Eastern Hemisphere, must wear white clothing. Violators of the law will be banished to Subterranean Rehabilitation Centers."

2. Do a future wheel for one of the following future worlds:
   a. everybody looks alike
   b. everybody dresses alike
   c. everybody thinks alike
   d. everybody talks alike

THE SUBLIMINAL MAN

—J. G. Ballard

"The signs, Doctor! Have you seen the signs?"

Frowning with annoyance, Dr. Franklin quickened his pace and hurried down the hospital steps toward the line of parked cars. Over his shoulder he caught a glimpse of a man in ragged sandals and lime-stained jeans waving to him from the far side of the drive, then break into a run when he saw Franklin try to evade him.

"Dr. Franklin! The signs!"

Head down, Franklin swerved around an elderly couple approaching the out-patients department. His car was over a hundred yards away. Too tired to start running himself, he waited for the young man to catch him up.

"All right, Hathaway, what is it this time?" he snapped irritably. "I'm getting sick of you hanging around here all day."

Hathaway lurched to a halt in front of him, uncut black hair like an awning over his eyes. He brushed it back with a claw-like hand and turned on a wild smile, obviously glad to see Franklin and oblivious of the latter's hostility.

"I've been trying to reach you at night, Doctor, but your wife always puts the phone down on me," he explained without a hint of rancor, as if well-used to this kind of snub. "And I didn't want to look for you inside the Clinic." They were standing by a privet hedge that shielded them from the lower windows of the main administrative block, but Franklin's regular rendezvous with Hathaway and his strange messianic cries had already been the subject of amused comment.

Franklin began to say: "I appreciate that—" but Hathaway brushed this aside. "Forget it, Doctor, there are more important things happening now. They've started to build the first big signs! Over a hundred feet high, on the traffic islands just outside town. They'll soon have all the approach roads covered. When they do we might as well stop thinking."

"Your trouble is that you're thinking too much," Franklin told him. "You've been rambling about these signs for weeks now. Tell me, have you actually seen one signalling?"

Hathaway tore a handful of leaves from the hedge, exasperated by this irrelevancy. "Of course I haven't, that's the whole point, Doctor." He dropped his voice as a group of nurses walked past, watching him uneasily out of the corners of their eyes. "The construction gangs were out again last night, laying huge power cables. You'll see them on the way home. Everything's nearly ready now."

"They're traffic signs," Franklin explained patiently. "The flyover has just been completed. Hathaway, for God's sake relax. Try to think of Dora and the child."

"I *am* thinking of them!" Hathaway's voice rose to a controlled scream. "Those cables were 40,000-volt lines, Doctor, with terrific switch-gear. The trucks were loaded with enormous metal scaffolds. Tomorrow they'll start lifting them up all over the city, they'll block off half the sky! What do you think Dora will be like after six months of that? We've got to stop them, Doctor, they're trying to transistorize our brains!"

Embarrassed by Hathaway's high-pitched shouting, Franklin had momentarily lost his sense of direction and helplessly searched the sea of cars for his own. "Hathaway, I can't waste any more time talking to you. Believe me, you need skilled help, these obsessions are beginning to master you."

Hathaway started to protest, and Franklin raised his right hand firmly. "Listen. For the last time, if you can show me one of these new signs, and prove that it's transmitting subliminal commands, I'll go to the police with you. But you haven't got a shred of evidence, and you know it. Subliminal advertising was banned thirty years ago, and the laws have never been repealed. Anyway, the technique was unsatisfactory; any success it had was marginal. Your idea of a huge conspiracy with all these thousands of giant signs everywhere is preposterous."

"All right, Doctor." Hathaway leaned against the bonnet of one of the cars. His moods seemed to switch abruptly from one level to the next. He watched Franklin amiably. "What's the matter—lost your car?"

"All your damned shouting has confused me." Franklin pulled out his ignition key and read the number off the tag: "NYN 299-566-367-21— can you see it?"

Hathaway leaned around lazily, one sandal up on the bonnet, survey-ing the square of a thousand or so cars facing them. "Difficult, isn't it, when they're all identical, even the same color? Thirty years ago there were about ten different makes, each in a dozen colors."

Franklin spotted his car, began to walk toward it. "Sixty years ago there were a hundred makes. What of it? The economies of standardization are obviously bought at a price."

Hathaway drummed his palm lightly on the roofs. "But these cars aren't all that cheap, Doctor. In fact, comparing them on an average income basis with those of thirty years ago they're about forty percent more expensive. With only one make being produced you'd expect a substantial reduction in price, not an increase."

"Maybe," Franklin said, opening his door. "But mechanically the cars of today are far more sophisticated. They're lighter, more durable, safer to drive."

Hathaway shook his head sceptically. "They *bore* me. The same model, same styling, same color, year after year. It's a sort of communism." He rubbed a greasy finger over the windshield. "This is a new one again, isn't it, Doctor? Where's the old one—you only had it for three months?"

"I traded it in," Franklin told him, starting the engine. "If you ever had any money you'd realize that it's the most economical way of owning a car. You don't keep driving the same one until it falls apart. It's the same with everything else—television sets, washing machines, refrigerators. But you aren't faced with the problem—you haven't got any."

Hathaway ignored the gibe and leaned his elbow on Franklin's window. "Not a bad idea, either, Doctor. It gives me time to think. I'm not working a twelve-hour day to pay for a lot of things I'm too busy to use before they're obsolete."

He waved as Franklin reversed the car out of its line, then shouted into the wake of exhaust: "Drive with your eyes closed, Doctor!"

On the way home Franklin kept carefully to the slowest of the four-speed lanes. As usual after his discussions with Hathaway he felt vaguely depressed. He realized that unconsciously he envied Hathaway's foot-loose existence. Despite the grimy cold-water apartment in the shadow and roar of the flyover, despite his nagging wife and their sick child, and the endless altercations with the landlord and the supermarket credit manager, Hathaway still retained his freedom intact. Spared any responsibilities, he could resist the smallest encroachment upon him by the rest of society, if only by generating obsessive fantasies, such as his latest one about subliminal advertising.

The ability to react to stimuli, even irrationally, was a valid criterion of freedom. By contrast, what freedom Franklin possessed was peripheral, sharply demarked by the manifold responsibilities in the center of his life—the three mortgages on his home, the mandatory rounds of cocktail and TV parties, the private consultancy occupying most of Saturday which paid the instalments on the multitude of household gadgets, clothes and past holidays. About the only time he had to himself was driving to and from work.

But at least the roads were magnificent. Whatever other criticisms might be leveled at the present society, it certainly knew how to build roads. Eight-, ten- and twelve-lane expressways interlaced across the continent, plunging from overhead causeways into the giant car parks in the center of the cities, or dividing into the great suburban arteries with their multiacre parking aprons around the marketing centers. Together the roadways and car parks covered more than a third of the country's entire area, and in the neighborhood of the cities the proportion was higher. The old cities were surrounded by the vast, dazzling abstract sculptures of the clover-leaves and flyovers, but even so the congestion was unremitting.

The ten-mile journey to his home in fact covered over twenty-five miles and took him twice as long as it had done before the construction of the expressway, the additional miles contained within the three giant clover-leaves. New cities were springing from the motels, cafés and car marts around the highways. At the slightest hint of an intersection a shanty town of shacks and filling stations sprawled away among the forest of electric signs and route indicators, many of them substantial cities.

All around him cars bulleted along, streaming toward the suburbs. Relaxed by the smooth motion of the car, Franklin edged outward into the next speed-lane. As he accelerated from 40 to 50 mph a strident ear-jarring noise drummed out from his tires, shaking the chassis of the car. Ostensibly an aid to lane discipline, the surface of the road was covered with a mesh of small rubber studs, spaced progressively further apart in each of the lanes so that the tire hum resonated exactly on 40, 50, 60, and 70 mph. Driving at an intermediate speed for more than a few seconds became physiologically painful, and soon resulted in damage to the car and tires.

When the studs wore out they were replaced by slightly different patterns, matching those on the latest tires, so that regular tire changes were necessary, increasing the safety and efficiency of the expressway. It also increased the revenues of the car and tire manufacturers, for most cars over six months old soon fell to pieces under the steady battering, but this was regarded as a desirable end, the greater turnover reducing the unit price and making necessary more frequent model changes, as well as ridding the roads of dangerous vehicles.

A quarter of a mile ahead, at the approach to the first of the clover-leaves, the traffic stream was slowing, huge police signs signaling "Lanes Closed Ahead" and "Drop Speed by 10 mph." Franklin tried to return to the previous lane, but the cars were jammed bumper to bumper. As the chassis began to shudder and vibrate, jarring his spine, he clamped his teeth and tried to restrain himself from sounding the horn. Other drivers were less self-controlled, and everywhere engines were plunging and snarling, horns blaring. Road taxes were now so high, up to 30 percent of income (by contrast, income taxes were a bare 2 percent) that any delay on the expressways called for an immediate government inquiry, and the major departments of state were concerned with the administration of the road systems.

Nearer the clover-leaf the lanes had been closed to allow a gang of construction workers to erect a massive metal sign on one of the traffic islands. The palisaded area swarmed with engineers and surveyors and Franklin assumed that this was the sign Hathaway had seen unloaded the previous night. His apartment was in one of the gimcrack buildings in the settlement that straggled away around a nearby flyover, a low-rent area inhabited by service station personnel, waitresses and other migrant labor.

The sign was enormous, at least a hundred feet high, fitted with heavy concave grilles similar to radar bowls. Rooted in a series of concrete caissons, it reared high into the air above the approach roads, visible for miles. Franklin craned up at the grilles, tracing the power cables from the transformers up into the intricate mesh of metal coils that covered their surface. A line of red aircraft-warning beacons was already alight along the top strut, and Franklin assumed that the sign was part of the ground approach system of the city airport ten miles to the east.

Three minutes later, as he accelerated down the two-mile link of straight highway to the next clover-leaf, he saw the second of the giant signs looming up into the sky before him.

Changing down into the 40 mph lane, Franklin uneasily watched the great bulk of the second sign recede in his rearview mirror. Although there were no graphic symbols among the wire coils covering the grilles, Hathaway's warnings still sounded in his ears. Without knowing why, he felt sure that the signs were not part of the airport approach system. Neither of them was in line with the principal airlanes. To justify the expense of siting them in the center of the expressway—the second sign required elaborate angled buttresses to support it on the narrow island—obviously meant that their role related in some way to the traffic streams.

Two hundred yards away was a roadside auto-mart, and Franklin abruptly remembered that he needed some cigarettes. Swinging the car down the entrance ramp, he joined the queue slowly passing the self-service dispenser at the far end of the rank. The auto-mart was packed with cars, each of the five purchasing ranks lined with tired-looking men hunched over their wheels.

Inserting his coins (paper money was no longer in circulation, unmanageable by the automats) he took a carton from the dispenser. This was the only brand of cigarettes available—in fact there was only one brand of everything—though giant economy packs were an alternative. Moving off, he opened the dashboard locker.

Inside, still sealed in their wrappers, were three other cartons.

A strong fish-like smell pervaded the house when he reached home, steaming out from the oven in the kitchen. Sniffing it uneagerly, Franklin took off his coat and hat, and found his wife crouched over the TV set in the lounge. An announcer was dictating a stream of numbers, and Judith scribbled them down on a pad, occasionally cursing under her breath. "What a muddle!" she snapped finally. "He was talking so quickly I took only a few things down."

"Probably deliberate," Franklin commented. "New panel game?"

Judith kissed him on the cheek, discreetly hiding the ashtray loaded with cigarette butts and chocolate wrappings. "Hullo, darling, sorry not to have a drink ready for you. They've started this series of Spot Bargains. They give you a selection of things on which you get a ninety percent trade-in discount at the local stores, if you're in the right area and have the right serial numbers. It's all terribly complicated."

"Sounds good, though. What have you got?"

Judith peered at her checklist. "Well, as far as I can see the only thing is the infra-red barbecue spit. But we have to be there before eight o'clock tonight. It's seven-thirty already."

"Then that's out. I'm tired, angel, I need something to eat." When Judith started to protest he added firmly: "Look, I don't want a new infra-red barbecue spit; we've only had this one for two months. Damn it, it's not even a different model."

"But, darling, don't you see, it makes it cheaper if you keep buying new ones. We'll have to trade ours in at the end of the year anyway, we signed the contract, and this way we save at least twenty dollars. These Spot Bargains aren't just a gimmick, you know. I've been glued to that set all day." A note of irritation had crept into her voice, but Franklin sat his ground, doggedly ignoring the clock.

"Right, we lose twenty dollars. It's worth it." Before she could remonstrate he said, "Judith, please, you probably took the wrong number down anyway." As she shrugged and went over to the bar he called, "Make it a stiff one. I see we have health foods on the menu."

"They're good for you, darling. You know you can't live on ordinary foods all the time. They don't contain any proteins or vitamins. You're always saying we ought to be like people in the old days and eat nothing but health foods."

"I would, but they smell so awful." Franklin lay back, nose in the glass of whiskey, gazing at the darkened skyline outside.

A quarter of a mile away, gleaming out above the roof of the neighborhood supermarket, were the five red beacon lights. Now and then, as the headlamps of the Spot Bargainers swung up across the face of the building, he could see the square massive bulk of the giant sign clearly silhouetted against the evening sky.

"Judith!" He went into the kitchen and took her over to the window. "That sign, just behind the supermarket. When did they put it up?"

"I don't know." Judith peered at him curiously. "Why are you so worried, Robert? Isn't it something to do with the airport?"

Franklin stared thoughtfully at the dark hull of the sign. "So everyone probably thinks."

Carefully he poured his whiskey into the sink.

After parking his car on the supermarket apron at seven o'clock the next morning, Franklin carefully emptied his pockets and stacked the coins in the dashboard locker. The supermarket was already busy with early morning shoppers and the line of thirty turnstiles clicked and slammed. Since the introduction of the "twenty-four-hour spending day" the shopping complex was never closed. The bulk of the shoppers were discount buyers, housewives contracted to make huge volume purchases of food, clothing and appliances against substantial overall price cuts, and forced to drive around all day from supermarket to supermarket, frantically trying to keep pace with their purchase schedules and grappling with the added incentives inserted to keep the schemes alive.

Many of the women had teamed up, and as Franklin walked over to the entrance a pack of them charged toward their cars, stuffing their pay slips into their bags and gesticulating at each other. A moment later their cars roared off in a convoy to the next marketing zone.

A large neon sign over the entrance listed the latest discount—a mere 5 percent—calculated on the volume of turnover. The highest discounts, sometimes up to 25 percent, were earned in the housing estates where junior white-collar workers lived. There, spending had a strong social incentive, and the desire to be the highest spender in the neighborhood was given moral reinforcement by the system of listing all the names and their accumulating cash totals on a huge electric sign in the supermarket foyers. The higher the spender, the greater his contribution to the discounts enjoyed by others. The lowest spenders were regarded as social criminals, free-riding on the backs of others.

Luckily this system had yet to be adopted in Franklin's neighborhood. Not because the professional men and their wives were able to exercise more discretion, but because their higher incomes allowed them to contract into more expensive discount schemes operated by the big department stores in the city.

Ten yards from the entrance Franklin paused, looking up at the huge metal sign mounted in an enclosure at the edge of the car park. Unlike the other signs and hoardings that proliferated everywhere, no attempt had been made to decorate it, or disguise the gaunt bare rectangle of riveted steel mesh. Power lines wound down its sides, and the concrete surface of the car park was crossed by a long scar where a cable had been sunk.

Franklin strolled along, then fifty feet from the sign stopped and turned, realizing that he would be late for the hospital and needed a new carton of cigarettes. A dim but powerful humming emanated from the transformers below the sign, fading as he retraced his steps to the supermarket.

Going over to the automats in the foyer, he felt for his change, then whistled sharply when he remembered why he had deliberately emptied his pockets.

"The cunning thing!" he said, loud enough for two shoppers to stare at him. Reluctant to look directly at the sign, he watched its reflection in one of the glass doorpanes, so that any subliminal message would be reversed.

Almost certainly he had received two distinct signals—"Keep Away" and "Buy Cigarettes." The people who normally parked their cars along the perimeter of the apron were avoiding the area under the enclosure, the cars describing a loose semicircle fifty feet around it.

He turned to the janitor sweeping out the foyer. "What's that sign for?"

The man leaned on his broom, gazing dully at the sign. "Dunno," he said, "must be something to do with the airport." He had an almost fresh cigarette in his mouth, but his right hand reached unconsciously to his hip pocket and pulled out a pack. He drummed the second cigarette absently on his thumbnail as Franklin walked away.

Everyone entering the supermarket was buying cigarettes.

Cruising quietly along the 40 mph lane, Franklin began to take a closer interest in the landscape around him. Usually he was either too tired or too preoccupied to do more than think about his driving, but now he examined the expressway methodically, scanning the roadside cafés for any smaller versions of the new signs. A host of neon displays covered the doorways and windows, but most of them seemed innocuous, and he turned his attention to the larger billboards erected along the open stretches of the expressway. Many of these were as high as four-story houses, elaborate three-dimensional devices in which giant glossy-skinned housewives with electric eyes and teeth jerked and postured around their ideal kitchens, neon flashes exploding from their smiles.

The areas on either side of the expressway were wasteland, continuous junkyards filled with cars and trucks, washing machines and refrigerators, all perfectly workable but jettisoned by the economic pressure of the succeeding waves of discount models. Their intact chrome hardly tarnished, the mounds of metal shells and cabinets glittered in the sunlight. Nearer the city the billboards were sufficiently close together to hide them, but now and then, as he slowed to approach one of the flyovers, Franklin caught a glimpse of the huge pyramids of metal, gleaming silently like the refuse grounds of some forgotten El Dorado.

That evening Hathaway was waiting for him as he came down the hospital steps. Franklin waved him across the court, then led the way quickly to his car.

"What's the matter, Doctor?" Hathaway asked as Franklin wound up the windows and glanced around the lines of parked cars. "Is someone after you?"

Franklin laughed somberly. "I don't know. I hope not, but if what you say is right, I suppose there is."

Hathaway leaned back with a chuckle, propping one knee up on the dashboard. "So you've seen something, Doctor, after all."

"Well, I'm not sure yet, but there's just a chance you may be right. This morning at the Fairlawne supermarket—" He broke off, uneasily remembering the huge blank sign and the abrupt way in which he had turned back to the supermarket as he approached it, then described his encounter.

Hathaway nodded slowly. "I've seen the sign there. It's big, but not as big as some that are going up. They're building them everywhere now. All over the city. What are you going to do, Doctor?"

Franklin gripped the wheel tightly. Hathaway's thinly veiled amusement irritated him. "Nothing, of course. Damn it, it may be just auto-suggestion, you've probably got me imagining—"

Hathaway sat up with a jerk, his face mottled and savage. "Don't be absurd, Doctor! If you can't believe your own senses what chance have you left? They're invading your brain; if you don't defend yourself they'll take it over completely! We've got to act now, before we're all paralyzed."

Wearily Franklin raised one hand to restrain him. "Just a minute. Assuming that these signs *are* going up everywhere, what would be their object? Apart from wasting the enormous amount of capital invested in all the other millions of signs and billboards, the amounts of discretionary spending power still available must be infinitesimal. Some of the present mortgage and discount schemes reach half a century ahead, so there can't be much slack left to take up. A big trade war would be disastrous."

"Quite right, Doctor," Hathaway rejoined evenly, "but you're forgetting one thing. What would supply that extra spending power? A big increase in production. Already they've started to raise the working day from twelve hours to fourteen. In some of the appliance plants around the city Sunday working is being introduced as a norm. Can you visualize it, Doctor—a seven-day week, everyone with at least three jobs."

Franklin shook his head. "People won't stand for it."

"They will. Within the last twenty-five years the gross national product has risen by fifty percent, but so have the average hours worked. Ultimately we'll all be working and spending twenty-four hours a day, seven days a week. No one will dare refuse. Think what a slump would mean— millions of lay-offs, people with time on their hands and nothing to spend it on. Real leisure, not just time spent buying things." He seized Franklin by the shoulder. "Well, Doctor, are you going to join me?"

Franklin freed himself. Half a mile away, partly hidden by the four-story bulk of the Pathology Department, was the upper half of one of the giant signs, workmen still crawling across its girders. The airlines over the city had deliberately been routed away from the hospital, and the sign obviously had no connection with approaching aircraft.

"Isn't there a prohibition on subliminal living? How can the unions accept it?"

"The fear of a slump. You know the new economic dogmas. Unless output rises by a steady inflationary 5 percent the economy is stagnating. Ten years ago increased efficiency alone would raise output, but the advantages there are minimal now and only one thing is left. More work. Increased consumption and subliminal advertising will provide the spur."

"What are you planning to do?"

"I can't tell you, Doctor, unless you accept equal responsibility for it."

"Sounds rather Quixotic," Franklin commented. "Tilting at windmills. You won't be able to chop those things down with an axe."

· "I won't try." Hathaway suddenly gave up and opened the door. "Don't wait too long to make up your mind, Doctor. By then it may not be yours to make up." With a wave he was gone.

On the way home Franklin's scepticism returned. The idea of the conspiracy was preposterous, and the economic arguments were too plausible. As usual, though, there had been a hook in the soft bait Hathaway dangled before him—Sunday working. His own consultancy had been extended into Sunday morning with his appointment as visiting factory doctor to one of the automobile plants that had started Sunday shifts. But instead of resenting this incursion into his already meager hours of leisure he had been glad. For one frightening reason—he needed the extra income.

Looking out over the lines of scurrying cars, he noticed that at least a dozen of the great signs had been erected along the expressway. As Hathaway had said, more were going up everywhere, rearing over the supermarkets in the housing developments like rusty metal sails.

Judith was in the kitchen when he reached home, watching the TV program on the hand-set over the cooker. Franklin climbed past a big cardboard carton, its seals still unbroken, which blocked the doorway, and kissed her on the cheek as she scribbled numbers down on her pad. The pleasant odor of pot-roast chicken—or, rather, a gelatine dummy of a chicken fully flavored and free of any toxic or nutritional properties—mollified his irritation at finding her still playing the Spot Bargains.

He tapped the carton with his foot. "What's this?"

"No idea, darling, something's always coming these days, I can't keep up with it all." She peered through the glass door at the chicken—an economy twelve-pounder, the size of a turkey, with stylized legs and wings and an enormous breast, most of which would be discarded at the end of the meal (there were no dogs or cats these days, the crumbs from the rich man's table saw to that) and then glanced at him pointedly.

"You look rather worried, Robert. Bad day?"

Franklin murmured noncommittally. The hours spent trying to detect false clues in the faces of the Spot Bargain announcers had sharpened Judith's perceptions, and he felt a pang of sympathy for the legion of husbands similarly outmatched.

"Have you been talking to that crazy beatnik again?"

"Hathaway? As a matter of fact I have. He's not all that crazy." He stepped backward into the carton, almost spilling his drink. "Well, what is this thing? As I'll be working for the next fifty Sundays to pay for it I'd like to find out."

He searched the sides, finally located the label. "*A TV set?* Judith, do we need another one? We've already got three. Lounge, dining room, and the hand-set. What's the fourth for?"

"The guest room, dear, don't get so excited. We can't leave a hand-set in the guest room, it's rude. I'm trying to economize, but four TV sets is the bare minimum. All the magazines say so."

"*And* three radios?" Franklin stared irritably at the carton. "If we do invite a guest here how much time is he going to spend alone in his room watching television? Judith, we've got to call a halt. It's not as if these things were free, or even cheap. Anyway, television is a total waste of time. There's only one program. It's ridiculous to have four sets."

"Robert, there are *four* channels."

"But only the commercials are different." Before Judith could reply the telephone rang. Franklin lifted the kitchen receiver, listened to the gabble of noise that poured from it. At first he wondered whether this was some off-beat prestige commercial, then realized it was Hathaway in a manic swing.

"Hathaway!" he shouted back. "Relax, man! What's the matter now?"

"—Doctor, you'll have to believe me this time. I tell you I got on to one of the islands with a stroboscope; they've got hundreds of high-speed shutters blasting away like machine-guns straight into people's faces and they can't see a thing, it's fantastic! The next big campaign's going to be cars and TV sets, they're trying to swing a two-month model change—can you imagine it, Doctor, a new car every two months? God Almighty, it's just—"

Franklin waited impatiently as the five-second commercial break cut in (all telephone calls were free, the length of the commercial extending with range—for long-distance calls the ratio of commercial to conversation was as high as 10:1, the participants desperately trying to get a word in edgeways between the interminable interruptions), but just before it ended he abruptly put the telephone down, then removed the receiver from the cradle.

Judith came over and took his arm. "Robert, what's the matter? You look terribly strained."

Franklin picked up his drink and walked through into the lounge. "It's just Hathaway. As you say, I'm getting a little too involved with him. He's starting to prey on my mind."

He looked at the dark outline of the sign over the supermarket, its red warning lights glowing in the night sky. Blank and nameless, like an area forever closed-off in an insane mind, what frightened him was its total anonymity.

"Yet I'm not sure," he muttered. "So much of what Hathaway says makes sense. These subliminal techniques are the sort of last-ditch attempt you'd expect from an overcapitalized industrial system."

He waited for Judith to reply, then looked up at her. She stood in the center of the carpet, hands folded limply, her sharp, intelligent face curiously dull and blunted. He followed her gaze out over the rooftops, then with an effort turned his head and quickly switched on the TV set.

"Come on," he said grimly. "Let's watch television. God, we're going to need that fourth set."

A week later Franklin began to compile his inventory. He saw nothing more of Hathaway; as he left the hospital in the evening the familiar scruffy figure was absent. When the first of the explosions sounded dimly around the city and he read of the attempts to sabotage the giant signs he automatically assumed that Hathaway was responsible, but later he

heard on a newscast that the detonations had been set off by construction workers excavating foundations.

More of the signs appeared over the rooftops, isolated on the palisaded
islands near the suburban shopping centers. Already there were over
thirty on the ten-mile route from the hospital, standing shoulder to shoulder over the speeding cars like giant dominoes. Franklin had given up his
attempt to avoid looking at them, but the slim possibility that the explosions might be Hathaway's counterattack kept his suspicions alive.

He began his inventory after hearing the newscast, discovered that in
the previous fortnight he and Judith had traded in their

    Car (previous model 2 months old)
    2 TV sets (4 months)
    Power mower (7 months)
    Electric cooker (5 months)
    Hair dryer (4 months)
    Refrigerator (3 months)
    2 radios (7 months)
    Record player (5 months)
    Cocktail bar (8 months)

Half these purchases had been made by himself, but exactly when he
could never recall realizing at the time. The car, for example, he had left
in the garage near the hospital to be greased; that evening he had signed
for the new model as he sat at its wheel, accepting the salesman's assurance that the depreciation on the two-month trade-in was virtually less
than the cost of the grease-job. Ten minutes later, as he sped along the
expressway, he suddenly realized that he had bought a new car. Similarly,
the TV sets had been replaced by identical models after developing the
same irritating interference pattern (curiously, the new sets also displayed
the pattern, but as the salesman assured them, this promptly vanished
two days later).

*Not once had he actually decided of his own volition that he wanted
something and then gone out to a store and bought it!*

He carried the inventory around with him, adding to it as necessary,
quietly and without protest analyzing these new sales techniques, wondering whether total capitulation might be the only way of defeating
them. As long as he kept up even a token resistance, the inflationary
growth curve would show a controlled annual 10 percent climb. With
that resistance removed, however, it would begin to rocket upward out
of control. . . .

Then, driving home from the hospital two months later, he saw one
of the signs for the first time.

He was in the 40 mph lane, unable to keep up with the flood of new cars, had just passed the second of the three clover-leaves when the traffic half a mile away began to slow down. Hundreds of cars had driven up on to the grass verge, and a large crowd was gathering around one of the signs. Two small black figures were climbing up the metal face, and a series of huge grid-like patterns of light flashed on and off, illuminating the evening air. The patterns were random and broken, as if the sign was being tested for the first time.

Relieved that Hathaway's suspicions had been completely groundless, Franklin turned off onto the soft shoulder, then walked forward through the spectators as the lights blinked and stuttered in their faces. Below, behind the steel palisades around the island, was a large group of police and engineers, craning up at the men scaling the sign a hundred feet over their heads.

Suddenly Franklin stopped, the sense of relief fading instantly. With a jolt he saw that several of the police on the ground were armed with shot-guns, and that the two policemen climbing the sign carried submachine-guns slung over their shoulders. They were converging on a third figure, crouched by a switchbox on the penultimate tier, a ragged bearded man in a grimy shirt, a bare knee poking through his jeans.

Hathaway!

Franklin hurried toward the island, the sign hissing and spluttering, fuses blowing by the dozen.

Then the flicker of lights cleared and steadied, blazing out continuously, and together the crowd looked up at the decks of brilliant letters. The phrases, and every combination of them possible, were entirely familiar, and Franklin knew that he had been reading them unconsciously in his mind for weeks as he passed up and down the expressway.

BUY NOW BUY NOW BUY NOW BUY NOW BUY NOW NEW CAR NOW NEW CAR NOW NEW CAR NOW YES YES YES YES YES YES YES YES YES YES YES

Sirens blaring, two patrol cars swung up onto the verge through the crowd and plunged across the damp grass. Police spilled from its doors, batons in their hands, and quickly began to force back the crowd. Franklin held his ground as they approached, started to say: "Officer, I know the man—" but the policeman punched him in the chest with the flat of his hand. Winded, he stumbled back among the cars, leaned helplessly against a fender as the police began to break the windshields, the hapless drivers protesting angrily, those further back rushing for their vehicles.

The noise fell away abruptly when one of the submachine-guns fired a brief roaring burst, then rose in a massive gasp of horror as Hathaway, arms outstretched, let out a cry of triumph and pain, and jumped.

"But, Robert, what does it really matter?" Judith asked as Franklin sat inertly in the lounge the next morning. "I know it's tragic for his wife and daughter, but Hathaway was in the grip of an obsession. If he hated advertising signs so much why didn't he dynamite those we·*can* see, instead of worrying so much about those we can't?"

Franklin stared at the TV screen, hoping the program would distract him.

"Hathaway was *right,*" he said simply.

"Was he? Advertising is here to stay. We've no real freedom of choice, anyway. We can't spend more than we can afford, the finance companies soon clamp down."

"You accept that?" Franklin went over to the window. A quarter of a mile away, in the center of the estate, another of the signs was being erected. It was due east from them, and in the early morning light the shadows of its rectangular superstructure fell across the garden, reaching almost to the steps of the French windows at his feet. As a concession to the neighborhood, and perhaps to allay any suspicions while it was being erected by an appeal to petty snobbery the lower sections had been encased in mock-Tudor paneling.

Franklin stared at it numbly, counting the half-dozen police lounging by their patrol cars as the construction gang unloaded prefabricated grilles from a couple of trucks. Then he looked at the sign by the supermarket, trying to repress his memories of Hathaway and the pathetic attempts the man had made to convince Franklin and gain his help.

He was still standing there an hour later when Judith came in, putting on her hat and coat, ready to visit the supermarket.

Franklin followed her to the door: "I'll drive you down there, Judith," he said in a flat dead voice. "I have to see about booking a new car. The next models are coming out at the end of the month. With luck we'll get one of the early deliveries."

They walked out into the trim drive, the shadows of the great signs swinging across the quiet neighborhood as the day progressed, sweeping over the heads of the people on their way to the supermarket like the dark blades of enormous scythes.

PROBINGS

1. In your opinion, what does it mean to be "nice"? What is the nicest thing that anyone has said to you or done for you? What is the nicest thing you have said or done for someone else?
2. Construct a model of an "ideal" person. What qualities does she or he have? How does she or he behave? What kind of a personality does she or he have?
3. Analyze at least ten TV, magazine, or newspaper advertisements for some of the following products: soap, underarm deodorant, perfume or cologne, shaving cream, eye shadow, hair spray, toothpaste, mouth wash, cigarettes, other. What is promised if you use the product? How will you supposedly be different? Is any sex appeal promised? How about popularity? Remember, often the message is hidden and you'll have to dig for it. What special words and images are used in the ad? For example, some skin cream ads promise "silky skin" or "skin like velvet." I don't know how this skin would feel, but it doesn't sound appealing to me.

    If you use newspaper or magazine ads, bring them into class and as a group analyze them. Underline key words; circle key images.
4. Why *do* most people conform in a society? What do they fear? What pressures do they feel? In your opinion, why don't most of us rebel as Hathaway did? What would move you to rebel? What would have to happen in our society to turn you into Hathaway?
5. Since this is a story that is also about the government, what uses could the government find for subliminal advertising? Write a short story developing the idea that the government would or could use subliminal advertising to force people to think alike.
6. How often does *your* family trade in or buy a new:
    a. car
    b. TV
    c. stereo
    d. furniture
    e. house
    f. electrical appliances
    g. other
        Why?

NONCONFORMITY

10

There are always those few people who don't fit in or, perhaps more appropriately, who *won't* fit in. In the words of Henry David Thoreau, these are the people who march to the beat of a different drummer. Of course, nonconformists pay a price for their "difference"; they are often rejected and scorned by their relatives, friends, and society. Words such as "odd" and "weird" are attached to them, and they usually live their lives as outcasts.

The important question, though, is what specifically separates such people from the rest of the crowd? In some instances, physical and cultural differences have caused whole groups of people to be labeled as "strange." Chicanos, Blacks, and American Indians to this day still suffer discrimination in many areas of the country.

In the late 19th and early 20th centuries, immigrants who came to the United States from Southern and Eastern Europe didn't find the land of their dreams; they found instead much bigotry. They were laughed at because of their customs and their dress, and they were ridiculed in ethnic jokes and by nicknames. To "native" Americans, these more recent immigrants were unwanted, so they had to seek out areas of the cities where their "difference" was mutual. Now we can see that because of "them" our culture has been enriched by new foods, customs, and ideas.

What happens to the individual who thinks differently from the great majority? One Jewish rabbi tearfully indicted his fellow Germans during the Civil Rights March on Washington in 1963. He charged that they were guilty of the "crime of silence"; they stood silently by as Hitler had the Jews exterminated. It was the rare person who had the courage of his or her beliefs to stand up and resist the Nazis.

Sometimes even a different lifestyle can lead to discrimination. For example, Murray in the film *A Thousand Clowns* wanted to raise his young nephew his way—without working for a living. To society in general, anyone who does not work is immediately stigmatized as a bum.

In the following story, we meet a little boy who is very different from his peers. Like Luke in the film *Cool Hand Luke,* this boy is pressured to get "his mind right." However, he is a strong-willed little boy and instead helps his psychiatrist to "get his mind right."

1. Headlines from Tomorrow:

"GOVERNMENT BANS MASS PRODUCTION OF CLOTHING"

You are living in the 21st century. You tune in the news on the videoscreen and hear a report about a clothing manufacturer who is going bankrupt because of the new law that prohibits people from dressing alike. Write the news report you have heard in the form of an interview. Describe or draw the clothing of the news commentator and of the manufacturer.

PROJECTIONS

IT'S SUCH A BEAUTIFUL DAY

—Isaac Asimov

On April 12, 2117, the field-modulator brake-valve in the Door belonging to Mrs. Richard Hanshaw depolarized for reasons unknown. As a result, Mrs. Hanshaw's day was completely upset and her son, Richard, Jr., first developed his strange neurosis.

It was not the type of thing you would find listed as a neurosis in the usual textbooks and certainly young Richard behaved, in most respects, just as a well-brought-up twelve-year-old in prosperous circumstances ought to behave.

And yet from April 12 on, Richard Hanshaw, Jr., could only with regret ever persuade himself to go through a Door.

Of all this, on April 12, Mrs. Hanshaw had no premonition. She woke in the morning (an ordinary morning) as her mekkano slithered gently into her room, with a cup of coffee on a small tray. Mrs. Hanshaw was planning a visit to New York in the afternoon and she had several things to do first that could not quite be trusted to a mekkano, so after one or two sips, she stepped out of bed.

The mekkano backed away, moving silently along the diamagnetic field that kept its oblong body half an inch above the floor, and moved back to the kitchen, where its simple computer was quite adequate to set the proper controls on the various kitchen appliances in order that an appropriate breakfast might be prepared.

Mrs. Hanshaw, having bestowed the usual sentimental glance upon the cubograph of her dead husband, passed through the stages of her morning ritual with a certain contentment. She could hear her son across the hall clattering through his, but she knew she need not interfere with him. The mekkano was well adjusted to see to it, as a matter of course, that he was showered, that he had on a change of clothing, and that he would eat a nourishing breakfast. The tergo-shower she had had installed the year before made the morning wash and dry so quick and pleasant that, really, she felt certain Dickie would wash even without supervision.

On a morning like this, when she was busy, it would certainly not be necessary for her to do more than deposit a casual peck on the boy's cheek before he left. She heard the soft chime the mekkano sounded to indicate approaching school time and she floated down the force-lift to the lower floor (her hair-style for the day only sketchily designed, as yet) in order to perform that motherly duty.

She found Richard standing at the door, with his textreels and pocket projector dangling by their strap and a frown on his face.

"Say, Mom," he said, looking up, "I dialed the school's co-ords but nothing happens."

She said, almost automatically, "Nonsense, Dickie. I never heard of such a thing."

"Well, you try."

Mrs. Hanshaw tried a number of times. Strange, the school Door was always set for general reception. She tried other coordinates. Her friends' Doors might not be set for reception, but there would be a signal at least, and then she could explain.

But nothing happened at all. The Door remained an inactive gray barrier despite all her manipulations. It was obvious that the Door was out of order—and only five months after its annual fall inspection by the company.

She was quite angry about it.

It *would* happen on a day when she had much planned. She thought petulantly of the fact that a month earlier she had decided against installing a subsidiary Door on the ground that it was an unnecessary expense. How was she to know that Doors were getting to be so *shoddy?*

She stepped to the visiphone while the anger still burned in her and said to Richard, "You just go down the road, Dickie, and use the Williamsons' Door."

Ironically, in view of later developments, Richard balked. "Aw, gee, Mom, I'll get dirty. Can't I stay home till the Door is fixed?"

And, as ironically, Mrs. Hanshaw insisted. With her finger on the combination board of the phone, she said, "You won't get dirty if you put flexies on your shoes, and don't forget to brush yourself well before you go into their house."

"But, golly—"

"No back-talk, Dickie. You've got to be in school. Just let me see you walk out of here. And quickly, or you'll be late."

The mekkano, an advanced model and very responsive, was already standing before Richard with flexies in one appendage.

Richard pulled the transparent plastic shields over his shoes and moved down the hall with visible reluctance. "I don't even know how to work this thing, Mom."

"You just push that button," Mrs. Hanshaw called. "The red button. Where it says 'For Emergency Use.' And don't dawdle. Do you want the mekkano to go along with you?"

"Gosh, no," he called back, morosely, "what do you think I am? A baby? Gosh!" His muttering was cut off by a slam.

With flying fingers, Mrs. Hanshaw punched the appropriate combination on the phone board and thought of the things she intended saying to the company about this.

Joe Bloom, a reasonably young man, who had gone through technology school with added training in force-field mechanics, was at the

Hanshaw residence in less than half an hour. He was really quite competent, though Mrs. Hanshaw regarded his youth with deep suspicion.

She opened the movable house-panel when he first signaled and her sight of him was as he stood there, brushing at himself vigorously to remove the dust of the open air. He took off his flexies and dropped them where he stood. Mrs. Hanshaw closed the house-panel against the flash of raw sunlight that had entered. She found herself irrationally hoping that the step-by-step trip from the public Door had been an unpleasant one. Or perhaps that the public Door itself had been out of order and the youth had had to lug his tools even farther than the necessary two hundred yards. She wanted the Company, or its representative at least, to suffer a bit. It would teach them what broken Doors meant.

But he seemed cheerful and unperturbed as he said, "Good morning, ma'am. I came to see about your Door."

."I'm glad someone did," said, Mrs. Hanshaw, ungraciously. "My day is quite ruined."

"Sorry, ma'am. What seems to be the trouble?"

"It just won't work. Nothing at all happens when you adjust co-ords," said Mrs. Hanshaw. "There was no warning at all. I had to send my son out to the neighbors through that—that thing."

She pointed to the entrance through which the repairman had come.

He smiled and spoke out of the conscious wisdom of his own specialized training in Doors. "That's a door, too, ma'am. You don't give that kind a capital letter when you write it. It's a hand-door, sort of. It used to be the only kind once."

"Well, at least it works. My boy's had to go out in the dirt and germs."

"It's not bad outside today, ma'am," he said, with the connoisseur-like air of one whose profession forced him into the open nearly every day. "Sometimes it *is* real unpleasant. But I guess you want I should fix this here Door, ma'am, so I'll get on with it."

He sat down on the floor, opened the large tool case he had brought in with him and in half a minute, by use of a point-demagnetizer, he had the control panel removed and a set of intricate vitals exposed.

He whistled to himself as he placed the fine electrodes of the field-analyzer on numerous points, studying the shifting needles on the dials. Mrs. Hanshaw watched him, arms folded.

Finally, he said, "Well, here's something," and with a deft twist, he disengaged the brake-valve.

He tapped it with a fingernail and said, "This here brake-valve is depolarized, ma'am. There's your whole trouble." He ran his finger along the little pigeonholes in his tool case and lifted out a duplicate of the object he had taken from the door mechanism. "These things just go all of a sudden. Can't predict it."

He put the control panel back and stood up. "It'll work now, ma'am."

He punched a reference combination, blanked it, then punched another. Each time, the dull gray of the Door gave way to a deep, velvety

It's Such a Beautiful Day/Isaac Asimov

blackness. He said, "Will you sign here, ma'am? And put down your charge number, too, please? Thank you, ma'am."

He punched a new combination, that of his home factory, and with a polite touch of finger to forehead, he stepped through the Door. As his body entered the blackness, it cut off sharply. Less and less of him was visible and the tip of his tool case was the last thing that showed. A second after he had passed through completely, the Door turned back to dull gray.

Half an hour later, when Mrs. Hanshaw had finally completed her interrupted preparations and was fuming over the misfortune of the morning, the phone buzzed annoyingly and her real troubles began.

Miss Elizabeth Robbins was distressed. Little Dick Hanshaw had always been a good pupil. She hated to report him like this. And yet, she told herself, his actions were certainly queer. And she would talk to his mother, not to the principal.

She slipped out to the phone during the morning study period, leaving a student in charge. She made her connection and found herself staring at Mrs. Hanshaw's handsome and somewhat formidable head.

Miss Robbins quailed, but it was too late to turn back. She said, diffidently, "Mrs. Hanshaw, I'm Miss Robbins." She ended on a rising note.

Mrs. Hanshaw looked blank, then said, "Richard's teacher?" That, too, ended on a rising note.

"That's right. I called you, Mrs. Hanshaw," Miss Robbins plunged right into it, "to tell you that Dick was quite late to school this morning."

"He was? But that couldn't be. I saw him leave."

Miss Robbins looked astonished. She said, "You mean you saw him use the Door?"

Mrs. Hanshaw said quickly, "Well, no. Our Door was temporarily out of order. I sent him to a neighbor and he used that Door."

"Are you sure?"

"Of course I'm sure. I wouldn't lie to you."

"No, no, Mrs. Hanshaw. I wasn't implying that at all. I meant are you sure he found the way to the neighbor? He might have got lost."

"Ridiculous. We have the proper maps, and I'm sure Richard knows the location of every house in District A-3." Then, with the quiet pride of one who knows what is her due, she added, "Not that he ever needs to know, of course. The co-ords are all that are necessary at any time."

Miss Robbins, who came from a family that had always had to economize rigidly on the use of its Doors (the price of power being what it was) and who had therefore run errands on foot until quite an advanced age, resented the pride. She said, quite clearly, "Well, I'm afraid, Mrs. Hanshaw, that Dick did not use the neighbor's Door. He was over an hour late to school and the condition of his flexies made it quite obvious that he tramped cross-country. They were *muddy*."

"*Muddy?*" Mrs. Hanshaw repeated the emphasis on the word. "What did he say? What was his excuse?"

159

Miss Robbins couldn't help but feel a little glad at the discomfiture of the other woman. She said, "He wouldn't talk about it. Frankly, Mrs. Hanshaw, he seems ill. That's why I called you. Perhaps you might want to have a doctor look at him."

"Is he running a temperature?" The mother's voice went shrill.

"Oh, no. I don't mean physically ill. It's just his attitude and the look in his eyes." She hesitated, then said with every attempt at delicacy, "I thought perhaps a routine checkup with a psychic probe—"

She didn't finish. Mrs. Hanshaw, in a chilled voice and with what was as close to a snort as her breeding would permit, said, "Are you implying that Richard is *neurotic?*"

"Oh, no, Mrs. Hanshaw, but—"

"It certainly sounded so. The idea! He has always been perfectly healthy. I'll take this up with him when he gets home. I'm sure there's a perfectly normal explanation which he'll give to *me.*"

The connection broke abruptly, and Miss Robbins felt hurt and uncommonly foolish. After all she had only tried to help, to fulfill what she considered an obligation to her students.

She hurried back to the classroom with a glance at the metal face of the wall clock. The study period was drawing to an end. English Composition next.

But her mind wasn't completely on English Composition. Automatically, she called the students to have them read selections from their literary creations. And occasionally she punched one of those selections on tape and ran it through the small vocalizer to show the students how English *should* be read.

The vocalizer's mechanical voice, as always, dripped perfection, but, again as always, lacked character. Sometimes, she wondered if it was wise to try to train the students into a speech that was divorced from individuality and geared only to a mass-average accent and intonation.

Today, however, she had no thought for that. It was Richard Hanshaw she watched. He sat quietly in his seat, quite obviously indifferent to his surroundings. He was lost deep in himself and just not the same boy he had been. It was obvious to her that he had had some unusual experience that morning and, really, she was right to call his mother, although perhaps she ought not to have made the remark about the probe. Still it was quite the thing these days. All sorts of people got probed. There wasn't any disgrace attached to it. Or there shouldn't be, anyway.

She called on Richard, finally. She had to call twice, before he responded and rose to his feet.

The general subject assigned had been: "If you had your choice of traveling on some ancient vehicle, which would you choose, and why?" Miss Robbins tried to use the topic every semester. It was a good one because it carried a sense of history with it. It forced the youngster to think about the manner of living of people in past ages.

She listened while Richard Hanshaw read in a low voice.

"If I had my choice of ancient vehicles," he said, pronouncing the "h" in vehicles, "I would choose the stratoliner. It travels slow like all vehicles but it is clean. Because it travels in the stratosphere, it must be all enclosed so that you are not likely to catch disease. You can see the stars if it is night time almost as good as in a planetarium. If you look down you can see the Earth like a map or maybe see clouds—" He went on for several hundred more words.

She said brightly when he had finished reading, "It's pronounced vee-ick-ulls, Richard. No 'h.' Accent on the first syllable. And you don't say 'travels slow' or 'see good.' What do you say, class?"

There was a small chorus of responses and she went on, "That's right. Now what is the difference between an adjective and an adverb? Who can tell me?"

And so it went. Lunch passed. Some pupils stayed to eat; some went home. Richard stayed. Miss Robbins noted that, as usually he didn't.

The afternoon passed, too, and then there was the final bell and the usual upsurging hum as twenty-five boys and girls rattled their belongings together and took their leisurely place in line.

Miss Robbins clapped her hands together. "Quickly, children. Come, Zelda, take your place."

"I dropped my tape-punch, Miss Robbins," shrilled the girl, defensively.

"Well, pick it up, pick it up. Now children, be brisk, be brisk."

She pushed the button that slid a section of the wall into a recess and revealed the gray blankness of a large Door. It was not the usual Door that the occasional student used in going home for lunch, but an advanced model that was one of the prides of this well-to-do private school.

In addition to its double width, it possessed a large and impressively gear-filled "automatic serial finder" which was capable of adjusting the door for a number of different coordinates at automatic intervals.

At the beginning of the semester, Miss Robbins always had to spend an afternoon with the mechanic, adjusting the device for the coordinates of the homes of the new class. But then, thank goodness, it rarely needed attention for the remainder of the term.

The class lined up alphabetically, first girls, then boys. The door went velvety black and Hester Adams waved her hand and stepped through. "By-y-y—"

The "bye" was cut off in the middle, as it almost always was.

The door went gray, then black again, and Theresa Cantrocchi went through. Gray, black, Zelda Charlowicz. Gray, black, Patricia Coombs. Gray, black, Sara May Evans.

The line grew smaller as the Door swallowed them one by one, depositing each in her home. Of course, an occasional mother forgot to leave the house Door on special reception at the appropriate time and then the school Door remained gray. Automatically, after a minute-long wait, the Door went on to the next combination in line and the pupil in question had to wait till it was all over, after which a phone call to the forgetful parent would set things right. This was always bad for the pupils involved, especially the sensitive ones who took seriously the implication that they were little thought of at home. Miss Robbins always tried to impress this on visiting parents, but it happened at least once every semester just the same.

The girls were all through now. John Abramowitz stepped through and then Edwin Byrne—

Of course, another trouble, and a more frequent one, was the boy or girl who got into line out of place. They *would* do it despite the teacher's sharpest watch, particularly at the beginning of the term when the proper order was less familiar to them.

When that happened, children would be popping into the wrong houses by the half-dozen and would have to be sent back. It always meant a mix-up that took minutes to straighten out and parents were invariably irate.

Miss Robbins was suddenly aware that the line had stopped. She spoke sharply to the boy at the head of the line.

"Step through, Samuel. What are you waiting for?"

Samuel Jones raised a complacent countenance and said, "It's not my combination, Miss Robbins."

"Well, whose is it?" She looked impatiently down the line of five remaining boys. "Who was out of place?"

"It's Dick Hanshaw's, Miss Robbins."

"Where is he?"

Another boy answered, with the rather repulsive tone of self-righteousness all children automatically assume in reporting the deviations of their friends to elders in authority, "He went through the fire door, Miss Robbins."

"What?"

The schoolroom Door had passed on to another combination and Samuel Jones passed through. One by one, the rest followed.

Miss Robbins was alone in the classroom. She stepped to the fire door. It was a small affair, manually operated, and hidden behind a bend in the wall so that it would not break up the uniform structure of the room.

She opened it a crack. It was there as a means of escape from the building in case of fire, a device which was enforced by an anachronistic law that did not take into account the modern methods of automatic fire-fighting that all public buildings used. There was nothing outside, but the—outside. The sunlight was harsh and a dusty wind was blowing.

Miss Robbins closed the door. She was glad she had called Mrs. Hanshaw. She had done her duty. More than ever, it was obvious that something was wrong with Richard. She suppressed the impulse to phone again.

Mrs. Hanshaw did not go to New York that day. She remained home in a mixture of anxiety and an irrational anger, the latter directed against the impudent Miss Robbins.

Some fifteen minutes before school's end, her anxiety drove her to the

Door. Last year she had had it equipped with an automatic device which activated it to the school's coordinates at five of three and kept is so, barring manual adjustment, until Richard arrived.

Her eyes were fixed on the Door's dismal gray (why couldn't an inactive force-field be any other color, something more lively and cheerful?) and waited. Her hands felt cold as she squeezed them together.

The Door turned black at the precise second but nothing happened. The minutes passed and Richard was late. Then quite late. Then very late.

It was a quarter of four and she was distracted. Normally, she would have phoned the school, but she couldn't, she couldn't. Not after that teacher had deliberately cast doubts on Richard's mental well-being. How could she?

Mrs. Hanshaw moved about restlessly, lighting a cigarette with fumbling fingers, then smudging it out. Could it be something quite normal? Could Richard be staying after school for some reason? Surely he would have told her in advance. A gleam of light struck her; he knew she was planning to go to New York and might not be back till late in the evening—

No, he would surely have told her. Why fool herself?

Her pride was breaking. She would have to call the school, or even (she closed her eyes and teardrops squeezed through between the lashes) the police.

And when she opened her eyes, Richard stood before her, eyes on the ground and his whole bearing that of someone waiting for a blow to fall.

"Hello, Mom."

Mrs. Hanshaw's anxiety transmuted itself instantly (in a manner known only to mothers) into anger. "Where have you been, Richard?"

And then, before she could go further into the refrain concerning careless, unthinking sons and broken-hearted mothers, she took note of his appearance in greater detail, and gasped in utter horror.

She said, "You've been in the open."

Her son looked down at his dusty shoes (minus flexies), at the dirt marks that streaked his lower arms and at the small, but definite tear in his shirt. He said, "Gosh, Mom, I just thought I'd—" and he faded out.

She said, "Was there anything wrong with the school Door?"

"No, Mom."

"Do you realize I've been worried sick about you?" She waited vainly for an answer. "Well, I'll talk to you afterward, young man. First, you're taking a bath, and every stitch of your clothing is being thrown out. Mekkano!"

But the mekkano had already reacted properly to the phrase "taking a bath" and was off to the bathroom in its silent glide.

"You take your shoes off right here," said Mrs. Hanshaw, "then march after mekkano."

Richard did as he was told with a resignation that placed him beyond futile protest.

Mrs. Hanshaw picked up the soiled shoes between thumb and forefinger and dropped them down the disposal chute which hummed in faint dismay at the unexpected load. She dusted her hands carefully on a tissue which she allowed to float down the chute after the shoes.

She did not join Richard at dinner but let him eat in the worse-than-lack-of-company of the mekkano. This, she thought, would be an active sign of her displeasure and would do more than any amount of scolding or punishment to make him realize that he had done wrong. Richard, she frequently told herself, was a sensitive boy.

But she went up to see him at bedtime.

She smiled at him and spoke softly. She thought that would be the best way. After all, he had been punished already.

She said, "What happened today, Dickie-boy?" She had called him that when he was a baby and just the sound of the name softened her nearly to tears.

But he only looked away and his voice was stubborn and cold. "I just don't like to go through those darn Doors, Mom."

"But why ever not?"

He shuffled his hands over the filmy sheet (fresh, clean, antiseptic and, of course, disposable after each use) and said, "I just don't like them."

"But then how do you expect to go to school, Dickie?"

"I'll get up early," he mumbled.

"But there's nothing wrong with Doors."

"Don't like 'em." He never once looked up at her.

She said, despairingly, "Oh, well, you have a good sleep and tomorrow morning, you'll feel much better."

She kissed him and left the room, automatically passing her hand through the photo-cell beam and in that manner dimming the room-lights.

But she had trouble sleeping herself that night. Why should Dickie dislike Doors so suddenly? They had never bothered him before. To be sure, the Door had broken down in the morning but that should make him appreciate them all the more.

Dickie was behaving so unreasonably.

Unreasonably? That reminded her of Miss Robbins and her diagnosis and Mrs. Hanshaw's soft jaw set in the darkness and privacy of her bedroom. Nonsense! The boy was upset and a night's sleep was all the therapy he needed.

But the next morning when she arose, her son was not in the house. The mekkano could not speak but it could answer questions with gestures of its appendages equivalent to a yes or no, and it did not take Mrs. Hanshaw more than half a minute to ascertain that the boy had arisen thirty minutes earlier than usual, skimped his shower, and darted out of the house.

But not by way of the Door.

Out the other way—through the door. Small "d."

Mrs. Hanshaw's visiphone signaled genteelly at 3:10 P.M. that day. Mrs.

Hanshaw guessed the caller and having activated the receiver, saw that she had guessed correctly. A quick glance in the mirror to see that she was properly calm after a day of abstracted concern and worry and then she keyed in her own transmission.

"Yes, Miss Robbins," she said coldly.

Richard's teacher was a bit breathless. She said, "Mrs. Hanshaw, Richard has deliberately left through the fire door although I told him to use the regular Door. I do not know where he went."

Mrs. Hanshaw said, carefully, "He left to come home."

Miss Robbins looked dismayed, "Do you approve of this?"

Pale-faced, Mrs. Hanshaw set about putting the teacher in her place. "I don't think it is up to you to criticize. If my son does not choose to use the Door, it is his affair and mine. I don't think there is any school ruling that would force him to use the Door, is there?" Her bearing quite plainly intimated that if there were she would see to it that it was changed.

Miss Robbins flushed and had time for one quick remark before contact was broken. She said, "I'd have him probed. I really would."

Mrs. Hanshaw remained standing before the quartzinium plate, staring blindly at its blank face. Her sense of family placed her for a few moments quite firmly on Richard's side. Why *did* he have to use the Door if he chose not to? And then she settled down to wait and pride battled the gnawing anxiety that something after all was wrong with Richard.

He came home with a look of defiance on his face, but his mother, with a strenuous effort at self-control, met him as though nothing were out of the ordinary.

For weeks, she followed that policy. It's nothing, she told herself. It's a vagary. He'll grow out of it.

It grew into an almost normal state of affairs. Then, too, every once in a while, perhaps three days in a row, she would come to breakfast to find Richard waiting sullenly at the Door, then using it when school time came. She always refrained from commenting on the matter.

Always, when he did that, and especially when he followed it up by arriving home via the Door, her heart grew warm and she thought, "Well, its over." But always with the passing of one day, two or three, he would return like an addict to his drug and drift silently out by the door—small "d"—before she woke.

And each time she thought despairingly of psychiatrists and probes, and each time the vision of Miss Robbins' low-bred satisfaction at (possibly) learning of it, stopped her, although she was scarcely aware that that was the true motive.

Meanwhile, she lived with it and made the best of it. The mekkano was instructed to wait at the door—small "d"—with a Tergo kit and a change of clothing. Richard washed and changed without resistance. His underthings, socks and flexies were disposable in any case, and Mrs. Hanshaw bore uncomplainingly the expense of daily disposal of shirts.

Trousers she finally allowed to go a week before disposal on condition of rigorous nightly cleansing.

One day she suggested that Richard accompany her on a trip to New York. It was more a vague desire to keep him in sight than part of any purposeful plan. He did not object. He was even happy. He stepped right through the Door, unconcerned. He didn't hesitate. He even lacked the look of resentment he wore on those mornings he used the Door to go to school.

Mrs. Hanshaw rejoiced. This could be a way of weaning him back into Door usage, and she racked her ingenuity for excuses to make trips with Richard. She even raised her power bill to quite unheard-of-heights by suggesting, and going through with, a trip to Canton for the day in order to witness a Chinese festival.

That was on a Sunday, and the next morning Richard marched directly to the hole in the wall he always used. Mrs. Hanshaw, having wakened particularly early, witnessed that. For once, badgered past endurance, she called after him plaintively, "Why not the Door, Dickie?"

He said, briefly, "It's all right for Canton," and stepped out of the house.

So that plan ended in failure. And then, one day, Richard came home soaking wet. The mekkano hovered about him uncertainly and Mrs. Hanshaw, just returned from a four-hour visit with her sister in Iowa, cried, "Richard Hanshaw!"

He said, hangdog fashion, "It started raining. All of a sudden, it started raining."

For a moment, the word didn't register with her. Her own school days and her studies of geography were twenty years in the past. And then she remembered and caught the vision of water pouring recklessly and endlessly down from the sky—a mad cascade of water with no tap to turn off, no button to push, no contact to break.

She said, "And you stayed out in it?"

He said, "Well, gee, Mom, I came home fast as I could. I didn't know it was going to rain."

Mrs. Hanshaw had nothing to say. She was appalled and the sensation filled her too full for words to find a place.

Two days later, Richard found himself with a running nose, and a dry, scratchy throat. Mrs. Hanshaw had to admit that the virus of disease had found a lodging in her house, as though it were a miserable hovel of the Iron Age.

It was over that that her stubbornness and pride broke and she admitted to herself that, after all, Richard had to have psychiatric help.

Mrs. Hanshaw chose a psychiatrist with care. Her first impulse was to find one at a distance. For a while, she considered stepping directly into the San Francisco Medical Center and choosing one at random.

And then it occurred to her that by doing that she would become merely an anonymous consultant. She would have no way of obtaining any greater consideration for herself than would be forthcoming to any public-Door user of the city slums. Now if she remained in her own community, her word would carry weight——

She consulted the district map. It was one of that excellent series prepared by Doors, Inc., and distributed free of charge to their clients. Mrs. Hanshaw couldn't quite suppress that little thrill of civic pride as she unfolded the map. It wasn't a fine-print directory of Door coordinates only. It was an actual map, with each house carefully located.

And why not? District A-3 was a name of moment in the world, a badge of aristocracy. It was the first community on the planet to have been established on a completely Doored basis. The first, the largest, the wealthiest, the best-known. It needed no factories, no stores. It didn't even need roads. Each house was a little secluded castle, the Door of which had entry anywhere the world over where other Doors existed.

Carefully, she followed down the keyed listing of the five thousand families of District A-3. She knew it included several psychiatrists. The learned professions were well represented in A-3.

Doctor Hamilton Sloane was the second name she arrived at and her finger lingered upon the map. His office was scarcely two miles from the Hanshaw residence. She liked his name. The fact that he lived in A-3 was evidence of worth. And he was a neighbor, practically a neighbor. He would understand that it was a matter of urgency—and confidential.

Firmly, she put in a call to his office to make an appointment.

Doctor Hamilton Sloane was a comparatively young man, not quite forty. He was of good family and he had indeed heard of Mrs. Hanshaw.

He listened to her quietly and then said, "And this all began with the Door breakdown."

"That's right, Doctor."

"Does he show any fear of the Doors?"

"Of course not. What an idea!" She was plainly startled.

"It's possible, Mrs. Hanshaw, it's possible. After all, when you stop to think of how a Door works it is rather a frightening thing, really. You step into a Door, and for an instant your atoms are converted into field-energies, transmitted to another part of space and reconverted into matter. For that instant you're not alive."

"I'm sure no one thinks of such things."

"But your son may. He witnessed the breakdown of the Door. He may be saying to himself, 'What if the Door breaks down just as I'm halfway through?' "

"But that's nonsense. He still uses the Door. He's even been to Canton with me; Canton, China. And as I told you, he uses it for school about once or twice a week."

"Freely? Cheerfully?"

"Well," said Mrs. Hanshaw, reluctantly, "he does seem a bit put out by it. But really, Doctor, there isn't much use talking about it, is there?

If you would do a quick probe, see where the trouble was," and she finished on a bright note, "why, that would be all. I'm sure it's quite a minor thing."

Dr. Sloane sighed. He detested the word "probe" and there was scarcely any word he heard oftener.

"Mrs. Hanshaw," he said patiently, "there is no such thing as a quick probe. Now I know the mag-strips are full of it and it's a rage in some circles, but it's much overrated."

"Are you serious?"

"Quite. The probe is very complicated and the theory is that it traces mental circuits. You see, the cells of the brains are interconnected in a large variety of ways. Some of those interconnected paths are more used than others. They represent habits of thought, both conscious and unconscious. Theory has it that these paths in any given brain can be used to diagnose mental ills early and with certainty."

"Well, then?"

"But subjection to the probe is quite a fearful thing, especially to a child. It's a traumatic experience. It takes over an hour. And even then, the results must be sent to the Central Psychoanalytical Bureau for analysis, and that could take weeks. And on top of all that, Mrs. Hanshaw, there are many psychiatrists who think the theory of probe-analysis to be most uncertain."

Mrs. Hanshaw compressed her lips. "You mean nothing can be done."

Dr. Sloane smiled. "Not at all. There were psychiatrists for centuries before there were probes. I suggest that you let me talk to the boy."

"Talk to him? Is that all?"

"I'll come to you for background information when necessary, but the essential thing, I think, is to talk to the boy."

"Really, Dr. Sloane, I doubt if he'll discuss the matter with you. He won't talk to me about it and I'm his mother."

"That often happens," the psychiatrist assured her. "A child will sometimes talk more readily to a stranger. In any case, I cannot take the case otherwise."

Mrs. Hanshaw rose, not at all pleased. "When can you come, Doctor?"

"What about this coming Saturday? The boy won't be in school. Will you be busy?"

"We will be ready."

She made a dignified exit. Dr. Sloane accompanied her through the small reception room to his office Door and waited while she punched the coordinates of her house. He watched her pass through. She became a half-woman, a quarter-woman, an isolated elbow and foot, a nothing.

It *was* frightening.

Did a Door ever break down during passage, leaving half a body here and half there? He had never heard of such a case, but he imagined it could happen.

He returned to his desk and looked up the time of his next appointment. It was obvious to him that Mrs. Hanshaw was annoyed and disappointed at not having arranged for a psychic probe treatment.

Why, for God's sake? Why should a thing like the probe, an obvious piece of quackery in his own opinion, get such a hold on the general public? It must be part of this general trend toward machines. Anything man can do, machines can do better. Machines! More machines! Machines for anything and everything! O tempora! O mores!

Oh, hell!

His resentment of the probe was beginning to bother him. Was it a fear of technological unemployment, a basic insecurity on his part, a mechanophobia, if that was the word—

He made a mental note to discuss this with his own analyst.

Dr. Sloane had to feel his way. The boy wasn't a patient who had come to him, more or less anxious to talk, more or less anxious to be helped.

Under the circumstances it would have been best to keep his first meeting with Richard short and noncommittal. It would have been sufficient merely to establish himself as something less than a total stranger. The next time he would be someone Richard had seen before. The time after he would be an acquaintance, and after that a friend of the family.

Unfortunately, Mrs. Hanshaw was not likely to accept a long-drawn-out process. She would go searching for a probe and, of course, she would find it.

And harm the boy. He was certain of that.

It was for that reason he felt he must sacrifice a little of the proper caution and risk a small crisis.

An uncomfortable ten minutes had passed when he decided he must try. Mrs. Hanshaw was smiling in a rather rigid way, eyeing him narrowly, as though she expected verbal magic from him. Richard wriggled in his seat, unresponsive to Dr. Sloane's tentative comments, overcome with boredom and unable not to show it.

Dr. Sloane said, with casual suddenness, "Would you like to take a walk with me, Richard?"

The boy's eyes widened and he stopped wriggling. He looked directly at Dr. Sloane. "A walk, sir?"

"I mean, outside."

"Do you go—outside?"

"Sometimes. When I feel like it."

Richard was on his feet, holding down a squirming eagerness. "I didn't think anyone did."

"I do. And I like company."

The boy sat down, uncertainly. "Mom—?"

Mrs. Hanshaw had stiffened in her seat, her compressed lips radiating horror, but she managed to say, "Why certainly, Dickie. But watch yourself."

And she managed a quick and baleful glare at Dr. Sloane.

In one respect, Dr. Sloane had lied. He did *not* go outside "sometimes." He hadn't been in the open since early college days. True, he had been athletically inclined (still was to some extent) but in his time the indoor ultraviolet chambers, swimming pools and tennis courts had flourished. For those with the price, they were much more satisfactory than the outdoor equivalents, open to the elements as they were, could possibly be. There was no occasion to go outside.

So there was a crawling sensation about his skin when he felt wind touch it, and he put down his flexied shoes on bare grass with a gingerly movement.

"Hey, look at that." Richard was quite different now, laughing, his reserve broken down.

Dr. Sloane had time only to catch a flash of blue that ended in a tree. Leaves rustled and he lost it.

"What was it?"

"A bird," said Richard. "A blue kind of bird."

Dr. Sloane looked about him in amazement. The Hanshaw residence was on a rise of ground, and he could see for miles. The area was only lightly wooded and between clumps of trees, grass gleamed brightly in the sunlight.

Colors set in deeper green made red and yellow patterns. They were flowers. From the books he had viewed in the course of his lifetime and from the old video shows, he had learned enough so that all this had an eerie sort of familiarity.

And yet the grass was so trim, the flowers so patterned. Dimly, he realized he had been expecting something wilder. He said, "Who takes care of all this?"

Richard shrugged. "I dunno. Maybe the mekkanos do it."

"Mekkanos?"

"There's loads of them around. Sometimes they got a sort of atomic knife they hold near the ground. It cuts the grass. And they're always fooling around with the flowers and things. There's one of them over there."

It was a small object, half a mile away. Its metal skin cast back highlights as it moved slowly over the gleaming meadow, engaged in some sort of activity that Dr. Sloane could not identify.

Dr. Sloane was astonished. Here it was a perverse sort of estheticism, a kind of conspicuous consumption—

"What's that?" he asked suddenly.

Richard looked. He said, "That's a house. Belongs to the Froehlichs. Coordinates, A-3, 23, 461. That little pointy building over there is the public Door."

Dr. Sloane was staring at the house. Was that what it looked like from the outside? Somehow he had imagined something much more cubic, and taller.

"Come along," shouted Richard, running ahead.

Dr. Sloane followed more sedately. "Do you know all the houses about here?"

"Just about."

170

"Where is A-23, 26, 475?" It was his own house, of course.

Richard looked about. "Let's see. Oh, sure, I know where it is—you see that water there?"

"Water?" Dr. Sloane made out a line of silver curving across the green.

"Sure. Real water. Just sort of running over rocks and things. It keeps running all the time. You can get across it if you step on the rocks. It's called a river."

More like a creek, thought Dr. Sloane. He had studied geography, of course, but what passed for the subject these days was really economic and cultural geography. Physical geography was almost an extinct science except among specialists. Still, he knew what rivers and creeks were, in a theoretical sort of way.

Richard was still talking. "Well, just past the river, over that hill with the big clump of trees and down the other side a way is A-23, 26, 475. It's a light green house with a white roof."

"It is?" Dr. Sloane was genuinely astonished. He hadn't known it was green.

Some small animal disturbed the grass in its anxiety to avoid the oncoming feet. Richard looked after it and shrugged. "You can't catch them. I tried."

A butterfly flitted past, a wavering bit of yellow. Dr. Sloane's eyes followed it.

There was a low hum that lay over the fields, interspersed with an occasional harsh, calling sound, a rattle, a twittering, a chatter that rose, then fell. As his ear accustomed itself to listening, Dr. Sloane heard a thousand sounds, and none were man-made.

A shadow fell upon the scene, advancing toward him, covering him. It was suddenly cooler and he looked upward, startled.

Richard said, "It's just a cloud. It'll go away in a minute—look at these flowers. They're the kind that smell."

They were several hundred yards from the Hanshaw residence. The cloud passed and the sun shone once more. Dr. Sloane looked back and was appalled at the distance they had covered. If they moved out of sight of the house and if Richard ran off, would he be able to find his way back?

He pushed the thought away impatiently and looked out toward the line of water (nearer now) and past it to where his own house must be. He thought wonderingly: Light green?

He said, "You must be quite an explorer."

Richard said, with a shy pride, "When I go to school and come back, I always try to use a different route and see new things."

"But you don't go outside every morning, do you? Sometimes you use the Doors, I imagine."

"Oh, sure."

"Why is that, Richard?" Somehow, Dr. Sloane felt there might be significance in that point.

But Richard quashed him. With his eyebrows up and a look of astonishment on his face, he said, "Well, gosh, some mornings it rains and I *have* to use the Door. I hate that, but what can you do? About two weeks ago,

I got caught in the rain and I—" he looked about him automatically, and his voice sank to a whisper "—caught a cold, and wasn't Mom upset, though."

Dr. Sloane sighed. "Shall we go back now?"

There was a quick disappointment on Richard's face. "Aw, what for?"

"You remind me that your mother must be waiting for us."

"I guess so." The boy turned reluctantly.

They walked slowly back. Richard was saying, chattily, "I wrote a composition at school once about how if I could go on some ancient vehicle" (he pronounced it with exaggerated care) "I'd go in a stratoliner and look at stars and clouds and things. Oh, boy, I was sure nuts."

"You'd pick something else now?"

"You bet, I'd go in an aut'm'bile, real slow. Then I'd see everything there was."

Mrs. Hanshaw seemed troubled, uncertain. "You don't think it's abnormal, then, Doctor?"

"Unusual, perhaps, but not abnormal. He likes the outside."

"But how can he? It's so dirty, so unpleasant."

"That's a matter of individual taste. A hundred years ago our ancestors were all outside most of the time. Even today, I dare say there are a million Africans who have never seen a Door."

"But Richard's always been taught to behave himself the way a decent person in District A-3 is supposed to behave," said Mrs. Hanshaw, fiercely. "Not like an African or—or an ancestor."

"That may be part of the trouble, Mrs. Hanshaw. He feels this urge to go outside and yet he feels it to be wrong. He's ashamed to talk about it to you or to his teacher. It forces him into sullen retreat and it could eventually be dangerous."

"Then how can we persuade him to stop?"

Dr. Sloane said, "Don't try. Channel the activity instead. The day your Door broke down, he was forced outside, found he liked it, and that set a pattern. He used the trip to school and back as an excuse to repeat that first exciting experience. Now suppose you agree to let him out of the house for two hours on Saturdays and Sundays. Suppose he gets it through his head that after all he can go outside without necessarily having to go anywhere in the process. Don't you think he'll be willing to use the Door to go to school and back thereafter? And don't you think that will stop the trouble he's now having with his teacher and probably with his fellow-pupils?"

"But then will matters remain so? Must they? Won't he ever be normal again?"

Dr. Sloane rose to his feet. "Mrs. Hanshaw, he's as normal as need be right now. Right now, he's tasting the joys of the forbidden. If you cooperate with him, show that you don't disapprove, it will lose some of its attraction right there. Then, as he grows older, he will become more aware of the expectations and demands of society. He will learn to

172

conform. After all, there is a little of the rebel in all of us, but it generally dies down as we grow old and tired. Unless, that is, it is unreasonably suppressed and allowed to build up pressure. Don't do that. Richard will be all right."

He walked to the Door.

Mrs. Hanshaw said, "And you don't think a probe will be necessary, Doctor?"

He turned and said vehemently, "No, definitely not! There is nothing about the boy that requires it. Understand? Nothing."

His fingers hesitated an inch from the combination board and the expression on his face grew lowering.

"What's the matter, Dr. Sloane?" asked Mrs. Hanshaw.

But he didn't hear her because he was thinking of the Door and the psychic probe and all the rising, choking tide of machinery. There is a little of the rebel in all of us, he thought.

So he said in a soft voice, as his hand fell away from the board and his feet turned away from the Door, "You know, it's such a beautiful day that I think I'll walk."

PROBINGS

1. Would you like a "mekkano" for your own that would help you regulate your life? Why? Why not? Consider how you would use such a machine?
2. Consider how we are already mechanized. How many clocks does your family own? How many "labor-saving" devices do you own: electric toothbrush? Electric knife? Can opener? Power mower? Why do you need so many of these devices?
3. What is the purpose of "The Door"? How would you react to "The Door"? Do you see advantages of the "Door"? Where would you like to travel, if you could go via "The Door"?
4. What makes Richard such a different boy? Would you try to change him? Why? Why not?
5. Think of people that you know who are similar to Richard; those people who are considered "weird," "different," or "strange." What sets them apart? How do you and your friends react to "them"?
6. It's easy to admire and to identify with characters such as Richard or Luke in the film *Cool Hand Luke,* but would you really want a nonconformist as a brother, friend, father or mother, husband or wife? Why or why not?

7. Role play the following situation (which is, incidentally, based on real life). A neighbor of yours is a bit "weird" and decides to paint his house like a gigantic American flag. Your fellow neighbors are very upset with the man. Role play the confrontation between the "weird" neighbor and the other neighbors. What arguments would probably be used to force him to change his mind? What pressures might be brought to bear?

8. "Your dress, hair style, and lifestyle are your own business, and *nobody* has any right to insist that you change them." Do you agree with this statement? Under what conditions might you change your opinion?

9. A famous artist, Vincent van Gogh, decided in a fit of depression or madness to chop off his ear. Does an individual have the right to do anything that he/she wishes to his/her own body? Who should determine the limits in this area?

10. Develop a future wheel around the idea that everybody is totally different—we look, act, and think differently in order to express our individuality.

CONSCIENCE

11

In literature we have been fascinated by the lives of those who in time of great moral crises followed the will of their consciences rather than submit to the smothering pressure of the group or the state. In the Greek play *Antigone*, a young woman insists on paying respect to her warrior brother who has been killed. In order to bury her brother, she must defy the King who had decreed the brother is not to receive a proper burial. To Antigone, there was only one clear voice to be heard and that was her conscience telling her to do what she felt was right.

Plato recounted how Socrates also faced a moral dilemma, which eventually cost him his life. Socrates was asked to renounce a lifetime of teaching and ideas because the elders feared Socrates was corrupting the youth of Athens. He could not meet the elders' demands. He was then given an option to leave Athens; this, too, would have been a cowardly thing for him to do—so he drank the cup of poison hemlock. To some people, Socrates did a very brave thing; others feel that he was foolish because he lost his life. In countless other plays, films, and stories, tragic characters are torn between a troubled conscience and the overwhelming pressure to conform.

In real life there have also been numerous people who made courageous moral decisions that put their lives, careers, and reputations in jeopardy. John F. Kennedy wrote accounts of these decisions that he called "profiles in courage." One such "profile in courage" was lived by John Peter Altgeld, governor of the State of Illinois, who pardoned three anarchists accused of inciting the famous Haymarket riot in Chicago. The evidence against the anarchists was contrived, but popular feeling ran against them at the time. Since this was an unpopular decision, Altgeld knowingly suffered dearly for his decision: the end of his political career. Why did he make the decision? He thought it was the only right course.

Dr. Martin Luther King, Jr., was the subject of another "profile in courage" when he stood alone and advocated nonviolent protest against laws that discriminated against black people. Even though those laws were in force, Dr. King and others felt that they were "bad" laws because they degraded an entire race. Dr. King recognized that when we decide to disobey laws, we must suffer the consequences, and he did go to jail on a number of occasions.

We need not dwell, however, just on the "profiles in courage" of the famous. The anonymous Americans who helped to run the underground railroad before and during the Civil War were certainly defying the law and following what they thought was "the right" path. Many who marched with Dr. King were in the same category, as were the demonstrators who protested the war in Viet Nam. Nobody claims that people can just pick and choose what laws they will obey, because if we all did this, we would soon live in a jungle where the person with the biggest club would dominate. However, there are those times when some individuals have had the moral courage to stand up against the state.

In Avram Davidson's "Now Let Us Sleep," one very unusual man decides to commit a very unusual act because he knows it is the only right thing to do.

1. Headlines from Tomorrow:

INTERGALACTIC WAR ERUPTS OVER SPACE RIGHTS

For the first time since the end of conventional wars in the 20th century, new draft laws have been established. Anyone between the ages of 5 and 60 is eligible for the draft. These draft laws will go into effect as of 12:00 PM tonight, as a

PROJECTIONS

result of the outbreak of the latest intergalactic war. In anticipation of these laws, thousands of eligible Earth people have defected to Galaxy Z with the help of the Universal Pacifists Organization.

Anyone with information about UPO activities should report it to the nearest Galactic Headquarters.

You have discovered that your best friend is an active member of the UPO. What would you do? Why?

NOW LET US SLEEP

—Avram Davidson

A pink-skinned young cadet ran past Harper, laughing and shouting and firing his stungun. The wind veered about, throwing the thick scent of the Yahoos into the faces of the men, who whooped loudly to show their revulsion.

"I got three!" the chicken cadet yelped at Harper. "Did you see me pop those two together? Boy, what a stink they have!"

Harper looked at the sweating kid, muttered, "You don't smell so sweet yourself," but the cadet didn't wait to hear. All the men were running now, running in a ragged semicircle with the intention of driving the Yahoos before them, to hold them at bay at the foot of the gaunt cliff a quarter-mile off.

The Yahoos loped awkwardly over the rough terrain, moaning and grunting grotesquely, their naked bodies bent low. A few hundred feet ahead one of them stumbled and fell, his arms and legs flying out as he hit the ground, twitched, and lay still.

A bald-headed passenger laughed triumphantly, paused to kick the Yahoo, and trotted on. Harper kneeled beside the fallen Primitive, felt for a pulse in the hairy wrist. It seemed slow and feeble, but then, no one actually knew what the normal pulse-beat should be. And—except for Harper—no one seemed to give a damn.

Maybe it was because he was the grandson of Barret Harper, the great naturalist—back on Earth, of course. It seemed as if man could be fond of nature only on the planet of man's origin, whose ways he knew so well. Elsewhere, it was too strange and alien—you subdued it, or you adjusted to it, or you were perhaps even content with it. But you almost never *cared* about the flora or fauna of the new planets. No one had the feeling for living things that an earth-born had.

The men were shouting more loudly now, but Harper didn't lift his head to see why. He put his hand to the shaggy grey chest. The heart was still beating, but very slowly and irregularly. Someone stood beside him.

"He'll come out of it in an hour or so," the voice of the purser said. "Come on—you'll miss all the fun—you should see how they act when they're cornered! They kick out and throw sand and—" he laughed at the thought—"they weep great big tears, and go, *'Oof! Oof!'* "

Harper said, "An ordinary man *would* come out of it in an hour or so. But I think their metabolism is different . . . Look at all the bones lying around."

The purser spat. "Well, don't that prove they're not human, when they won't even bury their dead? . . .*Oh*, oh!—look at that!" He swore.

Harper got to his feet. Cries of dismay and disappointment went up from the men.

"What's wrong?" Harper asked.

The purser pointed. The men had stopped running, were gathering together and gesturing. "Who's the damn fool who planned this drive?" the purser asked, angrily. "He picked the wrong cliff! The damned Yahoos *nest* in that one! Look at them climb, will you—" He took aim, fired the stungun. A figure scrabbling up the side of the rock threw up its arms and fell, bounding from rock to rock until it hit the ground. "*That* one will never come out of it!" the purser said, with satisfaction.

But this was the last casualty. The other Yahoos made their way to safety in the caves and crevices. No one followed them. In those narrow, stinking confines a Yahoo was as good as a man, there was no room to aim a stungun, and the Yahoos had rocks and clubs and their own sharp teeth. The men began straggling back.

"This one a she?" The purser pushed at the body with his foot, let it fall back with an annoyed grunt as soon as he determined its sex. "There'll be Hell to pay in the hold if there's more than two convicts to a she." He shook his head and swore.

Two lighters came skimming down from the big ship to load up.

"Coming back to the launch?" the purser asked. He had a red shiny face. Harper had always thought him a rather decent fellow—before. The purser had no way of knowing what was in Harper's mind; he smiled at him and said, "We might as well get on back, the fun's over now."

Harper came to a sudden decision. "What're the chances of my taking a souvenir back with me? This big fellow, here, for example?"

The purser seemed doubtful. "Well, I dunno, Mr. Harper. We're only supposed to take females aboard, and unload *them* as soon as the convicts are finished with their fun." He leered. Harper, suppressing a strong urge to hit him right in the middle of his apple-red face, put his hand in his pocket. The purser understood, looked away as Harper slipped a bill into the breast pocket of his uniform.

"I guess it can be arranged. See, the Commissioner-General on Selopé III wants one for his private zoo. Tell you what: We'll take one for him and one for you—I'll tell the supercargo it's a spare. But if one croaks, the C-G has to get the other. Okay?"

At Harper's nod the purser took a tag out of his pocket, tied it around the Yahoo's wrist, waved his cap to the lighter as it came near. "Although why anybody'd *want* one of these beats me," he said, cheerfully. "They're dirtier than animals. I mean, a pig or a horse'll use the same corner of the enclosure, but these things'll dirty anywhere. Still, if you *want* one—" He shrugged.

As soon as the lighter had picked up the limp form (the pulse was still fluttering feebly) Harper and the purser went back to the passenger launch. As they made a swift ascent to the big ship the purser gestured to the two lighters. "That's going to be a mighty slow trip *those* two craft will make back up," he remarked.

Harper innocently asked why. The purser chuckled. The coxswain laughed.

"The freight-crewmen want to make their points before the convicts. *That's* why."

The chicken cadet, his face flushed a deeper pink than usual, tried to sound knowing. "How about that, purser? Is it pretty good stuff?"

The other passengers wiped their perspiring faces, leaned forward eagerly. The purser said. "Well, rank has its privileges, but that's one I figure I can do without."

His listeners guffawed, but more than one looked down towards the lighters and then avoided other eyes when he looked back again.

Barnum's Planet (named, as was the custom then, after the skipper who'd first sighted it) was a total waste, economically speaking. It was almost all water and the water supported only a few repulsive-looking species of no discernible value. The only sizable piece of land—known, inevitably, as Barnumland, since no one else coveted the honor—was gaunt and bleak, devoid alike of useful minerals or arable soil. Its ecology seemed dependent on a sort of fly: A creature rather like a lizard ate the flies and the Yahoos ate the lizards. If something died at sea and washed ashore, the Yahoos ate that, too. What the flies ate no one knew, but their larvae ate the Yahoos, dead.

They were small, hairy, stunted creatures whose speech—if speech it was—seemed confined to moans and clicks and grunts. They wore no clothing, made no artifacts, did not know the use of fire. Taken away captive, they soon languished and died. Of all the Primitives discovered by man, they were the most primitive. They might have been left alone on their useless planet to kill lizards with tree branches forever—except for one thing.

Barnum's Planet lay equidistant between Coulter's System and the Selopés, and it was a long, long voyage either way. Passengers grew restless, crews grew mutinous, convicts rebellious. Gradually the practice developed of stopping on Barnum's Planet "to let off steam"—archaic expression, but although the nature of the machinery man used had changed since it was coined, man's nature hadn't.

And, of course, no one *owned* Barnum's Planet, so no one cared what happened there.

Which was just too bad for the Yahoos.

It took some time for Harper to settle the paperwork concerning his "souvenir," but finally he was given a baggage check for "One Yahoo, male, live," and hurried down to the freight deck. He hoped it would be still alive.

Pandemonium met his ears as he stepped out of the elevator. A rhythmical chanting shout came from the convict hold. "Hear that?" one of the duty officers asked him, taking the cargo chit. Harper asked what the men were yelling. "I wouldn't care to use the words," the officer said. He was a paunchy, gray-haired man, one who probably loved to tell his grandchildren about his "adventures." This was one he wouldn't tell them.

"I don't like this part of the detail," the officer went on. "Never did, never will. Those creatures *seem human* to me—stupid as they are. And if they're *not* human," he asked, "then how can we sink low enough to bring their females up for the convicts?"

The lighters grated on the landing. The noise must have penetrated to the convict hold, because all semblance of words vanished from the shouting. It became a mad cry, louder and louder.

"Here's your pet," the gray-haired officer said. "Still out, I see . . . I'll let you have a baggage-carrier. Just give it to a steward when you're done with it." He had to raise his voice to be heard over the frenzied howling from the hold.

The Ship's Surgeon was out having tea at the Captain's Table. The duty medical officer was annoyed. "What, another one? We're not veterinarians, you know . . . Well, wheel him in. My intern is working on the other one . . . *whew!*" He held his nose and hastily left.

The intern, a pale young man with close-cropped dark hair, looked up from the pressure-spray he had just used to give an injection to the specimen Yahoo selected for the Commissioner-General of Selopé III. He smiled faintly.

"Junior will have company, I see . . . Any others?"

Harper shook his head. The intern went on, "This should be interesting. The young one seems to be in shock. I gave him two cc's of anthidar sulfate, and I see I'd better do the same for yours. Then . . . Well, I guess there's still nothing like serum albumen, is there? But you'd better help me strap them down. If they come to, there's a cell back aft we can put them in, until I can get some cages rigged up." He shot the stimulant into the flaccid arm of Harper's Yahoo.

"Whoever named these beasties knew his Swift," the young medico said. "You ever read that old book, *Gulliver's Travels?*"

Harper nodded.

"Old Swift went mad, didn't he? He hated humanity, they all seemed like Yahoos to him . . . In a way I don't blame him. I think that's why everybody despises these Primitives: they seem like caricatures of ourselves. Personally, I look forward to finding out a lot about them, their metabolism and so on . . . What's *your* interest?"

He asked the question casually, but shot a keen look as he did so. Harper shrugged. "I hardly know, exactly. It's not a scientific one, because I'm a businessman." He hesitated. "You ever hear or read about the Tasmanians?"

The intern shook his head. He thrust a needle into a vein in the younger Yahoo's arm, prepared to let the serum flow in. "If they lived on Earth,

I wouldn't know. Never was there. I'm a third generation Coulterboy, myself."

Harper said, "Tasmania is an island south of Australia. The natives were the most primitive people known on Earth. They were almost all wiped out by the settlers, but one of them succeeded in moving the survivors to a smaller island. And then a curious thing happened."

Looking up from the older Primitive, the intern asked what that was.

"The Tasmanians—the few that were left—decided that they'd had it. They refused to breed. And in a few more years they were all dead . . . I read about them when I was just a kid. Somehow, it moved me very much. Things like that *did*—the dodo, the great auk, the quagga, the Tasmanians. I've never been able to get it out of my mind. When I began hearing about the Yahoos, it seemed to me that they were like the old Tasmanians. Only there are no settlers on Barnumland."

The intern nodded. "But that won't help our hairy friends here a hell of a lot. Of course no one knows how many of them there are—or ever were. But I've been comparing the figures in the log as to how many females are caught and taken aboard." He looked directly at Harper. "And on every trip there are less by far."

Harper bowed his head. He nodded. The intern's voice went on: "The thing is, Barnum's Planet is no one's responsibility. If the Yahoos could be used for labor, they'd be exploited according to a careful system. But as it is, no one cares. If half of them die from being stungunned, no one cares. If the lighter crews don't bother to actually land the females—if any of the wretched creatures are still *alive* when the convicts are done—but just dump them out from twenty feet up, why, again: no one cares. Mr. Harper?"

Their eyes met. Harper said, "Yes?"

"Don't misunderstand me . . . I've got a career here. I'm not jeopardizing it to save the poor Yahoos—but if *you* are interested—if you think you've got any influence—and if you want to try to do anything—" He paused. "Why, now is the the time to start. Because after another few stop-overs there aren't going to *be* any Yahoos. No more than there are any Tasmanians."

Selopé III was called "The Autumn Planet" by the poets. At least, the P.R. picture-tapes always referred to it as "Selopé III, The Autumn Planet of the poets," but no one knew who the poets were. It was true that the Commission Territory, at least, did have the climate of an almost-perpetual early New England November. Barnumland had been dry and warm. The Commissioner-General put the two Yahoos in a heated cage as large as the room Harper occupied at his company's Bachelor Executive Quarters.

"Here, boy," the C-G said, holding out a piece of fruit. He made a chirping noise. The two Yahoos huddled together in a far corner.

"They don't seem very bright," he said, sadly. "All my *other* animals eat out of my hand." He was very proud of his private zoo, the only one in the Territory. On Sundays he allowed the public to visit it.

Sighing, Harper repeated that the Yahoos were Primitives, not animals. But, seeing the C-G was still doubtful, he changed his tactics. He told the C-G about the great zoos on Earth, where the animals went loose in large enclosures rather than being caged up. The C-G nodded thoughtfully. Harper told him of the English dukes who—generation after ducal generation—preserved the last herd of wild White Cattle in a park on their estate.

The C-G stroked his chin. "Yes, yes," he said. "I see your point," he said. He sighed gustily. "Can't be done," he said.

"But why not, sir?" Harper cried.

It was simple. "No money. Who's to pay? The Exchequer-Commissioner is weeping blood trying to get the Budget through Council. If he adds a penny more— No, young fellow. I'll do what *I* can: I'll feed these two, here. But that's all I can do."

Trying to pull all the strings he could reach, Harper approached the Executive-Fiscal and the Procurator-General, the President-in-Council, the Territorial Advocate, the Chairman of the Board of Travel. But no one could do anything. Barnum's Planet, it was carefully explained to him, remained No Man's Land only because no man presumed to give any orders concerning it. If any government did, this would be a Presumption of Authority. And then every other government would feel obliged to deny that presumption and issue a claim of its own.

There was a peace on now—a rather tense, uneasy one. And it wasn't going to be disturbed for Harper's Yahoos. Human, were they? Perhaps. But who cared? As for Morality, Harper didn't even bother to mention the word. It would have meant as little as Chivalry.

Meanwhile, he was learning something of the Yahoos' language. Slowly and arduously, he gained their confidence. They would shyly take food from him. He persuaded the C-G to knock down a wall and enlarge their quarters. The official was a kindly old man, and he seemed to grow fond of the stooped, shaggy, splay-footed Primitives. And after a while he decided that they were smarter than animals.

"Put some clothes on 'em, Harper," he directed. "If they're people, let 'em start acting like people. They're too big to go around naked."

So, eventually, washed and dressed, Junior and Senior were introduced to Civilization via 3-D, and the program was taped and shown everywhere.

Would you like a cigarette, Junior? Here, let me light it for you. Give Junior a glass of water, Senior. Let's see you take off your slippers, fellows, and put them on again. And now do what I say in you own language . . .

But if Harper thought that might change public opinion, he thought wrong. Seals perform, too, don't they? And so do monkeys. They talk? Parrots talk better. And anyway, who cared to be bothered about animals *or* Primitives? They were okay for fun, but that was all.

And the reports from Barnumland showed fewer and fewer Yahoos each time.

Then one night two drunken crewmen climbed over the fence and went carousing in the C-G's zoo. Before they left, they broke the vapor-light tubes, and in the morning Junior and Senior were found dead from the poisonous fumes.

That was Sunday morning. By Sunday afternoon Harper was drunk, and getting drunker. The men who knocked on his door got no answer. They went in anyway. He was slouched, red-eyed, over the table.

"People," he muttered. "Tell you they were *human!*" he shouted.

"Yes, Mr. Harper, we know that," said a young man, pale, with close-cropped dark hair.

Harper peered at him, boozily. "Know you," he said. "Thir' gen'ration Coulterboy. Go 'way. Spoi' your c'reer. Whaffor. Smelly ol' Yahoo?" The young medico nodded to his companion, who took a small flask from his pocket, opened it. They held it under Harper's nose by main force. He gasped and struggled, but they held on, and in a few minutes he was sober.

"That's rough stuff," he said, coughing and shaking his head. "But—thanks, Dr. Hill. Your ship in? Or are you stopping over?"

The former intern shrugged. "I've left the ships," he said. "I don't have to worry about spoiling my new career. This is my superior, Dr. Anscomb."

Anscomb was also young, and, like most men from Coulter's System, pale. He said, "I understand you can speak the Yahoos' language."

Harper winced. "What good's that now? They're dead, poor little bastards."

Anscomb nodded. "I'm sorry about that, believe me. Those fumes are so quick . . . But there are still a few alive on Barnum's Planet who can be saved. The Joint Board for Research is interested. Are you?"

It had taken Harper fifteen years to work up to a room of this size and quality in Bachelor Executives' Quarters. He looked around it. He picked up the letter which had come yesterday. ". . . neglected your work and become a joke . . . unless you accept a transfer and reduction in grade . . ." He nodded slowly, putting down the letter. "I guess I've already made my choice. What are your plans. . . . ?"

Harper, Hill, and Anscomb sat on a hummock on the north coast of Barnumland, just out of rock-throwing range of the gaunt escarpment of the cliff which rose before them. Behind them a tall fence had been erected. They only Yahoos still alive were "nesting" in caves of the cliff. Harper spoke into the amplifier again. His voice was hoarse as he forced it into the clicks and moans of the Primitives' tongue.

Hill stirred restlessly. "Are you sure that means, *'Here is food. Here is water'*—and not, *'Come down and let us eat you'*? I think I can almost say it myself by now."

Shifting and stretching, Anscomb said, "It's been two days. Unless they've determined to commit race suicide a bit more abruptly than your ancient Tasmanians—" He stopped as Harper's fingers closed tightly on his arm.

There was a movement on the cliff. A shadow. A pebble clattered. Then a wrinkled face peered fearfully over a ledge. Slowly, and with many stops and hesitations, a figure came down the face of the cliff. It was an old she. Her withered and pendulous dugs flapped against her sagging belly as she made the final jump to the ground, and—her back to the wall of rock—faced them.

"Here is food," Harper repeated softly. "Here is water." The old woman sighed. She plodded wearily across the ground, paused, shaking with fear, and then flung herself down at the food and the water.

"The Joint Board for Research has just won the first round," Hill said. Anscomb nodded. He jerked his thumb upward. Hill looked.

Another head appeared at the cliff. Then another. And another. They watched. The crone got up, water dripping from her dewlaps. She turned to the cliff. "Come down," she cried. "Here is food and water. Do not die. Come down and eat and drink." Slowly, her tribes-people did so. There were thirty of them.

Harper asked, "Where are the others?"

The crone held out her dried and leathery breasts to him. "Where are those who have sucked? Where are those your brothers took away?" She uttered a single shrill wail; then was silent.

But she wept—and Harper wept with her.

"I'll guess we'll swing it all right," Hill said. Anscomb nodded. "Pity there's so few of them. I was afraid we'd have to use gas to get at them. Might have lost several that way."

Neither of them wept.

For the first time since ships had come to their world, Yahoos *walked* aboard one. They came hesitantly and fearfully, but Harper had told them that they were going to a new home and they believed him. He told them that they were going to a place of much food and water, where no one would hunt them down. He continued to talk until the ship was on its way, and the last Primitive had fallen asleep under the dimmmed-out vapor tube lights. Then he staggered to his cabin and fell asleep himself. He slept for thirty hours.

He had something to eat when he awoke, then strolled down to the hold where the Primitives were. He grimaced, remembered his trip to the hold of the other ship to collect Senior, and the frenzied howling of the convicts awaiting the females. At the entrance to the hold he met Dr. Hill, greeted him.

"I'm afraid some of the Yahoos are sick," Hill said. "But Dr. Anscomb is treating them. The others have been moved to this compartment here."

Harper stared. "Sick? How can they be sick? What from? And how many?"

Dr. Hill said, "It appears to be Virulent Plague ... Fifteen of them are down with it. You've *had* all six shots, haven't you? Good. Nothing to worry—"

Harper felt the cold steal over him. He stared at the pale young physician. "No one can enter or leave any system or planet without having had all six shots for Virulent Plague," he said, slowly. "So if we are all immune, how could the Primitives have gotten it? And how is it that only fifteen have it? Exactly half of them. What about the other fifteen, Dr. Hill? *Are they the control group for your experiment?*"

Dr. Hill looked at him calmly. "As a matter of fact, yes. I hope you'll be reasonable. Those were the only terms the Joint Board for Research would agree to. After all, not even convicts will volunteer for experiments in Virulent Plague."

Harper nodded. He felt frozen. After a moment he asked, "Can Anscomb do anything to pull them through?"

Dr. Hill raised his eyebrows. "Perhaps. We've got something we wanted to try. And at any rate, the reports should provide additional data on the subject. We must take the long-range view."

Harper nodded. "I suppose you're right," he said.

By noon all fifteen were dead.

"Well, that means an uneven control group," Dr. Anscomb complained. "Seven against eight. Still, that's not *too* bad. And it can't be helped. We'll start tomorrow."

"Virulent Plague again?" Harper asked.

Anscomb and Hill shook their heads. "Dehydration," the latter said. "And after that, there's a new treatment for burns we're anxious to try … It's a shame, when you think of the Yahoos being killed off by the thousands, year after year, *uselessly*. Like the dodo. We came along just in time—thanks to you, Harper."

He gazed at them. *"Quis custodiet ipsos custodes?"* he asked. They looked at him, politely blank. "I'd forgotten. Doctors don't study Latin anymore, do they? An old proverb. It means: 'Who shall guard the guards themselves?' … Will you excuse me, Doctors?"

Harper let himself into the compartment. "I come," he greeted the fifteen.

"We see you," they responded. The old woman asked how their brothers and sisters were "in the other cave."

"They are well … Have you eaten, have you drunk? Yes? Then let us sleep," Harper said.

The old woman seemed doubtful. "Is it time? The light still shines." She pointed to it. Harper looked at her. She had been so afraid. But she had trusted him. Suddenly he bent over and kissed her. She gaped.

"Now the light goes out," Harper said. He slipped off a shoe and shattered the vapor tube. He groped in the dark for the air-switch, turned it off. Then he sat down. He had brought them here, and if they had to die, it was only fitting that he should share their fate. There no longer seemed any place for the helpless, or for those who cared about them.

"Now let us sleep," he said.

PROBINGS

1. Why did Harper kill the remaining "primitives"? Was this an act of murder or an act of mercy? Was Harper "right" in doing what he did?
2. Recently a young man who was paralyzed in a motorcycle accident asked his brother to kill him because, even though his brain was alert, he didn't want to spend the rest of his life paralyzed from the neck down. One evening, the man's brother brought a shotgun to the hospital and killed him. The state charged the brother with murder and put him on trial. Was this a "right" decision? Have your class discuss the merits of the case, acting as a jury. Construct a defense for the surviving brother. Construct a prosecution.
3. While at work, you notice some of your friends are stealing merchandise. Your boss asks if you know anything about the thefts. What would you do? Tell him? Avoid answering? Tell on your friends? Why?
4. While you are babysitting one night, your friends come over and discover beer in the refrigerator. You don't drink but they do. Should you allow them to drink the beer if they want? Tell them they can't drink the beer? Let them drink the beer and then tell your employer?
5. What is the greatest act of conscience that you personally know about? Did you respect that person's decision?
6. Many SF stories and novels have used the theme that a future society will develop in which no one follows their conscience. Write an SF story using this theme.

SECTION 3
WHAT KIND
OF SOCIETY
DO I WANT?

WHAT KIND OF SOCIETY DO I WANT?

The term "society" is a difficult one to define. If asked to clarify it, many of us might say something like "the United States is a society." Certainly we blame "society" for many of our ills and some of our accomplishments. For example, if something goes wrong in our lives, it's often "society's fault."

But what is this thing called society and what kind of an ideal society would you like? These are the questions posed in this third section.

As humans with many different interests and values, as we have seen in sections one and two, we have a tendency to answer the above questions from a very personal perspective. For example, what is the good life and what role should society play in securing this good life? These questions can be answered very personally. To some, the good life means a guaranteed job, to others it is security in the form of an adequate pension and health care, while to still others the good life is simply being happy—whatever that may mean.

As an extension of the good life, we must consider the question of status—how we achieve it, hold it, or lose it. No discussion of an ideal society can leave out this important ingredient, which contributes significantly to the good life.

Our society is much more mechanized and computerized than that of a generation ago, and the society of your grandchildren is going to be even more automated. But so what? Why not develop airplanes that can span oceans and continents in an hour and develop even more sophisticated computers that can store massive amounts of data? These inventions are simply the hallmarks of an advancing society, some people would argue. To others, though, mechanization leads to dehumanization as the machines perhaps become more important than their masters, or as the question of who or what *is* the master is raised.

Many young people in the past ten or fifteen years have reacted very negatively to "technology" and have sought a simpler life. Other young people, however, have seemed to draw sustenance from stereophonic sound and the rumble of cars and motorcycles. Any discussion of an ideal society must raise this question: How much technology is enough?

Nothing is guaranteed to fray more nerves and aggravate more tempers than the issue of equality in a society. When we consider equality, we are really talking about justice— how just is a society? Are people treated alike? This, then, leads us back to an individual's status. Many claim that the higher one's status, the more justice one receives. In this part of the book, there is another intriguing consideration to ponder—What role can technology play in ensuring justice? In Ron Goulart's story, the answer is very simple. Technology can play a very large role.

Another consideration in judging a society is the quality of medical care. Medical science has made some startling breakthroughs that are going to change our society radically. But no area of futuristics has caused more controversy than bio-ethics. For example, consider the idea of immortality. Perhaps we will be able to live for hundreds of years and will be able literally to see our great-great-great grandchildren. Imagine a world in which you would be able to influence generations of your offspring—or would you want to?

THE GOOD LIFE 12

We often hear people speak of "the happy life" or "the good life." One beer jingle insists that "you only go around once in life." As the commercial tempts the viewer with steins of frothy beer, the real message is obvious: Enjoy! Enjoy while you can! But what is this good life that we are to seek? The Greek philosopher Aristotle told us centuries ago that we could never judge whether a life was a good one or not until we had reached the end of it. Then, of course, we could look back and make the judgment on whether or not it was a good life.

Most of us, however, are far too impatient to wait forty or fifty years to judge the good life. To some, the good life is associated with having the newest car or the biggest home, as we saw in section one. To others, a quiet life of serenity and contemplation is the good life. Certainly, we are not going to come up with a magical solution to the question of what is a good life, but you are being asked to think about some important questions: What is the good life for you? What would make you happiest?

In Aldous Huxley's novel *Brave New*

World, everyone is perpetually happy because the government programs all people before birth to be contented. There are few natural births in Huxley's world, and most embryos are developed in artificial wombs. Drop a few chemicals into this embryo and you retard it, making the person happy to be a menial laborer; give other chemicals to another embryo and, presto, you have created a person of high intelligence. Everyone belongs to a caste in *Brave New World:* Alphas, Betas, Gammas, Deltas, Epsilons. The Alphas do the jobs that need high intelligence; the Epsilons do the dirty work. Of course, this has all been decided before birth, so no one is unhappy. For those who do have temporary problems there is always soma, a drug to calm the nerves and keep one on a perpetual high.

In Frederik Pohl's "What to Do Till the Analyst Comes," we are offered an even more interesting kind of high—"cheery gum." Chew a stick of this wonderful gum and all of your problems will disappear.

PROJECTIONS

Headlines from Tomorrow:

HAPPINESS PILL APPROVED—NO SIDE EFFECTS

Design an advertisement or present a television commercial for the Happiness Pill. At whom would you direct the ad? What features would you stress to boost sales?

"WHAT TO DO TILL THE ANALYST COMES"

—Frederik Pohl

I just sent my secretary out for a container of coffee and she brought me back a lemon Coke.

I can't even really blame her. Who in all the world do I have to blame, except myself? Hazel was a good secretary to me for fifteen years, fine at typing, terrific at brushing off people I didn't want to see, and the queen of them all at pumping office gossip out of the ladies' lounge. She's a little fuzzy-brained most of the time now, sure. But after all!

I can say this for myself, I didn't exactly know what I was getting into. No doubt you remember the—. Well, let me start that sentence over again, because naturally there is a certain doubt. Perhaps, let's say, *perhaps* you remember the two doctors and their headline report about cigarettes and lung cancer. It hit us pretty hard at Vanden-Blumer & Silk, because we've been eating off the Mason-Dixon Tobacco account for twenty years. Just figure what our fifteen per cent amounted to on better than ten million dollars net billing a year, and you'll see that for yourself. What happened first was all to the good, because naturally the first thing that the client did was scream and reach for his checkbook and pour another couple million dollars into special promotions to counteract the bad press, but that couldn't last. And we knew it. V.B. & S. is noted in the trade as an advertising agency that takes the long view; we saw at once that if the client was in danger, no temporary spurt of advertising was going to pull him out of it, and it was time for us to climb up on top of the old mountain and take a good long look at the countryside ahead.

The Chief called a special Plans meeting that morning and laid it on the line for us. "There goes the old fire bell, boys," he said, "and it's up to us to put the fire out. I'm listening, so start talking."

Baggott cleared his throat and said glumly, "It may only be the paper, Chief. Maybe if they make them without paper . . ." He's the a.e. for Mason-Dixon, so you couldn't really blame him for taking the client's view.

The Chief twinkled: "If they make them without paper they aren't cigarettes any more, are they? Let's not wander off into side issues, boys. I'm still listening."

None of us wanted to wander off into side issues, so we all looked patronizingly at Baggott for a minute. Finally Ellen Silk held up her hand.

194

"I don't want you to think," she said, "that just because Daddy left me a little stock I'm going to push my way into things, Mr. VandenBlumer, but—well, did you have in mind finding some, uh, angle to play on that would take the public's mind off the report?"

You have to admire the Chief. "Is that your recommendation, my dear?" he inquired fondly, bouncing the ball right back to her.

She said weakly, "*I* don't know. I'm confused."

"Naturally, my dear," he beamed. "So are we all. Let's see if Charley here can straighten us out a little. Eh, Charley?"

He was looking at me. I said at once, "I'm glad you asked me for an opinion, Chief. I've been doing a little thinking, and here's what I've come up with." I ticked off the points on my fingers. "One, tobacco makes you cough. Two, liquor gives you a hangover. Three, reefers and the other stuff—well, let's just say they're against the law." I slapped the three fingers against the palm of my other hand. "So what's left for us, Chief? That's my question. Can we come up with something new, something different, something that, one, is not injurious to the health, two, does not give you a hangover, three, is not habit-forming and therefore against the law?"

Mr. VandenBlumer said approvingly, "That's good thinking, Charley. When you hear that fire bell, you really jump, boy."

Baggott's hand was up. He said, "Let me get this straight, Chief. Is it Charley's idea that we recommend to Mason-Dixon that they go out of the tobacco business and start making something else?"

The old man looked at him blandly for a moment. "Why should it be Mason-Dixon?" he asked softly, and left it at that while we all thought of the very good reasons why it *shouldn't* be Mason-Dixon. After all, loyalty to a client is one thing, but you've got an obligation to your own people too.

The old man let it sink in, then he turned back to me. "Well, Charley?" he asked. "We've heard you pinpoint what we need. Got any specific suggestions?"

They were all looking at me to see if I had anything concrete to offer. Unfortunately, I had.

I just asked Hazel to get me the folder on Leslie Clary Cloud, and she came in with a copy of my memo putting him on the payroll two years back. "That's all there was in the file," she said dreamily, her jaw muscles moving rhythmically. There wasn't any use arguing with her, so I handed her the container of lemon Coke and told her to ditch it and bring me back some *coffee,* C-O-F-F-E-E, coffee. I tried going through the files myself when she was gone, but *that* was a waste of time.

So I'll have to tell you about Leslie Clary Cloud from memory. He came into the office without an appointment and why Hazel ever let him in to see me I'll never know. But she did. He told me right away, "I've been fired, Mr. McGory. Canned. After eleven years with the Wyoming Bureau of Standards as a senior chemist."

"That's too bad, Dr. Cloud," I said, shuffling the papers on my desk. "I'm afraid, though, that our organization doesn't—"

"No, no," he said hastily. "I don't know anything about advertising. Organic chemistry's my field. I have a, well, a suggestion for a process that might interest you. You have the Mason-Dixon Tobacco account, don't you? Well, in my work for my doctorate I—" He drifted off into a fog of long-chain molecules and short-chain molecules and pentose sugars and common garden herbs. It took me a little while, but I listened patiently and I began to see what he was driving at. There was, he was saying, a substance in a common plant which, by cauliflamming the whingdrop and di-tricolating the residual glom, or words something like that, you could convert into another substance which appeared to have many features in common with what is sometimes called hop, snow or joy-dust. In other words, dope.

I stared at him aghast. "Dr. Cloud," I demanded, "do you know what you're suggesting? If we added this stuff to our client's cigarettes we'd be flagrantly violating the law. That's the most unheard-of thing I ever heard of! Besides, we've already looked into this matter, and the cost estimates are—"

"No, no!" he said again. "You don't understand, Mr. McGory. This isn't any of the drugs currently available, it's something new and different."

"Different?"

"Non-habit-forming, for instance."

"Non-habit-forming?"

"Totally. Chemically it is entirely unrelated to any narcotic in the pharmacopeia. Legally—well, I'm no lawyer, but I swear, Mr. McGory, this isn't covered by any regulation. No reason it should be. It doesn't hurt the user, it doesn't form a habit, it's cheap to manufacture, it—"

"Hold it," I said, getting to my feet. "Don't go away—I want to catch the boss before he goes to lunch."

So I caught the boss, and he twinkled thoughtfully at me. No, he didn't want me to discuss it with Mason-Dixon just yet, and yes, it did seem to have some possibilities, and certainly, put this man on the payroll and see if he turns up with something.

So we did; and he did.

Auditing raised the roof when the vouchers began to come through, but I bucked them up to the Chief and he calmed them down. It took a lot of money, though, and it took nearly six months. But then Leslie Clary Cloud called up one morning and said, "Come on down, Mr. McGory. We're in."

The place we'd fixed up for him was on the lower East Side and it reeked of rotten vegetables. I made a mental note to double-check all our added-chlorophyll copy and climbed up the two flights of stairs to Cloud's private room. He was sitting at a lab bench, beaming at a row of test tubes in front of him.

196

"This is it?" I asked, glancing at the test tubes.

"This is it." He smiled dreamily at me and yawned. "Excuse me," he blinked amiably. "I've been sampling the little old product."

I looked him over very carefully. He had been sampling something or other, that was clear enough. But no whiskey breath; no dilated pupils; no shakes; no nothing. He was relaxed and cheerful, and that was all you could say.

"Try a little old bit," he invited, gesturing at the test tubes.

Well, there are times when you have to pay your dues in the club. V.B. & S. had been mighty good to me, and if I had to swallow something unfamiliar to justify the confidence the Chief had in me, why I just had to go ahead and do it. Still, I hesitated for a moment.

"Aw," said Leslie Clary Cloud, "don't be scared. Look, I just had a shot but I'll take another one." He fumbled one of the test tubes out of the rack and, humming to himself, slopped a little of the colorless stuff into a beaker of some other colorless stuff—water, I suppose. He drank it down and smacked his lips. "Tastes awful," he observed cheerfully, "but we'll fix that. Whee!"

I looked him over again, and he looked back at me, giggling. "Too strong," he said happily. "Got it too strong. We'll fix that too." He rattled beakers and test tubes aimlessly while I took a deep breath and nerved myself up to it.

"All right," I said, and took the fresh beaker out of his hand. I swallowed it down almost in one gulp. It tasted terrible, just as he said, tasted like the lower floors had smelled, but that was all I noticed right away. Nothing happened for a moment except that Cloud looked at me thoughtfully and frowned.

"Say," he said, "I guess I should have diluted that." I guess he should have. *Wham.*

But a couple of hours later I was all right again.

Cloud was plenty apologetic. "Still," he said consolingly, standing over me as I lay on the lab bench, "it proves one thing. You had a dose about the equivalent of ten thousand normal shots, and you have to admit it hasn't hurt you."

"I do?" I asked, and looked at the doctor. *He* swung his stethoscope by the earpieces and shrugged.

"Nothing organically wrong with you, Mr. McGory—not that I can find, anyway. Euphoria, yes. Temporarily high pulse, yes. Delirium there for a little while, yes—though it was pretty mild. But I don't think you even have a headache now."

"I don't," I admitted. I swung my feet down and sat up, apprehensively. But no hammers started in my head. I had to confess it: I felt wonderful.

Well, between us we tinkered it into what Cloud decided would be a "normal" dosage—just enough to make you feel good—and he saturated some sort of powder and rolled it into pellets and clamped them in a press and came out with what looked as much like aspirins as anything else. "They'd probably work that way too," he said. "A psychogenic headache would melt away in five minutes with one of those."

"We'll bear that in mind," I said.

What with one thing and another, I couldn't get to the old man that day before he left, and the next day was the weekend and you *don't* disturb the Chief's weekends, and it was Monday evening before I could get him alone for long enough to give him the whole pitch. He was delighted.

"Dear, dear," he twinkled. "So much out of so little. Why, they hardly look like anything at all."

"Try one, Chief," I suggested.

"Perhaps I will. You checked the legal angle?"

"On the quiet. It's absolutely clean."

He nodded and poked at the little pills with his finger. I scratched the back of my neck, trying to be politely inconspicuous, but the Chief doesn't miss much. He looked at me inquiringly.

"Hives," I explained, embarrassed. "I, uh, got an overdose the first time, like I said. I don't know much about these things, but what they told me at the clinic was I set up an allergy."

"Allergy?" Mr. VandenBlumer looked at me thoughtfully. "We don't want to spread allergies with this stuff, do we?"

"Oh, no danger of that, Chief. It's Cloud's fault, in a way; he handed me an undiluted dose of the stuff, and I drank it down. The clinic was very positive about that: Even twenty or thirty times the normal dose won't do you any harm."

"Um." He rolled one of the pills in his finger and thumb and sniffed it thoughtfully. "How long are you going to have your hives?"

"They'll go away. I just have to keep away from the stuff. I wouldn't have them now, but—well, I liked it so much I tried another shot yesterday." I coughed, and added, "It works out pretty well, though. You see the advantages, of course, Chief. I have to give it up, and I can swear that there's no craving, no shakes, no kick-off symptoms, no nothing. I, well, I wish I could enjoy it like anyone else, sure. But I'm here to testify that Cloud told the simple truth: It isn't habit-forming."

"Um," he said again; and that was the end of the discussion.

Oh, the Chief is a cagey man. He gave me my orders: Keep my mouth shut about it. I have an idea that he was waiting to see what happened to my hives, and whether any craving would develop, and what the test series on animals and Cloud's Bowery-derelict volunteers would show. But even more, I think he was waiting until the time was exactly, climactically right.

Like at the Plans meeting, the day after the doctors' report and the panic at Mason-Dixon.

And that's how Cheery-Gum was born.

Hazel just came in with the cardboard container from the drug store, and I could tell by looking at it—no steam coming out from under the lid, beads of moisture clinging to the sides—that it wasn't the coffee I ordered. "Hey!" I yelled after her as she was dreamily waltzing through the door. "Come back here!"

"Sure 'nough, Massa," she said cheerfully, and two-stepped back. "S'matter?"

I took a grip on my temper. "Open that up," I ordered. "Take a look at what's in it."

She smiled at me and plopped the lid off the container. Half the contents spilled across my desk. "Oh, dear," said Hazel, "excuse me while I get a cloth."

"Never mind the cloth," I said, mopping at the mess with my handkerchief. "What's in there?"

She gazed wonderingly into the container for a moment; then she said, "Oh, *honestly,* boss! I see what you mean. Those idiots in the drug store, they're gummed up higher than a kite, morning, noon and night. I always say, if you can't handle it, you shouldn't touch it during working hours. I'm sorry about this, boss. No lemon! How can they call it a lemon Coke when they forget the—"

"Hazel," I said, "what I wanted was coffee. Coffee."

She looked at me. "You mean *I* got it wrong? Oh, I'm sorry, Mr. McGory. I'll go right down and get it now." She smiled repentantly and hummed her way toward the door. With her hand on the knob, she stopped and turned to look at me. "All the same, boss," she said, "that's a funny combination. Coffee *and* Coke. But I'll see what I can do."

And she was gone, to bring me heaven knows what incredible concoction. But what are you going to do?

No, that's no answer. I know it's what *you* would do. But it makes me break out in hives.

The first week we were delighted, the second week we were triumphant, the third week we were millionaires.

The sixth week I skulked along the sidewalks all the way across town and down, to see Leslie Clary Cloud. Even so I almost got it when a truckdriver dreamily piled into the glass front of a saloon a yard or two behind me.

When I saw Cloud sitting at his workbench, feet propped up, hands clasped behind his head, eyes half-closed, I could almost have kissed him. For his jaws were not moving. Alone in New York, except for me, he wasn't chewing Cheery-Gum.

"Thank heaven!" I said sincerely.

He blinked and smiled at me. "Mr. McGory," he said in a pleasant drawl. "Nice of you."

His manner disturbed me, and I looked more closely. "You're not—you're not gummed up, are you?"

He said gently, "Do I look gummed up? I never chew the stuff."

"Good!" I unfolded the newspaper I had carried all the way from

199

Madison Avenue and showed him the inside pages—the ones that were not a mere smear of ink. "See here, Cloud. Planes crashing into Radio City. Buses driving off the George Washington Bridge. Ships going aground at the Battery. We did it, Cloud, you and I!"

"Oh, I wouldn't get upset about it, old man," he said comfortably. "All local, isn't it?"

"Isn't that bad enough? And it isn't local—it can't be. It's just that there isn't any communication outside the city any more—outside of any city, I guess. The shipments of Cheery-Gum, that's all that ever gets delivered anywhere. Because that's all that anybody cares about any more, and we did it, you and I!"

He said sympathetically, "That's too bad, McGory."

"Curse you!" I shrieked at him. "You said it wasn't a drug! You said it wasn't habit-forming! You said—"

"Now, now," he said with gentle firmness. "Why not chew a stick yourself?"

"Because I can't! It gives me hives!"

"Oh, that's right." He looked self-reproachful. "Well," he said dreamily at last, "I guess that's about the size of it, McGory." He was staring at the ceiling again.

"*What* is?"

"What is what?"

"What's about the—Oh, the devil with it. Cloud, you got us into this, you have to get us out of it. There must be some way of curing this habit."

"But there isn't any habit to cure, McGory," he pointed out.

"But there is!"

"Tem-per," he said waggishly, and took a corked test tube out of his workbench. He drank it down, every drop, and tossed the tube in a wastebasket. "You see?" He demanded severely. "*I* don't chew Cheery-Gum."

So I appealed to a Higher Authority.

In the eighteenth century I would have gone to the Church, in the nineteenth, to the State. I went to an office fronting on Central Park where the name on the bronze plaque was *Theodor Yust, Analyst.*

It wasn't easy. I almost walked out on him when I saw that his jaws were chewing as rhythmically as his secretary's. But Cloud's concoction is not, as he kept saying, a drug, and though it makes you relax and makes you happy and, if you take enough of it, makes you drunk, it doesn't make you unfit to talk to. So I took a grip on my temper, the only bad temper left, and told him what I wanted.

He laughed at me—in the friendliest way. "Put a stop to Cheery-Gum? Mr. McGory!"

"But the plane crashes—"

"No more suicides, Mr. McGory!"

"The train wrecks—"

200

"Not a murder or a mugging in the whole city in a month."

I said hopelessly, "But it's *wrong!*"

"Ah," he said in the tone of a discoverer, "now we come down to it. Why is it wrong, Mr. McGory?"

That was the second time I almost walked out. But I said "Let's get one thing straight: I don't want you digging into my problems. That's not why I'm here. Cheery-Gum *is* wrong, and I am *not* biased against it. You can take a detached view of collisions and sudden death if you want to, but what about slow death? All over the city, all over the country, people are lousing up their jobs. Nobody cares. Nobody does anything but go through the motions. They're happy. What happens when they get hungry because the farmers are feeling too good to put in their crops?"

He sighed patiently. He took the wad of gum out of his mouth, rolled it neatly into a Kleenex and dropped it in the wastebasket. He took a fresh stick out of a drawer and unwrapped it, but stopped when he saw me looking at him. He chuckled. "Rather I didn't, Mr. McGory? Well, why not oblige you? It's not habit-forming, after all." He dropped the gum back into the drawer and said: "Answering your questions, they won't starve. The farmers are farming, the workers are working, the policemen are policing, and I'm analyzing. And you're worrying. Why? Work's getting done."

"But my secretary—"

"Forget about your secretary, Mr. McGory. Sure, she's a little fuzzy-brained, a little absent-minded. Who isn't? But she comes to work, because why shouldn't she?"

"Sure she does, but—"

"But she's happy. Let her be happy, Mr. McGory!"

I looked scandalized at him. "You, a doctor! How can you say that? Suppose *you* were fuzzy-brained and so on when a patient desperately needed—"

He stopped me. "In the past three weeks," he said gently, "you're the first to come in that door."

I changed tack: "All right, you're an analyst. What about a G.P. or a surgeon?"

He shrugged. "Perhaps," he conceded, "perhaps in one case out of a thousand—somebody hurt in an accident, say—he'd get to the hospital too late, or the surgeon would make some little mistake. Perhaps. Not even one in a thousand—one in a million, maybe. But Cheery-Gum isn't a drug. A quarter-grain of sodium amytol, and your surgeon's as good as new." Absent-mindedly he reached into the drawer for the stick of gum.

"And you say," I said accusingly, "that it's not habit-forming!"

He stopped with his hand halfway to his mouth. "Well," he said wryly, "it *is* a habit. Don't confuse semantics, Mr. McGory. It is not a narcotic addiction. If my supply were cut off this minute, I would feel bad—as bad as if I couldn't play bridge any more for some reason, and no worse." He put the stick of gum away again and rummaged through the bottom drawers of his desk until he found a dusty pack of cigarettes. "Used to smoke three packs a day," he wheezed, choking on the first drag.

He wiped his streaming eyes. "You know, Mr. McGory," he said sharply, "you're a bit of a prig. You don't want people to be happy."

"I—"

He stopped me before I could work up a full explosion. "Wait! Don't think that you're the only person who thinks about what's good for the world. When I first heard of Cheery-Gum, I worried." He stubbed the cigarette out distastefully, still talking. "Euphoria is well and good, I said, but what about emergencies? And I looked around, and there weren't any. Things were getting done, maybe slowly and erratically, but they were getting done. And then I said, on a high moral plane that's well and good, but what about the ultimate destiny of man? Should the world be populated by cheerful near-morons? And that worried me, until I began looking at my patients." He smiled reflectively. "I had 'em all, Mr. McGory. You name it, I had it coming in to see me twice a week. The worst wrecks of psyches you ever heard of, twisted and warped and destroying themselves; and they stopped. They stopped eating themselves up with worry and fear and tension, and then they weren't my patients any more. And what's more, they weren't morons. Give them a stimulus, they respond. Interest them, they react. I played bridge the other night with a woman who was catatonic last month; we had to put the first stick of gum in her mouth. She beat the hell out of me, Mr. McGory. I had a mathematician coming here who—well, never mind. It was bad. He's happy as a clam, and the last time I saw him he had finished a paper he began ten years ago, and couldn't touch. Stimulate them—they respond. When things are dull—Cheery-Gum. What could be better?"

I looked at him dully, and said, "So you can't help me."

"I didn't say that. Do you want me to help you?"

"Certainly!"

"Then answer my question: Why don't you chew a stick yourself?"

"Because I can't!" It all tumbled out, the Plans meeting and Leslie Clary Cloud and the beaker that hadn't been diluted and the hives. "A terrific allergy," I emphasized. "Even antihistamines don't help. They said at the clinic that the antibodies formed after a massive initial—"

He said comfortably, "Soma over psyche, eh? Well, what would you expect? But believe me, Mr. McGory, allergies are psychogenic. Now, if you'll just—"

Well, if you can't lick 'em, join 'em, that's what the old man used to say.

But I can't join them. Theodor Yust offered me an invitation, but I guess I was pretty rude to him. And when, at last, I went back, ready to crawl and apologize, there was a scrawled piece of cardboard over the bronze nameplate; it said: *Gone fishing.*

I tried to lay it on the line with the Chief. I opened the door of the Plans room, and there he was with Baggott and Wayber, from Mason-Dixon. They were sitting there whittling out model ships, and so intent on what they were doing that they hardly noticed me. After a while the Chief said idly, "Bankrupt yet?" And moments passed, and Wayber finally replied, in an absent-minded tone:

"Guess so. Have to file some papers or something." And they went on with their whittling.

So I spoke sharply to them, and the minute they looked up and saw me, it was like the Rockettes: The hands into the pockets, the paper being unwrapped, the gum into the mouth. And naturally I couldn't make any sense with them after that. So what are you going to do?

No! I can't!

Hazel hardly comes in to see me any more, even. I bawled her out for it—what would happen, I demanded, if I suddenly had to answer a letter. But she only smiled dreamily at me. "There hasn't been a letter in a month," she pointed out amiably. "Don't worry, though. If anything comes up, I'll be with you in a flash. This stuff isn't a habit with me, I can stop it any time, you just say the word and ol' Hazel'll be there. . . ."

And she's right because, when you get right down to it, there's the trouble. It isn't a habit.

So how can you break it?

You can stop Cheery-Gum any time. You can stop it this second, or five minutes from now, or tomorrow.

So why worry about it?

It's completely voluntary, entirely under your control; it won't hurt you, it won't make you sick.

I wish Theodor Yust would come back. Or maybe I'll just cut my throat.

PROBINGS

1. Is Cheery-Gum a good idea? Why or why not? Would you be personally willing to try it?

2. What might be some of the consequences of Cheery-Gum for the following:

    Home
    School
    Church
    Sports
    Marriage
    Funerals
    Other areas of our lives

3. Do you see any particular trends in our own society that could eventually lead to "cheery-gum"?

4. What to you is the "good life"? Do you ever hope to achieve it? If so, how?

5. Of all of the adults you have known, does any one of them lead what you would call "the good life"?

6. Write an SF story about a society where everyone is happy. Why are they happy? Would you like to live in such a society?

7. When are you most content? (listening to music?, hiking in the woods?, working on your car?, dancing?, reading?, being with friends?)

8. Even though we talk about the good life, is there such a thing as a bad life? an in-between life? Are such labels even valid? Why or why not?

STATUS 13

Every society has a way of conferring status on its members. For some people, high or low status is determined by birth. To be born a Rockefeller is much different from being born John Doe. However, through education, athletic ability, and musical or artistic talent, numerous persons of ordinary birth have received the reward of high status.

In some societies, people have high status if they own a lot of cattle. In other cultures, it is hunting ability that can elevate a person. In our culture, money and material possessions are valued by many. An expensive house, car, or boat may be signs of what one economist called conspicuous consumption —consuming goods simply to prove to people that you have the money to consume these goods. A cheap car is sufficient for moving people around; a Rolls Royce, though, says that you are someone special.

Certainly, consumption is vital to the type of economy that we have. If everyone cut their consumption of goods in half at the same time, the economy would be in deep trouble. Consumption is also a measure of status as we have mentioned. Let's consider a unique society where consumption is very different from what we are used to, one where consumers and producers are at war with each other.

1. Headlines from Tomorrow:

BE THE FIRST TO TAKE A TIME TRAVEL VACATION

Before you are permitted to go on a Time Travel Vacation, the Time Travel Bureau must compare your qualifications against a profile of the ideal time traveler. The bureau will consider financial position, age, level of education, reasons for going, etc. Only about

PROJECTIONS

10 percent of the population will be permitted to go.

Construct the profile. Based on the profile, would you be able to travel in time. Why or why not?

2. What "things" might give people status in the future?

Consider the following:
a. 3-D television
b. personal rocket ship
c. a real live tree
d. a private outer space resort area
e. other

CONSUMER'S REPORT

—Theodore R. Cogswell

CON●SUM●ER /ken-süm-mer/, n: 1: a person who destroys, uses up, or wastes industrial production in order to control the size of the population and make possible the full employment that is necessary for a healthy economy 2: one who has not yet achieved producer status 3: any person under twenty-one 4: *archaic:* a person who uses goods or services to satisfy his needs rather than to resell them or to produce other goods with them.

The Authorized Dictionary, New Washington, Kansas: The Federal Printing Office, 3rd ed., 1984.

IT was Saturday so Alan had to go out and get the mail. Just as the letter carrier's tank clanked away, he got his cousin Alf to man the front door turret and went zigzagging down the communication trench that led to the street. As he reached cautiously up to open the small door in the bottom of the armored mailbox, there was a sudden crack from across the way and the whine of a near miss sent him tumbling back into a slit trench. A moment later there was a coughing stutter as Alf opened up with fifty and pounded a burst into the tungsten steel shutters of the house across the street. Alan jumped to his feet, dumped the mail out of the box, and then made a quick dive for safety just in case Alf's fire hadn't discouraged the Higgens kid.

The mail didn't look particularly exciting. There wasn't anything for him, and, aside from a few letters for his uncle, most of what had come consisted of advertisements for sniper-scopes and stuff like that. The only exceptions were two small black boxes. They looked like samples of something, and since, as the only consumer left in the family, samples were Alan's prerequisite, he promptly stuffed them into his worn grenade carrier and just as promptly forgot about them. Until that evening when the man from Consolidated Munitions stopped by, that is.

Mr. Flugnet was so disturbed that he'd forgotten to take off his white truce hat. "We think the promotion crew passed out a batch on this street," he said as Alan slipped into the room and sat down quietly in the far corner. "But we're not sure."

"Why not?" asked Alan's uncle, a weedy little man with a somewhat nasal voice.

"Because some damn kid dropped a mortar shell on their halftrack while they were on the way back to the warehouse to pick up another load. Got every one of them. Were any samples dropped off here?"

"Alan brought in the mail," volunteered Alf.

"Was there anything in it that somebody wanted that they didn't get?" asked Alan in a small voice. They all turned and looked at him, aware of his presence for the first time.

"I'm from Consolidated Munitions," said Mr. Flugnet.

"Yes, sir?"

"Did you find a small black box in the mail? We've been passing out samples of our new concussion grenade and we just discovered today that several . . . uh . . . overpowered experimental models had got mixed in with them by mistake. We're trying to track them down before it's— well, before something unfortunate happens."

Alan was just about to reach into his grenade case and produce the two little cartons when the word "overpowered" registered. He struggled briefly against temptation and lost.

"I dumped all the advertising stuff on the hall table." He felt suddenly that his grenade case had become transparent and that the little black boxes inside, now grown to quadruple size, were visible to everybody in the room. He knew it couldn't be, but even so he let his hand drop casually over the carrier just in case there might be a revealing bulge. "I'll go check."

Once the door was safely shut behind him, he took the two boxes out, opened them, and examined their contents. There was a little metallic globe in each, but one had a roughly soldered seam that made it look like a hand-production job. He gave a little whistle of excitement and stowed it away carefully in his pocket. If he was going to make it through the game with North, he was going to need super power. And replacing the other grenade in his box and putting it back in his carrier, he squatted down on his haunches and listened at the keyhole. He wanted to find out something more about his new weapon.

"Fine young consumer, that," he heard Mr. Flugnet say in the voice that producers use when they want to say something nice that they really don't mean. Aunt Martha let out a long sniff.

"Too spindly! It's a wonder to us that he's made it this far. He just hasn't got the stuff that my boys have. Made it through, both of them, with hardly a scratch."

She nodded fondly over toward Reuban and Alf. Alf was sniggering through a comic book, one of the new improved kind without any words to distract the reader. Reuban just sat, a thin driblet of saliva drooling from one corner of his mouth, and plucked aimlessly at the buttons on his shirt. As they looked at him, he began to squirm back and forth and to make little whimpering sounds.

"Better take Reuban upstairs before he dirties himself again," said Aunt Martha. Alf obediently took his younger brother by the arm and herded him out of the room. Alan ducked under the hall table until they had gone by.

"Which shock is he on?" asked Mr. Flugnet politely.

"He got his third today. That's always the worst."

Mr. Flugnet nodded his agreement.

"Another couple of weeks, though, and he'll be ready to start his reconditioning. And by spring he'll be ready to settle down as a full-fledged producer and start raising little consumption units of his own." She sighed. "I do wish they'd work out a faster method. For three weeks now I've had to take care of him just like I would a baby. It's no easy job for a woman of my age."

Alan's uncle clucked impatiently. "We all had to go through it once— and somebody had to take care of us. It's never pretty, but it's just the way things are."

Alan was just about to give up and go back in the room when he heard his uncle say, "This new grenade you have in production, it's something special?"

"It was supposed to be," said the visitor unhappily. "We figured it would be the hottest consumer's item to hit the market in years."

"What do you mean, 'supposed to be'? Did some bugs show up after you got it into production?"

Mr. Flugnet shook his head. "There's nothing wrong with the grenade itself. It'll knock out anything within a radius of ten feet and not even bother anybody standing just the other side of the blast area. We thought we had the perfect consumer item. No flying fragments to bother inno-cent producers, no danger of misfire. New Washington was so impressed that they gave us a heavy enough subsidy to make it possible for us to put three man-hours in each one and still retail them for four dollars and twenty-seven cents a gross. And then . . . ."

"Yes?" Alan's uncle leaned forward eagerly in his chair.

For some reason or other, Mr. Flugnet changed the subject hurriedly. "What line are you in?"

"Small arms. But getting to those experimental models you're looking for . . . ."

Mr. Flugnet wasn't about to get back. "How's production?" he asked.

Unwillingly, Alan's uncle moved off in the new direction. "Not bad, considering. We're always the last to feel the pinch. Things are still tighter than I like, though. Shirey down the street got laid off at the burp-gun plant last week and he doesn't know when he'll be taken back. I don't see why the government doesn't shorten the truce periods so as to give the kids more consuming time."

"It's not that simple," said Mr. Flugnet pontifically. "If you increase consumption much over what it is now, you'll decrease the number of consumers too fast. That causes overproduction, and pretty soon more factories start shutting down. Then bingo! we've got ourselves a fine recession."

"I hadn't thought about it that way," said Alan's uncle slowly. "And after all, things aren't too bad. Even if some of the arms plants do have to shut down once in a while, most of the producers do have jobs most of the time. And we are able to keep the population down to the point where the land that escaped the dusting during the big war can produce enough food for everybody."

One of Alan's feet was going to sleep and the conversation didn't make much sense to him, so he decided that now was as good a time as any to make his entrance.

"I found it," he said, holding out the second sample.

"Took you long enough," grumbled his uncle. Mr. Flugnet didn't say anything; he just came over and took the box from Alan. Dumping the sphere that was inside out into the palm of his hand, he examined it closely.

"No soap," he said wearily and handed it back. "That's one of the regulars. Here, you can keep it."

"Thanks." Alan placed the little grenade carefully in his carrier. "I'll need this tonight. We're playing North and every little bit will help. Coach Blauman says that even if we haven't much in the way of equipment it's the spirit that counts. He says that if we really get in there and fight we'll be able to stop North cold."

"That's nice," murmured Mr. Flugnet vaguely as he reached for his hat. He obviously had his mind on other things.

"Sorry the boy didn't have what you were looking for," said Alan's uncle. "But probably the other men have rounded up the rest of them by now."

Mr. Flugnet looked dubious. "I doubt it. Kids are like pack rats. When Security finally broke Harris down—he's the guy that's responsible for this whole mess—he admitted to having made at least three hundred and slipping them into sample cases. As of an hour ago we'd recovered exactly thirty-seven."

He caught himself with a start. "Shouldn't be talking about it. Though I can't see where it makes any difference now." He let out a long sigh. "Well, you're the last house on my list and I've done all that I can. Guess I'd better be going." He picked up his truce hat and planted it firmly on his head.

"Guess I'd better be going too," said Alan. "I've got to be getting over to the stadium to get dressed for the game."

"Don't rush off," said Alan's uncle. He didn't intend to let the visitor escape until he found out exactly what it was that was causing him so much concern. "No, not you, Alan. You run on. I'm talking to Mr. Flugnet. Why not wait until the cease-fire siren sounds? It's getting dark outside and some of the kids might take a potshot at you before they see your truce hat."

"Thanks just the same, but . . . ."

"Aw, stay! I'll fix you a good stiff drink. You look as though you could use one."

Mr. Flugnet hesitated and then sat down again. "I guess I could at that," he said.

Alan's uncle hurried over to the liquor cabinet and poured two long ones. After he'd handed a drink to Mr. Flugnet, he settled back in his own chair and said as casually as he could, "You were saying something about somebody named Harris who did something to some grenades and got hauled in by Security?"

Mr. Flugnet didn't answer right away. Instead he took a long pull at his glass, coughed, and then took another. Alan looked at his watch and then started out of the room. He was almost to the door when his aunt said sharply, "Alan!"

He turned.

"If you get hit tonight, mind that you see that they do a proper job of patching you up at the aid station. I don't want my sheets all messed up like last time."

"Yes, ma'am," Alan said obediently. As he went out nobody said good-bye. They were all waiting for Mr. Flugnet to say something.

Alan stopped automatically at the front door and made a quick check of the street through the periscope. Nothing seemed to be moving, but he didn't take any chances. Sliding the door open just wide enough to get through, he made a running dive for the communication trench. The kid across the street had got a sniper-scope for Christmas and a guy wasn't even safe after dark.

The field lights were already on and the stadium a quarter full when Alan slipped into the locker room. He was ten minutes late and had to hurry with his dressing, but for once the coach didn't bawl him out. Coach Blauman didn't even notice him—Coach Blauman had troubles of his own. He was over in one corner telling them to Dan Ericson, the sports reporter for the *Tribune* who covered most of the high school events.

The coach was a fat, florid man, and there was a slight thickness to his speech that indicated that he had gotten to the bottle he kept in the back of his locker earlier than usual.

"You want a quote?" he snorted. "I'll give you a quote. I'll give you enough quotes to fill that whole damn fishwrapper you call a newspaper from front to back. You can put my picture on page one and put a great big *Coach Blauman says* right underneath it."

Ericson gave a tired grin. "Go ahead, coach. What's the beef for the evening?"

"That damn PTA, that's what. I go to them and ask for four mortars, four stinking mortars, and all I get is the brush-off. Three thousand bucks they got salted away, and it's all going for new body armor for the band. I say, 'What's the use of having a pretty band when the team's so hard up for equipment that a bunch of sandlot grade school players could knock them over.' So old Stevens gives me the fish eye and throws me a line about how it ain't whether you win or lose but how you play the game."

"Don't let it get you down, Blauman," said the reporter. "Think of all the character you're building!"

Alan was lugged off the field at the end of the second action with a gash in his head that took six stitches to close. During the rest of the quarter he sat woodenly on the bench in the players' dugout. A telescreen at the far end was following the play, but he didn't lift his head to look at it. He looked like a clockwork manikin that had been temporarily turned off.

He was sent back in just before the end of the half. Illegally, it is true—the enemy had already received credit for one wounded, and according to NAA rules he was supposed to be ineligible to continue playing. Blauman didn't have any choice, however. The last drive of North's had torn up his whole center and he didn't have much left in the way of reserves.

As Alan trotted out toward the foxholes that marked his side's last stand, he passed stretcher-bearers bringing back the dead and injured from the last play. Most of them were wearing the green helmet of Marshall. The PA system announced the substitution and there was a feeble cheer from the Marshall side of the stadium.

Alan went up to the referee's tank and threw a quick salute at the vision slit.

"Wetzel substituting for Mitchell."

"Check," said the bored voice of the official inside. "Fight clean and fight hard and may the best team win." The formula came mechanically. Neither the referee nor anybody else had any doubt that the best team had won.

Alan was halfway to the hastily dug trenches that marked his team's position when a mortar shell exploded forty feet away and knocked him off his feet. There was a sudden outraged blast from the enemies' siren, and then the enemy captain bobbed out of his foxhole.

"Sorry, sir," he yelled. "One of my mortar crews was sighting in and accidentally let off a round."

The referee wasn't impressed.

"That'll cost you exactly twenty yards," he said.

A yell came from the Marshall bleachers as the penalty for backfield illegally in motion was announced. The Marshall team was too tired to do any cheering. They just trudged forward and planted themselves in the defensive lines they had been thrown out of five minutes before.

The North team was more careful this time. There wasn't a quiver of motion from their side until the referee's siren signaled the beginning of play. Then they opened up with everything they had. It seemed to Alan that every mortar North owned was zeroed in on his position and that everyone of their grenade men was out to get him. Blast followed blast in such steady succession that the night air seemed one solid mass of jagged shrapnel. He'd had it bad before, but nothing like this. He flattened against the moist earth of his foxhole and waited numbly for the knife edges to rip him open. Then suddenly it stopped and without thinking he found himself rising into a defensive position. There was a savage spatter of victory yells from the other line and then they came swarming out of their positions, their bayonets gleaming wickedly in the overhead lights.

They were repeating the play that they had been using all evening, a hard punching thrust through center. The guidon bearer came charging forward, his tommy-gunners fanned out in front of him in a protecting screen, their guns showing the Marshall position with quick accurate bursts.

Alan forced himself to lift his head enough to sight accurately and opened up on the flag bearer. He was a difficult target as he came dancing forward, bobbing and shifting at every step. Alan fired methodically, remembering not to jerk his trigger finger as he squeezed off his shots. And then his gun jammed. He got a moment's breathing spell as Marshall's two surviving mortars opened up to give him some covering fire, but the Northers didn't stop altogether; they kept coming in short rushes.

Alan was singled out for their special attention. With him knocked out they could carry their flag right through the center of Marshall's line. With a sudden yell, four of them threw themselves into a crouching run and came charging down on his position. Alan hammered at the clearing lever of his rifle but it was stuck fast. Throwing it angrily off to one side, he tore open the cover of his grenade case and fumbled inside until his fingers closed around the sphere with the roughly soldered edge. He waited until the Northers were almost on him and then threw it at the middle man as hard as he could.

There was a blast. A blast of harsh purple light that punched through the protecting ramparts of his foxhole as if they weren't there. He felt a sudden wave of nausea, and then a stabbing tearing pain inside the back of his head as old neural channels were ripped out and new ones opened up. When he finally staggered to his feet he looked the same. Outside that is. Inside he wasn't the same sort of a human any longer. Neither was any other consumer in the stadium.

When Alan got back to the house, everybody was still in the living room. Mr. Flugnet was somewhat drunk and all the pressure that had been built up inside him was hissing out in speech. Alan stood silently in the doorway and listened.

". . . and then it was too late," said Mr. Flugnet. "Somebody must have slipped up in shock therapy or else something went haywire with the reconditioning machinery. Whatever it was, Harris came out with the job only half done. He waited ten years for a chance to strike back for what had been done to him while he was still a consumer. When he was put to work on the development of the new concussion grenade, he had his chance and he made the most of it."

"How?"

"He worked out a deconditioner that was so tiny it would fit into a grenade case and so powerful that it could blanket an area half a mile across."

"Deconditioner?" said Alan's uncle in a puzzled voice.

"You went through one while you were being changed. The old patterns have to be taken out before new ones can be put in."

"All that I remember is sitting in a long room with a silver helmet on my head that had a lot of wires attached to it. But I still don't understand about that Harris fellow."

"It's simple enough. He came out remembering."

"Remembering what?"

"Remembering what it was like to be a consumer," said Mr. Flugnet grimly.

"But everybody remembers that."

Mr. Flugnet shook his head. "You just think you do. Part of the reconditioning process is the introduction of a protective amnesia. Being a consumer isn't nice, isn't nice at all. The postnatal blocks only operate on the conscious level. Underneath a tremendous pressure of anger and hatred and fear is built up over the years. The consumer pattern that has been conditioned in runs directly contrary to the instinct for self-preservation, or whatever you want to call it. That's why the change to producer status takes so long. The accumulated charge has to be drained off slowly before the reconditioning can take place. But if the blocks were to be removed at once, if the youngsters were to suddenly wake up and see their world as it actually is . . . ." Mr. Flugnet's voice shuddered to a stop. "Do you mind if I have another drink? Just a short one?" Without waiting for an answer he went and helped himself. "Maybe they'd understand," he muttered.

"Understand what?" said Alan's uncle blankly. "Who?"

"The consumers. Maybe they'd understand that there wasn't any other way to do it. The factories produce so fast that when everybody has all they want they have to shut down—except the war plants, that is. That gets used up as fast as it's made. But when there was nobody left to fight, when everybody else was dead, we had to keep reproducing. And if you produce, somebody has to consume. And . . . ." His voice trailed off.

"I still don't see what you're so upset about," said Alan's uncle.

Alan stepped into the room. "I do," he said in a strange flat voice.

Mr. Flugnet took one good look at him, made a funny little squawking sound, and huddled back in his chair.

"I almost got killed tonight," said Alan.

His uncle shot him a surprised look. "That's a funny remark for a consumer to make."

"Yeah," said Alan. "I guess it is."

"Well, forget about it. If you've got what it takes, you'll make it through like Alf and Reuban did. If you haven't—well, that's just the way things are."

"And that's the way things should be," announced Alf. "Only the strong deserve the jobs. By the way, what happened to the celebration? We used to tear the town up after games."

"We're having it tomorrow."

"You are not!" snapped his uncle indignantly. "Tomorrow's Sunday. You kids have the streets to yourself three days a week as it is. If you think you're going to be allowed to throw lead around while your elders are on their way to church, you've got another think coming!"

"I don't think the producers will mind," said Alan softly. He made a quick mental calculation and took one step backward. When his hand came out of his worn grenade case, it wasn't empty.

There had been two little black boxes.

Mr. Flugnet had been right, the new concussion grenade did have a beautifully defined blast area. Aside from a slight ringing in his ears, Alan felt fine as he walked out of the house. For the first time in his life during a consumption period, he didn't dive into the communication trench that led to the street. Instead he walked slowly across the lawn. When he got to the sidewalk he sat down on the curb and waited. There was a brief staccato rattle of a burp gun from across the way and a moment later the Higgens kid came out of his house.

"Over here," yelled Alan. "The rest will be along in a minute."

From houses all up and down the street began to come sharp crashing explosions.

"Those new hand grenades are sure something," said the Higgens kid.

"They sure are," said Alan. He sighed comfortably and cupped his chin in his hands. "But tomorrow we'll have to start collecting all the ones that are left over. You leave stuff like that lying around and somebody might get hurt."

PROBINGS

1. If you could own one thing, and one thing only, that would give you instant status, what would it be? Why would this give you status?
2. In your opinion, what is high status? Middle status? Low status? Construct a lifestyle profile for persons in each of those three groups. You decide whether they are male or female.

	HIGH STATUS	MIDDLE STATUS	LOW STATUS
House or Apartment (Describe)			
Furniture (Describe)			
Job (What does he or she do? How much do they make?)			
Recreation Hobbies Sports			
Car			
Food (What do they enjoy)			
Type of Restaurant they go to			
Favorite drink			

3. What examples of status can you find in your school? Do certain students take certain types of courses? Are there cliques? What kinds of people belong to these cliques?
4. Locate a magazine such as *Town and Country, Gentleman's Quarterly,* or *Vogue* and see how status is depicted in the ads and the articles. Compare some of these magazines to *Sports Illustrated, Family Circle,* etc.—how do the approaches to status differ? Now take a newspaper. Look at the *New York Times Magazine* (Sunday) and compare it to, say, *Reader's Digest.* How do their advertisements differ? What does a person imply by saying that he/she couldn't get along without the *New York Times?* Does this imply a kind of intellectual status? What other kinds of status symbols are there? Tennis vs. bowling. *Carol Burnett Show* vs. *Monty Python's Flying Circus.* Harvard vs. Podunk U. Hot dogs vs. quiche lorraine.
5. Assuming that all levels of status are really artificial, create your own society with as many social strata as you wish. What is a symbol of status in your society?
6. What could give a person status in the future? One SF writer developed a story around status reversal. People of low status were forced to consume the most goods; people of higher status consumed the least. Using this idea, write an SF story about status in the future.

TECHNOLOGY

14

Less than a century ago, if two people wished to speak to one another, they had to, of course, meet physically in order to do so. If distant relatives wished to share news about a marriage, a birth, a death, it could take weeks and even months to send and receive the information. With the invention of the telephone, this all changed. Now, relatives many hundreds and even thousands of miles apart could be in almost instantaneous contact.

In 1900 people who wanted to hear the most current popular tune had to buy a copy of sheet music to play on the piano. First the phonograph and then the radio quickly changed our entertainment habits. Popular music today is only a flick of a dial away. Radio has also brought sports, drama, public events, and comedy right into the average American living room. With the invention of television, sight was wedded to sound, and even more marvelous events began appearing in our homes. Indeed, this was science fiction turned science fact—and what of the future? The Japanese have perfected a wall-sized TV and a number of American companies are experimenting with laser beams and holography, which will eventually result in 3-D TV. Imagine, three-dimensional actors, sports heroes, and other public figures, projected right into your house. However, we have paid a serious price for our advances in communication. Many of our contacts with our fellow humans are now electronic ones through telephones, televisions, stereos, and radios. It seems that we have lost much of the old-fashioned, personal contact.

Some people are arguing that we have

become dehumanized by our mechanical wonders; that we have become too dependent upon them. Others are asking where does humanity end and the machine begin.

Since World War II, transistors, along with the computer, have revolutionized our world. Today it takes a computer seconds to do what it took a human weeks to do thirty years ago. Computers keep track of our credit, our school and military records, and our income tax—and who knows what else is stored in their mechanical maw "for future use." Computers may be a wonder of our age; however, if a computer makes an error, it is difficult and frustrating to try correcting that error. In the following story, a mistake is made by a computer, with some very deadly results.

PROJECTIONS

1. Headlines from Tomorrow:

ROBOT HOMEMAKERS STRIKE

Either write a news story on this idea or write twelve more headlines showing how our society reached this point.

FIRST HUMAN/ROBOT MARRIAGE REVEALED

Where did it occur? Why? What were the reactions of the human's relatives and friends?

2. Write a story about the final confrontation between humans and computers. The winner will live, the loser perish. What would the battlefield be like?

COMPUTERS DON'T ARGUE

—Gordon R. Dickson

Mr: Walter A. Child Balance: $4.98
Dear Customer: Enclosed is your latest book selection. "Kidnapped," by Robert Louis Stevenson.

> 437 Woodlawn Drive
> Panduk, Michigan
> Nov. 16, 1965

Treasure Book Club
1823 Mandy Street
Chicago, Illinois

Dear Sirs:
  I wrote you recently about the computer punch card you sent, billing me for "Kim," by Rudyard Kipling. I did not open the package containing it until I had already mailed you my check for the amount on the card. On opening the package, I found the book missing half its pages. I sent it back to you, requesting either another copy or my money back. Instead, you have sent me a copy of "Kidnapped," by Robert Louis Stevenson. Will you please straighten this out?
  I hereby return the copy of "Kidnapped."

> Sincerely yours,
> Walter A. Child

Mr: Walter A. Child Balance: $4.98
For "Kidnapped," by Robert Louis Stevenson
(If remittance has been made for the above, please disregard this notice)

437 Woodlawn Drive
Panduk, Michigan
Jan. 21, 1966

Treasure Book Club
1823 Mandy Street
Chicago, Illinois

Dear Sirs:

May I direct your attention to my letter of November 16, 1965? You are still continuing to dun me with computer punch cards for a book I did not order. Whereas, actually, it is your company that owes *me* money.

Sincerely yours,
Walter A. Child

Treasure Book Club
1823 Mandy Street
Chicago, Illinois
Feb. 1, 1966

Mr. Walter A. Child
437 Woodlawn Drive
Panduk, Michigan

Dear Mr. Child:

We have sent you a number of reminders concerning an amount owing to us as a result of book purchases you have made from us. This amount which is $4.98 is now long overdue.

This situation is disappointing to us, particularly since there was no hesitation on our part in extending you credit at the time original arrangements for these purchases were made by you. If we do not receive payment in full by return mail, we will be forced to turn the matter over to a collection agency.

Very truly yours,
Samuel P. Grimes
Collection Mgr.

437 Woodlawn Drive
Panduk, Michigan
Feb. 5, 1966

Dear Mr. Grimes:

Will you stop sending me punch cards and form letters and make me some kind of a direct answer from a human being?

I don't owe you money. *You* owe me money. Maybe I should turn your company over to a collection agency.

Walter A. Child

FEDERAL COLLECTION OUTFIT

88 Prince Street
Chicago, Illinois
Feb. 28, 1966

Mr. Walter A. Child
437 Woodlawn Drive
Panduk, Michigan

Dear Mr. Child:
Your account with the Treasure Book Club, of $4.98 plus interest and charges has been turned over to our agency for collection. The amount due is now $6.83. Please send your check for this amount or we shall be forced to take immediate action.

Jacob N. Harshe
Vice President

FEDERAL COLLECTION OUTFIT

88 Prince Street
Chicago, Illinois
April 8, 1966

Mr. Walter A. Child
437 Woodlawn Drive
Panduk, Michigan

Dear Mr. Child:
You have seen fit to ignore our courteous requests to settle your long overdue account with Treasure Book Club, which is now, with accumulated interest and charges, in the amount of $7.51.
If payment in full is not forthcoming by April 11, 1966, we will be forced to turn the matter over to our attorneys for immediate court action.

Ezekiel B. Harshe
President

MALONEY, MAHONEY,
MACNAMARA and PRUITT
Attorneys

89 Prince Street
Chicago, Illinois
April 29, 1966

Mr. Walter A. Child
437 Woodlawn Drive
Panduk, Michigan

Dear Mr. Child:
   Your indebtedness to the Treasure Book Club has been referred to us for legal action to collect.
   This indebtedness is now in the amount of $10.01. If you will send us this amount so that we may receive it before May 5, 1966, the matter may be satisfied. However, if we do not receive satisfaction in full by that date, we will take steps to collect through the courts.
   I am sure you will see the advantage of avoiding a judgment against you, which as a matter of record would do lasting harm to your credit rating.

Very truly yours,
Hagthorpe M. Pruitt, Jr.
Attorney at law

437 Woodlawn Drive
Panduk, Michigan
May 4, 1966

Mr. Hagthorpe M. Pruitt, Jr.
Maloney, Mahoney, MacNamara and Pruitt
89 Prince Street
Chicago, Illinois

Dear Mr. Pruitt:
   You don't know what a pleasure it is to me in this matter to get a letter from a live human being to whom I can explain the situation.
   This whole matter is silly. I explained it fully in my letters to the Treasure Book Company. But I might as well have been trying to explain to the computer that puts out their punch cards, for all the good it seemed to do. Briefly, what happened was I ordered a copy of "Kim," by Rudyard Kipling, for $4.98. When I opened the package they sent me, I found the book had only half its pages, but I'd previously mailed a check to pay them for the book.
   I sent the book back to them, asking either for a whole copy or my money back. Instead, they sent me a copy of "Kidnapped," by Robert Louis Stevenson—which I had not ordered; and for which they have been trying to collect from me.

Meanwhile, I am still waiting for the money back that they owe me for the copy of "Kim" that I didn't get. That's the whole story. Maybe you can help me straighten them out.

Relievedly yours,
Walter A. Child

P.S.: I also sent them back their copy of "Kidnapped," as soon as I got it, but it hasn't seemed to help. They have never even acknowledged getting it back.

MALONEY, MAHONEY,
MACNAMARA and PRUITT
Attorneys

89 Prince Street
Chicago, Illinois
May 9, 1966

Mr. Walter A. Child
437 Woodlawn Drive
Panduk, Michigan

Dear Mr. Child:

I am in possession of no information indicating that any item purchased by your from the Treasure Book Club has been returned.

I would hardly think that, if the case had been as you stated, the Treasure Book Club would have retained us to collect the amount owing from you.

If I do not receive your payment in full within three days, by May 12, 1966, we will be forced to take legal action.

Very truly yours,
Hagthorpe M. Pruitt, Jr.

COURT OF MINOR CLAIMS
Chicago, Illinois

Mr. Walter A. Child
437 Woodlawn Drive
Panduk, Michigan

Be informed that a judgment was taken and entered against you in this court this day of May 26, 1966, in the amount of $15.66 including court costs.

Payment in satisfaction of this judgment may be made to this court or to the adjudged creditor. In the case of payment being made to the creditor, a release should be obtained from the creditor and filed with this court in order to free you of legal obligation in connection with this judgment.

Under the recent Reciprocal Claims Act, if you are a citizen of a different state, a duplicate claim may be automatically entered and judged against you in your own state so that collection may be made there as well as in the State of Illinois.

COURT OF MINOR CLAIMS
Chicago, Illinois
PLEASE DO NOT FOLD, SPINDLE
OR MUTILATE THIS CARD

Judgment was passed this day of May 27, 1966, under Statute $15.66
Against: Child, Walter A. of 347 Woodlawn Drive, Panduk, Michigan.
Pray to enter a duplicate claim for judgment.
In: Picayune Court—Panduk, Michigan
For Amount: Statute 941

> 437 Woodlawn Drive
> Panduk, Michigan
> May 31, 1966

Samuel P. Grimes
Vice President, Treasure Book Club
1823 Mandy Street
Chicago, Illinois

Grimes:
   This business has gone far enough. I've got to come down to Chicago on business of my own tomorrow. I'll see you then and we'll get this straightened out once and for all, about who owes what to whom, and how much!

> Yours,
> Walter A. Child

> From the desk of the Clerk
> Picayune Court

> June 1, 1966

Harry:
   The attached computer card from Chicago's Minor Claims Court against A. Walter has a 1500-series Statute number on it. That puts it over in Criminal with you, rather than Civil, with me. So I herewith submit it for your computer instead of mine. How's business?

> Joe

CRIMINAL RECORDS
Panduk, Michigan
PLEASE DO NOT FOLD, SPINDLE
OR MUTILATE THIS CARD

Convicted: (Child) A. Walter
On: May 26, 1966
Address: 437 Woodlawn Drive
Panduk, Mich.
Crim: Statute: 1566 (Corrected) 1567
Crime: Kidnap
Date: Nov. 16, 1965
Notes: At large. To be picked up at once.

POLICE DEPARTMENT, PANDUK, MICHIGAN. TO POLICE DEPARTMENT CHICAGO ILLINOIS. CONVICTED SUBJECT A. (COMPLETE FIRST NAME UNKNOWN) WALTER, SOUGHT HERE IN CONNECTION REF. YOUR NOTIFICATION OF JUDGMENT FOR KIDNAP OF CHILD NAMED ROBERT LOUIS STEVENSON, ON NOV. 16, 1965. INFORMATION HERE INDICATES SUBJECT FLED HIS RESIDENCE, AT 437 WOODLAND DRIVE, PANDUK, AND MAY BE AGAIN IN YOUR AREA.

POSSIBLE CONTACT IN YOUR AREA: THE TREASURE BOOK CLUB, 1823 MANDY STREET, CHICAGO, ILLINOIS. SUBJECT NOT KNOWN TO BE DANGEROUS. PICK UP AND HOLD, ADVISING US OF CAPTURE . . .

TO POLICE DEPARTMENT, PANDUK, MICHIGAN. REFERENCE YOUR REQUEST TO PICK UP AND HOLD A. (COMPLETE FIRST NAME UNKNOWN) WALTER, WANTED IN PANDUK ON STATUTE 1567, CRIME OF KIDNAPPING.

SUBJECT ARRESTED AT OFFICES OF TREASURE BOOK CLUB, OPERATING THERE UNDER ALIAS WALTER ANTHONY CHILD AND ATTEMPTING TO COLLECT $4.98 FROM ONE SAMUEL P. GRIMES, EMPLOYEE OF THAT COMPANY.

DISPOSAL: HOLDING FOR YOUR ADVICE.

POLICE DEPARTMENT PANDUK, MICHIGAN TO POLICE DEPARTMENT CHICAGO, ILLINOIS

REF: A. WALTER (ALIAS WALTER ANTHONY CHILD) SUBJECT WANTED FOR CRIME OF KIDNAP, YOUR AREA, REF: YOUR COMPUTER PUNCH CARD NOTIFICATION OF JUDGMENT, DATED MAY 27, 1966. COPY OUR CRIMINAL RECORDS PUNCH CARD HEREWITH FORWARDED TO YOUR COMPUTER SECTION.

CRIMINAL RECORDS
Chicago, Illinois
PLEASE DO NOT FOLD, SPINDLE
OR MUTILATE THIS CARD

SUBJECT (CORRECTION—OMITTED RECORD SUPPLIED)
APPLICABLE STATUTE NO. 1567
JUDGMENT NO. 456789
TRIAL RECORD: APPARENTLY MISFILED AND UNAVAILABLE
DIRECTION: TO APPEAR FOR SENTENCING BEFORE JUDGE JOHN
ALEXANDER MCDIVOT, COURTROOM A JUNE, 9 1966

From the Desk of
Judge Alexander J. McDivot

June 2, 1966

Dear Tony:
I've got an adjudged criminal coming up before me for sentencing
Thursday morning—but the trial transcript is apparently misfiled.
I need some kind of information (Ref: A. Walter—Judgment No.
456789, Criminal). For example, what about the victim of the kidnap-
ping. Was victim harmed?

Jack McDivot

June 3, 1966

Records Search Unit
Re: Ref: Judgment No. 456789—was victim harmed?

Tonio Malagasi
Records Division

June 3, 1966

To: United States Statistics Office
Attn.: Information Section
Subject: Robert Louis Stevenson
Query: Information concerning

Records Search Unit
Criminal Records Division
Police Department
Chicago, Ill.

June 5, 1966

To: Records Search Unit
Criminal Records Division
Police Department
Chicago, Illinois
Subject: Your query re Robert Louis Stevenson (File no. 189623)

Action: Subject deceased. Age at death, 44 yrs. Further information requested?

A. K.
Information Section
U.S. Statistics Office

June 6, 1966

To: United States Statistics Office
Attn.: Information Division
Subject: RE: File no. 189623
No further information required.

Thank you.
Records Search Unit

Criminal Records Division
Police Department
Chicago, Illinois

June 7, 1966

To: Tonio Malagasi
Records Division
Re: Ref: judgment No. 456789—victim is dead.

Records Search Unit

June 7, 1966

To: Judge Alexander J. McDivot's Chambers
Dear Jack:
Ref: Judgment No. 456789. The victim in this kidnap case was apparently slain.
From the strange lack of background information on the killer and his victim, as well as the victim's age, this smells to me like a gangland killing. This for your information. Don't quote me. It seems to me, though, that Stevenson—the victim—has a name that rings a faint bell with me. Possibly, one of the East Coast Mob, since the association comes back to me as something about pirates—possibly New York dockage hijackers—and something about buried loot.
As I say, above is only speculation for your private guidance.
Any time I can help . . .

Best,
Tony Malagasi
Records Division

MICHAEL R. REYNOLDS
Attorney-at-law

49 Water Street
Chicago, Illinois
June 8, 1966

Dear Tim:

Regrets: I can't make the fishing trip. I've been court-appointed here
to represent a man about to be sentenced tomorrow on a kidnapping
charge.

Ordinarily, I might have tried to beg off, and McDivot, who is doing
the sentencing, would probably have turned me loose. But this is the
damndest thing you ever heard of.

The man being sentenced has apparently been not only charged, but
adjudged guilty as a result of a comedy of errors too long to go into here.
He not only isn't guilty—he's got the best case I ever heard of for
damages against one of the larger Book Clubs headquartered here in
Chicago. And that's a case I wouldn't mind taking on.

It's inconceivable—but damnably possible, once you stop to think of
it in this day and age of machine-made records—that a completely inno-
cent man could be put in this position.

There shouldn't be much to it. I've asked to see McDivot tomorrow
before the time for sentencing, and it'll just be a matter of explaining to
him. Then I can discuss the damage suit with my freed client at his leisure.

Fishing next weekend?

Yours,
Mike

MICHAEL R. REYNOLDS
Attorney-at-law

49 Water Street
Chicago, Illinois
June 10

Dear Tim:

In haste—

No fishing this coming week either. Sorry.

You won't believe it. My innocent-as-a-lamb-and-I'm-not-kidding client has just been sentenced to death for first-degree murder in connection with the death of his kidnap victim.

Yes, I explained the whole thing to McDivot. And when he explained
his situation to me, I nearly fell out of my chair.

It wasn't a matter of my not convincing him. It took less than three minutes to show him that my client should never have been within the walls of the County Jail for a second. But—get this—McDivot couldn't do a thing about it.

The point is, my man had already been judged guilty according to the computerized records. In the absence of a trial record—of course there never was one (but that's something I'm not free to explain to you now)—the judge has to go by what records are available. And in the case of an adjudged prisoner, McDivot's only legal choice was whether to sentence to life imprisonment, or execution.

The death of the kidnap victim, according to the statute, made the death penalty mandatory. Under the new laws governing length of time for appeal, which has been shortened because of the new system of computerizing records, to force an elimination of unfair delay and mental anguish to those condemned, I have five days in which to file an appeal, and ten to have it acted on.

Needless to say, I am not going to monkey with an appeal. I'm going directly to the Governor for a pardon—after which we will get this farce reversed. McDivot has already written the governor, also, explaining that his sentence was ridiculous, but that he had no choice. Between the two of us, we ought to have a pardon in short order.

Then, I'll make the fur fly . . .

And we'll get in some fishing.

Best,
Mike

OFFICE OF THE
GOVERNOR OF ILLINOIS

June 17, 1966

Mr. Michael R. Reynolds
49 Water Street
Chicago, Illinois

Dear Mr. Reynolds:

In reply to your query about the request for pardon for Walter A. Child (A. Walter), may I inform you that the Governor is still on his trip with the Midwest Governors Committee, examining the Wall in Berlin. He should be back next Friday.

I will bring your request and letters to his attention the minute he returns.

Very truly yours,
Clara B. Jilks
Secretary to the Governor

229

June 27, 1966

Michael R. Reynolds
49 Water Street
Chicago, Illinois

Dear Mike:
   Where is that pardon?
   My execution date is only five days from now!

Walt

June 29, 1966

Walter A. Child (A. Walter)
Cell Block E
Illinois State Penitentiary
Joliet, Illinois

Dear Walt:
   The Governor returned, but was called away immediately to the White House in Washington to give his views on interstate sewage.
   I am camping on his doorstep and will be on him the moment he arrives here.
   Meanwhile, I agree with you about the seriousness of the situation. The warden at the prison there, Mr. Allen Magruder will bring this letter to you and have a private talk with you. I urge you to listen to what he has to say; and I enclose letters from your family also urging you to listen to Warden Magruder.

Yours,
Mike

June 30, 1966

Michael R. Reynolds
49 Water Street
Chicago, Illinois

Dear Mike: (This letter being smuggled out by Warden Magruder)
   As I was talking to Warden Magruder in my cell, here, news was brought to him that the Governor has at last returned for a while to Illinois, and will be in his office early tomorrow morning, Friday. So you will have time to get the pardon signed by him and delivered to the prison in time to stop my execution on Saturday.

Accordingly, I have turned down the Warden's kind offer of a chance to escape; since he told me he could by no means guarantee to have all the guards out of my way when I tried it; and there was a chance of my being killed escaping.

But now everything will straighten itself out. Actually, an experience as fantastic as this had to break down sometime under its own weight.

Best,
Walt

FOR THE SOVEREIGN
STATE OF ILLINOIS

I, Hubert Daniel Willikens, Governor of the State of Illinois, and invested with the authority and powers appertaining thereto, including the power to pardon those in my judgment wrongfully convicted or otherwise deserving of executive mercy, do this day of July 1, 1966, announce and proclaim that Walter A. Child (A. Walter) now in custody as a consequence of erroneous conviction upon a crime of which he is entirely innocent, is fully and freely pardoned of said crime. And I do direct the necessary authorities having custody of the said Walter A. Child (A. Walter) in whatever place or places he may be held, to immediately free, release, and allow unhindered departure to him . . .

Interdepartmental Routing Service
PLEASE DO NOT FOLD, MUTILATE,
OR SPINDLE THIS CARD

Failure to route Document properly.
To: Governor Hubert Daniel Willikens
Re: Pardon issued to Walter A. Child, July 1, 1966

Dear State Employee:

You have failed to attach your Routing Number.

PLEASE: Resubmit document with this card and form 876, explaining your authority for placing a TOP RUSH category on this document. Form 876 must be signed by your Departmental Superior.

RESUBMIT ON: Earliest possible date ROUTING SERVICE office is open. In this case, Tuesday, July 5, 1966.

WARNING: Failure to submit form 876 WITH THE SIGNATURE OF YOUR SUPERIOR may make you liable to prosecution for misusing a Service of the State Government. A warrant may be issued for your arrest.

There are NO exceptions. YOU have been WARNED.

PROBINGS

1. Do a careful room-by-room survey of your home or apartment and list all the machines and motors that you can find. Examples include the electric clock, electric can opener, furnace, radio, television, hair dryer, and electric shaver.

    Bedroom(s)   Family Room

    Bathroom   Garage

    Living Room   Kitchen

    Dining Room

    Which person in the class had the most items? How does he or she feel about having these items?
2. Construct a scale from your list of those mechanical things that you are most/least dependent upon.

MOST DEPENDENT
     1.
     2.
     3.
     4.
     5.
     6.
     7.
     8.
     9.
    10.
LEAST DEPENDENT

3. Develop an advertisement for a new mechanical toy, appliance, or tool. For example, one man is developing mechanical pets for people who live in the city. Before you scoff at such an invention, consider how attached some people are to their cars. How would the electric pet be marketed? What appeals might be used to motivate people to buy? Consider doing an ad for androids, bionic parts of the body, etc.
4. Examine your family's mail for at least two weeks and save all the "junk" mail that you can. This is advertising or marketing mail that results from a person's name being put on a computerized list. This list is then sold to mail-order companies, who, in turn, sell it to other companies.
5. How has your personal life been changed by the computer?

   At home
   At school
   In recreation (some campgrounds use the computer to assign sites)
   At church

6. Develop an ad or a story that would encourage people to use a computer mating service before they become engaged, go steady, live together, or marry.
7. Several years ago, using a calculator to do your math homework was considered "cheating." Now there are classes designed to teach you how to use the calculator. What do you think will happen ten years from now? Will anyone know how to add, subtract, etc. without calculators? What will this do to the human mind? Already there are people who wouldn't think of doing their income tax or balancing their checkbook without having a calculator in hand; do you know anyone like that?

8. In 1947 The Gallup Poll asked Americans what they thought were the greatest inventions ever made. The results:

Electric light and appliances 29%
Atomic bomb 17%
Radio 12%
The wheel 6%
Airplane 6%
Telephone 4%
Automobile 4%
Steam engine 2%
Radar 2%
Printing press 2%
Washing machine 1%
Television 1%
Others 9%
No opinion 5%

a. Do a similar poll for this year. Which inventions mentioned in 1947 were not mentioned in this year's poll? Why? Ask your parents and grandparents to rate the greatest inventions or the inventions that most changed their lives. Ask open-ended questions; don't give them the Gallup list.

b. Construct a list of what you think will be considered the most important inventions in the year 2026.

JUSTICE

15

At one time, we settled our differences among ourselves very quickly, if often fatally, by the club or sword. If one member of a family or group was killed or injured by a member of another family or group, the answer of how to settle the problem was simple. The first group simply injured or killed a person from the second group. As a result of this principle, in American history we have had numerous family feuds in which blood flowed freely for many generations. In fact, the most famous such feud, between the Hatfields and the McCoys, was settled only recently. Recall also the image that films and TV give us of the frontier days of the American West, when the only justice was administered quickly by a rope or gun.

However, at another stage in history, blood money was paid to the victim's family. If a wrong was done by one family to another, rather than physically resolving the problem, the first family simply paid a proper sum of money.

Humans consider themselves "civilized" when the State assumes the responsibility for protecting its citizens from harm by bringing criminals to something called justice. But what is justice and how should it be administered? To some, the rich receive the best form of justice because they can afford it, and the poor receive unequal treatment.

There is another angle to this question of justice, too. Not only do many Americans feel that justice is uneven; they also feel that it isn't quick enough. While nobody seems to want to return to the law of the jungle, many feel that we must find a way to ensure the safety of law-abiding citizens. Too many criminals, the argument goes, are able to walk the streets while awaiting a trial. New York state even passed a law authorizing payments to the victims of crime, on the theory that if the state can't properly protect its citizens from harm, then the state should be financially responsible for some types of crimes committed.

In Ron Goulart's story, "Into The Shop," this question of justice is most important, and justice is administered very, very speedily.

PROJECTIONS

1. Headlines from Tomorrow:

EZ TRIAL CORPORATION ANNOUNCES ITS TENTH-GENERATION COMPUTER JUSTICE PROGRAM

Following the breakdown of the judicial process, leading to an enormous backlog of cases, it was decided to administer justice by a computerized trial system, known as Computer Justice.

Make a future wheel on Computer Justice.

2. What do you think will be a crime in the year 2500? What kind of punishment will there be? Will we still have courts? Will crime and criminals be publicized as they are today?

INTO
THE SHOP

—Ron Goulart

The waitress screamed, that was the trouble with live help, and made a flapping motion with her extended arm. Stu Clemens swung sideways in the booth and looked out through the green-tinted window at the parking lot. A dark-haired man in his early thirties was slumping to his knees, his hands flickering at his sides. Silently the lawagon spun back out of its parking place and rolled nearer to the fallen man. "There's nobody in that car," said the waitress, dropping a cup of coffee.

She must be new to this planet, from one of the sticks systems maybe. "It's my car," said Clemens, flipping the napkin toggle on the table and then tossing her one when it popped up. "Here, wipe your uniform off. That's a lawagon and it knows what it's doing."

The waitress put the napkin up to her face and turned away.

Out in the lot the lawagon had the man trussed up. It stunned him again for safety and then it flipped him into the back seat for interrogation and identification. "It never makes a mistake," said Clemens to the waitress's back. "I've been marshal in Territory 23 for a year now and that lawagon has never made a mistake. They build them that way."

The car had apparently given the suspect an injection and he had fallen over out of sight. Three more napkins popped up out of the table unasked. "Damn it," said Clemens and pounded the outlet with his fist once, sharply.

"It does that sometimes," said the waitress, looking again at Clemens, but no further. She handed him his check card.

Clemens touched the waitress's arm as he got up. "Don't worry now. The law is always fair on Barnum. I'm sorry you had to see a criminal up close like that."

"He just had the businessman's lunch," the waitress said.

"Well, even criminals have to eat." Clemens paid the cash register and it let him out of the drive-in oasis.

The cars that had been parked near the lawagon were gone now. When people were in trouble they welcomed the law but other times they stayed clear. Clemens grimaced, glancing at the dry yellow country beyond the oasis restaurant. He had just cleaned up an investigation and was heading back to his office in Hub 23. He still had an hour to travel. Lighting a cigarette he started for the lawagon. He was curious to see whom his car had apprehended.

"This is a public service announcement," announced the lawagon from its roof speakers. "Sheldon Kloog, wanted murderer, has just been captured by Lawagon A10. Trial has been held, a verdict of guilty brought in, death sentenced and the sentence carried out as prescribed by law. This has been a public service announcement from the Barnum Law Bureau."

Clemens ran to the car. This was a break. Sheldon Kloog was being hunted across eleven territories for murdering his wife and dismantling all their household androids. At the driver's door the marshal took his ID cards out of his grey trouser pocket and at the same time gave the day's passwords to the lawagon. He next gave the countersigns and the oath of fealty and the car let him in.

Behind the wheel Clemens said, "Congratulations. How'd you spot him?"

The lawagon's dash speaker answered, "Made a positive identification five seconds after Kloog stepped out of the place. Surprised you didn't spot him. Was undisguised and had all the telltale marks of a homicide prone."

"He wasn't sitting in my part of the restaurant. Sorry." Clemens cocked his head and looked into the empty back seat. The lawagons had the option of holding murderers for full cybernetic trial in one of the territorial hubs or, if the murderer checked out strongly guilty and seemed dangerous, executing them on the spot. "Where is he?"

The glove compartment fell open and an opaque white jar rolled out. Clemens caught it. *Earthly Remains of Sheldon Kloog,* read the label. The disintegrator didn't leave much.

Putting the jar back, Clemens said, "Did you send photos, prints, retinal patterns and the rest on to my office."

"Of course," said the car. "Plus a full transcript of the trial. Everything in quadruplicate."

"Good," said Clemens. "I'm glad we got Kloog and he's out of the way." He lit a fresh cigarette and put his hands on the wheel. The car could drive on automatic or manual. Clemens preferred to steer himself. "Start up and head for the hub. And get my junior marshal on the line."

"Yes, sir," said the car.

"Your voice has a little too much treble," said Clemens, turning the lawagon on to the smooth black six-lane roadway that pointed flat and straight towards Hub 23.

"Sorry. I'll fix it. This is a public announcement. This is a public announcement. Better?"

"Fine. Now get me Kepling."

"Check, sir."

Clemens watched a flock of dot-sized birds circle far out over the desert. He moistened his lips and leaned back slightly.

"Jr. Marshal Kepling here," came a voice from the dash.

"Kepling," said Clemens, "a packet of assorted ID material should have come out of the teleport slot a few minutes ago. Keep a copy for our files and send the rest on to Law Bureau Central in Hub 1."

"Right, sir."

"We just got that murderer, Sheldon Kloog."

"Good work. Shall I pencil him in for a trial at Cybernetics hall?"

"We already had the trial," said Clemens. "Anything else new?"

"Looks like trouble out near Townten. Might be a sex crime."

"What exactly?"

"I'm not sure, sir," said Kepling. "The report is rather vague. You know how the android patrols out in the towns are. I dispatched a mechanical deputy about an hour ago and he should reach there by mid-afternoon. If there's a real case I can drive our lawagon over after you get back here."

Clemens frowned. "What's the victim's name?"

"Just a minute. Yeah, here it is. Marmon, Dianne. Age twenty-five, height five feet six inches, weight . . ."

Clemens had twisted the wheel violently to the right. "Stop," he said to the lawagon as it shimmied off the roading. "Dianne Marmon, Kepling."

"That's right. Do you know her?"

"What are the details you have on the crime?"

"The girl is employed at Statistics Warehouse in Townten. She didn't appear at work this morning and a routine check by a personnel andy found evidence of a struggle in her apartment. The patrol says there are no signs of theft. So kidnapping for some purpose seems likely. You may remember that last week's report from Crime Trends said there might be an upswing of sex crimes in the outlying areas like Townten this season. That's why I said it might be a sex crime. Do you know the girl?"

Clemens had known her five years ago, when they had both been at the Junior Campus of Hub 23 State College together. Dianne was a pretty blonde girl. Clemens had dated her fairly often but lost track of her when he'd transferred to the Police Academy for his final year. "I'll handle this case myself," he said. "Should take me a little over two hours to get to Townten. I'll check with you en route. Let me know at once if anything important comes in before that."

"Yes, sir. You do know her then?"

"I know her," said Clemens. To the lawagon he said, "Turn around and get us to Townten fast."

"Yes, sir," said the car.

Beyond Townseven, climbing the wide road that curved between the flat fields of yellow grain, the call from Jr. Marshal Kepling came. "Sir," said Kepling. "The patrol androids have been checking out witnesses. No one saw the girl after eleven last night. That was when she came home to her apartment. She was wearing a green coat, orange dress, green accessories. There was some noise heard in the apartment but no one thought much of it. That was a little after eleven. Seems like someone jimmied the alarm system for her place and got in. That's all so far. No prints or anything."

"Damn it," said Clemens. "It must be a real kidnapping then. And I'm an hour from Townten. Well the lawagon will catch the guy. There has to be time."

"One other thing," said Kepling.

"About Dianne Marmon?"

"No, about Sheldon Kloog."

"What?"

"Central has a report that Sheldon Kloog turned himself in at a public surrender booth in a park over in Territory 20 this morning. All the ID material matches. Whereas the stuff we sent shows a complete negative."

"What are they talking about? We caught Kloog."

"Not according to Central."

"It's impossible. The car doesn't make mistakes, Kepling."

"Central is going to make a full check-up as soon as you get back from this kidnapping case."

"They're wrong," said Clemens. "Okay. So keep me filled in on Dianne Marmon."

"Right, sir," said the Jr. Marshal, signing off.

To his lawagon Clemens said, "What do you think is going on? You couldn't have made a mistake about Sheldon Kloog. Could you?"

The car became absolutely silent and coasted off the road, brushing the invisible shield around the grain fields. Everything had stopped functioning.

"I didn't order you to pull off," said Clemens.

The car did not respond.

Lawagons weren't supposed to break down. And if they did, which rarely happened, they were supposed to repair themselves. Clemens couldn't get Lawagon A10 to do anything. It was completely dead. There was no way even to signal for help.

"For God's sake," said Clemens. There was an hour between him and Dianne. More than an hour now. He tried to make himself not think of her, of what might be happening. Of what might have already happened.

Clemens got out of the lawagon, stood back a few feet from it. "One more time," he said, "will you start?"

Nothing.

He turned and started jogging back towards Townseven. The heat of the day seemed to take all the moisture out of him, to make him dry and brittle. This shouldn't have happened. Not when someone he cared for was in danger. Not now.

Emergency Central couldn't promise him a repairman until the swing shift came on in a quarter of an hour. Clemens requested assistance, a couple of lawagons at least from the surrounding territories. Territory 20 had had a reactor accident and couldn't spare theirs. Territory 21 promised to send a lawagon and a Jr. Marshal over to Townten to pick up the trail of Dianne Marmon's kidnapper as soon as the lawagon was free. Territory 22 promised the same, although they didn't think their car would be available until after nightfall. Clemens finally ordered his own Jr. Marshal to fly over to Townten and do the best he could until a lawagon arrived. A live Jr. Marshal sure as hell couldn't do much, though. Not what a lawagon could.

The little Townseven café he was calling from was fully automatic and Clemens sat down at a coffee table to wait for the repairman to arrive. The round light-blue room was empty except for a hunched old man who was sitting at a breakfast table, ordering side orders of hash browns one after another. When he'd filled the surface of the table he started a second layer. He didn't seem to be eating any of the food.

Clemens drank the cup of coffee that came up out of his table and ignored the old man. It was probably a case for a Psych Wagon but Clemens didn't feel up to going through the trouble of turning the man in. He finished his coffee. A car stopped outside and Clemens jumped up. It was just a customer.

"How can I do that?" said the repairman as he and Clemens went down the ramp of the automatic café. "Look." He pointed across the parking area at his small one man scooter.

Clemens shook his head. "It's nearly sundown. A girl's life is in danger. Damn, if I have to wait here until you fix the lawagon and bring it back I'll lose that much more time."

"I'm sorry," said the small sun-worn man. "I can't take you out to where the car is. The bureau says these scooters are not to carry passengers. So if I put more than two hundred pounds on it it just turns off and won't go at all."

"Okay, okay." There were no cars in the parking lot, no one to commandeer.

"You told me where your lawagon is. I can find it if it's right on the highway. You wait."

"How long?"

The repairman shrugged. "Those babies don't break down much. But when they do . . . Could be a while. Overnight maybe."

"Overnight?" Clemens grabbed the man's arm. "You're kidding."

"Don't break my damn arm or it'll take that much longer."

"I'm sorry. I'll wait here. You'll drive the lawagon back?"

"Yeah. I got a special set of ID cards and passwords so I can get its hood up and drive it. Go inside and have a cup of coffee."

"Sure," said Clemens. "Thanks."

"Do my best."

"Do you know anything about the dinner-for-two tables?" the thin loose-suited young man asked Clemens.

Clemens had taken the table nearest the door and was looking out at the twilight roadway. "Beg pardon?"

"We put money in for a candle and nothing happened, except that when the asparagus arrived its ends were lit. This is my first date with this girl, marshal, and I want to make a good impression."

"Hit the outlet with your fist," said Clemens, turning away.

"Thank you, sir."

Clemens got up and went in to call the Law Bureau answering service in Townten. The automatic voice told him that Jr. Marshal Kepling had just arrived and reported in. He was on his way to the victim's apartment. No other news.

"She's not a victim," said Clemens and cut off.

"Arrest those two," said the old man, reaching for Clemens as he came out of the phone alcove.

"Why?"

"They shot a candle at my table and scattered my potatoes to here and gone."

The young man ran up. "I hit the table like you said and the candle came out. Only it went sailing all the way across the room."

"Young people," said the old man.

"Here," said Clemens. He gave both of them some cash. "Start all over again."

"That's not—" started the old man.

Clemens saw something coming down the dark road. He pushed free and ran outside.

As he reached the roadway the lawagon slowed and stopped. There was no one inside.

"Welcome aboard," said the car.

Clemens went through the identification ritual, looking off along the roadway, and got in. "Where's the repairman? Did he send you on in alone."

"I saw through him, sir," said the lawagon. "Shall we proceed to Townten?"

"Yes. Step on it," said Clemens. "But what do you mean you saw through him?"

The glove compartment dropped open. There were two white jars in it now. "Sheldon Kloog won't bother us any more, sir. I have just apprehended and tried him. He was disguised as a repairman and made an attempt to dismantle an official Law Bureau vehicle. That offense, plus his murder record, made only one course of action possible."

Clemens swallowed, making himself not even tighten his grip on the wheel. If he said anything the car might stop again. There was something wrong. As soon as Dianne was safe Lawagon A10 would have to go into the shop for a thorough check-up. Right now Clemens needed the car badly, needed what it could do. They had to track down whoever had kidnapped Dianne. "Good work," he said evenly.

The headlights hit the cliffs that bordered the narrow road and long ragged shadows crept up the hillside ahead of them.

"I think we're closing in," said Clemens. He was talking to Jr. Marshal Kepling whom he'd left back at the Law Bureau answering service in Townten. He had cautioned Kepling to make no mention of the Kloog business while the car could hear them.

"Central verifies the ID on the kidnapper from the prints we found," said Kepling. Surprisingly Kepling had found fingerprints in Dianne's apartment that the andy patrol and the mechanical deputy had missed. "It is Jim Otterson. Up to now he's only done short sentence stuff."

"Good," said Clemens. That meant that Otterson might not harm Dianne. Unless this was the time he'd picked to cross over. "The lawagon," said Clemens, "is holding on to his trail. We should get him now any time. He's on foot now and the girl is definitely still with him the car says. We're closing in."

"Good luck," said Kepling.

"Thanks." Clemens signed off.

Things had speeded up once he and the lawagon had reached Townten. Clemens had known that. The lawagon had had no trouble picking up the scent. Now, late at night, they were some twenty-five miles out of Townten. They'd found Otterson's car seven miles back with its clutch burned out. The auto had been there, off the unpaved back road, for about four hours. Otterson had driven around in great zigzags. Apparently he had spent the whole of the night after the kidnapping in a deserted storehouse about fifty miles from Townten. He had left there, according to the lawagon, about noon and headed towards Towneleven. Then he had doubled back again, swinging in near Townten. Clemens and the lawagon had spent hours circling around on Otterson's trail. With no more car Otterson and the girl couldn't have come much further than where Clemens and the lawagon were now.

The lawagon turned off the road and bumped across a rocky plateau. It swung around and stopped. Up above was a high flat cliffside, dotted with caves. "Up there, I'd say," said the lawagon. It had silenced its engine.

"Okay," said Clemens. There wasn't much chance of sneaking up on Otterson if he was up in one of those caves. Clemens would have to risk trying to talk to him. "Shoot the lights up there and turn on the speakers."

Two spotlights hit the cliff and a hand mike came up out of the dash. Taking it, Clemens climbed out of the lawagon. "Otterson, this is Marshal Clemens. I'm asking you to surrender. If you don't I'll have to use stun gas on you. We know you're in one of those caves, we can check each one off if we have to. Give up."

Clemens waited. Then half way up the cliffside something green flashed and then came hurtling down. It pinwheeled down the mountain and fell past the plateau.

"What the hell." Clemens ran forward. There was a gully between the cliff and the plateau, narrow and about thirty feet deep. At its bottom now was something. It might be Dianne, arms tangled over interlaced brush.

"Get me a handlight and a line," he called to the lawagon.

Without moving the car lobbed a handbeam to him and sent a thin cord snaking over the ground. "Check."

"Cover the caves. I'm going down to see what that was that fell."

"Ready?"

Clemens hooked the light on his belt and gripped the line. He backed over the plateau edge. "Okay, ready."

The line was slowly let out and Clemens started down. Near the brush he caught a rock and let go of the line. He unhitched the light and swung it. He exhaled sharply. What had fallen was only an empty coat. Otterson was trying to decoy them. "Watch out," Clemens shouted to his car. "It's not the girl. He may try to make a break now."

He steadied himself and reached for the rope. Its end snapped out at him and before he could catch it it whirred up and out of sight. "Hey, the rope. Send it back."

"Emergency," announced the lawagon, its engine coming on.

Up above a blaster sizzled and rock clattered. Clemens yanked out his pistol and looked up. Down the hillside a man was coming, carrying a bound up girl in his arms. His big hands showed and they held pistols. Dianne was gagged but seemed to be alive. Otterson zigzagged down, using the girl for a shield. He was firing not at Clemens but at the lawagon. He jumped across the gully to a plateau about twenty yards from where Clemens had started over.

Holstering his gun Clemens started to climb. He was half way up when he heard Otterson cry out. Then there was no sound at all.

Clemens tried to climb faster but could not. The gully side was jagged and hard to hold on to. Finally he swung himself up on the plateau.

"This is a public service announcement." said the lawagon. "Sheldon Kloog and his female accomplice have been captured, tried, sentenced and executed. This message comes to you from the Law-Bureau. Thank you."

Clemens roared. He grabbed up a rock in each hand and went charging at the car. "You've killed Dianne," he shouted. "You crazy damn machine."

The lawagon turned and started rolling towards him. "No you don't, Kloog," it said.

PROBINGS

1. What message or point about justice is Goulart trying to make in his story? Do you agree or disagree with it? Remember, the good SF writer makes a statement about the present as well as the future.
2. Write an SF story, tape a play, or develop a scenario based on the idea that a Crime Computer can conduct trials for accused criminals and carry out sentences. You might want to think about some of the other consequences of using computers for law enforcement, like the "accident" in "Computers Don't Argue."
3. Following are some opinions about crime and punishment:

   "Bringing criminals to trial in this country is too slow."
   *

   "No person apprehended for committing a crime should be allowed to walk the streets while awaiting trial."
   *

   "The rights of accused criminals must be protected like the rights of anyone else."
   *

   "The rights of criminal must be as protected as the rights of the victim."
   *

   "If the government can't control crime, then the government should pay the victims of crime."
   *

   "Any person who commits a major crime such as rape, murder, or robbery should be permanently put away."
   *

   "The courts are just too soft on criminals."

"White collar criminals who pad their expense accounts, cheat on their income tax, and embezzle money get lighter sentences than the common man."

"When you steal from the company you work for, you are the same as a looter and should go to jail."

Do you agree with any of these statements? Which ones? Why? Set up debates on these topics.

4. What if we had time travel? Would you like to go backward or forward in time to see "the crime of the century"? Where would you like to go? What if we could cross the continent in 20 minutes? How might this change crime? What if we had 3-D videophones? What might happen to obscene phone calls?

5. Headline from Tomorrow:
"First 3-D Videophone Crime Discovered"

6. One man has invented a device that can be installed in criminals' brains; when activated, this device would force criminals to stay in an assigned area. If the criminals try to leave, shooting pains would drive them back to their assigned area. Some people feel that this would be more humane than putting people in cramped cells the way we do now. What do you think?

Develop a scenario or story using this idea. Perhaps, criminals could be assigned to special villages where they could even live with their families. Would there be any criminals you wouldn't like to see "loose" in this way? Which? Would it bother you to see convicted mass murderers Richard Speck or Charles Manson in such a village?

BIO-ETHICS: I

16

Before World War II, babies frequently died from pneumonia. Stroll through any cemetery and you can read the sad tales of many a family on the grave markers. With the discovery of penicillin and a battery of wonder drugs, numerous diseases such as pneumonia could be checked. Just a few decades ago, the word "polio" struck terror in the hearts of parents and their children. With the discovery of a polio vaccine, millions of Americans were spared death and the agony of being crippled. In this miraculous world of ours, pacemakers keep numerous hearts beating regularly, artificial limbs can be electronically controlled, and hundreds of new drugs save us from pain and even death. Consider that many of these medical marvels were only in the realm of science fiction not too many years ago.

The future holds still more astounding breakthroughs that will make television's bionic man and woman look simple by comparison. For example, scientists have already cloned a frog; by removing one cell from a donor frog, they were able, by means of a complicated process, to reproduce the frog *exactly*. If a human could be cloned at some point in the future, he or she could also be reproduced exactly. If the original human had been born with a mole or birthmark, so would the clone. Think about it, if you were twenty years old when you decided to have yourself cloned, you could watch yourself grow up again from babyhood. But would you want to? All of these medical breakthroughs raise serious moral, ethical, religious, and legal questions that we must think about now. These questions constitute the realm of bio-ethics. There is little doubt that profound and mind-boggling changes are going to affect the society that you will live in tomorrow; how we will cope with these changes is the central question of bio-ethics.

Consider, for example, organ transplants. On the one hand, doctors must hope for the right kind of a death in order to save another life. For years doctors have been able to replace the cornea of the eye, tissue, and some bones. Recently kidney and heart transplants have become more frequent, although they are not always successful. One scientist is experimenting in the area of brain transplants for monkeys, with the consequences of such research being all too obvious for humans. If you have watched the bionic man or woman, you also know that there is considerable interest in replacing human parts with mechanical ones. In fact, artificial hips, jaws, and joints are already being used.

One doctor has even suggested the idea of body farming, or raising human clones for spare parts. If you need a new leg or arm, it would be easy to make. In the following story, the author allows us to consider some of the hidden consequences of organ transplants. What he is really asking us to ponder, though, is how far are you willing to see this experimental kind of research go? Cloning humans? Creating bionic people? Raising babies in artificial wombs.?

1. Consider the *New Yorker* cartoon below:
    a. Why might the older man want himself cloned?
    b. Write a caption for the son's response to his father.

PROJECTIONS

"I'm afraid, Son, this will never be yours. I'm having myself cloned."

HEADLINES FROM TOMORROW:

GROW-A-CHILD

NOW POSSIBLE

Read carefully the following directive, mailed to you on May 1, 2026.

A.G.E.

by
Bernard Hollister
and Joy Joyce

Since Dr. Warren Wolski's dramatic medical breakthrough some twenty years ago, it has been possible to grow human embryos artificially; these embryos are now commonly known by the acronym A.G.E. In rural areas, doctors have taken on the responsibility of making periodic house calls to check on the A.G.E.s' development. In the bigger cities, computers are now used to monitor the embryos.

Before anyone may have an A.G.E., he or she must be approved by a special board of citizens. You have just been invited to sit on this board. If you accept, you have a variety of options open to you. You may disapprove all of the following applications individually, you may approve all of the applications individually, you may approve some and reject others. However, all the applications that you accept must be ranked in order of priority. For example, No. 1 means that this person has the first choice. The reason for this is that there are a limited number of A.G.E.'s and perhaps not all approved applicants can be accommodated. If you refuse, you may serve as an observer and take notes on the decision-making process.

A few background notes that you should be aware of follow: 1) It is possible to determine the sex of an A.G.E. If potential parents request a male or female, they can be accommodated if their application is accepted. 2) All potential parents over the age of 50 are required to submit to a "health-life" examination by the "Medi-Computer." Literally thousands of variables are fed into the machine, for example, age, present health, heredity, former diseases, occupation, sex, etc., and the Medi-Computer makes a statistical projection of how many healthy years the applicant may expect—barring, of course, accidents, wars, etc.

The applications follow. Remember that you must rank all the applicants that you accept by priority.

1. Mary and Tom Smith have had trouble with previous pregnancies. Mary has had three miscarriages and one still-born child. They now have a nine-month-old baby, but they would like another healthy child as soon as possible. Mary is 27 and Tom is 31. He is a mechanic, and Mary has done office work. They have serious reservations about raising an only child.

2. Jan O'Conner is a professional entertainer who wants a child. She feels very strongly that she cannot now leave her singing for a normal pregnancy, and so she has requested an A.G.E. She is mar-

ried for the third time—to another professional entertainer. She had one child when she was 18; that child now lives with her first husband. Jan is 30; her husband, 40.

3. Norma (37) and Timothy (30) McGuire have admitted that their marriage has become increasingly shaky in recent years. They hope that a child will bring them closer together and have applied for an A.G.E. Because Norma is in her late thirties, they feel that it would involve considerable risk for her to carry the baby.

4. Sheila Greene (37) had a hysterectomy for medical reasons during her late twenties, right after the birth of her first child. She and her husband, Morgan (37), would like to have more children. A.G.E. is the only option they are considering right now.

5. Marilyn Maski (34) is a world-renowned brain surgeon with a very active career. She would like very much to have a child, but she can't spare the time from her practice. She is unmarried, but lives with her widowed mother (55), who would help care for the child.

6. Janice Lewandowski (33) has been told that for her to have another child might well kill her, but she and her husband want more children. The only way they could safely have more is through A.G.E. Their children are a girl 12, a girl 10, a boy 7, a boy 3, a girl 2. Jan is a housewife and her husband is a well-to-do banker.

7. John Murphy retired early at 55. Now at 57 he and his wife, who is about the same age, are in good health, but they feel themselves unfulfilled. Because they both had very active careers at one time, they never had children; now they feel that they have many good qualities to share with a child. The Medi-Computer indicates that they have a projected Health-Life of 20–22

years. They have plenty of money to support themselves and any children whom they might be allowed to have through A.G.E.

8. Joan Krane (26) is tired of working and has agreed to have a child because her 29-year-old husband wants one. To Joan, though, having a baby is "so messy and painful." Tom Krane is an IBM analyst; Joan is a secretary.

9. Jerry X is an unmarried male homosexual, aged 25. He makes an excellent living in the restaurant he owns. He very much would like a child, but he can't stand women.

10. Chuck and Laura Walters (both are 30) had used various drugs very heavily during their twenties. They have recently reformed their lifestyle and intend to begin a family. However, in the light of their past drug use, Laura fears carrying a child, and they have consequently applied for an A.G.E.

11. Sybil Jones is a black woman of 29 who has never been married, and she has strong feelings against ever getting married. She feels that she can give a great deal to a child and is frank about being lonely. She is an attorney and can afford expensive day care.

12. Jane Sutton, a 27-year-old psychologist, is very much into Women's Liberation and, while she wants children, she feels that the woman should not have to carry one—if she doesn't wish to. As a result, she has applied for an A.G.E. Her husband, David (29), would not object to a child through A.G.E.

13. The Clarks, like the Murphys, are older —in their middle fifties. Unlike the Murphys, the Clarks have raised three children to adulthood. They are going to retire in about eight years and they would like an A.G.E. for companionship. He works in a factory on an assembly line; she is a sales clerk. Their

Health-Life projection is also 20–25 years.

14. James Hubbel (41) has had two unsuccessful marriages, but he very much wants to have a son to carry on his name. He is presently unmarried, and he intends to stay that way. He has two daughters from his former marriages who are living with their mother.

15. Morgan Xandu (33) is a black militant who wants a child without the "encumbrance" of a woman. He feels that in this way he can raise a son to be, in his words, "as tough as steel." Morgan is financially secure.

16. Drs. Joseph and Sarah Benson (both around 35) are not in a hurry to have children because of their careers. Their parents, however, are elderly and are anxious to have grandchildren. Sarah is unwilling at this time to carry a child. They have applied for an A.G.E. with the understanding that if their application is approved, the child will be raised by the grandparents for the first few years. Both Joe and Sarah feel that the grandparents would be responsible surrogate parents.

17. After repeated attempts to have a child, Maureen (28) and Eric Wolfe (27) sought medical advice. Tests determined that Eric was sterile and a sperm donor was the only alternative. Maureen consented to artificial insemination, but she later changed her mind for "sentimental" and "emotional" reasons. The Wolfes have applied to the A.G.E. board instead.

18. Jeremy (23) and Susan Lawson (28) have no children. Susan is of RH-negative blood type. Carrying a child has been declared unwise by her physician, although for the first child it may be safe. They would like to have at least two children.

19. Both children born to David and Allison Barker (both 24) have had fairly

severe physical handicaps. The Barkers want to have a normal child. The cause of their children's defects is not known.

20. Jason Andrews, 31, and Cathy Powers, 27, have lived together for three years. They are unmarried and don't want to become "entangled," as they put it, in marriage. However, they would like a child, and they feel that their relationship is secure.

CAUGHT IN THE ORGAN DRAFT

—Robert Silverberg

Look there, Kate, down by the promenade. Two splendid seniors, walking side by side near the water's edge. They radiate power, authority, wealth, assurance. He's a judge, a senator, a corporation president, no doubt, and she's—what?—a professor emeritus of international law, let's say. There they go toward the plaza, moving serenely, smiling, nodding graciously to passersby. How the sunlight gleams in their white hair! I can barely stand the brilliance of that reflected aura: it blinds me, it stings my eyes. What are they—eighty, ninety, a hundred years old? At this distance they seem much younger—they hold themselves upright, their backs are straight, they might pass for being only fifty or sixty. But I can tell. Their confidence, their poise, mark them for what they are. And when they were nearer I could see their withered cheeks, their sunken eyes. No cosmetics can hide that. These two are old enough to be our great-grandparents. They were well past sixty before we were even born, Kate. How superbly their bodies function! But why not? We can guess at their medical histories. She's had at least three hearts, he's working on his fourth set of lungs, they apply for new kidneys every five years, their brittle bones are reinforced with hundreds of skeletal snips from the arms and legs of hapless younger folk, their dimming sensory apparatus is aided by countless nerve grafts obtained the same way, their ancient arteries are freshly sheathed with sleek teflon. Ambulatory assemblages of second-hand human parts, spiced here and there with synthetic or mechanical organ substitutes, that's all they are. And what am I, then, or you? Nineteen years old and vulnerable. In their eyes I'm nothing but a ready stockpile of healthy organs, waiting to serve their needs. Come here, son. What a fine strapping young man you are! Can you spare a kidney for me? A lung? A choice little segment of intestine? Ten centimeters of your ulnar nerve? I need a few pieces of you, lad. You won't deny a distinguished elder leader like me what I ask, will you? *Will you?*

Today my draft notice, a small crisp document, very official looking, came shooting out of the data slot when I punched for my morning mail. I've been expecting it all spring: no surprise, no shock, actually rather an anticlimax now that it's finally here. In six weeks I am to report to Transplant House for my final physical exam—only a formality, they wouldn't have drafted me if I didn't already rate top marks as organ reservoir potential—and then I go on call. The average call time is about two months. By autumn they'll be carving me up. Eat, drink, and be merry, for soon comes the surgeon to my door.

A straggly band of senior citizens is picketing the central headquarters of the League for Bodily Sanctity. It's a counterdemonstration, an anti-anti-transplant protest, the worst kind of political statement, feeding on the ugliest of negative emotions. The demonstrators carry glowing signs that say:

Bodily Sanctity—or Bodily Selfishness?

And:

You Owe Your Leaders Your Very Lives

And:

Listen to the Voice of Experience

The picketers are low-echelon seniors, barely across the qualifying line, the ones who can't really be sure of getting transplants. No wonder they're edgy about the league. Some of them are in wheelchairs and some are encased right up to the eyebrows in portable life support systems. They croak and shout bitter invective and shake their fists. Watching the show from an upper window of the league building, I shiver with fear and dismay. These people don't just want my kidneys or my lungs. They'd take my eyes, my liver, my pancreas, my heart, anything they might happen to need.

I talked it over with my father. He's forty-five years old—too old to have been personally affected by the organ draft, too young to have needed any transplants yet. That puts him in a neutral position, so to speak, except for one minor factor: his transplant status is 5-G. That's quite high on the eligibility list, not the top priority class but close enough. If he fell ill tomorrow and the Transplant Board ruled that his life would be endangered if he didn't get a new heart or lung or kidney, he'd be given one practically immediately. Status like that simply has to influence his objectivity on the whole organ issue. Anyway, I told him I was planning to appeal and maybe even to resist. "Be reasonable," he said, "be rational, don't let your emotions run away with you. Is it worth jeopardizing your whole future over a thing like this? After all, not everybody who's drafted loses vital organs."

"Show me the statistics," I said. "Show me."

He didn't know the statistics. It was his impression that only about a quarter or a fifth of the draftees actually got an organ call. That tells you how closely the older generation keeps in touch with the situation—and my father's an educated man, articulate, well informed. Nobody over the age of thirty-five that I talked to could show me any statistics. So I showed them. Out of a league brochure, it's true, but based on certified National Institute of Health reports. Nobody escapes. They always clip you, once you qualify. The need for young organs inexorably expands to match the pool of available organpower. In the long run they'll get us all and chop us to bits. That's probably what they want, anyway. To rid themselves of the younger members of the species, always so troublesome, by cannibalizing us for spare parts, and recycling us, lung by lung, pancreas by pancreas, through their own deteriorating bodies.

Fig. 4. On March 23, 1964, this dog's own liver was removed and replaced with the liver of a non-related mongrel donor. The animal was treated with azathioprine for four months and all therapy then stopped. He remains in perfect health 6-2/3 years after transplantation.

The war goes on. This is, I think, its fourteenth year. Of course they're beyond the business of killing now. They haven't had any field engagements since '93 or so, certainly—not since the organ draft legislation went into effect. The old ones can't afford to waste precious young bodies on the battlefield. So robots wage our territorial struggles for us, butting heads with a great metallic clank, laying land mines and twitching their sensors at the enemy's mines, digging tunnels beneath his screens, et cetera, et cetera. Plus, of course, the quasi-military activity—economic sanctions, third-power blockades, propaganda telecasts beamed as overrides from merciless orbital satellites, and stuff like that. It's a subtler war than the kind they used to wage: nobody dies. Still, it drains national resources. Taxes are going up again this year, the fifth or sixth year in a row, and they've just slapped a special Peace Surcharge on all metal-containing goods, on account of the copper shortage. There once was a time when we could hope that our crazy old leaders would die off or at least retire for reasons of health, stumbling away to their country villas with ulcers or shingles or scabies or scruples and allowing new young peacemakers to take office. But now they just go on and on, immortal and insane, our senators, our cabinet members, our generals, our planners. And their war goes on and on too, their absurd, imcomprehensible, diabolical, self-gratifying war.

I know people my age or a little older who have taken asylum in Belgium or Sweden or Paraguay or one of the other countries where Bodily Sanctity laws have been passed. There are about twenty such countries, half of them the most progressive nations in the world and half of them the most reactionary. But what's the sense of running away? I don't want to live in exile. I'll stay here and fight.

Naturally they don't ask a draftee to give up his heart or his liver or some other organ essential to life, say his medulla oblongata. We haven't yet reached that stage of political enlightenment at which the government feels capable of legislating fatal conscription. Kidneys and lungs, the paired organs, the dispensable organs, are the chief targets so far. But if you study the history of conscription over the ages you see that it can always be projected on a curve rising from rational necessity to absolute lunacy. Give them a fingertip, they'll take an arm. Give them an inch of bowel, they'll take your guts. In another fifty years they'll be drafting hearts and stomachs and maybe even brains, mark my words; let them get the technology of brain transplants together and nobody's skull will be safe. It'll be human sacrifice all over again. The only difference between us and the Aztecs is one of method: we have anesthesia, we have antisepsis and asepsis, we use scalpels instead of obsidian blades to cut out the hearts of our victims.

MEANS OF OVERCOMING THE HOMOGRAFT REACTION

The pathway that has led from the demonstration of immunological nature of the homograft reaction and its universality to the development of relatively effective but by no means completely satisfactory means of overcoming it for therapeutic purposes is an interesting one that can only be touched upon very briefly. The year 1950 ushered in a new era in transplantation immunobiology in which the discovery of various means of weakening or abrogating a host's response to a homograft—such as sublethal whole body x-irradiation, or treatment with certain adrenal cortico-steroid hormones, notably cortisone—began to influence the direction of the mainstream of research and engender confidence that a workable clinical solution might not be too far off. By the end of the decade powerful immuno-suppressive drugs, such as 6-mercaptopurine, had been shown to be capable of holding in abeyance the reactivity of dogs to renal homografts, and soon afterwards this principle was successfully extended to man.

Is my resistance to the draft based on an ingrained abstract distaste for tyranny in all forms or rather on the mere desire to keep my body intact? Could it be both, maybe? Do I need an idealistic rationalization at all? Don't I have an inalienable right to go through my life wearing my own native-born kidneys?

The law was put through by an administration of old men. You can be sure that all laws affecting the welfare of the young are the work of doddering moribund ancients afflicted with angina pectoris, atherosclerosis, prolapses of the infundibulum, fulminating ventricles, and dilated viaducts. The problem was this: not enough healthy young people were dying of highway accidents, successful suicide attempts, diving board miscalculations, electrocutions, and football injuries; therefore there was a shortage of transplantable organs. An effort to restore the death penalty for the sake of creating a steady supply of state-controlled cadavers lost out in the courts. Volunteer programs of organ donation weren't working too well, since most of the volunteers were criminals who signed up in order to gain early release from prison: a lung reduced your sentence by five years, a kidney got you three years off, and so on. The exodus of convicts from the jails under this clause wasn't so popular among suburban voters. Meanwhile there was an urgent and mounting need for organs; a lot of important seniors might in fact die if something didn't get done fast. So a coalition of senators from all four parties rammed the organ draft measure through the upper chamber in the face of a filibuster threat from a few youth-oriented members. It had a much easier time in the House of Representatives, since nobody in the House ever pays much attention to the text of a bill up for a vote, and word had been circulated on this one that if it passed, everybody over sixty-five who had any political pull at all could count on living twenty or thirty extra years, which to a representative means a crack at ten to fifteen extra terms of office. Naturally there have been court challenges, but what's the use? The average age of the eleven justices of the Supreme Court is seventy-eight. They're human and mortal. They need our flesh. If they throw out the organ draft now, they're signing their own death warrants.

For a year and a half I was the chairman of the antidraft campaign on our campus. We were the sixth or seventh local chapter of the League for Bodily Sanctity to be organized in this country, and we were real activists. Mainly we would march up and down in front of the draft board offices carrying signs proclaiming things like:

KIDNEY POWER

And:

A MAN'S BODY IS HIS CASTLE

And:

THE POWER TO CONSCRIPT ORGANS IS THE POWER
TO DESTROY LIVES

We never went in for the rough stuff, though, like bombing organ transplant centers or hijacking refrigeration trucks. Peaceful agitation, that was our motto. When a couple of our members tried to swing us to a more violent policy, I delivered an extemporaneous two-hour speech arguing for moderation. Naturally I was drafted the moment I became eligible.

"I can understand your hostility to the draft," my college advisor said. "It's certainly normal to feel queasy about surrendering important organs of your body. But you ought to consider the countervailing advantages. Once you've given an organ you get a 6-A classification, Preferred Recipient, and you remain forever on the 6-A roster. Surely you realize that this means that if you ever need a transplant yourself, you'll automatically be eligible for one, even if your other personal and professional qualifications don't lift you to the optimum level. Suppose your career plans don't work out and you become a manual laborer, for instance. Ordinarily you wouldn't rate even a first look if you developed heart disease, but your Preferred Recipient status would save you. You'd get a new lease on life, my boy."

I pointed out the fallacy inherent in this. Which is that as the number of draftees increases, it will come to encompass a majority or even a totality of the population, and eventually everybody will have 6-A Preferred Recipient status by virtue of having donated, and the term Preferred Recipient will cease to have any meaning. A shortage of transplantable organs would eventually develop as each past donor stakes his claim to a transplant when his health fails, and in time they'd have to arrange the Preferred Recipients by order of personal and professional achievement anyway, for the sake of arriving at some kind of priorities within the 6-A class, and we'd be right back where we are now.

Fig. 7. The course of a patient who received antilymphocyte globulin (ALG) before and for the first four months after renal homotransplantation. The donor was an older brother. There was no early rejection. Prednisone therapy was started forty days postoperatively. Note the insidious onset of late rejection after cessation of globulin therapy. This was treated by a moderate increase in the maintenance doses of steroids. This delayed complication occurred in only two of the first twenty recipients of intrafamilial homografts who were treated with ALG. It has been seen with about the same low frequency in subsequent cases. (By permission of Surg. Gynec. Obstet. 126 (1968): p. 1023.)

So I went down to Transplant House today, right on schedule, to take my physical. A couple of my friends thought I was making a tactical mistake by reporting at all; if you're going to resist, they said, resist at every point along the line. Make them drag you in for the physical. In purely idealistic (and ideological) terms I suppose they're right. But there's no need yet for me to start kicking up a fuss. Wait till they actually say, "We need your kidney, young man." Then I can resist, if resistance is the course I ultimately choose. (Why am I wavering? Am I afraid of the damage to my career plans that resisting might do? Am I not entirely convinced of the injustice of the entire organ draft system? I don't know. I'm not even sure that I *am* wavering. Reporting for your physical isn't really a sellout to the system.) I went, anyway. They tapped this and x-rayed that and peered into the other thing. Yawn, please. Bend over, please. Cough, please. Hold out your left arm, please. They marched me in front of a battery of diagnostat machines and I stood there hoping for the red light to flash—*tilt,* get out of here!—but I was, as expected, in perfect physical shape, and I qualified for call. Afterward I met Kate and we walked in the park and held hands and watched the glories of the sunset and discussed what I'll do, when and if the call comes. *If?* Wishful thinking, boy!

If your number is called you become exempt from military service, and they credit you with a special $750 tax deduction every year. Big deal.

Another thing they're very proud of is the program of voluntary dona- tion of unpaired organs. This has nothing to do with the draft, which— thus far, at least—requisitions only paired organs, organs that can be spared without loss of life. For the last twelve years it's been possible to walk into any hospital in the United States and sign a simple release form allowing the surgeons to slice you up. Eyes, lungs, heart, intestines, pancreas, liver, anything, you give it all to them. This process used to be known as suicide in a simpler era and it was socially disapproved, espe- cially in times of labor shortages. Now we have a labor surplus, because even though our population growth has been fairly slow since the middle of the century, the growth of labor-eliminating mechanical devices and processes has been quite rapid, even exponential. Therefore to volunteer for this kind of total donation is considered a deed of the highest social utility, removing as it does a healthy young body from the overcrowded labor force and at the same time providing some elder statesman with the assurance that the supply of vital organs will not unduly diminish. Of course, you have to be crazy to volunteer, but there's never been any shortages of lunatics in our society.

If you're not drafted by the age of twenty-one, through some lucky fluke, you're safe. And a few of us do slip through the net, I'm told. So far there are more of us in the total draft pool than there are patients in need of transplants. But the ratios are changing rapidly. The draft legisla- tion is still relatively new. Before long they'll have drained the pool of eligible draftees, and then what? Birth rates nowadays are low; the supply of potential draftees is finite. But death rates are even lower; the demand for organs is essentially infinite. I can give you only one of my kidneys, if I am to survive; but you, as you live on and on, may require more than one kidney transplant. Some recipients may need five or six sets of kidneys or lungs before they finally get beyond hope of repair at age seventy-one or so. As those who've given organs come to requisition organs later on in life, the pressure on the under-twenty-one group will get even greater. Those in need of transplants will come to outnumber those who can donate organs, and everybody in the pool will get clipped. And then? Well, they could lower the draft age to seventeen or sixteen or even fourteen. But even that's only a short-term solution. Sooner or later, there won't be enough spare organs to go around.

Will I stay? Will I flee? Will I go to court? Time's running out. My call is sure to come up in another few weeks. I feel a tickling sensation in my back, now and then, as though somebody's quietly sawing at my kidneys.

Cannibalism. At Chou-kou-tien, Dragon Bone Hill, twenty-five miles southwest of Peking, paleontologists excavating a cave early in the twentieth century discovered the fossil skulls of Peking Man, *Pithecanthropus pekinensis.* The skulls had been broken away at the base, which led Franz Weidenreich, the director of the Dragon Bone Hill digs, to speculate that Peking Man was a cannibal who had killed his own kind, extracted the brains of his victims through openings in the base of their skulls, cooked and feasted on the cerebral meat—there were hearths and fragments of charcoal at the site—and left the skulls behind in the cave as trophies. To eat your enemy's flesh: to absorb his skills, his strengths, his knowledge, his achievements, his virtues. It took mankind five hundred thousand years to struggle upward from cannibalism. But we never lost the old craving, did we? There's still easy comfort to gain by devouring those who are younger, stronger, more agile than you. We've improved the techniques, is all. And so now they eat us raw, the old ones, they gobble us up, organ by throbbing organ. Is that really an improvement? At least Peking Man cooked his meat.

Our brave new society, where all share equally in the triumphs of medicine, and the deserving senior citizens need not feel that their merits and prestige will be rewarded only by a cold grave—we sing its praises all the time. How pleased everyone is about the organ draft! Except, of course, a few disgruntled draftees.

The ticklish question of priorities. Who gets the stockpiled organs? They have an elaborate system by which hierarchies are defined. Supposedly a big computer drew it up, thus assuring absolute godlike impartiality. You earn salvation through good works: accomplishments in career and benevolence in daily life win you points that nudge you up the ladder until you reach one of the high-priority classifications, 4-G or better. No doubt the classification system is impartial and is administered justly. But is it rational? Whose needs does it serve? In 1943, during World War II, there was a shortage of the newly discovered drug penicillin among the American military forces in North Africa. Two groups of soldiers were most in need of its benefits: those who were suffering from infected battle wounds and those who had contracted venereal disease. A junior medical officer, working from self-evident moral principles, ruled that the wounded heroes were more deserving of treatment than the self-indulgent syphilitics. He was overruled by the medical officer in charge, who observed that the VD cases could be restored to active duty more quickly, if treated; besides, if they remained untreated they served as vectors of further infection. Therefore he gave them the penicillin and left the wounded groaning on their beds of pain. The logic of the battle-field, incontrovertible, unassailable.

The great chain of life. Little creatures in the plankton are eaten by larger ones, and the greater plankton falls prey to little fishes, and little fishes to bigger fishes, and so on up to the tuna and the dolphin and the shark. I eat the flesh of the tuna and I thrive and flourish and grow fat, and store up energy in my vital organs. And am eaten in turn by the shriveled wizened seniors. All life is linked. I see my destiny.

In the early days rejection of the transplanted organ was the big prob-lem. Such a waste! The body failed to distinguish between a beneficial though alien organ and an intrusive, hostile microorganism. The mech-anism known as the immune response was mobilized to drive out the invader. At the point of invasion enzymes came into play, a brush fire was designed to rip down and dissolve the foreign substances. White corpus-cles poured in via the circulatory system, vigilant phagocytes on the march. Through the lymphatic network came antibodies, high-powered protein missiles. Before any technology of organ grafts could be devel-oped, methods had to be devised to suppress the immune response. Drugs, radiation treatment, metabolic shock—one way and another, the organ rejection problem was long ago conquered. I can't conquer my draft rejection problem. Aged and rapacious legislators, I reject you and your legislation.

My call notice came today. They'll need one of my kidneys. The usual request. "You're lucky," somebody said at lunchtime. "They might have wanted a lung."

Kate and I walk into the green glistening hills and stand among the blossoming oleanders and corianders and frangipani and whatever. How good it is to be alive, to breathe this fragrance, to show our bodies to the bright sun! Her skin is tawny and glowing. Her beauty makes me weep. She will not be spared. None of us will be spared. I go first, then she, or is it she ahead of me? Where will they make the incision? Here, on her smooth rounded back? Here, on the flat taut belly? I can see the high priest standing over the altar. At the first blaze of dawn his shadow falls across her. The obsidian knife that is clutched in his upraised hand has a terrible fiery sparkle. The choir offers up a discordant hymn to the god of blood. The knife descends.

My last chance to escape across the border. I've been up all night, weighing the options. There's no hope of appeal. Running away leaves a bad taste in my mouth. Father, friends, even Kate, all say stay, stay, stay, face the music. The hour of decision. Do I really have a choice? I have no choice. When the time comes, I'll surrender peacefully.

I report to Transplant House for conscriptive donative surgery in three hours.

After all, he said coolly, what's a kidney? I'll still have another one, you know. And if that one malfunctions, I can always get a replacement. I'll have Preferred Recipient status, 6-A, for what that's worth. But I won't settle for my automatic 6-A. I know what's going to happen to the priority system; I'd better protect myself. I'll go into politics. I'll climb. I'll attain upward mobility out of enlightened self-interest, right? Right. I'll become so important that society will owe me a thousand transplants. And one of these years I'll get that kidney back. Three of four kidneys, fifty kidneys, as many as I need. A heart or two. A few lungs. A pancreas, a spleen, a liver. They won't be able to refuse me anything. I'll show them. I'll show them. I'll out-senior the seniors. There's your Bodily Sanctity activist for you, eh? I suppose I'll have to resign from the league. Goodbye, idealism. Goodbye, moral superiority. Goodbye, kidney. Goodbye, goodbye, goodbye.

It's done. I've paid my debt to society. I've given up unto the powers that be my humble pound of flesh. When I leave the hospital in a couple of days, I'll carry a card testifying to my new 6-A status.
Top priority for the rest of my life.
Why, I might live for a thousand years.

PROBINGS

1. If you were the young man in the story who was caught in the organ draft, how would you react? Would you emigrate to escape the organ draft? Would such an organ draft be a good idea? Would your answer be different if you were 60 years old?
2. If you could be cloned, would you want to be? Why or why not?
3. If you could select any person from the past or present to be cloned, who would it be? Why? Consider some of the consequences if we could clone people many times; people such as Jesus, Buddha, Napoleon, Hitler, John F. Kennedy, Dr. King.
4. Write a science fiction story about some famous person of the past being cloned.
5. Some scientists talk about body farming, or "growing" bodies for their spare parts. Would you be in favor of such an idea? Develop arguments for both sides of this issue. Consider having a debate.
6. Develop an advertisement for TV, the newspaper, or magazines to market one or all of the following. What appeal would have to be made to get the American people to buy?

a. clone
   b. an embryo grown in an artificial womb
   c. organ transplants
7. Develop a scenario showing how our society could get to the point
    where we might have to draft young people for their internal organs.
8. Another science fiction writer developed a story about transplant
    organs, using the basic idea that organs were taken from criminals.
    Plot out a story on this theme? Incidentally, in the original story,
    capital punishment was extended to many types of crimes, to widen
    the donor pool. For example, jay-walking became a capital crime. In
    the story, people also engage in organ-napping; stealing organs the
    way some people kidnap people.
9. Still another SF writer developed a story around a wealthy young
    man's death. His family donates some of his organs to other needy
    humans with some interesting results; one donor's family sues the
    estate of the deceased, claiming that part of the deceased is still alive.
    Write a story about what happens to the lawsuit.

BIO-ETHICS: II

17

Humans always seem to have speculated about immortality. Every school child learns about the frustrating search for the fountain of youth by Ponce de León. It seems tempting, upon first consideration, to live for two or three hundred years.

Writers have dealt with the theme of immortality very creatively. For example, Bram Stoker's famous *Dracula* is really a story about man's immortality. As long as the fabled vampire has a source of fresh blood, he can live forever. Pierce his heart with a wooden stake and he is placed in a form of suspended animation; remove the stake and he comes back to life.

In H. G. Wells' *Time Machine* we have a unique science fiction twist added to the theme of immortality, and that is time travel. The hero is projected via time travel thousands of years into the future and gains a type of immortality. Of course, countless science fiction stories have been written on the theme of time travel.

But what if you never had to age? You could decide at any point in your life to stop aging, literally, and you would look this age for the rest of your life. Think of it, maybe you could live to be 100 and still look 20, but would you want to? In Maggie Naddler's story "The Pill" this is just what we have, a society in which one can elect to stop aging.

1. Headlines from Tomorrow
   Consider the following newspaper headline:

EIGHTY-YEAR-OLD MOTHER KEPT HER FIFTY-YEAR-OLD SON A BABY BY USING YOUTH PILLS

PROJECTIONS

Chicago . . . July 5, 1999. It was discovered today by Chicago medical authorities that an eighty-year-old woman had been feeding her son youth pills for decades. Today, although her son is fifty years old, he looks like a baby. The woman's only comment to the authorities was: "I wanted my darling baby with me always." What do you think of this possibility?

2. How old would you like to live to be? Why?

THE PILL

—Maggie Nadler

The woman who sat alone on the veranda staring out at the mountains was a beauty. Early morning sunlight glinted on the golden hair that fell loose past her shoulders, and played over the cameo face with its dark eyes and perfect features. Her deep tan was set off against a white summer dress which also brought out the youthful suppleness of her figure. She sat motionless for a long time, gazing far off.

A door opened and a second woman appeared on the porch, a tumbler in her hand. The newcomer was perhaps fifty-five, and dumpy, with lank gray hair and a puffy face that even in her prime could scarcely have been attractive. She approached the seated woman and touched her gently on the shoulder. "It's time for your pill, dear," she said. The other made no response. "Your medicine," she said, more loudly, and when there was still no reply she moved around to face the front of the chair. This time the seated woman raised blank, remote eyes to her. "That's right, darling. Let me help you. Now open your mouth—that's a good girl"—and as the mouth popped obediently open she poured the contents of the glass down the blonde woman's throat. There was a gasping, choking sound as perhaps half the liquid came back up, dribbling out around the even teeth. The dumpy woman forced her own mouth into a smile. "That's just fine. Now I'll go back inside and do a few little things and then we'll go for a nice ride. How will that be?" *I can't take any more,* she screamed inwardly, *I just can't take it. It's a good thing it's all arranged and she's going away today, because I just can't take any more.*

But the blonde hadn't heard her and was already back in her old position, staring unseeingly straight ahead into the distance.

A short time later the dumpy woman emerged from the house once more. In each hand she carried a small suitcase. These she loaded into the trunk of a battered green sedan. Then she returned to the porch for her companion. She helped her to her feet and, moving slowly, guided her carefully down the steps along the walkway and assisted her into the car. She herself took the driver's seat, and only minutes later they were on the main highway. It was a long, silent, tedious drive across barren desert land, the woman at the wheel tense and preoccupied, the other lolling vacantly beside her. At last, after several interminable hours, the rocky landscape gave way to renewed greenery and presently they were driving up a winding tree-lined road which ended abruptly at a pair of great iron gates bearing the legend: GREEN MANSIONS. The gates were open and they drove on through until they came to a sprawling and ancient but apparently well cared-for mansion with a small parking area nearby. They eased into a space near the entrance. The dumpy woman unloaded the suitcases and assisted her companion out of the car and up the two low steps to the slightly open door. Timidly she pushed it farther open and they stepped together, the blonde leaning on her for support, into a large immaculate reception room. The receptionist, a handsome, somewhat hard-faced woman in a smartly-tailored suit, looked up and stared. For a moment she seemed startled. Then, "Yes?" she asked sharply.

"I—I'm Margaret Duggins and this is Mrs. Nelson, the patient I called you about last Wednesday. I believe you were expecting us . . ." Her voice trailed off.

"Oh, yes . . . Duggins . . . that's right. You're expected," the receptionist said in a milder tone. "Dottie!" she called toward the open door beyond her desk. A thin, dark-haired girl of about twenty, clad in a nurse's uniform, immediately appeared. She glanced in some surprise at the newcomers.

"Yes, Miss Biggs?"

"We have a new guest. Mrs. Nelson, here." She indicated the blonde who stood gaping at her new surroundings, saliva trickling from one corner of her mouth. "A room should be ready for her—you know, No. 19. Perhaps you'd better take her there now and get her settled."

"Yes, Miss Biggs." The girl took the blonde's arm in a brisk, businesslike manner and led her away. The woman named Margaret made as if to follow, but the receptionist called her back.

"No, Miss Duggins. Not today. We find that it's better if the relatives and friends stay behind at first. It's less confusing to the patient, less upsetting. Later, when she's all settled and comfortable, you can visit her as often as you like. No, don't worry about her bags—Dottie will get them later." The dumpy woman dropped back but continued to peer after the two retreating figures. The corridor was dim; through the gloom, she could make out vague shapes propped up in chairs staring at what must have been a television screen down at the far end . . . She forced her attention back to the receptionist, who spoke once more. "And now, if you'll just fill out these papers, there's information we need to have . . ."

About forty-five minutes later, the nurse, Dottie, re-entered the office. "Well, I finally got her to sleep. Gave her two sleeping tablets. It wasn't easy, though. Would you believe it, she started fighting me."

"God, what a pathetic case," muttered Miss Biggs.

"You mean because she dribbles? They all do that," said Dottie indifferently. "She's past ninety; what do you expect?"

"No, not her. I mean the daughter. Did you notice her?"

A glimmer of understanding came into the nurse's eyes. "Did I! How could I avoid it? I wonder why people want to let themselves go like that, anyway. It's awful."

"Why anyone would let themselves become such an eyesore when the Youth Pill is so cheap is more than I'll ever see." The receptionist was fifty years and had a date with a college junior for that evening.

"I've got an aunt like that," said the nurse reflectively. "Won't take the Pill, lets herself go, you should just see her. She's eighty. Says if it can't make the rest of her young along with her skin she wants no part of it. She's one of those real old-fashioned New England rugged individualist types, so maybe you can excuse her. But I can't understand for the life of me why any Californian would want to act like that. I'm sure going to be taking the Pill by the time *I'm* 25 or 30."

The older woman sighed philosophically. "Well, you never can tell," she said, shaking her head. "It takes all kinds."

PROBINGS

1. If there were a youth pill similar to the one in the story, would you personally take it? Why or why not? At what age would you take it?
2. Write a story describing what it would be like if mothers, grandmothers, and children all looked the same age? Would you like living in such a society?
3. Develop a scenario or write another SF short story using one of the following ideas:
   a. A ninety-year-old woman weds a twenty-year-old man.
   b. A young man visits a nursing home where everyone is senile but looks twenty.
   c. What types of cosmetics are needed for a senior citizen with a youthful body? What kind of clothes do people wear?
4. Develop or design an ad to sell "The Pill."
5. If you could pick the three best years of your life, what would they be? These years may be from the past, present, or future. Why did you select the years you did?
6. Some people believe in cryogenics, a process in which a person can be quickly frozen upon death, to be thawed in one or two hundred years—after medical breakthroughs could be used to revive them. What might be some consequences of this process? Who could be frozen? Who not? What would happen to the relationships between generations? Develop a future wheel.

SECTION 4
WHAT KIND
OF WORLD
DO I SEEK?

WHAT KIND OF WORLD DO I SEEK?

Twenty-five years ago, the world was an American world—or at least it seemed that way. We gave aid to many countries while at the same time exporting our goods and our ideas throughout the globe. One could travel to Europe, Asia, and Africa and see such familiar American names as Coca Cola, Ford, and IBM.

In the sixties and seventies, however, the world changed drastically. Many countries began declaring that they did not want to be like the Americans. Some emulated the Russians or the Chinese; others insisted upon their independence. Like people, some countries seemed to be suffering the pangs of an identity crisis. They were, and are, seeking an image and a direction to follow as we move closer to a brand new century.

Regardless of whether other countries wish to model themselves after us—or whether they seek to discover their own destinies, one thing is clear. There is a growing recognition that we must all share this globe together. At present, however, Americans consume a disproportionate share of the world's resources. Paul Ehrlich, a noted ecologist, has said that it is a tragedy when an American child is born, because that child in its lifetime will consume more and waste more of the globe's precious resources than a child of any other nationality.

In this section, the question has been raised for you to ponder: What kind of a world do you really want for you and your children? Certainly in raising that question, we must also raise the question: How many people can this globe afford? How can we feed them? Or to put it another way: How many people can we allow to perish through starvation? Already many areas of our planet suffer from famine and malnutrition. Still another question to consider: What responsibility, if any, do the wealthier countries have for these starving millions?

We have learned an important lesson in the last ten years, and that lesson has to do with ecology. For more than a hundred years, industrialized nations consumed resources without much consideration for what we were really doing to our planet. We have now come to a time to reconsider our priorities: Is it more important to be an industrial giant with well-off millions or is it more important to have clean air and water? Or can we have both? To answer these questions we can't listen only to Americans or Russians because, as we have learned in this past decade, we are all riders together on a giant spaceship called Earth. What we do affects Africans, Asians, Europeans, and Latin-Americans.

Finally, any study of the world of tomorrow must also raise the ultimate question: Is there going to be any tomorrow? As one nation after another has sought and achieved membership in the nuclear power club, the more dangerous the world has become. We still must concern ourselves with that ultimate question: How are we as riders on earth going to cope with the realization that we have the potential to commit global suicide?

ECOLOGY: I

18

Use the term *ecology,* and many people think automatically of picking up the litter of aluminum beverage cans and nonreturnable bottles along the local highway. Fighting litter is important, but it's only one small part of the ecology problem. In the broadest sense, ecology is concerned with the thin layer of air, water, and land that is precariously inhabited by all of earth's species. This region is sometimes referred to as the biosphere.

Slight changes in the earth's climate can dramatically trigger a series of events that can virtually eliminate entire species of birds, fish, or mammal from the biosphere. This was the case when numerous prehistoric creatures, some of the largest creatures ever seen on earth, were doomed by climatic change. Today we can only see the skeletal remains of these beasts in our museums.

The greatest threat, however, to our biosphere is not from natural causes but from humans. In our maddening quest for technological progress, in this country alone, we have reduced the virgin timber forests to a sparse few, plowed up the plains, polluted the water and air, and in general upset the ecological balance like no other species, past or present. As the comic strip character Pogo has noted about the ecological mess we are in: "We have met the enemy and the enemy is us."

Some people have likened our planet to a giant spaceship moving through the heavens. Like any spaceship, we must provide food, air, and water for the crew. Also, all the crew's members should be sensitive to the reality that in order to survive they must be dependent one on the other. If we recognize our planet as Spaceship Earth, we must also be aware that all of the Earth's people are crew members, dependent one upon the other. Perhaps this means that we should subordinate our national identities to our common "earthness" in order to survive. If we dump DDT into one area of our spaceship, it must affect at least part of the crew. If we contaminate the ship's water and air supply, who suffers? Further, can we allow part of the crew to go hungry while others have full stomachs? These are a few vital questions that we must ponder.

For years science fiction writers have played with the idea of ecological collapse—or that time in the future when our spaceship may break down or blow up. In his novel *No Blade of Grass,* John Christopher foresaw a world in which all grain was mysteriously blighted. Of course, grain is the basic food for humans; it is used to make bread, pasta, cereals, and even beer and liquor.

Other writers have imagined worlds in which insects or animals come to dominate the earth. In Clifford Simak's novel *City,* the dogs take over; in *The Hellstrom Chronicles,* insects do. In the following story, it's birds that go berserk. As you read this story, that all important question appears: What kind of a world do I want to live in?

PROJECTIONS

Draw your own ecology cartoon, after considering the cartoon below.

THE BIRDS

—Daphne du Maurier

On December the third the wind changed overnight and it was winter. Until then the autumn had been mellow, soft. The earth was rich where the plow had turned it.

Nat Hocken, because of a wartime disability, had a pension and did not work full-time at the farm. He worked three days a week, and they gave him the lighter jobs. Although he was married, with children, his was a solitary disposition; he liked best to work alone.

It pleased him when he was given a bank to build up, or a gate to mend, at the far end of the peninsula, where the sea surrounded the farmland on either side. Then, at midday, he would pause and eat the meat pie his wife had baked for him and, sitting on the cliff's edge, watch the birds.

In autumn great flocks of them came to the peninsula, restless, uneasy, spending themselves in motion; now wheeling, circling in the sky; now settling to feed on the rich, new-turned soil; but even when they fed, it was as though they did so without hunger, without desire.

Restlessness drove them to the skies again. Crying, whistling, calling, they skimmed the placid sea and left the shore.

Make haste, make speed, hurry and begone; yet where, and to what purpose? The restless urge of autumn, unsatisfying, sad, had put a spell upon them, and they must spill themselves of motion before winter came.

Perhaps, thought Nat, a message comes to the birds in autumn, like a warning. Winter is coming. Many of them will perish. And like people who, apprehensive of death before their time, drive themselves to work or folly, the birds do likewise; tomorrow we shall die.

The birds had been more restless than ever this fall of the year, their agitation more remarked because the days were still.

As Mr. Trigg's tractor traced its path up and down the western hills, and Nat, hedging, saw it dip and turn, the whole machine and the man upon it were momentarily lost in the great cloud of wheeling, crying birds.

Nat remarked upon them to Mr. Trigg when the work was finished for the day.

"Yes," said the farmer, "there are more birds about than usual. I have a notion the weather will change. It will be a hard winter. That's why the birds are restless."

The farmer was right. That night the weather turned.

The bedroom in the cottage faced east. Nat woke just after two and heard the east wind, cold and dry. It sounded hollow in the chimney, and a loose slate rattled on the roof. Nat listened, and he could hear the sea roaring in the bay. He drew the blanket around him, leaned closer to the back of his wife, deep in sleep. Then he heard the tapping on the window-pane. It continued until, irritated by the sound, Nat got out of bed and went to the window. He opened it; and as he did so something brushed his hand, jabbing at his knuckles, grazing the skin. Then he saw the flutter of wings and the thing was gone again, over the roof, behind the cottage.

It was a bird. What kind of bird he could not tell. The wind must have driven it to shelter on the sill.

He shut the window and went back to bed, but feeling his knuckles wet, put his mouth to the scratch. The bird had drawn blood.

Frightened, he supposed, bewildered, seeking shelter, the bird had stabbed at him in the darkness. Once more he settled himself to sleep.

Presently the tapping came again—this time more forceful, more insistent. And now his wife woke at the sound, and turning in the bed, said to him, "See to the window, Nat; it's rattling."

• "I've already been to it," he told her. "There's some bird there, trying to get in."

"Send it away," she said. "I can't sleep with that noise."

He went to the window for the second time, and now when he opened it, there was not one bird on the sill but half a dozen; they flew straight into his face.

He shouted, striking out at them with his arms, scattering them; like the first one, they flew over the roof and disappeared.

He let the window fall and latched it.

Suddenly a frightened cry came from the room across the passage where the children slept.

"It's Jill," said his wife, roused at the sound.

There came a second cry, this time from both children. Stumbling into their room, Nat felt the beating of wings about him in the darkness. The window was wide open. Through it came the birds, hitting first the ceiling and the walls, then swerving in midflight and turning to the children in their beds.

"It's all right. I'm here," shouted Nat, and the children flung themselves, screaming, upon him, while in the darkness the birds rose, and dived, and came for him again.

"What is it, Nat? What's happened?" his wife called. Swiftly he pushed the children through the door to the passage and shut it upon them, so that he was alone in their bedroom with the birds.

He seized a blanket from the nearest bed, and using it as a weapon, flung it to right and left about him.

He felt the thud of bodies, heard the fluttering of wings; but the birds were not yet defeated, for again and again they returned to the assault, jabbing his hands, his head, their little stabbing beaks sharp as pointed forks.

The blanket became a weapon of defense. He wound it about his head, and then in greater darkness, beat at the birds with his bare hands. He dared not stumble to the door and open it lest the birds follow him.

How long he fought with them in the darkness he could not tell; but at last the beating of the wings about him lessened, withdrew; and through the dense blanket he was aware of light.

He waited, listened; there was no sound except the fretful crying of one of the children from the bedroom beyond.

He took the blanket from his head and stared about him. The cold gray morning light exposed the room.

Dawn and the open window had called the living birds; the dead lay on the floor.

Sickened, Nat went to the window and stared out across his patch of garden to the fields.

It was bitter cold, and the ground had all the hard, black look of the frost that the east wind brings. The sea, fiercer now with turning tide, whitecapped and steep, broke harshly in the bay. Of the birds there was no sign.

Nat shut the window and the door of the small bedroom and went back across the passage to his own room.

His wife sat up in bed, one child asleep beside her; the smaller one in her arms, his face bandaged.

"He's sleeping now," she whispered. "Something must have cut him; there was blood at the corners of his eyes. Jill said it was the birds. She said she woke up and the birds were in the room."

His wife looked up at Nat, searching his face for confirmation. She looked terrified, bewildered. He did not want her to know that he also was shaken, dazed almost, by the events of the past few hours.

"There are birds in there," he said. "Dead birds, nearly fifty of them. Robins, wrens, all of the little birds from here about. It's as though a madness seized them, with the east wind."

He sat down on the bed beside his wife, and held her hand.

"It's the hard weather," he said. "It must be that; it's the hard weather. They aren't the birds, maybe, from around here. They've been driven down from upcountry."

"But Nat," whispered his wife, "it's only this night that the weather turned. They can't be hungry yet. There's food for them out there in the fields."

"It's the weather," repeated Nat. "I tell you, it's the weather."

His face, too, was drawn and tired, like hers. They stared at one another for a while without speaking.

Nat went to the window and looked out. The sky was hard and leaden, and the brown hills that had gleamed in the sun the day before looked dark and bare. Black winter had descended in a single night.

The children were awake now. Jill was chattering, and young Johnny was crying once again. Nat heard his wife's voice, soothing, comforting them as he went downstairs.

Presently they came down. He had breakfast ready for them.

"Did you drive away the birds?" asked Jill.

"Yes, they've all gone now," Nat said. "It was the east wind brought them in."

"I hope they won't come again," said Jill.

"I'll walk with you to the bus," Nat said to her.

Jill seemed to have forgotten her experience of the night before. She danced ahead of him, chasing the leaves, her face rosy under her pixie hood.

All the while Nat searched the hedgerows for the birds, glanced over them to the fields beyond, looked to the small wood above the farm where the rooks and jackdaws gathered; he saw none. Soon the bus came ambling up the hill.

Nat saw Jill onto the bus, then turned and walked back toward the farm. It was not his day for work, but he wanted to satisfy himself that all was well. He went to the back door of the farmhouse; he heard Mrs. Trigg singing, the wireless making a background for her song.

"Are you there, missus?" Nat called.

She came to the door, beaming, broad, a good-tempered woman.

"Hullo, Mr. Hocken," she said. "Can you tell me where this cold is coming from? Is it Russia? I've never seen such a change. And it's going on, the wireless says. Something to do with the Arctic Circle."

"We didn't turn on the wireless this morning," said Nat. "Fact is, we had trouble in the night."

"Kiddies poorly?"

"No." He hardly knew how to explain. Now, in daylight, the battle of the birds would sound absurd.

He tried to tell Mrs. Trigg what had happened, but he could see from her eyes that she thought his story was the result of nighmare following a heavy meal.

"Sure they were real birds?" she said, smiling.

"Mrs. Trigg," he said, "there are fifty dead birds, robins, wrens, and such, lying low on the floor of the children's bedroom. I suppose the weather brought them; once in the bedroom they went for me; they tried to go for young Johnny's eyes."

Mrs. Trigg stared at him doubtfully. "Well, now," she answered. "I suppose the weather brought them; once in the bedroom they wouldn't know where they were. Foreign birds maybe, from that Arctic Circle."

"No," said Nat. "They were the birds you see about here every day."

"Funny thing," said Mrs. Trigg. "No explaining it, really. You ought to write up and ask the *Guardian*. They'd have some answer for it. Well, I must be getting on."

Nat walked back along the lane to his cottage. He found his wife in the kitchen with young Johnny.

"See anyone?" she asked.

"Mrs. Trigg," he answered. "I don't think she believed me. Anyway, nothing wrong up there."

"You might take the birds away," she said. "I daren't go into the room to make the beds until you do. I'm scared."

"Nothing to scare you now," said Nat. "They're dead, aren't they?"

He went up with a sack and dropped the stiff bodies into it, one by one. Yes, there were fifty of them all told. Just the ordinary, common birds of the hedgerow; nothing as large even as a thrush. It must have been fright that made them act the way they did.

He took the sack out into the garden and was faced with a fresh problem. The ground was frozen solid, yet no snow had fallen; nothing had happened in the past hours but the coming of the east wind. It was unnatural, queer. He could see the whitecapped seas breaking in the bay. He decided to take the birds to the shore and bury them.

When he reached the beach below the headland, he could scarcely stand, the force of the east wind was so strong. It was low tide; he crunched his way over the shingle to the softer sand and then, his back to the wind, opened up his sack.

He ground a pit in the sand with his heel, meaning to drop the birds into it; but as he did so, the force of the wind lifted them as though in flight again, and they were blown away from him along the beach, tossed like feathers, spread and scattered.

The tide will take them when it turns, he said to himself.

He looked out to sea and watched the crested breakers, combing green. They rose stiffly, curled, and broke again; and because it was ebb tide, the roar was distant, more remote, lacking the sound and thunder of the flood.

Then he saw them. The gulls. Out there, riding the seas.

What he had thought at first were the whitecaps of the waves were gulls. Hundreds, thousands, tens of thousands.

They rose and fell in the troughs of the seas, heads to the wind, like a mighty fleet at anchor, waiting on the tide.

Nat turned; leaving the beach, he climbed the steep path home.

Someone should know of this. Someone should be told. Something was happening because of the east wind and the weather, that he did not understand.

As he drew near the cottage, his wife came to meet him at the door. She called to him, excited. "Nat," she said, "it's on the wireless. They've just read out a special news bulletin. It's not only here, it's everywhere. In London, all over the country. Something has happened to the birds. Come listen; they're repeating it."

Together they went into the kitchen to listen to the announcement.

"Statement from the Home Office, at eleven A.M. this morning. Reports from all over the country are coming in hourly about the vast quantity of birds flocking above towns, villages, and outlying districts, causing obstruction and damage and even attacking individuals. It is thought that the Arctic air stream at present covering the British Isles is causing birds to migrate south in immense numbers, and that intense hunger may drive these birds to attack human beings. Householders are warned to see to their windows, doors, and chimneys, and to take reasonable precautions for the safety of their children. A further statement will be issued later."

A kind of excitement seized Nat. He looked at his wife in triumph. "There you are," he said. "I've been telling myself all morning there's something wrong. And just now, down on the beach, I looked out to sea and there were gulls, thousands of them, riding on the sea, waiting."

"What are they waiting for, Nat?" she asked.

He stared at her. "I don't know," he said slowly.

He went over to the drawer where he kept his hammer and other tools. "What are you going to do, Nat?"

"See to the windows and the chimneys, like they tell you to."

"You think they would break in with the windows shut? Those wrens and robins and such? Why, how could they?"

He did not answer. He was not thinking of the robins and the wrens. He was thinking of the gulls.

He went upstairs and worked there the rest of the morning, boarding the windows of the bedrooms, filling up the chimney bases.

"Dinner's ready." His wife called him from the kitchen.

"All right. Coming down."

When dinner was over and his wife was washing up, Nat switched on the one o'clock news. The same announcement was repeated, but the news bulletin enlarged upon it. "The flocks of birds have caused dislocation in all areas," said the announcer, "and in London the mass was so dense at ten o'clock this morning that it seemed like a vast black cloud. The birds settled on rooftops, on window ledges, and on chimneys. The species included blackbird, thrush, the common house sparrow, and as might be expected in the metropolis, a vast quantity of pigeons, starlings, and that frequenter of the London river, the black-headed gull. The sight was so unusual that traffic came to a standstill in many thoroughfares, work was abandoned in shops and offices, and the streets and pavements were crowded with people standing about to watch the birds."

The announcer's voice was smooth and suave; Nat had the impression that he treated the whole business as he would an elaborate joke. There would be others like him, hundreds of them, who did not know what it was to struggle in darkness with a flock of birds.

Nat switched off the wireless. He got up and started work on the kitchen windows. His wife watched him, young Johnny at her heels.

"What they ought to do," she said, "is to call the army out and shoot the birds."

"Let them try," said Nat. "How'd they set about it?"

"I don't know. But something should be done. They ought to do something."

Nat thought to himself that "they" were no doubt considering the problem at that very moment, but whatever "they" decided to do in London and the big cities would not help them here, nearly three hundred miles away.

"How are we off for food?" he asked.

"It's shopping day tomorrow, you know that. I don't keep uncooked food about. Butcher doesn't call till the day after. But I can bring back something when I go in tomorrow."

Nat did not want to scare her. He looked in the larder for himself and in the cupboard where she kept her tins.

They could hold out for a couple of days.

He went on hammering the boards across the kitchen windows. Candles. They were low on candles. That must be another thing she meant to buy tomorrow. Well, they must go early to bed tonight. That was, if—

He got up and went out the back door and stood in the garden, looking down toward the sea.

There had been no sun all day, and now, at barely three o'clock, a kind of darkness had already come; the sky was sullen, heavy, colorless like salt. He could hear the vicious sea drumming on the rocks.

He walked down the path halfway to the beach. And then he stopped. He could see the tide had turned. The gulls had risen. They were circling, hundreds of them, thousands of them, lifting their wings against the wind.

It was the gulls that made the darkening of the sky.

And they were silent. They just went on soaring and circling, rising, falling, trying their strength against the wind. Nat turned. He ran up the path back to the cottage.

"I'm going for Jill," he said to his wife.

"What's the matter?" she asked. "You've gone quite white."

"Keep Johnny inside," he said. "Keep the door shut. Light up now and draw the curtains."

"It's only gone three," she said.

"Never mind. Do what I tell you."

He looked inside the tool shed and took the hoe.

He started walking up the lane to the bus stop. Now and again he glanced back over his shoulder; and he could see the gulls had risen higher now, their circles were broader, they were spreading out in huge formation across the sky.

He hurried on. Although he knew the bus would not come before four o'clock, he had to hurry.

He waited at the top of the hill. There was half an hour still to go.

The east wind came whipping across the fields from the higher ground. In the distance he could see the clay hills, white and clean against the heavy pallor of the sky.

Something black rose from behind them, like a smudge at first, then widening, becoming deeper. The smudge became a cloud; and the cloud divided again into five other clouds, spreading north, east, south, and west; and then they were not clouds at all but birds.

He watched them travel across the sky, within two or three hundred feet of him. He knew, from their speed, that they were bound inland; they had no business with the people here on the peninsula. They were rooks, crows, jackdaws, magpies, jays, all birds that usually preyed upon the smaller species, but bound this afternoon on some other mission.

He went to the telephone call box, stepped inside, lifted the receiver. The exchange would pass the message on. "I'm speaking from the highway," he said, "by the bus stop. I want to report large formations of birds traveling upcountry. The gulls are also forming in the bay."

"All right," answered the voice, laconic, weary.

"You'll be sure and pass this message on to the proper quarter?"

"Yes. Yes." Impatient now, fed up. The buzzing note resumed.

She's another, thought Nat. She doesn't care.

The bus came lumbering up the hill. Jill climbed out.

"What's the hoe for, Dad?"

"I just brought it along," he said. "Come on now, let's get home. It's cold; no hanging about. See how fast you can run."

He could see the gulls now, still silent, circling the fields, coming in toward the land.

"Look, Dad; look over there. Look at all the gulls."

"Yes. Hurry now."

"Where are they flying to? Where are they going?"

"Upcountry, I dare say. Where it's warmer."

He seized her hand and dragged her after him along the lane.

"Don't go so fast. I can't keep up."

The gulls were copying the rooks and the crows. They were spreading out, in formation, across the sky. They headed, in bands of thousands, to the four compass points.

"Dad, what is it? What are the gulls doing?"

They were not intent upon their flight, as the crows, as the jackdaws, had been. They still circled overhead. Nor did they fly so high. It was as though they waited upon some signal; as though some decision had yet to be given.

"I wish the gulls would go away." Jill was crying. "I don't like them. They're coming closer to the lane."

He started running, swinging Jill after him. As they went past the farm turning, he saw the farmer backing his car into the garage. Nat called to him.

"Can you give us a lift?" he said.

Mr. Trigg turned in the driver's seat and stared at them. Then a smile came to his cheerful, rubicund face. "It looks as though we're in for some fun," he said. "Have you seen the gulls? Jim and I are going to take a crack at them. Everyone's gone bird crazy, talking of nothing else. I hear you were troubled in the night. Want a gun?"

Nat shook his head.

The small car was packed, but there was room for Jill on the back seat.

"I don't want a gun," said Nat, "but I'd be obliged if you'd run Jill home. She's scared of the birds."

"Okay," said the farmer. "I'll take her home. Why don't you stop behind and join the shooting match? We'll make the feathers fly."

Jill climbed in, and turning the car, the driver sped up the lane. Nat followed after. Trigg must be crazy. What use was a gun against a sky of birds?

They were coming in now toward the farm, circling lower in the sky. The farm, then, was their target. Nat increased his pace toward his own cottage. He saw the farmer's car turn and come back along the lane. It drew up beside him with a jerk.

"The kid has run inside," said the farmer. "Your wife was watching for her. Well, what do you make of it? They're saying in town the Russians have done it. The Russians have poisoned the birds."

"How could they do that?" asked Nat.

"Don't ask me. You know how stories get around."

"Have you boarded your windows?" Asked Nat.

"No. Lot of nonsense. I've had more to do today than to go around boarding up my windows."

"I'd board them now if I were you."

"Garn. You're windy. Like to come to our place to sleep?"

"No, thanks all the same."

"All right. See you in the morning. Give you a gull breakfast."

The farmer grinned and turned his car to the farm entrance. Nat hurried on. Past the little wood, past the old barn, and then across the stile to the remaining field. As he jumped the stile, he heard the whirl of wings. A black-backed gull dived down at him from the sky. It missed, swerved in flight, and rose to dive again. In a moment it was joined by others—six, seven, a dozen.

Nat dropped his hoe. The hoe was useless. Covering his head with his arms, he ran toward the cottage.

They kept coming at him from the air—noiseless, silent, save for the beating wings. The terrible, fluttering wings. He could feel the blood on his hands, his wrists, upon his neck. If only he could keep them from his eyes. Nothing else mattered.

With each dive, with each attack, they became bolder. And they had no thought for themselves. When they dived low and missed, they crashed, bruised and broken, on the ground.

As Nat ran he stumbled, kicking their spent bodies in front of him.

He found the door and hammered upon it with his bleeding hands. "Let me in," he shouted. "It's Nat. Let me in."

Then he saw the gannet, poised for the dive, above him in the sky.

The gulls circled, retired, soared, one with another, against the wind.

Only the gannet remained. One single gannet, above him in the sky. Its wings folded suddenly to its body. It dropped like a stone.

Nat screamed; and the door opened.

He stumbled across the threshold, and his wife threw her weight against the door.

They heard the thud of the gannet as it fell.

His wife dressed his wounds. They were not deep. The backs of his hands had suffered most, and his wrists. Had he not worn a cap, the birds would have reached his head. As for the gannet—the gannet could have split his skull.

The children were crying, of course. They had seen the blood on their father's hands.

"It's all right now," he told them. "I'm not hurt."

His wife was ashen. "I saw them overhead," she whispered. "They began collecting just as Jill ran in with Mr. Trigg. I shut the door fast, and it jammed. That's why I couldn't open it at once when you came."

"Thank God the birds waited for me," he said. "Jill would have fallen at once. They're flying inland, thousands of them. Rooks, crows, all the bigger birds. I saw them from the bus stop. They're making for the towns."

"But what can they do, Nat?"

"They'll attack. Go for everyone out in the streets. Then they'll try the windows, the chimneys."

"Why don't the authorities do something? Why don't they get the army, get machine guns?"

"There's been no time. Nobody's prepared. We'll hear what they have to say on the six o'clock news."

"I can hear the birds," Jill said. "Listen, Dad."

Nat listened. Muffled sounds came from the windows, from the door. Wings brushing the surface, sliding, scraping, seeking a way of entry. The sound of many bodies pressed together, shuffling on the sills. Now and again came a thud, a crash, as some bird dived and fell.

Some of them will kill themselves that way, he thought, but not enough. Never enough.

"All right," he said aloud. "I've got boards over the windows, Jill. The birds can't get in."

He went and examined all the windows. He found wedges—pieces of old tin, strips of wood and metal—and fastened them at the sides of the windows to reinforce the boards.

His hammering helped to deafen the sound of the birds, the shuffling, the tapping, and—more ominous—the splinter of breaking glass.

"Turn on the wireless," he said.

He went upstairs to the bedrooms and reinforced the windows there. Now he could hear the birds on the roof—the scraping of claws, a sliding, jostling sound.

He decided the whole family must sleep in the kitchen and keep up the fire. He was afraid of the bedroom chimneys. The boards he had placed at their bases might give way. In the kitchen they would be safe because of the fire.

He would have to make a joke of it. Pretend to the children they were playing camp. If the worst happened and the birds forced an entry by way of the bedroom chimneys, it would be hours, days perhaps, before they could break down the doors. The birds would be imprisoned in the bedrooms. They could do no harm there. Crowded together, they would stifle and die. He began to bring the mattresses downstairs.

At sight of them, his wife's eyes widened in apprehension.

"All right," he said cheerfully. "We'll all sleep together in the kitchen tonight. More cozy, here by the fire. Then we won't be worried by those silly old birds tapping at the windows."

He made the children help him rearrange the furniture, and he took the precaution of moving the dresser against the windows.

We're safe enough now, he thought. We're snug and tight. We can hold out. It's just the food that worries me. Food and coal for the fire. We've enough for two or three days, not more. By that time—

No use thinking ahead as far as that. And they'd be given directions on the wireless.

And now, in the midst of many problems, he realized that only dance music was coming over the air. He knew the reason. The usual programs had been abandoned; this only happened at exceptional times.

At six o'clock the records ceased. The time signal was given. There was a pause, and then the announcer spoke. His voice was solemn, grave. Quite different from midday.

"This is London," he said. "A national emergency was proclaimed at four o'clock this afternoon. Measures are being taken to safeguard the lives and property of the population, but it must be understood that these are not easy to effect immediately, owing to the unforeseen and unparalleled nature of the present crisis. Every householder must take precautions about his own building. Where several people live together, as in flats and hotels, they must unite to do the utmost that they can to prevent entry. It is absolutely imperative that every individual stay indoor tonight.

"The birds, in vast numbers, are attacking anyone on sight, and have already begun an assault upon buildings; but these, with due care, should be impenetrable.

"The population is asked to remain calm.

"Owing to the exceptional nature of the emergency, there will be no further transmission from any broadcasting station until seven A.M. tomorrow."

They played "God Save the Queen." Nothing more happened.

Nat switched off the set. He looked at his wife. She stared back at him.

"We'll have supper early," suggested Nat. "Something for a treat— toasted cheese, eh? Something we all like."

He winked and nodded at his wife. He wanted the look of dread, of apprehension, to leave her face.

He helped with the supper, whistling, singing, making as much clatter as he could. It seemed to him that the shuffling and the tapping were not so intense as they had been at first, and presently he went up to the bedrooms and listened. He no longer heard the jostling for place upon the roof.

They've got reasoning powers, he thought. They know it's hard to break in here. They'll try elsewhere.

Supper passed without incident. Then, when they were clearing away, they heard a new sound, a familiar droning.

His wife looked up at him, her face alight.

"It's planes," she said. "They're sending out planes after the birds. That will get them. Isn't that gunfire? Can't you hear guns?"

It might be gunfire, out at sea. Nat could not tell. Big naval guns might have some effect upon the gulls out at sea, but the gulls were inland now. The guns couldn't shell the shore because of the population.

"It's good, isn't it," said his wife, "to hear the planes?"

Catching her enthusiasm, Jill jumped up and down with Johnny. "The planes will get the birds."

Just then they heard a crash about two miles distant. Followed by a second, then a third. The droning became more distant, passed away out to sea.

"What was that?" asked his wife.

"I don't know," answered Nat. He did not want to tell her that the sound they had heard was the crashing of aircraft.

It was, he had no doubt, a gamble on the part of the authorities to send out reconnaissance forces, but they might have known the gamble was suicidal. What could aircraft do against birds that flung themselves to death against propeller and fuselage but hurtle to the ground themselves?

"Where have the planes gone, Dad?" asked Jill.

"Back to base," he said. "Come on now, time to tuck down for bed."

There was no further drone of aircraft, and the naval guns had ceased. Waste of life and effort, Nat said to himself. We can't destroy enough of them that way. Cost too heavy. There's always gas. Maybe they'll try spraying with gas, mustard gas. We'll be warned first, of course, if they do. There's one thing, the best brains of the country will be on it tonight.

Upstairs in the bedrooms all was quiet. No more scraping and stabbing at the windows. A lull in battle. The wind hadn't dropped, though. Nat could still hear it roaring in the chimneys. And the sea breaking down on the shore.

Then he remembered the tide. The tide would be on the turn. Maybe the lull in battle was because of the tide. There was some law the birds obeyed, and it had to do with the east wind and the tide.

He glanced at his watch. Nearly eight o'clock. It must have gone high water an hour ago. That explained the lull. The birds attacked with the flood tide.

He reckoned the time limit in his head. They had six hours to go without attack. When the tide turned again, around 1:20 in the morning, the birds would come back.

He called softly to his wife and whispered to her that he would go out and see how they were faring at the farm, see if the telephone was still working there so that they might get news from the exchange.

"You're not to go," she said at once, "and leave me alone with the children. I can't stand it."

"All right," he said, "all right. I'll wait till morning. And we can get the wireless bulletin then, too, at seven. But when the tide ebbs again, I'll try for the farm; they may let us have bread and potatoes."

His mind was busy again, planning against emergency. They would not have milked, of course, this evening. The cows would be standing by the gate, waiting; the household would be inside, battened behind boards as they were here at the cottage.

That is, if they had had time to take precautions.

Softly, stealthily, he opened the back door and looked outside.

It was pitch-dark. The wind was blowing harder than ever, coming in steady gusts, icy, from the sea.

He kicked at the step. It was heaped with birds. These were the suicides, the divers, the ones with broken necks. Wherever he looked, he saw dead birds. The living had flown seaward with the turn of the tide. The gulls would be riding the seas now, as they had done in the forenoon.

In the far distance on the hill, something was burning. One of the aircraft that had crashed; the fire, fanned by the wind, had set light to a stack.

He looked at the bodies of the birds. He had a notion that if he stacked them, one upon the other, on the window sills, they would be added protection against the next attack.

Not much, perhaps, but something. The bodies would have to be clawed at, pecked and dragged aside before the living birds gained purchase on the sills and attacked the panes.

He set to work in the darkness. It was queer. He hated touching the dead birds, but he went on with his work. He noticed grimly that every window pane was shattered. Only the boards had kept the birds from breaking in.

He stuffed the cracked panes with the bleeding bodies of the birds and felt his stomach turn. When he had finished, he went back into the cottage and barricaded the kitchen door, making it doubly secure.

His wife had made him cocoa; he drank it thirstily. He was very tired. "All right," he said, smiling, "don't worry. We'll get through."

He lay down on his mattress and closed his eyes.

He dreamed uneasily because, through his dreams, ran the dread of something forgotten. Some piece of work that he should have done. It was connected, in some way, with the burning aircraft.

It was his wife, shaking his shoulder, who awoke him finally.

"They've begun," she sobbed. "They've started this last hour. I can't listen to it any longer alone. There's something smells bad too, something burning."

Then he remembered. He had forgotten to make up the fire.

The fire was smoldering, nearly out. He got up swiftly and lighted the lamp.

The hammering had started at the windows and the door, but it was not that he minded now. It was the smell of singed feathers.

The smell filled the kitchen. He knew what it was at once. The birds were coming down the chimney, squeezing their way down to the kitchen range.

He got sticks and paper and put them on the embers, then reached for the can of kerosene.

"Stand back," he shouted to his wife. He threw some of the kerosene onto the fire.

The flame roared up the pipe, and down into the fire fell the scorched, blackened bodies of the birds.

The children waked, crying. "What is it?" asked Jill. "What's happened?"

Nat had no time to answer her. He was raking the bodies from the chimney, clawing them out onto the floor.

The flames would drive away the living birds from the chimney top. The lower joint was the difficulty though. It was choked with the smoldering, helpless bodies of the birds caught by fire.

He scarcely heeded the attack on the windows and the door. Let them beat their wings, break their backs, lose their lives, in the desperate attempt to force an entry into his home. They would not break in.

"Stop crying," he called to the children. "There's nothing to be afraid of. Stop crying."

. He went on raking out the burning, smoldering bodies as they fell into the fire.

This'll fetch them, he said to himself. The draft and the flames together. We're all right as long as the chimney doesn't catch.

Amid the tearing at the window boards came the sudden homely striking of the kitchen clock. Three o'clock.

A little more than four hours to go. He could not be sure of the exact time of high water. He reckoned the tide would not turn much before half past seven.

He waited by the range. The flames were dying. But no more blackened bodies fell from the chimney. He thrust his poker up as far as it could go and found nothing.

The danger of the chimney's being choked up was over. It could not happen again, not if the fire was kept burning day and night.

I'll have to get more fuel from the farm tomorrow, he thought. I can do all that with the ebb tide. It can be worked; we can fetch what we need when the tide's turned. We've just got to adapt ourselves, that's all.

They drank tea and cocoa, ate slices of bread. Only half a loaf left, Nat noticed. Never mind, though; they'd get by.

If they could hang on like this until seven, when the first news bulletin came through, they would not have done too badly.

"Give us a smoke," he said to his wife. "It will clear away the smell of the scorched feathers."

"There's only two left in the packet," she said. "I was going to buy you some."

"I'll have one," he said.

He sat with one arm around his wife and one around Jill, with Johnny on his lap, the blankets heaped about them on the mattress.

"You can't help admiring the beggars," he said. "They've got persistency. You'd think they'd tire of the game, but not a bit of it."

Admiration was hard to sustain. The tapping went on and on; and a new, rasping note struck Nat's ear, as though a sharper beak than any hitherto had come to take over from its fellows.

He tried to remember the names of birds; he tried to think which species would go for this particular job.

It was not the tap of the woodpecker. That would be light and frequent. This was more serious; if it continued long, the wood would splinter as the glass had done.

Then he remembered the hawks. Could the hawks have taken over from the gulls? Were there buzzards now upon the sills, using talons as well as beaks? Hawks, buzzards, kestrels, falcons; he had forgotten the birds of prey. He had forgotten the gripping power of the birds of prey. Three hours to go; and while they waited, the sound of the splintering wood, the talons tearing at the wood.

Nat looked about him, seeing what furniture he could destroy to fortify the the door.

The windows were safe because of the dresser. He was not certain of the door. He went upstairs; but when he reached the landing, he paused and listened.

There was a soft patter on the floor of the children's bedroom. The birds had broken through.

The other bedroom was still clear. He brought out the furniture to pile at the head of the stairs should the door of the children's bedroom go.

"Come down, Nat. What are you doing?" called his wife.

"I won't be long," he shouted. I'm just making everything shipshape up here."

He did not want her to come. He did not want her to hear the pattering in the children's bedroom, the brushing of those wings against the door.

After he suggested breakfast, he found himself watching the clock, gazing at the hands that went so slowly around the dial. If his theory was not correct, if the attack did not cease with the turn of the tide, he knew they were beaten. They could not continue through the long day without air, without rest, without fuel.

A crackling in his ears drove away the sudden, desperate desire for sleep.

"What is it? What now?" he said sharply.

"The wireless," said his wife. "I've been watching the clock. It's nearly seven."

The comfortable crackling of the wireless brought new life.

They waited. The kitchen clock struck seven.

The crackling continued. Nothing else. No chimes. No music.

They waited until a quarter past. No news bulletin came through.

"We heard wrong," he said. "They won't be broadcasting until eight o'clock."

They left the wireless switched on. Nat thought of the battery, wondered how much power was left in the battery. If it failed, they would not hear the instructions.

"It's getting light," whispered his wife. "I can't see it but I can feel it. And listen! The birds aren't hammering so loud now."

She was right. The rasping, tearing sound grew fainter every moment.

So did the shuffling, the jostling for place upon the step, upon the sills. The tide was on the turn.

By eight there was no sound at all. Only the wind. And the crackling of the wireless. The children, lulled at last by the stillness, fell asleep.

At half past eight Nat switched the wireless off.

"We'll miss the news," said his wife.

"There isn't going to be any news," said Nat. "We've got to depend upon ourselves."

He went to the door and slowly pulled away the barricades. He drew the bolts, and kicking the broken bodies from the step outside the door, breathed the cold air.

He had six working hours before him, and he knew he must reserve his strength to the utmost, not waste it in any way.

Food and light and fuel; these were the most necessary things. If he could get them, they could endure another night.

He stepped into the garden; and as he did so, he saw the living birds. The gulls had gone to ride the sea, as they had done before. They sought sea food and the buoyancy of the tide before they returned to the attack.

Not so the land birds. They waited, and watched.

Nat saw them on the hedgerows, on the soil, crowded in the trees, outside in the field—line upon line of birds, still, doing nothing. He went to the end of his small garden.

The birds did not move. They merely watched him.

I've got to get food, Nat said to himself. I've got to go to the farm to get food.

He went back to the cottage. He saw to the windows and the door.

"I'm going to the farm," he said.

His wife clung to him. She had seen the living birds from the open door.

"Take us with you," she begged. "We can't stay here alone. I'd rather die than stay here alone."

"Come on, then," he said. "Bring baskets and Johnny's pram. We can load up the pram."

They dressed against the biting wind. His wife put Johnny in the pram, and Nat took Jill's hand.

"The birds," Jill whimpered. "They're all out there in the fields."

"They won't hurt us," he said. "Not in the light."

They started walking across the field toward the stile, and the birds did not move. They waited, their heads turned to the wind.

When they reached the turning to the farm, Nat stopped and told his wife to wait in the shelter of the hedge with the two children. "But I want to see Mrs. Trigg," she protested. "There are lots of things we can borrow if they went to market yesterday, and—"

"Wait here," Nat interrupted. "I'll be back in a moment."

The cows were lowing, moving restlessly in the yard, and he could see a gap in the fence where the sheep had knocked their way through to roam unchecked in the front garden before the farmhouse.

No smoke came from the chimneys. Nat was filled with misgiving. He did not want his wife or children to go down to the farm.

He went down alone, pushing his way through the herd of lowing cows, who turned this way and that, distressed, their udders full.

He saw the car standing by the gate. Not put away in the garage.

All the windows of the farmhouse were smashed. There were many dead gulls lying in the yard and around the house.

The living birds perched on the group of trees behind the farm and on the roof of the house. They were quite still. They watched him. Jim's body lay in the yard. What was left of it. His gun was beside him.

The door of the house was shut and bolted, but it was easy to push up a smashed window and climb through.

Trigg's body was close to the telephone. He must have been trying to get through to the exchange when the birds got him. The receiver was off the hook, and the instrument was torn from the wall.

No sign of Mrs. Trigg. She would be upstairs. Was it any use going up? Sickened, Nat knew what he would find there.

Thank God, he said to himself, there were no children.

He forced himself to climb the stairs, but halfway up he turned and descended again. He could see Mrs. Trigg's legs protruding from the open bedroom door. Beside her were the bodies of black-backed gulls and an umbrella, broken. It's no use doing anything, Nat thought. I've only got five hours; less than that. The Triggs would understand. I must load up with what I can find.

He tramped back to his wife and children.

"I'm going to fill up the car with stuff," he said. "We'll take it home and return for a fresh load."

"What about the Triggs?" asked his wife.

"They must have gone to friends," he said.

"Shall I come and help you then?"

"No, there's a mess down there. Cows and sheep all over the place. Wait; I'll get the car. You can sit in the car."

Her eyes watched his all the time he was talking. He believed she understood. Otherwise she certainly would have insisted on helping him find the bread and groceries.

They made three journeys altogether, to and from the farm, before he was satisfied they had everything they needed. It was surprising, once he started thinking, how many things were necessary. Almost the most important of all was planking for the windows. He had to go around searching for timber. He wanted to renew the boards on all the windows at the cottage.

On the final journey he drove the car to the bus stop and got out and went to the telephone box.

He waited a few minutes, jangling the hook. No good, though. The line was dead. He climbed onto a bank and looked over the countryside, but there was no sign of life at all, nothing in the fields but the waiting, watching birds.

Some of them slept; he could see their beaks tucked into their feathers.

You'd think they'd be feeding, he said to himself, not just standing that way.

Then he remembered. They were gorged with food. They had eaten their fill during the night. That was why they did not move this morning.

He lifted his face to the sky. It was colorless, gray. The bare trees looked bent and blackened by the east wind.

The cold did not affect the living birds, waiting out there in the fields.

This is the time they ought to get them, Nat said to himself. They're a sitting target now. They must be doing this all over the country. Why don't our aircraft take off now and spray them with mustard gas? What are all our chaps doing? They must know; they must see for themselves.

He went back to the car and got into the driver's seat.

"Go quickly past that second gate," whispered his wife. "The postman's lying there. I don't want Jill to see."

It was a quarter to one by the time they reached the cottage. Only an hour to go.

"Better have dinner," said Nat. "Heat up something for yourself and the children, some of that soup. I've no time to eat now. I've got to unload all this stuff from the car."

He got everything inside the cottage. It could be sorted later. Give them all something to do during the long hours ahead.

First he must see to the windows and the door.

He went around the cottage methodically, testing every window and the door. He climbed onto the roof also, and fixed boards across every chimney except the kitchen's.

The cold was so intense he could hardly bear it, but the job had to be done. Now and again he looked up, searching the sky for aircraft. None came. As he worked, he cursed the inefficiency of the authorities.

He paused, his work on the bedroom chimney finished, and looked out to sea. Something was moving out there. Something gray and white among the breakers.

"Good old navy," he said. "They never let us down. They're coming down channel; they're turning into the bay."

He waited, straining his eyes toward the sea. He was wrong, though. The navy was not there. It was the gulls rising from the sea. And the massed flocks in the fields, with ruffled feathers, rose in formation from the ground and, wing to wing, soared upward to the sky.

The tide had turned again.

Nat climbed down the ladder and went inside the cottage. The family were at dinner. It was a little after two.

He bolted the door, put up the barricade, and lighted the lamp.

"It's nighttime," said young Johnny.

His wife had switched on the wireless once again. The crackling sound came, but nothing else.

"I've been all around the dial," she said, "foreign stations and all. I can't get anything but the crackling."

"Maybe they have the same trouble," he said. "Maybe it's the same right through Europe."

They ate in silence.

The tapping began at the windows, at the doors, the rustling, the jostling, the pushing for position on the sills. The first thud of the suicide gulls upon the step.

When he had finished dinner, Nat planned, he would put the supplies away, stack them neatly, get everything shipshape. The boards were strong against the windows and across the chimneys. The cottage was filled with stores, with fuel, with all they needed for the next few days.

His wife could help him, and the children too. They'd tire themselves out between now and a quarter to nine, when the tide would ebb; then he'd tuck them down on their mattresses, see that they slept good and sound until three in the morning.

He had a new scheme for the windows, which was to fix barbed wire in front of the boards. He had brought a great roll of it from the farm. The nuisance was, he'd have to work at this in the dark, when the lull came between nine and three. Pity he had not thought of it before. Still, as long as the wife and kids slept—that was the main thing.

The smaller birds were at the windows now. He recognized the light tap-tapping of their beaks and the soft brush of their wings.

The hawks ignored the windows. They concentrated their attack upon the door.

Nat listened to the tearing sound of splintering wood, and wondered how many million years of memory were stored in those little brains, behind the stabbing beaks, the piercing eyes, now giving them this instinct to destroy mankind with all the deft precision of machines.

"I'll smoke that last cigarette," he said to his wife. "Stupid of me. It was the one thing I forgot to bring back from the farm."

He reached for it, switched on the crackling wireless.

He threw the empty packet onto the fire and watched it burn.

PROBINGS

1. This story, of course, was eventually made into Alfred Hitchcock's famous film of the same name. Write a diary (fictional, of course) or keep a journal documenting how you would react to an invasion of one of the following. What would you do first, second, third, etc.?
    a. insects (pick your own)
    b. rats
    c. worms
    d. mammals (pick your own)
    e. bacteria
    f. other
2. Of course, man has tampered with ecology to the point that some species have died off, while others have multiplied beyond control, like the "Birds." There has been still another result of our dabbling with Mother Nature; we have created new forms of life. For example, one man bred African honey bees with Brazilian bees and produced a third strain of bees—killer bees. These killers are progressing slowly towards Florida. Find other ways that humanity has tampered with nature only to have our efforts backfire. Remember the warning on the TV commercial: "IT'S NOT NICE TO FOOL MOTHER NATURE!"
3. Role play a situation in which your neighbor decides to allow his yard to go natural by allowing the indigenous plants (which we call "weeds") to take over. Would any pressures be brought to bear against him? What kinds? Why?

4. Make a tour of your own school campus or surrounding neighborhood and identify as many varieties of the following as you can:

trees   animals
native plants(weeds)   birds
flowers   insects

Who had the largest list?

5. Go through your kitchen and bathroom cupboards. Make a list of all the ingredients in prepared products such as cake mixes, cheese spreads, cheese dips, patent medicines. Which of the ingredients are unfamiliar to you? Do some research, if necessary, to find out which of the ingredients are artificial and which are potentially harmful.

6. Headlines from Tomorrow:

January 3, 1999. "Porpoises Complain to Humans—File List of Grievances"

Develop this idea into a story, using the fact that our current communications research with porpoises allows us to talk with them.

7. Develop a series of "Headlines from Tomorrow" based on the idea that we have learned to communicate with plants.

8. Develop a future wheel for no. 7. What might happen to our dietary habits? Our clothing?

ECOLOGY: II

19

René Dubos, a famous biologist, has made an interesting observation about his fellow humans: we are too adaptable. Dinosaurs are extinct because they couldn't adapt to change. How strange it is that our species has so many limitations and yet we have survived. Homo sapiens can't run or climb as well as many other species; we can't swim very well and we certainly can't fly naturally. We aren't as strong as the proverbial bull, nor is our eyesight as keen as an eagle's. However, because of our brain capacity humans have compensated brilliantly. As you know, we have invented machines that allow us to fly faster than a bird, stay under water as long as many fish, or see better (with microscopes and telescopes) than any creature. In the process of becoming ruler of the jungle, we have paid a price: adaptability. We have adapted all too well to ingesting harmful gases and smoke into our lungs, and to eating and drinking polluted foods and water. Yes, we have adjusted to an inferior existence, and this is what Dubos is saying to us.

In "Frog Pond," we meet a young person who has adapted in a dramatic way to the deterioration of the environment.

1. Headlines from Tomorrow:

**LAST DOMESTIC COLLIE
PLACED IN ZOO**

PROJECTIONS

2. Develop a future advertisement
    for the following:
    a. fresh air in bottles
    b. 100% unpolluted ·water
    c. real grass
    d. live fish
    e. farm Resort—with live cows
        and chickens; real corn and
        wheat fields.

FROG POND

—Chelsea Quinn Yarbro

No matter what Mr. Thompson said, it was a good day for frogging and fishing. The morning sun had that bright double halo that meant the whole day would be clear. I got up before Mom, took some old pie from where she hid it last night, grabbed my wading shoes and net and lit out for the creek. I had to leave real quiet. I'm not supposed to be going down to the creek any more. They say it's dangerous down there.

But the creek ain't dangerous if you know what you're doing. You just have to stay away from pink water spots and you're safe all the way.

I took the long way around the Baxter place. I think Pop was right about them; something's wrong there. Dr. Baxter ain't been at Town Meeting for a long time—Pop thinks that maybe some sick people moved in on the Baxters.

So I walked through the brambles on the edge of the woods where the new trees are growing. It was sunny and fine and the breeze came in nice and sweet from the north. No cities up that way, not for hundreds of miles.

Caught some crickets along the way, the big kind with the long wings. They make good bait for the stickery fish in the shallows. All I got to do is tangle them up in the net and put it down in the water. The stickery fish go right for 'em. Mr. Thompson, he says that it ain't safe to eat 'em, which just shows you how much he knows. I eat 'em all the time.

I headed right for Rotten Log Hollow. There's a nice big hole in there and a gravel bar and you can catch lots of frogs there if you're careful. They like to hide under that old broken pipe, under the foam. I got maybe a dozen there, last time out.

First I walked along the bank, looking down into the water to see what was there, you know. It was still and there wasn't a lot of foam piling up. There wasn't any fish either, so I sat down in the warm gravel, ate my pie and pulled on my wading shoes. They've got high tops that Pop always tells me to pull all the way up, but I ain't bothered with that for years. Heck, a little water can't kill me.

After a little while I went into the water real cautious—careful not to scare the frogs. I worked my way out into mid-stream and started peering around for frogs. I had my net in my belt but I don't use it much—not for frogs.

So there I was in the creek, careful as could be, when all of a sudden this bunch of rocks and grass comes rolling down the bank and this city fellow comes down after it, trying to grab hold of bushes on the way. He hit the pipe and it stopped him, but he sure messed up the water.

A couple of minutes went by and he started to get up. He had a heck of a time doing it. He kept flailing his arms around and pulling himself back onto the pipe.

I was mad because he'd scared the frogs, so I yelled out, "Hey, mister, don't do that!"

Boy, did he look up fast. You'd of thought I was a C.D. man or something the way he snapped around. His eyes got wild and he shook all over. Before he could fall again I called out. "It's just me, mister, down in the creek."

He turned around, grabbing the pipe for balance. I waited till he'd steadied himself and then I said, "You're scaring the frogs."

"Scaring the frogs?" he yelled back, sounding like frogs were monsters.

"Yeah, I'm trying to catch some. Can you just sit there a minute?"

I could see he was thinking this over. Finally he sat back on the pipe like he was worn out and said real quiet, "Why not?" And he leaned his head back and closed his eyes.

I got three frogs while he was sleeping there. They were big and fat. I put a stick through their throats and let 'em dangle in the creek to keep fresh. I almost had the fourth one when the city guy woke up.

"Listen," he called to me. "Where am I?"

"Rotten Log Hollow."

"Where is that?"

I sure couldn't see the point in yelling all the time, so I told him to come closer and we could talk. "Talk makes less noise. Maybe I can still catch some frogs if we're just talking."

He hustled off the pipe and scrambled along the shore, splashing dirt and stones into the water.

"Hi," I said when he got closer.

"Hello." He was still awful nervous and had that funny white look around his eyes, sort of like turtle skin. "What's your name?"

He was really trying to be friendly and even if Mr. Thompson says in that spooly voice of his that there ain't any friendly strangers, well, this guy wasn't anything I couldn't handle.

"My name is Althea," I told him, polite like Mom tells me to be. "But mostly my friends call me Thorny. Who are you?"

"Uh—" He looked around then back. "Stan!—Stan—just call me Stan."

You could see that he was lying. He wasn't even good at it. So I said, sure, his name was Stan. Then I waited for him to say something.

"You like this place?" he asked.

"Yeah. I come here lots of times."

"You live around here, then?"

A dumb question. He was really all city. Maybe he thought we had subways out here in the country. He kept looking around like he expected a whole herd of people to come running out of the pipe.

"Yeah, I live at the Baxter place." It was a lie but he'd told me one—

and besides, Pop said I wasn't to tell people where we live, just in case.

"Where's that?" He said it like he wasn't really interested, like he didn't give a damn where the Baxter place was. He just wanted to talk to someone. I pointed back toward the Baxter place and told him it was about a mile along the road.

"Do a lot of people live there, at the Baxter place?"

"Not too many. About six or seven. You planning on moving in, mister?"

He laughed at that. It was one of those high laughs that sounds like crying. My brother Davey cries like that a lot. It ain't right a six-year-old kid should cry like that. About this Stan—or whoever—I didn't know.

"What's funny, mister?" I would have gone and left him there, but I saw that he was standing almost in some green gunk that comes out of the pipe and washes on shore so I said to him a little louder, "And you better get away from there."

He stopped laughing. "From where? Why?"

Wow, he was nervous.

"From that." I pointed so he would not get panicked again. "That stuff is bad for you. It can give you burns if you're not used to it." That isn't quite right. Some people can't get used to it, but it never burned me, not even the first time. Mr. Thompson says that means selective mutations are adapting to the new demands of the environment. Mr Thompson thinks that just because he's a geneticist he knows everything.

Stan leaped away from the green stuff like it was about to bite him. "What is it?"

"I don't know. Just stuff that comes out of the pipe. When the Santa Rosa pumping station got blown up a couple of years back this broke and started dripping that green stuff." I shrugged. "It won't hurt you if you don't touch it." Stan looked like he was going to start laughing again, so I said, real quick, "I bet you're from Santa Rosa, huh?"

"Santa Rosa? What makes you think that?" He sure got jumpy if you asked him anything.

"Nothing. Santa Rosa's the first big city south of here. I just figured you probably had to come from there. Or maybe Sonoma or Napa, but those ain't too likely."

"Why do you say that?" He was real close now and his hands were balling into fists.

"Simple," I said, trying to keep my eyes off his fists. He must have been sick or something, the way he kept tightening and loosening his fingers. "The big highway north is still open, but not the one between Sonoma and Santa Rosa."

He wobbled his head up and down at that. "Yes, yes of course. That would be why." He looked at me, letting his hands open up again. I was glad to see that. "Sorry, Thorny. I guess I'm jumpier than I thought."

"That's okay," I told him. I didn't want to set him off again.

So Stan stood back and watched me while I looked for frogs.

After a while he asked me, "Is there anyone needing some help on their farms around here? Anyone you know of?"

I said no.

"Maybe there's a school somewhere that needs a teacher. Unless I miss my guess I could teach a few things. You kids probably don't have too many good teachers."

What a spooly thing to say. "My Pop teaches at the high school. Maybe he could help you find work." We didn't need teachers, but if Stan knew about teaching maybe one of the other towns could use him.

"Were you born around here?" Stan was looking around the hollow like anyone's having been born here was real special and unlikely.

"Nope. Over at Davis." That was where Pop had been doing the research into plant viruses, before he and the Baxters and the Thompsons and the Wainwrights and the Aumendsens and the Leventhals bought this place here.

"On a farm?"

"Sort of."

His voice sounded like being born on a farm was something great like saving the seaweed or maybe going back to the moon some day.

"I've always wanted to live in the country. Maybe now I can." He stumbled along the bank to the sandy spot opposite the gravel bar and sat down. Boy, he was really dumb.

"There's snakes there," I said, real gentle. Sure enough, up he shot, squealing like Mrs. Wainwright's pig.

"They won't hurt you. Just watch out for them. They only bite if you hurt 'em or scare 'em."

And with him jumping up and down I wasn't going to get any more frogs, that was for sure. So I decided to settle just for conversation.

"Is any place safe in this bank?" he asked.

"Sure," I said with a smile. "Right where you were sitting. Just keep an eye out for the snakes. They're about two feet long and sort of red. About the color of those pine needles." I pointed up the bank. "Like that."

"Dear God. How long have the pine needles been that way?"

I slogged over into the deep water. "About the last five, six years. The smog does it."

"Smog?" He gave me a real blank look. "There isn't any smog here."

"Can't see it or even smell it. Mr. Thompson says there's too much of it everywhere so we can't tell it's there any more. But the trees know it. That's why they turn that color."

"But they'll die," he said. He sounded real upset.

"Maybe. Maybe they'll change."

"How can they? This is terrible."

"Well, the pines are holding up. Most of the redwoods south of the Navarro River died years ago. Lots of them are still standing," I explained, seeing him go blank again. "But they aren't alive any more. But the pines here, they haven't died yet and maybe they aren't going to." A real sharp shine was coming into his eyes and I knew I had said more than I should have. I tried to cover up as best as I could. "We learn about this in school. They say we'll have to find ways to handle all the trouble when we grow up. Mr. Thompson tells us about biology." That last part was true, at least.

"Biology. At your age."

That kind of talk can still make me mad. "Look, mister, I'm fifteen years old, and that's plenty old to know about biology. And chemistry, too. Just because this is a long way from Santa Rosa, don't think we can't read or like that."

I was really angry. I know I'm little, but, heck, lots of people are small now.

"I didn't mean anything. I was just surprised that you have such good schools here." Boy, that Stan really couldn't lie at all.

"What do they teach where you come from?" I knew that might make him jumpy again, but I wanted to get back at him for that.

"Nothing important. They teach history and language and art with no emphasis on survival. Why, when some of the students last semester requested that the administration include courses in things like forestry, basket making and plant grafting, they called out the C.D. and there was a riot. One of the C.D.—" Stan licked his lips in an odd way—"was ambushed and left hanging from a lamppost by his heels."

"That's bad," I said. It was, too. That was the first time I found out how bad it had got in the cities. Stan was still smiling when he told me what had been done to the C.D. It wasn't nice to hear. He kept trying to make it better by calling it gelding. He said that the last time they did it was during the black-white trouble.

And that guy wanted to teach in our schools. He said that he knew what it was really like with people all over and could contribute to our system. I could see Pop's face getting real set and hard at what Stan was saying. But Stan insisted he thought that it was very important for people to understand "The System"—like it was a religious thing. You know? I was beginning to get scared.

"Fifteen is too old," he went on. "Do you have any brothers or sisters younger than yourself?"

I was pretty cautious about answering him. "Yes. I got two brothers. And one sister." I didn't tell him that Jamie was already doing research work or that Davey didn't do anything. Or that Lisa was getting ready to board in the next town so that we could keep the families from interbreeding too much.

"Older or younger."

"Mostly older." So I lied again. At least I was good at it. He didn't think to ask anything more about them.

"Too bad. We are going to have to change what's been happening. Martial law, searches without warrants, confiscations. It's terrible, Thorny, terrible."

He must have thought that living out here we didn't hear anything or see anything. He kept telling me how bad it was to have soldiers everywhere and how they were doing awful things. I knew about that and a lot of other things, too. And I knew about how there were gangs that killed people and robbed them—and murder clubs that just killed people for fun. Heck, Jules Leventhal used to be a clinical psychologist and he taught us a lot about the way mobs act and how too many people make problems for everybody.

"How are things north of here?" Stan was asking.

"Not too bad. Humboldt County is doing pretty good and there are more people around the Klamath River now." I sure didn't want a guy like him staying with us. I figured that maybe telling him about conditions up north might encourage him to move on. But he just looked tense and nodded, like that crazy preacher who wanted us all to die for god, a couple of years back. "Of course, that's redwood country so they might have trouble there in a few years."

He looked at me real hard. "Thorny, do you think you could tell me how to get to Humboldt county?"

Dumb, dumb, I told you. All he had to do is keep going up old 101 and there it would be. That crazy guy hadn't even looked at a map. Or else he had and was trying to trap me, but I ain't easy to trap.

"You can keep going up the main highway," I said, talking real sincere-like. "But there might be C.D. men up ahead, you know, near Ukiah. Or Willits. The best way is to cut over to the coast and just follow it up."

There, I thought. That ought to get him; he was jumpy enough before.

"Yes, yes, that would work. And Eureka is a port—there would be the ocean for access—"

He went on like that for about five minutes. He wanted to launch some kind of attack against The System, to protect the People, but for another System. He kept talking about rights and saying how he knew what the People really wanted and he would change things so that they could have it. He said he knew what was best for them. Wow, I wish Mr. Leventhal could have heard him.

"And what about you? You should be in school, right?"

"Nope," I said. "We have school just two days in the week. The rest of the time is free."

I wondered if that much had been all right to tell. We weren't supposed to let out much about our school.

"But it's a waste, don't you see?" Stan crouched down on the bank, looking like a huge skinny rabbit squatting there. "This is the time when you must learn political philosophy. You should be learning about how society works. It's terribly important."

"I know how society works," I said.

Heck, all the kids who learned from Mr. Wainwright know about that. After all, one of the reasons the Wainwrights came along with the rest of us was that the politicians in Sacramento didn't like what he was teaching about the way *they* worked. And they were society.

"Not this society," he said in a real haughty way, like Mr. Thompson when he's crossed. "Society in the cities, in the population centers."

He was going on that way when I saw a couple of frogs moving on the bottom. I watched where they were going and then I reached down for them, holding my breath as my face hit the water. I dragged one of them out but the other got away.

"Spending your time catching frogs," Stan spat.

"Sure. They taste real good. Mom fixes 'em up with batter and fries 'em."

"You mean you eat them?" he squeaked, looking gray.

"Of course. They're meat ain't they?" I waded over to the other frogs on the stick and stuck the new one on, too. He wiggled and jerked for a bit and them stopped.

"But frogs? How can you eat frogs?"

"Easy." I didn't think he was going to get over it: that we eat frogs. Just to be sure, I reached over and grabbed the stick with the frogs on it. "See? This one," I put my thumb on one's belly, "is the fattest. It'll taste real good."

"And do you really chase after them without seeing them?"

I turned around and looked at him. He was standing up on the other bank and the frightened look was back in his eye. "No. You got to see what you're after."

"But in that water—"

"Oh, I don't open my eyes like you do," I said, real casual-like. "I go after them with these." And I slid up the membranes.

Stan looked like he'd swallowed a salamander. "What was that?" he demanded, looking more scared than ever.

"Nictitating membranes—I was engineered for it," I said.

"Mutants," he gibbered. "Already!"

He started trying to back up the bank watching me like he thought I was a werewolf or something. He slipped and stumbled until he got to the top and then he ran away—I could hear him crashing through the brush making more noise than a herd of deer.

By the time he left the whole hole was filled with leaves and sticks and rocks and I knew that there wouldn't be any more frogs or fish that day, so I took the frogs on the stick, got off my wading shoes and started back˙ for the house. I knew Mom would be mad but I was hoping that the frogs would help her get over it. I guessed I had to tell them about Stan. They didn't like people coming here.

They were real mad about it. The funny thing is that they were maddest about my having shown my eyes. But cripes, that was just one little flap of skin that Mr. Thompson got us to breed. Just one lousy bit of extra skin near the eye.

But to hear him tell it, you'd think he'd changed the whole world.

PROBINGS

1. If you have ever moved from one community to another, or one state to another, list all of the ways in which you had to adapt. (Better yet, if you have moved from one country to another, do the same.) Consider how your friends changed, your lifestyle, your housing, the scenery; how foods might have varied, or climate, or clothing. How did you feel making all of these adaptations? Of course, your changes weren't as radical as those in "Frog Pond," but you probably get the idea!

2. Think of all of the ways in which we have learned how to substitute mechanical devices for the human body. For example, we don't walk so much because we drive more.

3. What physical adaptations can you predict might happen to the human body if we continue to pollute the water, air, and food we use? How might we compensate mechanically for these changes? Obviously, when poisonous gases are present, we use gas masks. When dangerous chemicals flood an area, we adopt protective clothing. Write an SF story or play on how the human body changes as a result of pollution. If you are good at art, consider sketching The Future Human.

4. What exactly is Yarbro's message in "Frog Pond"? This isn't an easy story so you might want to summarize the plot just to make sure you understand it. What exactly has happened in this society?

5. Why don't Thorny's parents want people to know about the young-ster's special mutation?

POPULATION: I

20

In the first century A.D., by best estimates, there were approximately 250 million people on Earth. In the United States alone, our population today exceeds 225 million humans, and a mind-boggling four billion people now claim Earth as their home. By the year 2000, we can expect at least an additional two billion people to join us.

Unfortunately, millions of our planet's people are already starving, and countless Americans are seriously malnourished. As indicated, we must remember that we are all on this spaceship together, and at this point the ship is getting to be a very crowded one. How many crew members we will add is a critical question for the next few decades.

Population increases are often hard to predict, and population trends are very complex. For example, the World Health Organization introduced DDT to Ceylon as a humanitarian gesture to kill the mosquitoes that cause malaria. Malaria was controlled, but the population doubled within ten years, resulting in a torturous moral question with no answer: Was it better to die from malaria or starvation?

In the United States, there is little concern that we will have too little space for our population. Our concern is of a different nature; the *quality* of our existence is endangered. More than three-quarters of Americans now live in urban areas, if you include cities and suburbs alike. In fact, the distinction between the city and its suburbs has become unclear: Where does the city stop, and where do the suburbs begin? We are at last realizing that urban areas face common problems of crime, transportation, and the quality of our air and water, to name just a few.

Perhaps the real population problem in our country is one of density. Too many people living too closely together on a limited piece of land. For example, during the average workday, Isaac Asimov estimates that Manhattan has a population density of 100,000 people per square mile.

In a famous study done by Cornell Medical School, it was discovered that overcrowding in urban areas can lead to both physical and psychological stress. The physical stress is evidenced by increased heart attacks, high blood pressure, ulcers, and other stress diseases. Psychological stress has resulted in irritability, neuroses, and even psychoses.

Just how would you adapt to a world that was so overcrowded that people work, sleep, and play in shifts? This is just the world that J. G. Ballard creates for us in his story "Billenium."

1. Develop a scenario or a series of headlines for the following dates showing how we might overpopulate the Earth.

1976	**World Population Hits 4 Billion**
1984	
1997	
2001	
2009	
2017	
2025	
2040	
2050	**U.S. Tops One Billion People**

2. Examine the cartoon below; what is the cartoonist's message?

PROJECTIONS

BILLENIUM

—J. G. Ballard

All day long, and often into the early hours of the morning, the tramp of feet sounded up and down the stairs outside Ward's cubicle. Built into a narrow alcove in a bend of the staircase between the fourth and fifth floors, its plywood walls flexed and creaked with every footstep like the timbers of a rotting windmill. Over a hundred people lived in the top three floors of the old rooming house, and sometimes Ward would lie awake on his narrow bunk until 2 or 3 a.m. mechanically counting the last residents returning from the all-night movies in the stadium half a mile away. Through the window he could hear giant fragments of the amplified dialogue booming among the rooftops. The stadium was never empty. During the day the huge four-sided screen was raised on its davit and athletics meetings or football matches ran continuously. For the people in the houses abutting the stadium the noise must have been unbearable.

Ward, at least, had a certain degree of privacy. Two months earlier, before he came to live on the staircase, he had shared a room with seven others on the ground floor of a house in 755th Street, and the ceaseless press of people jostling past the window had reduced him to a state of chronic exhaustion. The street was always full, an endless clamor of voices and shuffling feet. By six-thirty, when he woke, hurrying to take his place in the bathroom queue, the crowds already jammed it from sidewalk to sidewalk, the din punctuated every half minute by the roar of the elevated trains running over the shops on the opposite side of the road. As soon as he saw the advertisement describing the staircase cubicle (like everyone else, he spent most of his spare time scanning the classifieds in the newspapers, moving his lodgings an average of once every two months) he had left despite the higher rental. A cubicle on a staircase would almost certainly be on its own.

However, this had its drawbacks. Most evenings his friends from the library would call in, eager to rest their elbows after the bruising crush of the public reading room. The cubicle was slightly more than four and a half square meters in floor area, half a square meter over the statutory maximum for a single person, the carpenters having taken advantage, illegally, of a recess beside a nearby chimney breast. Consequently Ward had been able to fit a small straight-backed chair into the interval between the bed and the door, so that only one person at a time need sit on the bed—in most single cubicles host and guest had to sit side by side on the bed, conversing over their shoulders and changing places periodically to avoid neck strain.

"You were lucky to find this place," Rossiter, the most regular visitor, never tired of telling him. He reclined back on the bed, gesturing at the cubicle. "It's enormous, the perspectives really zoom. I'd be surprised if

315

you hadn't got at least five meters here, perhaps even six."

Ward shook his head categorically. Rossiter was his closest friend, but the quest for living space had forged powerful reflexes. "Just over four and a half, I've measured it carefully. There's no doubt about it."

Rossiter lifted one eyebrow. "I'm amazed. It must be the ceiling then."

Manipulating the ceiling was a favorite trick of unscrupulous landlords —most assessments of area were made upon the ceiling, out of convenience, and by tilting back the plywood partitions the rated area of a cubicle could be either increased, for the benefit of a prospective tenant (many married couples were thus bamboozled into taking a single cubicle), or decreased temporarily on the visit of the housing inspectors. Ceilings were crisscrossed with pencil marks staking out the rival claims of tenants on opposite sides of a party wall. Someone timid of his rights could be literally squeezed out of existence—in fact, the advertisement "quiet clientele" was usually a tacit invitation to this sort of piracy.

"The wall does tilt a little," Ward admitted. "Actually, it's about four degrees out—I used a plumb line. But there's still plenty of room on the stairs for people to get by."

Rossiter grinned. "Of course, John. I'm just envious, that's all. My room's driving me crazy." Like everyone, he used the term "room" to describe his tiny cubicle, a hangover from the days fifty years earlier when people had indeed lived one to a room, sometimes, unbelievably, one to an apartment or house. The microfilms in the architecture catalogs at the library showed scenes of museums, concert halls, and other public buildings in what appeared to be everyday settings, often virtually empty, two or three people wandering down an enormous gallery or staircase. Traffic moved freely along the center of streets, and in the quieter districts sections of sidewalk would be deserted for fifty yards or more.

Now, of course, the older buildings had been torn down and replaced by housing batteries, or converted into apartment blocks. The great banqueting room in the former City Hall had been split horizontally into four decks, each of these cut up into hundreds of cubicles.

As for the streets, traffic had long since ceased to move about them. Apart from a few hours before dawn when only the sidewalks were crowded, every thoroughfare was always packed with a shuffling mob of pedestrians, perforce ignoring the countless "Keep Left" signs suspended over their heads, wrestling past each other on their way to home and office, their clothes dusty and shapeless. Often "locks" would occur when a huge crowd at a street junction became immovably jammed. Sometimes these locks would last for days. Two years earlier Ward had been caught in one outside the stadium; for over forty-eight hours he was trapped in a gigantic pedestrian jam containing over twenty thousand people, fed by the crowds leaving the stadium on one side and those approaching it on the other. An entire square mile of the local neighborhood had been paralyzed, and he vividly remembered the nightmare of swaying helplessly on his feet as the jam shifted and heaved, terrified of losing his balance and being trampled underfoot. When the police had

316

finally sealed off the stadium and dispersed the jam he had gone back to his cubicle and slept for a week, his body blue with bruises.

"I hear they may reduce the allocation to three and a half meters," Rossiter remarked.

Ward paused to allow a party of tenants from the sixth floor to pass down the staircase, holding the door to prevent it jumping off its latch. "So they're always saying," he commented. "I can remember that rumor ten years ago."

"It's no rumor," Rossiter warned him. "It may well be necessary soon. Thirty million people packed into this city now, a million increase in just one year. There's been some pretty serious talk at the Housing Department."

Ward shook his head. "A drastic revaluation like that is almost impossible to carry out. Every single partition would have to be dismantled and nailed up again; the administrative job alone is so vast it's difficult to visualize. Millions of cubicles to be redesigned and certified, licenses to be issued, plus the complete resettlement of every tenant. Most of the buildings put up since the last revaluation are designed around a four-meter module—you can't simply take half a meter off the end of each cubicle and then say that makes so many new cubicles. They may be only six inches wide." He laughed. "Besides, how can you live in just three and a half meters?"

Rossiter smiled. "That's the ultimate argument, isn't it? They used it twenty-five years ago at the last revaluation, when the minimum was cut from five to four. It couldn't be done they all said, no one could stand living in only four square meters; it was enough room for a bed and suitcase, but you couldn't open the door to get in." Rossiter chuckled softly. "They were all wrong. It was merely decided that from then on all doors would open outward. Four square meters was here to stay."

Ward looked at his watch. It was seven-thirty. "Time to eat. Let's see if we can get into the food bar across the road."

Grumbling at the prospect, Rossiter pulled himself off the bed. They left the cubicle and made their way down the staircase. This was crammed with luggage and packing cases so that only a narrow interval remained around the bannister. On the floors below the congestion was worse. Corridors were wide enough to be chopped up into single cubicles, and the air was stale and dead, cardboard walls hung with damp laundry and makeshift larders. Each of the five rooms on the floors contained a dozen tenants, their voices reverberating through the partitions.

People were sitting on the steps above the second floor, using the staircase as an informal lounge, although this was against the fire regulations, women chatting with the men queueing in their shirtsleeves outside the washroom, children diving around them. By the time they reached the entrance Ward and Rossiter were having to force their way through the tenants packed together on every landing, loitering around the notice boards or pushing in from the street below.

Taking a breath at the top of the steps, Ward pointed to the food bar on the other side of the road. It was only thirty yards away, but the throng moving down the street swept past like a river at full tide, crossing them from right to left. The first picture show at the stadium started at nine o'clock and people were setting off already to make sure of getting in.

"Can't we go somewhere else?" Rossiter asked, screwing his face up at the prospect of the food bar. Not only would it be packed and take them half an hour to be served, but the food was flat and unappetizing. The journey from the library four blocks away had given him an appetite.

Ward shrugged. "There's a place on the corner, but I doubt if we can make it." This was two hundred yards upstream; they would be fighting the crowd all the way.

"Maybe you're right." Rossiter put his hand on Ward's shoulder. "You know, John, your trouble is that you never go anywhere, you're too disengaged, you just don't realize how bad everything is getting."

Ward nodded. Rossiter was right. In the morning, when he set off for the library, the pedestrian traffic was moving with him toward the downtown offices; in the evening, when he came back, it was flowing in the opposite direction. By and large he never altered his routine. Brought up from the age of ten in a municipal hostel, he had gradually lost touch with his father and mother, who lived on the east side of the city and had been unable, or unwilling, to make the journey to see him. Having surrendered his initiative to the dynamics of the city he was reluctant to try to win it back merely for a better cup of coffee. Fortunately his job at the library brought him into contact with a wide range of young people of similar interests. Sooner or later he would marry, find a double cubicle near the library, and settle down. If they had enough children (three was the required minimum) they might even one day own a small room of their own.

They stepped out into the pedestrian stream, carried along by it for ten or twenty yards, then quickened their pace and sidestepped through the crowd, slowly tacking across to the other side of the road. There they found the shelter of the shop fronts, slowly worked their way back to the food bar, shoulders braced against the countless minor collisions.

"What are the latest population estimates?" Ward asked as they circled a cigarette kiosk, stepping forward whenever a gap presented itself.

Rossiter smiled. "Sorry, John, I'd like to tell you but you might start a stampede. Besides, you wouldn't believe me."

Rossiter worked in the Insurance Department at the City Hall, had informal access to the census statistics. For the last ten years these had been classified information, partly because they were felt to be inaccurate, but chiefly because it was feared they might set off a mass attack of claustrophobia. Minor outbreaks had taken place already, and the official line was that world population had reached a plateau, leveling off at twenty thousand million. No one believed this for a moment, and Ward assumed that the 3 percent annual increase maintained since the 1960s was continuing.

How long it could continue was impossible to estimate. Despite the gloomiest prophecies of the Neo-Malthusians, world agriculture had managed to keep pace with the population growth, although intensive cultivation meant that 95 percent of the population was permanently trapped in vast urban conurbations. The outward growth of cities had at last been checked; in fact, all over the world former suburban areas were being reclaimed for agriculture and population additions were no longer confined within the existing urban ghettos. The countryside, as such, no longer existed. Every single square foot of ground sprouted a crop of one type or other. The one-time fields and meadows of the world were now, in effect, factory floors, as highly mechanized and closed to the public as any industrial area. Economic and ideological rivalries had long since faded before one overriding quest—the internal colonization of the city.

Reaching the food bar, they pushed themselves into the entrance and joined the scrum of customers pressing six deep against the counter.

"What is really wrong with the population problem," Ward confided to Rossiter, "is that no one has ever tried to tackle it. Fifty years ago shortsighted nationalism and industrial expansion put a premium on a rising population curve, and even now the hidden incentive is to have a large family so that you can gain a little privacy. Single people are penalized simply because there are more of them and they don't fit conveniently into double or triple cubicles. But it's the large family with its compact, space-saving logistic that is the real villain."

Rossiter nodded, edging nearer the counter, ready to shout his order. "Too true. We all look forward to getting married just so that we can have our six meters."

Directly in front of them, two girls turned around and smiled. "Six square meters," one of them, a dark-haired girl with a pretty oval face, repeated. "You sound like the sort of young man I ought to get to know. Going into the real estate business, Henry?"

Rossiter grinned and squeezed her arm. "Hello, Judith. I'm thinking about it actively. Like to join me in a private venture?"

The girl leaned against him as they reached the counter. "Well, I might. It would have to be legal, though."

The other girl, Helen Waring, an assistant at the library, pulled Ward's sleeve. "Have you heard the latest, John? Judith and I have been kicked out of our room. We're on the street right at this minute."

"What?" Rossiter cried. They collected their soups and coffee and edged back to the rear of the bar. "What on earth happened?"

Helen explained. "You know that little broom cupboard outside our cubicle? Judith and I have been using it as a sort of study hole, going in there to read. It's quiet and restful, if you can get used to not breathing. Well, the old girl found out and kicked up a big fuss, said we were breaking the law and so on. In short, out." Helen paused. "Now we've heard she's going to let it as a single."

Rossiter pounded the counter ledge. "A broom cupboard? Someone's going to live there? But she'll never get a license."

Judith shook her head. "She's got it already. Her brother works in the Housing Department."

Ward laughed into his soup. "But how can she let it? No one will live in a broom cupboard."

Judith stared at him somberly. "You really believe that, John?"

Ward dropped his spoon. "No, I guess you're right. People will live anywhere. God, I don't know who I feel more sorry for—you two, or the poor devil who'll be living in that cupboard. What are you going to do?"

"A couple in a place two blocks west are subletting half their cubicle to us. They've hung a sheet down the middle and Helen and I'll take turns sleeping on a camp bed. I'm not joking, our room's about two feet wide. I said to Helen that we ought to split up again and sublet one half at twice our rent."

They had a good laugh over all this and Ward said goodnight to the others and went back to his rooming house.

There he found himself with similar problems.

The manager leaned against the flimsy door, a damp cigar butt revolving around his mouth, an expression of morose boredom on his unshaven face.

"You got four point seven two meters," he told Ward, who was standing out on the staircase, unable to get into his room. Other tenants stepped past onto the landing, where two women in curlers and dressing gowns were arguing with each other, tugging angrily at the wall of trunks and cases. Occasionally the manager glanced at them irritably. "Four seven two. I worked it out twice." He said this as if it ended all possibility of argument.

"Ceiling or floor?" Ward asked.

"Ceiling, whaddya think? How can I measure the floor with all this junk?" He kicked at a crate of books protruding from under the bed.

Ward let this pass. "There's quite a tilt on the wall," he pointed out. "As much as three or four degrees."

The manager nodded vaguely. "You're definitely over the four. Way over." He turned to Ward, who had moved down several steps to allow a man and women to get past. "I can rent this as a double."

"What, only four and a half?" Ward said incredulously. "How?"

The man who had just passed him leaned over the manager's shoulder and sniffed at the room, taking in every detail in a one-second glance. "You renting a double here, Louie?"

The manager waved him away and then beckoned Ward into the room, closing the door after him.

"It's a nominal five," he told Ward. "New regulation, just came out. Anything over four five is a double now." He eyed Ward shrewdly. "Well, whaddya want? It's a good room, there's a lot of space here, feels more like a triple. You got access to the staircase, window slit—" He broke off as Ward slumped down on the bed and started to laugh.

"Whatsa matter? Look, if you want a big room like this you gotta pay for it. I want an extra half rental or you get out."

Ward wiped his eyes, then stood up wearily and reached for the shelves. "Relax, I'm on my way. I'm going to live in a broom cupboard. 'Access to the staircase'—that's really rich. Tell me, Louie, is there life on Uranus?"

Temporarily, he and Rossiter teamed up to rent a double cubicle in a semiderelict house a hundred yards from the library. The neighborhood was seedy and faded, the rooming houses crammed with tenants. Most of them were owned by absentee landlords or by the city corporation, and the managers employed were of the lowest type, mere rent collectors who cared nothing about the way their tenants divided up the living space, and never ventured beyond the first floors. Bottles and empty cans littered the corridors, and the washrooms looked like sumps. Many of the tenants were old and infirm, sitting about listlessly in their narrow cubicles, wheedling at each other back to back through the thin partitions.

Their double cubicle was on the third floor, at the end of a corridor that ringed the building. Its architecture was impossible to follow, rooms letting off at all angles, and luckily the corridor was a cul-de-sac. The mounds of cases ended four feet from the end wall and a partition divided off the cubicle, just wide enough for two beds. A high window overlooked the areaways of the building opposite.

Possessions loaded onto the shelf above his head, Ward lay back on his bed and moodily surveyed the roof of the library through the afternoon haze.

"It's not bad here," Rossiter told him, unpacking his case. "I know there's no real privacy and we'll drive each other insane within a week, but at least we haven't got six other people breathing into our ears two feet away."

The nearest cubicle, a single, was built into the banks of cases half a dozen steps along the corridor, but the occupant, a man of seventy, was deaf and bedridden.

"It's not bad," Ward echoed reluctantly. "Now tell me what the latest growth figures are. They might console me."

Rossiter paused, lowering his voice. "Four percent. *Eight hundred million extra people in one year*—just less than half the Earth's total population in 1950."

Ward whistled slowly. "So they will revalue. What to? Three and a half?"

"Three. From the first of next year."

"Three square meters." Ward sat up and looked around him. "It's unbelievable! The world's going insane, Rossiter. For God's sake, when are they going to do something about it? Do you realize there soon won't be room enough to sit down, let alone lie down?"

Exasperated, he punched the wall beside him, on the second blow knocked in one of the small wooden panels that had been lightly papered over.

"Hey!" Rossiter yelled. "You're breaking the place down." He dived across the bed to retrieve the panel, which hung downward supported by a strip of paper. Ward slipped his hand into the dark interval and carefully drew the panel back onto the bed.

"Who's on the other side?" Rossiter whispered. "Did they hear?"

Ward peered through the interval, eyes searching the dim light. Suddenly he dropped the panel and seized Rossiter's shoulder, pulled him down onto the bed.

"Henry! Look!"

Rossiter freed himself and pressed his face to the opening, focused slowly and then gasped.

Directly in front of them, faintly illuminated by a grimy skylight, was a medium-sized room, some fifteen feet square, empty except for the dust silted up against the skirting boards. The floor was bare, a few strips of frayed linoleum running across it, the walls covered with a drab floral design. Here and there patches of the paper had peeled off and segments of the picture rail had rotted away, but otherwise the room was in habitable condition.

Breathing slowly, Ward closed the open door of the cubicle with his foot, then turned to Rossiter.

"Henry, do you realize what we've found? Do you realize it, man?"

"Shut up. For Pete's sake keep your voice down." Rossiter examined the room carefully. "It's fantastic. I'm trying to see whether anyone's used it recently."

'Of course they haven't," Ward pointed out. "It's obvious. There's no door into the room. We're looking through it now. They must have paneled over this door years ago and forgotten about it. Look at that filth everywhere."

Rossiter was staring into the room, his mind staggered by its vastness.

"You're right," he murmured. "Now, when do we move in?"

Panel by panel, they pried away the lower half of the door, nailed it onto a wooden frame so that the dummy section could be replaced instantly.

Then picking an afternoon when the house was half empty and the manager asleep in his basement office, they made their first foray into the room, Ward going in alone while Rossiter kept guard in the cubicle.

For an hour they exchanged places, wandering silently around the dusty room, stretching their arms out to feel its unconfined emptiness, grasping at the sensation of absolute spatial freedom. Although smaller than many of the subdivided rooms in which they had lived, this room seemed infinitely larger, its walls huge cliffs that soared upward to the skylight.

Finally, two or three days later, they moved in.

For the first week Rossiter slept alone in the room, Ward in the cubicle outside, both there together during the day. Gradually they smuggled in a few items of furniture: two armchairs, a table, a lamp fed from the socket in the cubicle. The furniture was heavy and Victorian; the cheapest available, its size emphasized the emptiness of the room. Pride of place was taken by an enormous mahogany wardrobe, fitted with carved angels and castellated mirrors, which they were forced to dismantle and carry into the house in their suitcases. Towering over them, it reminded Ward of the microfilms of Gothic cathedrals, with their massive organ lofts crossing vast naves.

After three weeks they both slept in the room, finding the cubicle unbearably cramped. An imitation Japanese screen divided the room adequately and did nothing to diminish its size. Sitting there in the evenings, surrounded by his books and albums, Ward steadily forgot the city outside. Luckily he reached the library by a back alley and avoided the crowded streets. Rossiter and himself began to seem the only real inhabitants of the world, everyone else a meaningless by-product of their own existence, a random replication of identity which had run out of control.

It was Rossiter who suggested that they ask the two girls to share the room with them.

"They've been kicked out again and may have to split up," he told Ward, obviously worried that Judith might fall into bad company. "There's always a rent freeze after reevaluation, but all the landlords know about it so they're not reletting. It's getting damned difficult to find a room anywhere."

Ward nodded, relaxing back around the circular redwood table. He played with a tassel of the arsenic-green lampshade, for a moment felt like a Victorian man of letters, leading a spacious, leisurely life among overstuffed furnishings.

"I'm all for it," he agreed, indicating the empty corners. "There's plenty of room here. But we'll have to make damn sure they don't gossip about it."

After due precautions, they let the two girls into the secret, enjoying their astonishment at finding this private universe.

"We'll put a partition across the middle," Rossiter explained, "then take it down each morning. You'll be able to move in within a couple of days. How do you feel?"

"Wonderful!" They goggled at the wardrobe, squinting at the endless reflections in the mirrors.

There was no difficulty getting them in and out of the house. The turnover of tenants was continuous and bills were placed in the mail rack. No one cared who the girls were or noticed their regular calls at the cubicle.

However, half an hour after they arrived neither of them had unpacked her suitcase.

"What's up, Judith?" Ward asked, edging past the girls' beds into the narrow interval between the table and wardrobe.

Judith hesitated, looking from Ward to Rossiter, who sat on his bed, finishing off the plywood partition. "John, it's just that . . ."

Helen Waring, more matter of fact, took over, her fingers straightening the bedspread. "What Judith's trying to say is that our position here is a little embarrassing. The partition is—"

Rossiter stood up. "For heaven's sake, don't worry, Helen," he assured her, speaking in the loud whisper they had all involuntarily cultivated. "No funny business, you can trust us. This partition is as solid as a rock."

The two girls nodded. "It's not that," Helen explained, "but it isn't up all the time. We thought that if an older person were here, say Judith's aunt—she wouldn't take up much room and be no trouble, she's really awfully sweet—we wouldn't need to bother about the partition—except at night," she added quickly.

Ward glanced at Rossiter, who shrugged and began to scan the floor.

"Well, it's an idea," Rossiter said. "John and I know how you feel. Why not?"

"Sure," Ward agreed. He pointed to the space between the girls' beds and the table. "One more won't make any difference."

The girls broke into whoops. Judith went over to Rossiter and kissed him on the cheek. "Sorry to be a nuisance, Henry." She smiled at him. "That's a wonderful partition you've made. You couldn't do another one for Auntie—just a little one? She's very sweet but she is getting on."

"Of course," Rossiter said, "I understand. I've got plenty of wood left over."

Ward looked at his watch. "It's seven-thirty, Judith. You'd better get in touch with your aunt. She may not be able to make it tonight."

Judith buttoned her coat. "Oh, she will," she assured Ward. "I'll be back in a jiffy."

The aunt arrived within five minutes, three heavy suitcases soundly packed.

"It's amazing," Ward remarked to Rossiter three months later. "the size of this room still staggers me. It almost gets larger every day."

Rossiter agreed readily, averting his eyes from one of the girls changing behind the central partition. This they now left in place as dismantling it daily had become tiresome. Besides, the aunt's subsidiary partition was attached to it and she resented the continuous upsets. Ensuring she followed the entrance and exit drills through the camouflaged door and cubicle was difficult enough.

Despite this, detection seemed unlikely. The room had obviously been built as an afterthought into the central well of the house and any noise was masked by the luggage stacked in the surrounding corridor. Directly below was a small dormitory occupied by several elderly women, and Judith's aunt, who visited them socially, swore that no sounds came through the heavy ceiling. Above, the fanlight let out through a dormer window, its lights indistinguishable from the hundred other bulbs burning in the windows of the house.

Rossiter finished off the new partition he was building and held it upright, fitting it into the slots nailed to the wall between his bed and

Ward's. They had agreed that this would provide a little extra privacy.

"No doubt I'll have to do one for Judith and Helen," he confided to Ward.

Ward adjusted his pillow. They had smuggled the two armchairs back to the furniture shop as they took up too much space. The bed, anyway, was more comfortable. He had never got completely used to the soft upholstery.

"Not a bad idea. What about some shelving around the wall? I've got nowhere to put anything."

The shelving tidied the room considerably, freeing large areas of the floor. Divided by their partitions, the five beds were in line along the rear wall, facing the mahogany wardrobe. In between was an open space of three or four feet, a further six feet on either side of the wardrobe.

The sight of so much space fascinated Ward. When Rossiter mentioned that Helen's mother was ill and badly needed personal care he immediately knew where her cubicle could be placed—at the foot of his bed, between the wardrobe and the side wall.

Helen was overjoyed. "It's awfully good of you, John," she told him, "but would you mind if Mother slept beside me? There's enough space to fit an extra bed in."

So Rossiter dismantled the partitions and moved them closer together, six beds now in line along the wall. This gave each of them an interval two and a half feet wide, just enough room to squeeze down the side of their beds. Lying back on the extreme right, the shelves two feet above his head, Ward could barely see the wardrobe, but the space in front of him, a clear six feet to the wall ahead, was uniterrupted.

Then Helen's father arrived.

Knocking on the door of the cubicle, Ward smiled at Judith's aunt as she let him in. He helped her swing out the made-up bed which guarded the entrance, then rapped on the wooden panel. A moment later Helen's father, a small gray-haired man in an undershirt, braces tied to his trousers with string, pulled back the panel.

Ward nodded to him and stepped over the luggage piled around the floor at the foot of the beds. Helen was in her mother's cubicle, helping the old woman to drink her evening broth. Rossiter, perspiring heavily, was on his knees by the mahogany wardrobe, wrenching apart the frame of the central mirror with a jimmy. Pieces of the wardrobe lay on his bed and across the floor.

"We'll have to start taking these out tomorrow," Rossiter told him. Ward waited for Helen's father to shuffle past and enter his cubicle. He had rigged up a small cardboard door, and locked it behind him with a crude hook of bent wire.

Rossiter watched him, frowning irritably. "Some people are never happy. This wardrobe's a hell of a job. How did we ever decide to buy it?"

Ward sat down on his bed. The partition pressed against his knees and he could hardly move. He looked up when Rossiter was engaged and saw that the dividing line he had marked in pencil was hidden by the encroaching partition. Leaning against the wall, he tried to ease it back again, but Rossiter had apparently nailed the lower edge to the floor.

There was a sharp tap on the outside cubicle door—Judith returning from her office. Ward started to get up and then sat back. "Mr. Waring," he called softly. It was the old man's duty night.

Waring shuffled to the door of his cubicle and unlocked it fussily, clucking to himself.

"Up and down, up and down," he muttered. He stumbled over Rossiter's tool bag and swore loudly, then added meaningly over his shoulder: "If you ask me there's too many people in here. Down below they've only got six to our seven, and it's the same size room."

Ward nodded vaguely and stretched back on his narrow bed, trying not to bang his head on the shelving. Waring was not the first to hint that he move out. Judith's aunt had made a similar suggestion two days earlier. Since he left his job at the library (the small rental he charged the others paid for the little food he needed) he spent most of his time in the room, seeing rather more of the old man than he wanted to, but he had learned to tolerate him.

Settling himself, he noticed that the right-hand spire of the wardrobe, all he had been able to see for the past two months, was now dismantled.

It had been a beautiful piece of furniture, in a way symbolizing this whole private world, and the salesman at the store told him there were few left like it. For a moment Ward felt a sudden pang of regret, as he had done as a child when his father, in a mood of exasperation, had taken something away from him and he knew he would never see it again.

Then he pulled himself together. It was a beautiful wardrobe, without doubt, but when it was gone it would make the room seem even larger.

PROBINGS

1. Would you want to live in "Billenium?" Why or why not? What would you find hardest to adjust to? Easiest?
2. Have you ever felt really crowded in your life? If so, under what conditions? What were your feelings?
3. Should the government do anything to prevent "Billenium" from happening? For example, should the government subsidize people to move to North and South Dakota, where the population density is low? What would it take to get you to move to a less desirable area?
4. There is virtually no privacy in Ballard's future world. Where do you go to seek privacy? At home? Work? School? Develop a future wheel or write a story using the idea that there will be a world of tomorrow in which nobody has any privacy at any time.
5. Consider the following opinions about population. Which do you agree with?
   a. Just as we need Arab oil to power our industry, many parts of the world need our grain in order to live.
   b. The United States should take care of itself first, then worry about the rest of the world's population.

POPULATION: II

21

As we have seen, the increasing world's population poses a serious problem to the entire planet. Now, the time has come to ask: What can, we do about it?

In the early nineteenth century, Thomas Malthus, a famous economist, formulated a theory that population increases geometrically: 2, 4, 8, etc.; food increases arithmetically: 1, 2, 3, 4, etc. Of course, the conclusion is obvious: sooner or later, people will outstrip food. However, as Malthus noted, there are certain natural checks that keep population down, such as famine, disease, and war. As we saw in Ceylon, though, man is now controlling some of these natural checks such as disease.

An artificial check has become increasingly important in the twentieth century, and that is birth control. In the United States birth control has had a definite impact on the population growth rate. Unfortunately, birth control meets with resistance in many developing countries—where offspring are still regarded as a resource.

In Frederik Pohl's story, still another means of population control is suggested—as horrifying as it seems.

1. Headlines from Tomorrow:

PRESIDENT SIGNS
CHILD LIMIT BILL

The President today signed a bill, which had earlier passed Congress by an overwhelming majority, that permits couples to have only one child.

PROJECTIONS

2. Would you like to have children? If so, how many?
   a. What advantages or benefits do you think you would experience by having children? What disadvantages?
   b. Which of the following groups might influence your decision to have children: government; religious; family; friends; others? Why?

THE CENSUS TAKERS

—Frederik Pohl

It gets to be a madhouse around here along about the end of the first week. Thank heaven we only do this once a year, that's what I say! Six weeks on, and forty-six weeks off—that's pretty good hours, most people think. But they don't know what those six weeks are like.

It's bad enough for the field crews, but when you get to be an Area Boss like me it's frantic. You work your way up through the ranks, and then they give you a whole C.A. of your own; and you think you've got it made. Fifty three-man crews go out, covering the whole Census Area; a hundred and fifty men in the field, and twenty or thirty more in Area Command—and you boss them all. And everything looks great, until Census Period starts and you've got to work those hundred and fifty men; and six weeks is too unbearably long to live through, and too impossibly short to get the work done; and you begin living on black coffee and thiamin shots and dreaming about the vacation hostel on Point Loma.

Anybody can panic, when the pressure is on like that. Your best field men begin to crack up. But you can't afford to, because you're the Area Boss. . . .

Take Witeck. We were Enumerators together, and he was as good a man as you ever saw, absolutely nerveless when it came to processing the Overs. I counted on that man the way I counted on my own right arm; I always bracketed him with the greenest, shakiest new cadet Enumerators, and he never gave me a moment's trouble for years. Maybe it was too good to last; maybe I should have figured he would crack.

I set up my Area Command in a plush penthouse apartment. The people who lived there were pretty well off, you know, and they naturally raised the dickens about being shoved out. "Blow it," I told them. "Get out of here in five minutes, and we'll count you first." Well, that took care of *that;* they were practically kissing my feet on the way out. Of course, it wasn't strictly by the book, but you have to be a little flexible; that's why some men become Area Bosses, and others stay Enumerators.

Like Witeck.

Along about Day Eight things were really hotting up. I was up to my neck in hurry-ups from Regional Control—we were running a little slow —when Witeck called up. "Chief," he said, "I've got an In."

I grabbed the rotary file with one hand and a pencil with the other. "Blue-card number?" I asked.

Witeck sounded funny over the phone. "Well, Chief," he said, "he doesn't have a blue card. He says—"

"No blue card?" I couldn't believe it. Come in to a strange C.A.

without a card from your own Area Boss, and you're one In that's a cinch to be an Over. "What kind of a crazy C.A. does he come from, without a blue card?"

Witeck said, "He don't come from any C.A., Chief. He says—"

"You mean he isn't from this country?"

"That's right, Chief. He—"

"Hold it!" I pushed away the rotary file and grabbed the immigration roster. There were only a couple of dozen names on it, of course—we have enough trouble with our own Overs, without taking on a lot of foreigners, but still there were a handful every year who managed to get on the quotas. "I.D. number?" I demanded.

"Well, Chief," Witeck began, "he doesn't have an I.D. number. The way it looks to me—"

Well, you can fool around with these irregulars for a month, if you want to, but it's no way to get the work done. I said, "Over him!" and hung up. I was a little surprised, though; Witeck knew the ropes, and it wasn't like him to buck an irregular onto me. In the old days, when we were both starting out, I'd seen him Over a whole family just because the spelling of their names on their registry cards was different from the spelling on the checklist.

But we get older. I made a note to talk to Witeck as soon as the rush was past. We were old friends; I wouldn't have to threaten him with being Overed himself, or anything like that. He'd know, and maybe that would be all he would need to snap him back. I certainly would talk to him, I promised myself, as soon as the rush was over, or anyway as soon as I got back from Point Loma.

I had to run up to Regional Control to take a little talking-to myself just then, but I proved to them that we were catching up and they were only medium nasty. When I got back Witeck was on the phone again. "Chief," he said, real unhappy, "this In is giving me a headache. I—"

"Witeck," I snapped at him, "are you bothering me with another In? Can't you handle anything by yourself?"

He said, "It's the same one, Chief. He says he's a kind of ambassador, and—"

"Oh," I said. "Well, why the devil don't you get your facts straight in the first place? Give me his name and I'll check his legation."

"Well, Chief," he began again, "he, uh, doesn't have any legation. He says he's from the"— he swallowed— "from the middle of the earth."

"You're crazy." I'd seen it happen before, good men breaking under the strain of census taking. They say in cadets that by the time you process your first five hundred Overs you've had it; either you take a voluntary Over yourself, or you split wide open and they carry you off to a giggle farm. And Witeck was past the five hundred mark, way past.

There was a lot of yelling and crying from the filter center, which I'd put out by the elevators, and it looked like Jumpers. I stabbed the transfer button on the phone and called to Carias, my number-two man: "Witeck's flipped or something. Handle it!"

And then I forgot about it, while Carias talked to Witeck on the phone; because it was Jumpers, all right, a whole family of them.

There was a father and a mother and five kids—*five* of them. Aren't some people disgusting? The field Enumerator turned them over to the guards—they were moaning and crying—and came up and gave me the story. It was bad.

"You're the head of the household?" I demanded of the man.

He nodded, looking at me like a sick dog. "We—we weren't Jumping," he whined. "Honest to heaven, mister—you've got to believe me. We were—"

I cut in, "You were packed and on the doorstep when the field crew came by. Right?" He started to say something, but I had him dead to rights. "That's plenty, friend," I told him. "That's Jumping, under the law: Packing, with intent to move, while a census Enumeration crew is operating in your locale. Got anything to say?"

Well, he had plenty to say, but none of it made any sense. He turned my stomach, listening to him. I tried to keep my temper—you're not supposed to think of individuals, no matter how worthless and useless and generally unfit they are; that's against the whole principle of the Census—but I couldn't help telling him: "I've met your kind before, mister. Five kids! If it wasn't for people like you we wouldn't *have* any Overs, did you ever think of that? Sure you didn't—you people never think of anything but yourself! Five kids, and then when Census comes around you think you can get smart and Jump." I tell you, I was shaking. "You keep your little beady eyes peeled, sneaking around, watching the Enumerators, trying to count how many it takes to make an Over; and then you wait until they get close to you, so you can Jump. Ever stop to think what trouble that makes for us?" I demanded. "Census is supposed to be fair and square, everybody an even chance—and how can we make it that way unless everybody stands still to be counted?" I patted Old Betsy, on my hip. "I haven't Overed anybody myself in five years," I told him, "but I swear, I'd like to handle you personally!"

He didn't say a word once I got started on him. He just stood there, taking it. I had to force myself to stop, finally; I could have gone on for a long time, because if there's one thing I hate it's these lousy, stinking breeders who try to Jump when they think one of them is going to be an Over in the count-off. Regular Jumpers are bad enough, but when it's the people who make the mess in the first place—

Anyway, time was wasting. I took a deep breath and thought things over. Actually, we weren't too badly off; we'd started off Overing every two-hundred-and-fiftieth person, and it was beginning to look as though our preliminary estimate was high; we'd just cut back to Overing every three-hundredth. So we had a little margin to play with.

I told the man, dead serious; "You know I could Over the lot of you on charges, don't you?" He nodded sickly. "All right, I'll give you a chance. I don't want to bother with the red tape; if you'll take a voluntary Over for yourself, we'll start the new count with your wife."

Call me soft, if you want to; but I still say that it was a lot better than fussing around with charges and a hearing. You get into a hearing like that and it can drag on for half an hour or more; and then Regional Control is on your tail because you're falling behind.

It never hurts to give a man a break, even a Jumper, I always say—as long as it doesn't slow down your Census.

Carias was waiting at my desk when I got back; he looked worried about something, but I brushed him off while I initialed the Overage report on the man we'd just processed. He'd been an In, I found out when I canceled his blue card. I can't say I was surprised. He'd come from Denver, and you know how they keep exceeding their Census figures; no doubt he thought he'd have a better chance in my C.A. than anywhere else. And no doubt he was right, because we certainly don't encourage breeders like him—actually, if he hadn't tried to Jump it was odds-on that the whole damned family would get by without an Over for years.

Carias was hovering right behind me as I finished. "I hate these voluntaries," I told him, basketing the canceled card. "I'm going to talk to Regional Control about it; there's no reason why they can't be processed like any other Over, instead of making me okay each one individually. Now, what's the matter?"

He rubbed his jaw. "Chief," he said, "it's Witeck."

"Now what? Another In?"

Carias glanced at me, then away. "Uh, no, Chief. It's the same one. He claims he comes from, uh, the center of the earth."

I swore out loud. "So he has to turn up in my C.A.!" I complained bitterly. "He gets out of the nuthouse, and right away—"

Carias said, "Chief, he might not be crazy. He makes it sound pretty real."

I said: "Hold it, Carias. Nobody can live in the center of the earth. It's solid, like a potato."

"Sure, Chief," Carias nodded earnestly. "But he says it isn't. He says there's a what he calls neutronium shell, whatever that is, with dirt and rocks on both sides of it. We live on the outside. He lives on the inside. His people—"

"Carias!" I yelled. "You're as bad as Witeck. This guy turns up, no blue card, no I.D. number, no credentials of any kind. What's he going to say, 'Please sir, I'm an Over, please process me'? Naturally not! So he makes up a crazy story, and you fall for it!"

"I know, Chief," Carias said humbly.

"Neutronium shell!" I would have laughed out loud, if I'd had the time. "Neutronium my foot! Don't you know it's *hot* down there?"

"He says it's hot neutronium," Carias said eagerly. "I asked him that myself, Chief. He said it's just the shell that—"

"Get back to work!" I yelled at him. I picked up the phone and got Witeck on his wristphone. I tell you, I was boiling. As soon as Witeck answered I lit into him; I didn't give him a chance to get a word in. I gave it to him up and down and sidewise; and I finished off by giving him a

333

direct order. "You Over that man," I told him, "or I'll personally Over you! You hear me?"

There was a pause. Then Witeck said, "Jerry? Will you listen to me?"

That stopped me. It was the first time in ten years, since I'd been promoted above him, that Witeck had dared call me by my first name. He said, "Jerry, listen. This is something big. This guy is really from the center of the earth, no kidding. He—"

"Witeck," I said, "you've cracked."

"No, Jerry, honest! And it worries me. He's right there in the next room, waiting for me. He says he had no idea things were like this on the surface; he's talking wild about cleaning us off and starting all over again; he says—"

"*I* say he's an Over!" I yelled. "No more talk, Witeck. You've got a direct order—now carry it out!"

So that was that.

We got through the Census Period after all, but we had to do it shorthanded; and Witeck was hard to replace. I'm a sentimentalist, I guess, but I couldn't help remembering old times. We started even; he might have risen as far as I—but of course he made his choice when he got married and had a kid; you can't be a breeder and an officer of the Census both. If it hadn't been for his record he couldn't even have stayed on as an Enumerator.

I never said a word to anyone about his crackup. Carias might have talked, but after we found Witeck's body I took him aside. "Carias," I said reasonably, "we don't want any scandal, do we? Here's Witeck, with an honorable record; he cracks, and kills himself, and that's bad enough. We won't let loose talk make it worse, will we?"

Carias said uneasily, "Chief, where's the gun he killed himself with? His own processor wasn't even fired."

You can let a helper go just so far. I said sharply, "Carias, we still have at least a hundred Overs to process. You can be on one end of the processing—or you can be on the other. You understand me?"

He coughed. "Sure, Chief. I understand. We don't want any, loose talk."

And that's how it is when you're an Area Boss. But I didn't ever get my vacation at Point Loma; the tsunami there washed out the whole town the last week of the Census. And when I tried Baja California, they were having that crazy volcanic business; and the Yellowstone Park bureau wouldn't even accept my reservation because of some trouble with the geysers, so I just stayed home. But the best vacation of all was just knowing that the Census was done for another year.

Carias was all for looking for this In that Witeck was talking about, but I turned him down. "Waste of time," I told him. "By now he's a dozen C.A.'s away. We'll never see him again, him or anybody like him—I'll bet my life on that."

PROBINGS

1. Could you be an Enumerator? Why? Why not?
2. How did you feel about the Jumpers who tried to escape the Census?
3. By conservative estimates, we will add 25 to 50 million people to the U.S. population by the early twenty-first century, which will put even more pressure on you and your children not to have more children. Would you be in favor of the government's forcing parents to obtain licenses for parenthood? What criteria should be used for determining who should be parents?
4. Write an SF story on the idea of licensing parents.
5. Examine the Fischetti cartoon on population. Then draw your own cartoon, or develop an idea for a cartoon based on some of the consequences of overpopulation.

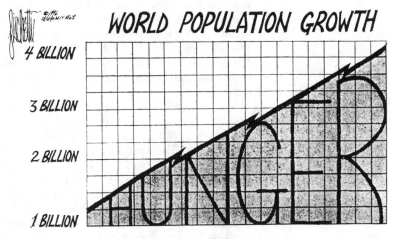

Deepening shadow

SURVIVAL

22

Nobody knows the exact day when humans stopped following wild animals and raised their own. Since humanity's beginnings, where the animals wandered, people had learned to follow. At some point, though —several thousand years ago—the hunters of animal flesh learned, perhaps by accident, that they could tame their own source of food and thus cease their eternal wanderings. With this change, humans began to settle down.

At what specific moment homo sapiens learned that they could also quit gathering their food and raise their own we don't know. Also we don't know at what specific moment humans learned that they didn't have to search to locate tools or weapons but could make them out of stone, bronze, and copper.

We do know, however, the exact day, hour, minute, and even second when we as humans entered the awesome reality of the atomic age. The first successful test bomb was exploded on July 16, 1945, in New Mexico. Then, on August 6, 1945, the U.S. dropped an atomic bomb on Japan, and the world entered a new era. In the past three decades, one nation after another has armed itself with an awesome array of atomic and hydrogen weapons.

The key to human survival is delicately balanced between hatred of those who are different from us and cooperation. If we look at the record, we earthlings have a poor one. Recorded history is filled with an unending series of wars—racial, tribal, nationalistic, and religious conflicts, to name the major types. But now we have to face the possibility, always hanging over our heads, that one nation might use The Bomb against another nation.

Science fiction writers have ably reflected the fear and distrust that we as humans have felt toward those who are different. When earthmen meet extraterrestrial beings in many science fiction stories, the latter are extremely ugly—bug-eyed, green, with grasping tentacles. "They" are also usually extremely intelligent and equally dangerous; therefore, any scheme or weapon used by earthmen to conquer "them" is acceptable. If you have watched a few grade B science fiction films on television, you have no doubt seen our extraterrestrial visitors slain by atomic bombs, germ warfare, and deadly plagues.

Science fiction also reflects the way in which we view our own neighbors on earth. During World War II, the Japanese and Germans were portrayed as monsters. During the 1950s and 60s the "bad guys" were the Russians and Chinese, and finally the Vietnamese.

In Philip K. Dick's "The Crawlers," we see one possible result of man's nuclear gambling, and it is a truly frightening result, at that.

1. Headlines from Tomorrow:

MESSAGE RECEIVED FROM OUTER SPACE

What is the message? Write a news story about how the message was received.

How did we greet "them"?

PROJECTIONS

2. Either describe in words or create an illustration of what the beings from outer space would look like.
3. a. What comes to mind when you hear the words, "mushroom cloud," "atomic war," "fall-out shelters"?
   b. What do your parents think of when they hear those words?

THE CRAWLERS

—Philip K. Dick

He built, and the more he built the more he enjoyed building. Hot sunlight filtered down; summer breezes stirred around him as he toiled joyfully. When he ran out of material he paused awhile and rested. His edifice wasn't large; it was more a practice model than the real thing. One part of his brain told him that, and another part thrilled with excitement and pride. It was at least large enough to enter. He crawled down the entrance tunnel and curled up inside in a contented heap.

Through a rent in the roof a few bits of dirt rained down. He oozed binder fluid and reinforced the weak place. In his edifice the air was clean and cool, almost dust-free. He crawled over the inner walls one last time, leaving a quick-drying coat of binder over everything. What else was needed? He was beginning to feel drowsy; in a moment he'd be asleep.

He thought about it, and then he extended a part of himself up through the still-open entrance. That part watched and listened warily, as the rest of him dozed off in a grateful slumber. He was peaceful and content, conscious that from a distance all that was visible was a light mound of dark clay. No one would notice it: no one would guess what lay beneath.

And if they did notice, he had methods of taking care of them.

The farmer halted his ancient Ford truck with a grinding shriek of brakes. He cursed and backed up a few yards. "There's one. Hop down and take a look at it. Watch the cars—they go pretty fast along here."

Ernest Gretry pushed the cabin door open and stepped down gingerly onto the hot mid-morning pavement. The air smelled of sun and drying grass. Insects buzzed around him as he advanced cautiously up the highway, hands in his trouser pockets, lean body bent forward. He stopped and peered down.

The thing was well mashed. Wheel marks crossed it in four places and its internal organs had ruptured and burst through. The whole thing was snail-like, a gummy elongated tube with sense organs at one end and a confusing mass of protoplasmic extensions at the other.

What got him most was the face. For a time he couldn't look directly at it: he had to contemplate the road, the hills, the big cedar trees, anything else. There was something in the little dead eyes, a glint that was rapidly fading. They weren't the lusterless eyes of a fish, stupid and vacant. The life he had seen haunted him, and he had got only a brief glimpse, as the truck bore down on it and crushed it flat.

"They crawl across here every once in awhile," the farmer said quietly. "Sometimes they get as far as town. The first one I saw was heading down the middle of Grant Street, about fifty yards an hour. They go pretty slow.

Some of the teenage kids like to run them down. Personally I avoid them, if I see them."

Gretry kicked aimlessly at the thing. He wondered vaguely how many more there were in the bushes and hills. He could see farmhouses set back from the road, white gleaming squares in the hot Tennessee sun. Horses and sleeping cattle. Dirty chickens scratching. A sleepy, peaceful countryside, basking in the late-summer sun.

"Where's the radiation lab from here?" he asked.

The farmer indicated. "Over there, on the other side of those hills. You want to collect the remains? They have one down at the Standard Oil Station in a big tank. Dead, of course. They filled the tank with kerosene to try to preserve it. That one's in pretty good shape, compared to this. Joe Jackson cracked its head with a two-by-four. He found it crawling across his property one night."

Gretry got shakily back into the truck. His stomach turned over and he had to take some long deep breaths. "I didn't realize there were so many. When they sent me out from Washington they just said a few had been seen."

"There's been quite a lot." The farmer started up the truck and carefully skirted the remains on the pavement. "We're trying to get used to them, but we can't. It's not nice stuff. A lot of people are moving away. You can feel it in the air, a sort of heaviness. We've got this problem and we have to meet it." He increased speed, leathery hands tight around the wheel. "It seems like there's more of *them* born all the time, and almost no normal children."

Back in town, Gretry called Freeman long distance from the booth in the shabby hotel lobby. "We'll have to do something. They're all around here. I'm going out at three to see a colony of them. The fellow who runs the taxi stand knows where they are. He says there must be eleven or twelve of them together."

"How do the people around there feel?"

"How the hell do you expect? They think it's God's Judgment. Maybe they're right."

"We should have made them move earlier. We should have cleaned out the whole area for miles around. Then we wouldn't have this problem." Freeman paused. "What do you suggest?"

"That island we took over for the H-bomb tests."

"It's a damn big island. There was a whole group of natives we moved off and resettled." Freeman choked. "Good God, are there *that* many of them?"

"The staunch citizens exaggerate, of course. But I get the impression there must be at least a hundred."

Freeman was silent a long time. "I didn't realize," he said finally. "I'll have to put it through channels, of course. We were going to make further tests on that island. But I see your point."

"I'd like it," Gretry said. "This is a bad business. We can't have things like this. People can't live with this sort of thing. You ought to drop out here and take a look. It's something to remember."

"I'll—see what I can do. I'll talk to Gordon. Give me a ring tomorrow."

Gretry hung up and wandered out of the drab, dirty lobby onto the blazing sidewalk. Dingy stores and parked cars. A few old men hunched over on steps and sagging cane-bottom chairs. He lit a cigarette and shakily examined his watch. It was almost three. He moved slowly toward the taxi stand.

The town was dead. Nothing stirred. Only the motionless old men in their chairs and the out-of-town cars zipping along the highway. Dust and silence lay over everything. Age, like a gray spider web, covered all the houses and stores. No laughter. No sound of any kind.

No children playing games.

A dirty blue taxicab pulled up silently beside him. "Okay, mister," the driver said, a rat-faced man in his thirties, toothpick hanging between his crooked teeth. He kicked the bent door open. "Here we go."

"How far is it?" Gretry asked, as he climbed in.

"Just outside town." The cab picked up speed and hurtled noisily along, bouncing and bucking. "You from the FBI?"

"No."

"I thought from your suit and hat you was." The driver eyed him curiously. "How'd you hear about the crawlers?"

"From the radiation lab."

"Yeah, it's that hot stuff they got there." The driver turned off the highway and onto a dirt side-road. "It's up here on the Higgins farm. The crazy damn things picked the bottom of old lady Higgins' place to build their houses."

"Houses?"

"They've got some sort of city, down under the ground. You'll see it—the entrances, at least. They work together, building and fussing." He twisted the cab off the dirt road, between two huge cedars, over a bumpy field, and finally brought it to rest at the edge of a rocky gully. "This is it."

It was the first time Gretry had seen one alive.

He got out of the cab awkwardly, his legs numb and unresponsive. The things were moving slowly between the woods and the entrance tunnels in the center of the clearing. They were bringing building material, clay and weeds. Smearing it with some kind of ooze and plastering it in rough forms which were carefully carried beneath the ground. The crawlers were two or three feet long; some were older than others, darker and heavier. All of them moved with agonizing slowness, a silent flowing motion across the sun-baked ground. They were soft, shelless, and looked harmless.

Again, he was fascinated and hypnotized by their faces. The weird parody of human faces. Wizened little baby features, tiny shoebutton eyes, slit of a mouth, twisted ears, and a few wisps of damp hair. What should have been arms were elongated pseudopods that grew and preceded like soft dough. The crawlers seemed incredibly flexible; they extended themselves, then snapped their bodies back, as their feelers made contact with obstructions. They paid no attention to the two men; they didn't even seem to be aware of them.

"How dangerous are they?" Gretry asked finally.

"Well, they have some sort of stinger. They stung a dog, I know. Stung him pretty hard. He swelled up and his tongue turned black. He had fits and got hard. He died." The driver added half-apologetically, "He was nosing around. Interrupting their building. They work all the time. Keep busy."

"Is this most of them?"

"I guess so. They sort of congregate here. I see them crawling this way." The driver gestured. "See, they're born in different places. One or two at each farmhouse, near the radiation lab."

"Which way is Mrs. Higgins' farmhouse?" Gretry asked.

"Up there. See it through the trees? You want to—"

"I'll be right back," Gretry said, and started abruptly off. "Wait here."

The old woman was watering the dark red geraniums that grew around her front porch, when Gretry approached. She looked up quickly, her ancient wrinkled face shrewd and suspicious, the sprinkling can poised like a blunt instrument.

"Afternoon," Gretry said. He tipped his hat and showed her his credentials. "I'm investigating the—crawlers. At the edge of your land."

"Why?" Her voice was empty, bleak, cold. Like her withered face and body.

"We're trying to find a solution." Gretry felt awkward and uncertain. "It's been suggested we transport them away from here, out to an island in the Gulf of Mexico. They shouldn't be here. It's too hard on people. It isn't right," he finished lamely.

"No. It isn't right."

"And we've already begun moving everybody away from the radiation lab. I guess we should have done that a long time ago."

The old woman's eyes flashed. "You people and your machines. See what you've done." She jabbed a bony finger at him excitedly. "Now you have to fix it. You have to do something."

"We're taking them away to an island as soon as possible. But there's one problem. We have to be sure about the parents. They have complete custody of them. We can't just—" He broke off futilely. "How do they feel? Would they let us cart up their—children, and haul them away?"

Mrs. Higgins turned and headed into the house. Uncertainly, Gretry followed her through the dim, dusty interior rooms. Musty chambers full of oil lamps and faded pictures, ancient sofas and tables. She led him through a great kitchen of immense cast iron pots and pans down a flight of wooden stairs to a painted white door. She knocked sharply.

Flurry and movement on the other side. The sound of people whispering and moving things hurriedly.

"Open the door," Mrs. Higgins commanded. After an agonized pause the door opened slowly. Mrs. Higgins pushed it wide and motioned Gretry to follow her.

In the room stood a young man and woman. They backed away as Gretry came in. The woman hugged a long pasteboard carton which the man had suddenly passed to her.

"Who are you?" the man demanded. He abruptly grabbed the carton back; his wife's small hands were trembling under the shifting weight.

Gretry was seeing the parents of one of them. The young woman, brown-haired, not more than nineteen. Slender and small in a cheap green dress, a full-breasted girl with dark frightened eyes. The man was bigger and stronger, a handsome dark youth with massive arms and competent hands gripping the pasteboard carton tight.

Gretry couldn't stop looking at the carton. Holes had been punched in the top; the carton moved slightly in the man's arms, and there was a faint shudder that rocked it back and forth.

"This man," Mrs. Higgins said to the husband, "has come to take it away."

The couple accepted the information in silence. The husband made no move except to get a better grip on the box.

"He's going to take all of them to an island," Mrs. Higgins said. "It's all arranged. Nobody'll harm them. They'll be safe and they can do what they want. Build and crawl around where nobody has to look at them."

The young woman nodded blankly.

"Give it to him," Mrs. Higgins ordered impatiently. "Give him the box and let's get it over with once and for all."

After a moment the husband carried the box over to a table and put it down. "You know anything about them?" he demanded. "You know what they eat?"

"We—" Gretry began helplessly.

"They eat leaves. Nothing but leaves and grass. We've been bringing in the smallest leaves we could find."

"It's only a month old," the young woman said huskily. "It already wants to go down with the others, but we keep it here. We don't want it to go down there. Not yet. Later, maybe, we thought. We didn't know what to do. We weren't sure." Her large dark eyes flashed briefly in mute appeal, then faded out again. "It's a hard thing to know."

The husband untied the heavy brown twine and took the lid from the carton. "Here. You can see it."

It was the smallest Gretry had seen. Pale and soft, less than a foot long. It had crawled in a corner of the box and was curled up in a messy web of chewed leaves and some kind of wax. A translucent covering spun clumsily around it, behind which it lay asleep. It paid no attention to them; they were out of its scope. Gretry felt a strange helpless horror rise up in him. He moved away, and the young man replaced the lid.

"We knew what it was," he said hoarsely. "Right away, as soon as it

343

was born. Up the road, there was one we saw. One of the first. Bog Douglas made us come over and look at it. It was his and Julie's. That was before they started coming down and collecting together by the gully."

"Tell him what happened," Mrs. Higgins said

"Douglas mashed its head with a rock. Then he poured gasoline on it and burned it up. Last week he and Julie packed and left."

"Have many of them been destroyed?" Gretry managed to ask.

"A few. A lot of men, they see something like that and they go sort of wild. You can't blame them." The man's dark eyes darted hopelessly. "I guess I almost did the same thing."

"Maybe we should have," his wife murmured. "Maybe I should have let you."

Gretry picked up the pasteboard carton and moved toward the door. "We'll get this done as quickly as we can. The trucks are on the way. It should be over in a day."

"Thank God for that," Mrs. Higgins exclaimed in a clipped, emotionless voice. She held the door open, and Gretry carried the carton through the dim, musty house, down the sagging front steps and out into the blazing mid-afternoon sun.

Mrs. Higgins stopped at the red geraniums and picked up her sprinkling can. "When you take them, take them all. Don't leave any behind. Understand?"

"Yes," Gretry muttered.

"Keep some of your men and trucks here. Keep checking. Don't let any stay where we have to look at them."

"When we get the people near the radiation lab moved away there shouldn't be any more of—"

He broke off. Mrs. Higgins had turned her back and was watering the geraniums. Bees buzzed around her. The flowers swayed dully with the hot wind. The old woman passed on around the side of the house, still watering and stooping over. In a few moments she was gone and Gretry was alone with his carton.

Embarrassed and ashamed, he carried the carton slowly down the hill and across the field to the ravine. The taxi driver was standing by his cab, smoking a cigarette and waiting patiently for him. The colony of crawlers was working steadily on its city. There were streets and passages. On some of the entrance-mounds he noticed intricate scratches that might have been words. Some of the crawlers were grouped together, setting up involved things he couldn't make out.

"Let's go," he said wearily to the driver.

The driver grinned and yanked the back door. "I left the meter running," he said, his ratty face bright with craft. "You guys all have a swindle sheet—you don't care."

He built, and the more he built the more he enjoyed building. By now the city was over eighty miles deep and five miles in diameter. The whole island had been converted into a single vast city that honeycombed and interlaced farther each day. Eventually it would reach the land beyond the ocean; then the work would begin in earnest.

To his right, a thousand methodically moving companions toiled silently on the structural support that was to reinforce the main breeding chamber. As soon as it was in place everyone would feel better; the mothers were just now beginning to bring forth their young.

That was what worried him. It took some of the joy out of building. He had seen one of the first born—before it was quickly hidden and the thing hushed up. A brief glimpse of bulbous head, foreshortened body, incredibly rigid extensions. It shrieked and wailed and turned red in the face. Gurgled and plucked aimlessly and kicked its *feet*.

In horror, somebody had finally mashed the throwback with a rock. And hoped there wouldn't be any more.

PROBINGS

1. What was your emotional reaction to the "crawlers"? Who or what were the "crawlers"?
2. Are you optimistic or pessimistic about atomic war? Why or why not?
3. If you had to spend the next twenty years in a fall-out shelter, who would you take with you? What would you take with you? Would you rather stay outside and commit suicide? What if your loved ones were excluded from the shelter?
4. One of the shortest SF stories ever written concerned a "last man on Earth" scene. The last man on Earth was sitting alone in a cabin when there came a knock on the door. You finish the story—who or what is out there?
5. If we established communications with someone or something, how should we greet them/it? How trusting should we be? Should we greet them with weapons?
6. Design a monument for peace to be placed in every American community. We already have many monuments dedicated to war.
7. Research what happened after the radio broadcast of "War of the Worlds" in the 1930s. Could the same thing happen today?

EPILOG

In the stories and activities in this book, you have been encouraged to take a unique journey, not unlike a space voyage, into your self, your associates, your society, and your world. We hope that you are now aware that science fiction isn't simply something for little kids and Trekkies, but that science fiction can be used to give us numerous insights into some possible worlds of tomorrow. Science fiction can help us experience a wide variety of options that we might never have thought about.

In section one, you evaluated the various roles that you play and might play in the future. On the one hand, occupational roles are certainly important, but—as you saw—leisure roles could very well dominate much of your personal future. Certainly, other types of roles, such as sexual roles, could change very dramatically in the future. And what of your values ten and twenty years from now? You were asked this all important question at the conclusion of section one, to motivate you to think seriously about how you want to live in a world of *tomorrows*.

Family, friends, and those assorted others with whom we surround ourselves help shape us into the unique creatures we become. In section two, you were asked to come to terms with these significant people who have had, and will continue to have, some influence in making you a unique you. Further, you were asked to examine the idea of what is conformity and why it is deemed important for most people to march to the same drummer. Every group sets up certain standards by which its members are supposed to abide, or they suffer the consequences. Obviously, some conformity is necessary, or a society would quickly collapse into the law of the jungle with each person only concerned about himself or herself. On the other hand, if a society is to remain vital and alive, we need models of new lifestyles and behavior, and this is where noncomformity is important. The people who march to a different drummer are not always popular; in fact, they are often scorned by their associates. Finally, we have those rarest of all humans, those who elect to follow their consciences rather than the law or the dictates of their friends and relatives. These are the few who, in time of moral crisis, step away from the crowd to stand up for what they think is right.

In section three, you were asked to consider what kind of a society you want to live in. Specifically, what is the good and happy life? What is status? How much technology do we need? How much can we endure? What is justice and how should it be administered and by whom? Finally, what kind of a society could be created through the numerous bioethical experiments that are being conducted? We truly have come full circle from science fiction to science fact when we talk about such things as cloning and immortality. We can't escape the realities of tomorrow— you are going to be living in a society that has the potential of being a wonderful utopia or a frightening nightmare straight out of *1984.* You will have some influence over the direction that society takes in the future, but you will have that influence only if you begin to think today about the type of society you want tomorrow.

In the final section of this book, you learned that we are all riding on an enormous spaceship and that when one country tampers with the spaceship we all suffer. Certainly, we can't add billions of people to the spaceship without crowding it too much; nor can one part of the crew monopolize the air, water, and food. Finally, the question of our survival was raised. By "our" is meant the entire crew of the ship. How far can we go in gambling with the lives of the planet's people?

We needn't end on a negative note, however. A theme runs throughout all four sections of this book, and that theme speaks directly to you—take responsibility! Already many of you are taking responsibility for your futures by planning the kind of work that you want to do or the kind of activities that you wish to pursue in your leisure time. Many females, and for that matter males, are breaking away from traditional roles to try to find out who they want to be. All around the world we are seeing many different people becoming aware that they don't necessarily have to follow the old ways—but that they can use new ways in order to establish lives that they are happy with.

What does responsibility have to do with the kind of society and world you want? Consider the number of young people (and older ones, too) who were a part of the ecology movement. While picking up beer cans or cleaning up a local park doesn't solve the ecology problem, it does indicate that many people are becoming aware that we are all responsible for the environment. And that we can do something about it.

So it is with all aspects of the world of tomorrow. On the one hand, we can have as many children as we wish. On the other hand, by adding too many new mouths to the planet we might hurt all of us. There is nothing more personal or responsible than deciding how large a family one wants. Also, we must become responsible about the world's resources. No longer can any nation use as much oil, iron ore, water, food, or even air without thinking of what the consequences might be for the rest of earth. Finally, if we are to live on this planet in peace, we all must consider just what is our personal responsibility for ensuring that peace. What's yours?